Donna Spivey Ellington

From Sacred Body to Angelic Soul

Understanding Mary in Late Medieval and Early Modern Europe

The Catholic University of America Press

Washington, D.C.

The paper used in this publication meets the minimum requirements
of American National Standards for Information Science—Permanence of Paper for Printed Library materials, ANSI Z39.48-1984.

∞

LIBRARY OF CONGRESS
CATALOGING-IN-PUBLICATION DATA

Ellington, Donna Spivey, 1955–
     From sacred body to angelic soul: understanding Mary in late
medieval and early modern Europe / Donna Spivey Ellington.
          p. cm.
     Includes bibliographical references and index.
     ISBN 0-8132-1014-3 (alk. paper)
          1. Mary, Blessed Virgin, Saint—History of doctrines.   2. Mary,
Blessed Virgin, Saint-History of doctrines—16th century.   I. Title.
BT610 .E45 2000
232.91′09′024-dc21
00-059040

*From Sacred Body
to Angelic Soul*

Campin, Robert (active by 1406–d. 1444). Triptych of the Annunciation:
central panel. *Reproduced with permission of The Metropolitan Museum of Art,*
The Cloisters Collection, 1956. (56.70)

Contents

Preface

I first began this study as an attempt to understand some of the massive changes occurring in religious perceptions in late medieval and early modern Europe. From the beginning, it seemed clear that Protestantism, even in some of its more radical forms, must be understood as a manifestation of religious trends that were affecting European religious life generally. Protestant theologians may have criticized the Catholic Church for practices and beliefs they deemed incorrect or unscriptural, but Catholic reformers as well, especially those such as Erasmus who were influenced by humanism, were also capable of mocking their fellow Catholics for their devotion to pilgrimages, the saints, and the relics associated with their cult. In short, even some loyal Catholics, independent of any Protestant critique, were beginning to back away from the material, concrete devotional forms so popular in the Middle Ages and move toward a more inward piety. How might I account for the many similarities among reformers in both camps, who otherwise were all too often prepared to view each other as heretics, responsible for leading the Church down the road to corruption and even damnation?

It was necessary first of all to select some aspect of Christian piety to act as a point of entry into the complex world of late medieval religion. There were obvious reasons for selecting devotion to the Virgin Mary as the focus for the study. The Virgin Mary was the most prominent figure in late medieval piety, after her son, and she remained at the heart of religious controversy in the sixteenth century. She could therefore serve as a powerful link between the two periods. As a woman, she could also be a means for exploring changing attitudes toward women in the period. Even more important, however, because Mary's religious significance stemmed from her bodily motherhood of Christ, she would necessarily be tied intimately to the concrete, sacramental piety of the late medieval period. An understanding of any possible changes in Marian devotion might therefore lead to greater comprehension of the wider religious transformation taking place in European Christianity generally. There is an extensive sermon literature in both the late Middle Ages and early modern period devoted to the Virgin Mary. I chose to explore Marian devotion in these sermons largely because the popular sermon existed at the crossroads of so many avenues of religious culture, joining together the formal theology of the schools where most preachers were trained and the popular attitudes and beliefs of the people to whom they preached. Finally, however, it must be said that my choice of subject and sources allowed me to explore a topic that has intrigued me ever since I began to study the Middle Ages. Even a casual acquaintance with the depth of feeling and the beauty of imagery engendered by the Blessed Virgin in this period, whether in sermons, visual art, or music, is enough to beckon any scholar toward further inquiries. It is almost as irresistible as the faint but distinct and compelling fragrance of roses that lures a hurried traveler into the quiet of an enclosed garden. And, as with any garden, once inside there are endless beautiful objects worthy of examination and reflection. I offer the reader my own conclusions, arranged and presented after much time spent in that kind of contemplation.

My central argument asserts that the Church's portrait of the Virgin gradually changed during the sixteenth century and became less focused on her body and more on her soul as religious life in Western Europe was increasingly dominated by a piety that stressed the inner life at the expense of the concrete and the material. During the late medieval period, preachers believed Mary's chief importance to be found in her bodily relationship to Jesus. Because she was his physical mother, the Virgin and Christ shared a common flesh and humanity which allowed her to participate mystically in all aspects of his incarnate life from birth to death. As European religion began to become less centered on concrete manifestations of the holy and more concerned with inward religious experience, the public portrait of Mary in Catholic sermon literature reflected this shift. Preachers began to emphasize Mary's "spiritual" motherhood of Jesus and to play down her physical involvement in all areas of Jesus' life.

The book sets these developments in the context of the growth of literacy and literate modes of thought during the sixteenth century. It also considers additional factors contributing to an altered portrait of Mary, including changing attitudes toward the body and toward women generally in early modern Europe. And it examines the growing development of a private sense of self resulting from newer confessional practices and from increased demands by Church and state for conformity to approved ideology and to codes of bodily control and deportment.

There are two distinct sections of the book. The introduction and chapters one through three concern late medieval devotion to Mary and the importance of its expression in popular sermons delivered to a culture still primarily governed by oral means of communication. Chapters four through six focus on the presentation of Mary largely by post-Tridentine preachers, and examine the effects which printing, the movement for ecclesiastical reform, and other cultural changes brought to the Church's public portrait of Mary.

In a detailed analysis of sermons or any piece of literature, the specific words used by the author are as important and revealing as the topics which are discussed. With this in mind, I have tried to provide extensive quotations from the original sermons in the notes, preserving as much as possible the spelling and punctuation as they appear in the text. This is especially important, since many of the sermons used in this study come from collections for which there is no modern edition. Any translations from the Latin, French, and, in one instance, from the Italian, are my own.

Many thanks to Ronald Witt and Kristen Neuschel, whose conversations with me helped me initially to clarify my ideas, and who have continued to offer encouragement and to believe in the importance of this work. I also need to express gratitude to Gardner-Webb University for granting me a sabbatical, without which I could not have completed the research for this study.

Portions of this work appeared previously as an article, "Impassioned Mother or Passive Icon: The Virgin's Role in Late Medieval and Early Modern Passion Sermons," *Renaissance Quarterly* 48 (1995): 227–61. Permission to use this material is gratefully acknowledged.

My greatest appreciation is reserved for my husband, Steven, who has never once expressed irritation or impatience with the long hours I have needed to spend in reading sermons and writing down my conclusions. Nor has he allowed me to waver in my own commitment. This book is dedicated to him, and to the Virgin herself, who was its inspiration from the beginning: Ave, gratia plena.

From Sacred Body
to Angelic Soul

Introduction

Marian Devotion, Popular Preaching, and the Power of Speech in Late Medieval Religious Life

*I say that the blessed Virgin is a garden of delights which God plant-
ed by his own hand. . . . and then God ordered a banquet to be prepared at the entrance to the garden, the sacred grove, which is the
womb of the Virgin, . . . for God prepared this banquet when he united human nature to his own divinity.*[1]

—Bernardino of Busti

AT LEAST SINCE THE FOURTH CENTURY, the Virgin Mary has occupied
an important place in the theology and piety of the Christian Church
in the West. As the mother of Christ, she was portrayed in St. Luke's
Gospel as the one whose consent had made possible the Incarnation itself.
Her body, whose womb provided the meeting place for the union of the
divine and human, was inevitably considered to be especially holy.

Mary remained significant in the lives of Christians during the early
Middle Ages, and devotion to her reached its apex in the twelfth century.
As Marian piety merged with the secular traditions of feudalism and
courtly love, the Virgin was honored increasingly as both bride of Christ
and his mother. Artists and theologians proclaimed that after her death,

---

1. Bernardino of Busti, *Mariale* (Milan: Leonardus Pachel, 1493), Sermon 1, "On Marian
Similes," pt. 1. The edition of Busti's work used for this study did not have page numbers
of any kind. References will supply the sermon number, larger division of the work in
which the sermon itself is located, and the part of the sermon where the citation occurs.

I

she had been welcomed into heaven by Christ himself and seated beside him, where she ruled in triumph as Queen of Heaven. As such, she must be served as lady and mistress, even as Christ is served as lord and master. Mary became the poetic lady of the troubadours, to be honored and obeyed with an absolute and pure devotion. "Notre Dame" took its place as the most popular title for Mary;[2] as a troubadour's lady, she was appropriately surrounded by songs and hymns composed in her honor.[3] Nor did Mary's popularity decline after the twelfth century.

Through the close of the Middle Ages, the figure of the Virgin continued to serve as the one key which could be counted on to unlock all of the major doors in the complex edifice of medieval piety, her central position guaranteed by the fact that her immaculate flesh had been given to become the body of Christ. In the minds of medieval Christians, Mary could therefore stand as the ultimate source of Jesus' suffering body on the cross and of his glorified body honored and received in the transubstantiated host. For many persons in the late Middle Ages, Mary's close physical connection to Jesus also meant that she was able to suffer with him at Calvary, thereby participating even more intimately in the act of redemption and earning the right to intercede with her son for sinners after her reception into heaven.

It was just this focus on the concrete and material aspects of the faith that caused a number of scholars and clergy in the late fifteenth and early sixteenth centuries to criticize medieval devotion and call for reform. Yet

2. Hilda Graef, *The Devotion to Our Lady* (New York: Hawthorn Books, 1963), 45–46. Graef quotes Ailred of Rievaulx (d. 1167), who said of Mary, "The spouse of our Lord is our mistress, the spouse of our King is our Queen, therefore let us serve her." Ailred specifically connects the honor due to Mary to the commandment to honor father and mother; however, his language immediately changes to that of the feudal relationship with which he would have been familiar. "Ecce quemadmodum mater nostra est; ideo debemus illi honorem. Hoc enim praecepit Dominus, sicut diximus: Honora patrem tuum et matrem tuam. Debemus etiam illi servitium, quia domina nostra est. Sponsa enim Domini nostri domina nostra est; sponsa regis nostri, regina nostra; ideo servamus illi." The reference is from one of Ailred's sermons on the Nativity of Mary and may be found in J. P. Migne, ed., *Patrologiae cursus completus: series latina*, 221 vols. (Paris: J. P. Migne, 1844–1866), 195:323–24. Migne's work will be referred to as PL in subsequent notes.

3. Hilda Graef, *Mary: A History of Doctrine and Devotion*, 2 vols. (New York: Sheed and Ward, 1964), 1:229. The "Salve Regina" was sung by the Dominicans each evening after Compline.

Mary also continued to hold an exalted position in the Catholic Church of the sixteenth and seventeenth centuries in spite of, and perhaps even because of, humanist critiques and Protestant attempts to abolish veneration of her altogether.

This prominence of the Virgin Mary in traditional Western Christianity meant that she was the subject of numerous sermons during the Middle Ages and the period of rapid Catholic reform in the sixteenth century. Yet there have been few attempts to explore in detail the ways in which Mary was portrayed in the popular sermons of the later Middle Ages, or the ways in which that portrait may have changed in response to the pressures of both Catholic and Protestant reform movements and the developments occurring in religious devotion generally in the early modern period.[4] There are, therefore, many questions which remain to be

4. Of course the literature covering some particular aspect of the Virgin's role in theology, art, religious practice, and ecclesiastical politics is vast. A few of the more important general works include Jaroslav Pelikan's *Mary Through the Centuries: Her Place in the History of Culture* (New Haven: Yale University Press, 1996); Graef, *Devotion* and *Mary;* Marina Warner, *Alone of All Her Sex: The Myth and Cult of the Virgin Mary* (New York: Alfred A. Knopf, 1976); and Nicholas Perry and Loreto Echeverría, *Under the Heel of Mary* (New York: Routledge, 1988). There is no major study that traces changes occurring in fifteenth- and sixteenth-century Marian doctrine and devotion as presented in the sermon literature. There are, however, studies of individual preachers of the later medieval period that deal with the preacher's Mariology. An important work is Heiko Oberman's book, *The Harvest of Medieval Theology: Gabriel Biel and Late Medieval Nominalism,* rev. ed. (Grand Rapids, Mich.: William B. Eerdmans Publishing Company, 1967). Oberman provides a thorough analysis of the formal aspects of Biel's Mariology as they appear in all of his works; and he contrasts Biel's effusive and creative approach to Mary in the sermons with the more restrained teaching found in his formal theological works. See also E. Jane Dempsey Douglass, *Justification in Late Medieval Preaching: A Study of John Geiler of Keisersberg* (Leiden: E. J. Brill, 1966). Douglass's book is useful because Geiler is often considered to be one of the "forerunners" of sixteenth-century reform. Hilda Graef's two-volume work on Marian devotion examines in a brief and limited way the sermons of some of the central medieval preachers. In general, the biographies of late medieval and early modern preachers do not give a great deal of information concerning their Marian teaching; most of the details provided come from their theological works and not their sermons. Caroline Walker Bynum has advised that there is a need for more work on Marian devotion in the later medieval period in *Holy Feast and Holy Fast: The Religious Significance of Food to Medieval Women* (Berkeley: University of California Press, 1987), 409 n. 43. In a 1982 article, John O'Malley called for more research on Catholic preaching as a whole during the Reformation era. He specifically says of sermons, "It is difficult to imagine material more appropriate for supporting comparisons between high and low culture, between theology and piety, between culture and religion." See "Catholic Reform," in *Reformation Europe: A Guide to Research,* ed.

answered about this crucial period in the history of the Church and the ways in which the Church communicated to the people through its preachers. Exactly what role did popular preachers encourage the people to believe that Mary would play in the drama of individual salvation? What are the connections between Marian piety and the hierarchical institutional Church? How did devotion to Mary operate within the structure of late medieval Christianity, and did its meaning change as a result of the struggle between Protestant and Catholic for religious control of Europe? If humanist scholars and Protestant theologians found it necessary to attack the concrete piety of devotion to the host, to relics, and to images, how would this affect devotion to Mary, whose primary connection to Christian history began with the physical act of conceiving and bearing Christ? Finally, in what ways is the discussion of Mary in public sermons a reflection of changing social forces and of newly emerging attitudes toward women and toward the human person in the fifteenth and sixteenth centuries? It is certainly significant that the Virgin is a woman, whose public portrayal was almost always carried out by men. She is therefore inescapably important for an understanding of gender relations in the period. For the most part, this study reserves a discussion of gender issues for the concluding chapter; however, it will be clear throughout the work that Mary is important to popular preachers because of her ability to serve as a model woman as well as a model Christian.

No single work could hope to answer fully all of these questions and concerns. This is particularly the case when one is examining a specific selection of one type of source, the popular sermon. I have tried in this study nevertheless to make a beginning by examining the published sermons of a number of fifteenth- and sixteenth-century preachers.

In addition, while sermons are the focal point of my study, I have also

---

Steven Ozment (St. Louis: Center for Reformation Research, 1982), 311. There are, however, some studies of preaching which deal specifically with either the earlier Middle Ages or the Renaissance/Reformation period. Particularly important are D. L. d'Avray, *The Preaching of the Friars: Sermons Diffused from Paris before 1300* (Oxford: Oxford University Press, 1985); Anscar Zawart, *The History of Franciscan Preaching and of Franciscan Preachers (1209–1927): A Bio-bibliographical Study* (New York: J. F. Wagner, 1928); and Larissa Taylor, *Soldiers of Christ: Preaching in Late Medieval and Reformation France* (Oxford: Oxford University Press, 1992).

attempted to demonstrate the interaction between the Marian themes prevalent in the sermons and those in the art, literature, popular prayers, and religious practices in which devotion to the Virgin also flowered.

The preachers whom I have selected were not only some of the most famous preachers of their day, but also men whose sermons were often deliberately intended for use by other preachers. Already by the thirteenth century, Latin editions of sermons by the mendicant friars were being distributed quite effectively from important international centers such as Paris. The system of distribution was so effective that D. L. d'Avray finds mendicant preaching to be one of the more prominent aspects of a shared culture among the European countries of the High Middle Ages.[5]

Among the preachers studied here, the mendicants, especially the Franciscans, predominate, because their own self-definition as religious orders meant that they would be intimately involved in preaching to the people on a regular basis. The mendicants were also known for their particular attachment to Mary and for promoting popular devotion to her. They therefore make up the largest percentage of the preachers examined in this study for both the late Middle Ages and the post-Tridentine period. For the fifteenth century, the Franciscans include two Italians, San Bernardino of Siena (1380–1444)[6] and Bernardino of Busti (c. 1450–1500);[7] a German, Johannes of Verden (d. 1437);[8] and two Frenchmen, Michel Menot (c. 1450–1518)[9] and Olivier Maillard (1430–1502).[10]

5. D'Avray, *Preaching of the Friars*, 3–4, 95. D'Avray describes the diffusion of sermons in this period as a type of "mass communication," and says of mendicant sermons that they are "not best studied within the framework of histories of preaching in one or another country. Latin transmission made mendicant preaching one of the common factors shared by the cultures of different regions."

6. San Bernardino of Siena, *Opera omnia*, ed. P. M. Perantoni, 5 vols. (Quaracchi: Collegium S. Bonaventurae, 1950–).

7. Bernardino of Busti, *Mariale*.

8. Johannes of Verden, *Sermones dominicales cum expositionibus evangeliorum, sive Dormi secure de tempore et de sanctis* (Basel: Johann Amerbach, 1484).

9. Michel Menot, *Sermons choisis de Michel Menot*, ed. J. Nève (Paris: Bibliothèque du XVe siècle, 1924).

10. Olivier Maillard, *Oeuvres françaises d'Olivier Maillard: sermons et poesies*, ed. A. de la Borderie (Nantes: Société des Bibliophiles Bretons, 1877); "Passio domini nostri Jesu Christi," in *Sermones quadragesimales* (Paris: Antoine Caillaut, 1498).

San Bernardino of Siena has long been known for his international influence on Marian devotion as well as for some of his more outrageous claims regarding her power and influence with God. The *Mariale* of Bernardino of Busti was generally recognized as a compendium of all of the current themes, legends, and symbols of the Marian cult of the late Middle Ages. It was a popular collection of sermons first published in 1492–93, which had already been through nine editions before the outbreak of the Reformation in 1517.[11] Johannes of Verden's *Dormi secure* was also immensely popular on into the early sixteenth century and went through eighty-nine editions within less than a century of its first publication in the late 1400's.[12] Finally, both Menot and Maillard represent the best of French Franciscan preaching on the eve of the Reformation. Maillard, whose Passion sermon is examined in this study, was known throughout Europe, having preached in Flanders, Spain, Germany, Hungary, and England, as well as throughout his native country;[13] Menot was known as "the new Chrysostom."[14]

In addition, I have examined the medieval sermons of the Italian Dominican Gabriel Barletta (c. 1470)[15] and the famous Parisian Chancellor Jean Gerson (1363–1429).[16] Gerson, in particular, was famous as an advocate of Marian prerogatives and his theological positions were influential throughout the Church.

The sixteenth century also produced a number of significant Franciscan preachers. Examined here are St. Lawrence of Brindisi (1559–1619), an Italian Capuchin;[17] Christopher Cheffontaines (d. 1595);[18] and a sermon

11. Zawart, *History of Franciscan Preaching*, 318.

12. Ibid., 328–29.

13. Alexandre Samouilllan, *Étude sur la chaire et la société française au quinzième siècle: Olivier Maillard, sa prédication et son temps* (Paris: E. Privat, 1891), 13.

14. Etienne Gilson, "Michel Menot et la technique du sermon médiévale," *Revue d'histoire Franciscaine* 2 (1925): 301.

15. Gabriel Barletta, *Sermones quadragesimales et de sanctis* (Brescia: Jacobus Britannicus, 1497). The Marian sermons of the Dominican Guillaume Pepin (1465–1533), *Rosareum aurem B. Mariae Virginis* (Antwerp: Guillelmus Lesteenius and Engelbertus Gymnicus, 1656), will also be examined in a more limited way.

16. Jean Gerson, *Oeuvres complètes,* ed. P. Glorieux, 8 vols. (Paris: Desclée and Cie, 1971).

17. Lawrence of Brindisi, *Opera omnia,* 10 vols. (Patavia: Ex officina typographica seminarii, 1928).

18. Christopher Cheffontaines, "Homilia in die immaculatae conceptionis sacratissimae

by the "Christian Demosthenes," Francis Panigarola (1548–94), whose sermons typify popular preaching at the papal court in the sixteenth century.[19] St. Lawrence engaged in highly effective international preaching missions in Germany, France, and Spain, and was singularly devoted to the Virgin Mary. Cheffontaines, along with his ardent Marian sermons, was especially important for fighting the spread of Calvinism in France.[20]

Because of the importance of the Jesuits in the Catholic effort to combat Protestant influence, and because of their unhesitating public defense of devotion to Mary, it was also necessary to look at a sample of their preaching. St. Peter Canisius of Holland (1521–91)[21] worked tirelessly to help rebuild Catholic piety in Germany in the wake of the ravages of Protestantism and, in 1577, he became the first Jesuit to publish a book in praise of Mary.[22] The Italian St. Robert Bellarmine (1542–1621)[23] became a model cleric of the Catholic Reformation, specializing in controversial theology and, like Canisius, in catechesis.[24] His sermons, therefore, represent a synthesis both of Jesuit and of general Catholic theology in the late sixteenth and early seventeenth century. Finally, no study of Catholic sermons in the Tridentine period could omit St. François de Sales (1576–1622), the bishop known internationally for his preaching and also for his ardent love for Mary.[25]

---

at dignissimae Virginis Mariae Matris Dei," in *Omnes epistolas quadragesimales homiliae* (Louvain: Johannes Bogardus, 1572), 161v–165v; "Sermo de Virginis Mariae laudibus et honore, qui in qualibet eius festivitate haberi ad populum potest," in *Novae illustrationes christianae fidei*, pt. 2 (Paris: Sittart, 1586), 1r–56v; "Sermo secundus qui de Virginis Mariae invocatione agit," in ibid., 57r–82r.

19. Francis Panigarola, "Predica di Maria Vergine, e Madre" (Rome: 1589).

20. Lazaro Iriarte, O.F.M.Cap., *Franciscan History: The Three Orders of St. Francis of Assisi* (Chicago: Franciscan Herald Press, 1983), 296.

21. Peter Canisius, *Meditationes seu notae in evangelicas lectiones*, 2d ed., ed. Frederick Streicher, S.J., 2 vols. (Munich: Officiana Salesiana, 1957).

22. John W. O'Malley, S.J., *The First Jesuits* (Cambridge: Harvard University Press, 1993), 270–76.

23. Robert Bellarmine, *Roberti cardinalis Bellarmini opera omnia*, 6 vols. (Naples: J. Giuliano, 1860).

24. Robert Bellarmine, *Robert Bellarmine: Spiritual Writings*, ed. and trans. John Patrick Donnelly, S.J., The Classics of Western Spirituality (New York: Paulist Press, 1989), 13–17.

25. François de Sales, *Oeuvres complètes de Saint François de Sales, éveque et prince de Genève*, 16 vols. (Paris: J. J. Blaise, 1821). Also of some importance to this study are the Marian sermons of François Le Picart (1504–56), *Les sermons et instructions chrestiennes, pour tous les jours*

These preachers were, in most cases, particularly well educated and skilled, and therefore the quality of their sermons, which reflected the latest beliefs and thinking of the Church, is not necessarily representative of that which people might regularly hear from their local parish priest. The popularity of these men nevertheless meant that many other preachers throughout Europe read the published editions of their sermons and used examples from them for their own preaching.

There is, in fact, considerable disagreement regarding the quality of sermons given by medieval preachers at the local level. Some scholars believe that excessive reliance on preaching aids resulted in unimaginative and boring sermons, while others find the overall nature of late medieval sermons to be quite good.[26] In any case, the homiletic efforts of the preachers studied here reflect the best that European preaching had to offer. I have used the sermons of these men as a window into the religious life of one of the most dynamic periods in the history of Western Christianity, and as a means of approaching, however haltingly, the devotional lives of the laity.

Popular Sermons and the Oral Society of Late Medieval Europe

It is never easy to determine the religious views and practices of those who have left little or no written evidence of their faith. Although the

---

de caresme, et feries de Pasques (Paris: Nicolas Chesneau, 1566). Le Picart, named Dean of Notre Dame in 1547, was highly popular as a preacher among the people of Paris.

26. Janet Coleman believes that the use of preaching manuals and collections of exempla was restrictive and resulted in hundreds of preachers preaching essentially the same sermons on the same topics. She cites Owst's famous study of medieval English preaching, which said that these preachers were "plagiarizing" from each other and "laying out the same dreary matter throughout the whole year—as with one voice from many pulpits came the same de tempore sermon"; G. R. Owst, *Preaching in Medieval England* (Cambridge: Cambridge University Press, 1926), 251, quoted in Janet Coleman, *Medieval Readers and Writers, 1350–1400* (New York: Columbia University Press, 1981), 176. Siegfried Wenzel, on the other hand, specifically criticizes Coleman for lumping all medieval English sermons into one category and labeling them boring and repetitive. He says that Coleman has distorted the "historical reality" and failed to take into account the great variety of sermon manuscripts that exists. Wenzel is rather impressed with the overall quality of medieval English sermons and believes that there is a close association between them and the development of English poetry in the period. Siegfried Wenzel, *Preachers, Poets, and the Early English Lyric* (Princeton: Princeton University Press, 1986), 15, 63.

invention of printing around 1450 made possible the spread of written materials on an unprecedented scale, the majority of people in Western Europe, even in the cities, remained unable to read and write in the late fifteenth and early sixteenth centuries.[27] Even when it is possible to know without doubt, however, that a person or group was exposed to a piece of literature or to the content of a sermon, there can be no hasty conclusions about the ways this material was received. People might accept, reject, or modify for their own purposes and according to their understanding the views presented in a book or sermon. Sarah Beckwith has shown that the single most potent religious symbol of the late Middle Ages, the body of Christ, could be appropriated by the laity to subvert the hierarchical structure many clergy sought to reinforce when they stressed the importance of the host in the Eucharistic liturgy and in Corpus Christi processions.[28] Also it is impossible to recreate precisely the exact social context of shared experiences in which the sermons were originally heard and which helped to determine the people's interpretation.[29] Among the communities which heard popular sermons, neither the preacher nor the audience was solely responsible for the meaning of the words spoken, for they were heard in the context of the common tradition.[30]

27. Literacy in this period was largely concentrated in the cities. Natalie Davis estimates that, in the countryside, even the more developed region outside Paris, the percentage of literate laborers and peasants was not likely much above 3 percent, and almost all of these would have been men. See her article, "Printing and the People," in *Society and Culture in Early Modern France* (Stanford: Stanford University Press, 1986), 195. Robert Scribner believes that approximately 90 percent of the people of Europe were illiterate at the time of the Reformation; "Oral Culture and the Diffusion of Reformation Ideas," *History of European Ideas* 5 (1984): 237.

28. Sarah Beckwith, *Christ's Body: Identity, Culture and Society in Late Medieval Writings* (New York: Routledge, 1993), 22–44. Beckwith suggests that the more the symbolism of Christ's body was made available to the people through processions and popular vernacular works, the more they were able to appropriate it for their own use.

29. Ward Parks, "The Textualization of Orality in Literary Criticism," in *Vox intexta: Orality and Textuality in the Middle Ages*, ed. A. N. Doane and Carol Braun Pasternack (Madison: University of Wisconsin Press, 1991), 55–57.

30. John Miles Foley, "Orality, Textuality and Interpretation," in *Vox intexta: Orality and Textuality in the Middle Ages*, ed. A. N. Doane and Carol Braun Pasternack (Madison: University of Wisconsin Press, 1991), 42. See also Ursula Schaefer, "Hearing from Books: The Rise of Fictionality in Old English Poetry," in ibid., 117–36. Like Parks and Foley, Schaefer argues that the formulas and references of oral performance are tied to the common understanding shared by the community.

Nor can it be assumed that popular preachers always gauged rightly their audience's religious capabilities and experiences. Gerald Strauss and David Sabean have demonstrated that even systematic attempts to indoctrinate cannot produce certain or predictable results.[31] Peter Bayley notes that many aspects of seventeenth-century Catholicism important to religious life in France are omitted from the sermons of the day as, perhaps, inappropriate for the pulpit.[32] Finally, Donald Weinstein suggests in his examination of Savonarola's sermons that the types of material which the urban preacher might deem suitable for a lay audience could be, in fact, out of step with the more subtle and sensitive spiritual needs of some of his hearers.[33] Preachers sometimes underestimated both the ability of their hearers to comprehend more advanced theological issues and their need to be reassured of the willingness of God to forgive their sins.

The "popular" sermons of these preachers often appeared in Latin rather than vernacular editions. The most common reason was that, as we have seen, a Latin version allowed the sermons to be circulated and used by preachers throughout the entire ecclesiastical community, regardless of

31. Gerald Strauss, *Luther's House of Learning: Indoctrination of the Young in the German Reformation* (Baltimore: Johns Hopkins University Press, 1978). Strauss examines efforts by leaders of both church and state to teach the religious and social principles of the German Reformation to the people through schools and catechism classes. His sources are largely visitation records and the exasperated statements of the reformers themselves. While there are certain problems with his choice of sources, he does demonstrate a considerable resistance on the part of the people toward efforts to alter radically their own religious understanding. See also David Warren Sabean, *Power in the Blood: Popular Culture and Village Discourse in Early Modern Germany* (Cambridge: Cambridge University Press, 1984). Especially important in the context of indoctrination is chapter 1, "Communion and Community," 37–60. Sabean identifies the conflicting views of the relationship between the individual, the community, and communion attendance held by literate Church authorities eager to implement Reformation doctrine, and by citizens of the town who have retained a more traditional understanding of the faith.

32. Peter Bayley, *French Pulpit Oratory 1598–1650: A Study in Themes and Styles, With a Descriptive Catalogue of Printed Texts* (Cambridge: Cambridge University Press, 1980), 14.

33. Donald Weinstein, "'The Art of Dying Well' and Popular Piety in the Preaching and Thought of Girolama Savonarola," in *Life and Death in Fifteenth-Century Florence*, ed. Marcel Tetel, Ronald G. Witt, and Rona Goffen (Durham, N.C.: Duke University Press, 1989), 88–104. Weinstein demonstrates the differences Savonarola believed existed between lay and clerical religion by comparing one of his popular sermons to his written theological works and to the spiritual advice he gave to monks and nuns.

their nationality;[34] and, of course, the more famous the preacher, the greater the international demand. A number of Gerson's sermons, for instance, were printed in both their original French and Latin. Likewise, certain sermons of San Bernardino of Siena may be found in Italian as well as Latin.[35] Works such as Johannes of Verden's *Dormi secure* were obviously intended to provide sermon material for other preachers.[36] St. Peter Canisius says in his own preface to the *Meditationes* that they are intended to be used by others, especially those less experienced in preaching.[37]

It is also true that medieval preachers often composed their sermons in Latin, even those that would be delivered eventually in the vernacular. Latin was the language of education and especially of theology. Most preachers were trained to some degree by the universities and would therefore be accustomed to using Latin for matters of religious discourse. Yet preachers followed the Church's instructions to preach to the people in their own language, even though they had prepared the sermon in Latin. If they were unfamiliar with the local dialect, they would employ a translator to help them with the language to be used in the actual delivery. At times, according to Hervé Martin, it is clear from the published editions that the preacher was struggling with language, for often there were words or phrases that were too unusual or too difficult to be translated into Latin. The preacher would then incorporate vernacular sections into the Latin text.[38] There are occasions, too, when sections of pub-

34. Samouillan, *Étude sur la chaire*, 59; Hervé Martin, *Le Métier de prédicateur en France septentrionale à la fin du moyen âge, 1350–1520* (Paris: Cerf, 1988), 13. With regard to the many late medieval French sermons he studied, Martin says, "Les manuscrits y circulent autant que les hommes; les manuels de prédication et parfois les sermons y sont les memes."

35. Zawart, *History of Franciscan Preaching*, 320.

36. Ibid., 328–29. Zawart specifically remarks that since the collection was published in Latin, other preachers would have had to translate Verden's work into the vernacular in order to use it in their preaching.

37. Canisius, *Meditationes*, 2,1:14. "Cum vero multis iam annis, ut dicere coeperam, in Germania verser et sacra publice doceam, non abs re fore putavi, si successivis saltem horis quaedam annotarem atque colligerem, quae nonnullis fratribus ac praesertim rudioribus ad sacras contiones in templis habendas aliquem usum et si sperare licet, auditoribus etiam utititatem et fructum possent adferre."

38. Martin, *Métier de prédicateur*, 560–61; Samouillan, *Étude sur la chaire*, 59. Samouillan states that Maillard's sermons were preached in French even though usually printed in a macaronic combination of French and Latin.

lished sermons move back and forth between Latin and the vernacular in a way that gives the impression that the mind of the preacher or scribe was doing the same thing as he composed the text. A good example is one of Bernardino of Busti's sermons portraying Mary's grief on Good Friday, in which he tells of a visionary encounter with both the prophet Jeremiah and a speaking image of the Virgin. All of Bernardino's narration is in Latin, while the words of Jeremiah and Mary are given in Italian.[39] It should not be assumed, therefore, that the Latin sermons of preachers such as St. Lawrence of Brindisi or Christopher Cheffontaines were never heard by audiences unfamiliar with Latin. The preacher would have translated them into Italian or French as he gave the sermon.[40] This process, in which sermons were often composed in Latin and later spoken in the vernacular, raises important questions for a study such as this one. How possible is it to recover a vernacular sermon from a Latin text, and does the fact that the sermon has been "textualized" for publication remove all traces of oral delivery? For the medieval period, the answer to both questions lies, to a certain extent, in the fact that at least since the eleventh century, "oral" and "literate" were not always two distinct categories, either

39. Bernardino of Busti, *Mariale*, Sermon 1, "On the Sorrows of Mary," pt. 1. According to Busti, the prophet Jeremiah appeared to him in a vision on Good Friday, ". . . non visione imaginaria sed in forma visibili corporalibus oculis. . . . intelligens desiderium meum interpellandi sacratissimam virginem: dixit mihi haec verba. 'O fili mio de non molestare la piatosa vergene Maria . . .'" Busti says that Jeremiah later ". . . apprehendit me per manum et duxit coram imagine ipsius virginis quae erat vidualibus vestimentis induta. . . . Ad cuius pedes ego protinus prostratus dixi, 'Per che ni vedo o vergene Maris. Tuta afflicta e plena di dolore: Sono venuto a farne compagnia. E esser participe del vostro gran merore. Con voi in sino al monte calvario.'" See also Barletta, *Sermones*, 103v. Larissa Taylor believes that macaronic sermons indicate the presence of a note taker, but that fully Latin editions were initially guided by the preacher through the publication process; Taylor, *Soldiers of Christ*, 54.

40. Zawart, *History of Franciscan Preaching*, 448; Iriarte, *Franciscan History*, 296. Zawart indicates that St. Lawrence, whose sermons are printed in Latin, engaged in successful popular preaching missions in several European countries. Iriarte identifies Cheffontaines as one of three major French preachers who fought the spread of Calvinism among the people "through pulpit and pen." The other two men were Noel Taillepied (d. 1589) and François Feuardent (d. c. 1610). Many later preachers simply composed their sermons in the vernacular to begin with. Louis Bourdaloue wrote out the entire text of his sermon as he planned to give it, in French, and memorized the complete text prior to delivery; see Bayley, *French Pulpit Oratory*, 15.

of persons or ways of communication.[41] This can be seen in the ways that various words having to do with what modern people would consider two different means of communicating, speaking and writing, are often mingled. "Dictare" was most often used to indicate the original composition of a text, while "scribere" referred only to the action of inscribing words on parchment.[42] The person who wrote down the actual words on the parchment would not necessarily be the one who created them and delivered them orally. Also, written texts, whether Scripture read contemplatively in a convent or formal public letters of communication between governments, were most often read aloud. As Karma Lochrie indicates, "The written word was viewed as an extension of the spoken word."[43] Nothing shows this more clearly than the fact that written devotional texts, intended to be read, and written sermon texts, intended to be preached publicly, both employed interactive dialogue to draw the reader/hearer into the drama of the story being presented.[44]

41. Brian Stock, *The Implications of Literacy: Written Language and Models of Interpretation in the Eleventh and Twelfth Centuries* (Princeton: Princeton University Press, 1983), 8–14. Stock concludes that there was no clear transition from an oral to a literate society in Western Europe, but that by the eleventh century, the presence of texts in larger numbers was beginning to restructure thought and social action. From that point on, both modes of communication worked equally to influence the literate (usually defined as literate in Latin), who read and used texts yet operated in a largely oral society, and the non-literate, through their association with people whose words and thoughts were more structured by literacy. Nevertheless, he admits that as late as the Reformation most Europeans, even aristocrats, remained in an oral/aural environment. See also William Graham, *Beyond the Written Word: Oral Aspects of Scripture in the History of Religion* (New York: Cambridge University Press, 1987), 31–40; Walter J. Ong, S.J., "Orality, Literacy and Medieval Textualization," *New Literary History* 16 (1984): 1–4; and M. T. Clanchy, *From Memory to Written Record: England, 1066–1307* (Cambridge: Harvard University Press, 1979). All of Clanchy's work deals with the gradual transformation of English politics and government through the use of written texts.

42. Suzanne Fleischman, "Philology, Linguistics, and the Discourse of the Medieval Text," *Speculum* 65 (1990): 20. Fleischman also uses the work of Jeffrey Kittay to remind her readers that early manuscripts were still very oral in style and required verbalization to make sense of them due to their lack of punctuation and separation between words and sentences. See Jeffrey Kittay, "Utterance Unmoored: The Changing Interpretations of the Act of Writing in the European Middle Ages," *Language in Society* 17 (1986): 209–30, cited in Fleischman, "Philology," 20 n. 4.

43. Karma Lochrie, *Margery Kempe and Translations of the Flesh* (Philadelphia: University of Pennsylvania Press, 1991), 102–4.

44. Beckwith, *Christ's Body*, 53. Beckwith examines works such as the Pseudo-Bernardine

Certainly Latin was a completely textualized language in the Middle Ages.[45] Even its spoken form was determined by the rules of written grammar.[46] This, in turn, could not help but influence the structure of sermons, even when eventually translated by the preacher into the people's language. Yet "traces of the oral infrastructure"[47] remain in such features as the extensive use of dialogue, frequent repetition of formulaic phrases to reiterate a point, and the macaronic character even of the published sermon texts already mentioned. Although it is true that the exact words heard by the people cannot be recovered with certainty from Latin editions, Latin sermons may still be a reliable guide to the general content of the preacher's message.[48]

During the fifteenth century, the people who lived in cities had the opportunity to hear more sermons than they had at any time in the past, perhaps as many as eight hundred over the course of a lifetime.[49] The great flurry of sermon activity was due in part to a renewed zeal for preaching within the Franciscan order. Having overcome a number of institutional problems which plagued the order throughout the fourteenth century, both branches of Franciscans, the Observants and the Conventuals, set about restoring popular preaching to a place of prominence in the urban milieu.[50]

Liber de passione Christi et doloribus et planctibus matris ejus and the Pseudo-Anselmian *Dialogus beatae Mariae et Anselmi de passione Domine.* She states that the reader "is asked to contemplate the Passion as a first-hand witness."

45. Ong, "Orality, Literacy and Medieval Textualization," 6; Fleischman, "Philology," 24.

46. Ong, "Orality, Literacy and Medieval Textualization," 6; Franz H. Bäuml, "Varieties and Consequences of Medieval Literacy and Illiteracy," *Speculum* 55, 2 (1980): 237–65.

47. Fleischman, "Philology," 24.

48. Zawart, *History of Franciscan Preaching,* 320. See also Oberman, *Harvest of Medieval Theology,* 21. According to Oberman, some scholars have said that Biel's sermons could not have been intended for popular audiences since they make "extensive use of scholastic authorities." He rejects this viewpoint on the grounds that Biel includes too many remarks obviously intended for lay persons. Of course, Biel's sermons also appeared in Latin editions. These "sermones predicabiles" were intended to help other preachers with their own sermons.

49. Martin, *Métier de prédicateur,* 618–19, 620 n. 4. Martin points out that, while most sermons were given in larger towns, some peasants occasionally came to town to hear famous preachers, especially during Lent; only rarely did mendicant preachers attempt to reach peasants by preaching in their small villages.

50. J. R. H. Moorman, *A History of the Franciscan Order from Its Origins to the Year 1517*

On the part of the laity, there was a corresponding desire to hear sermons and to participate more fully in religious life in all of its forms. Beginning already in the fourteenth century, parish sermons for Sundays and major feast days became common. Many churches, small parishes as well as cathedrals, established preachers' chairs staffed with men who were well qualified for the office. Not surprisingly, it was also the fourteenth century which saw the construction for the first time of permanent, stationary pulpits in church buildings.[51] Good preachers were paid by local bishops and by town officials for preaching cycles of Advent and Lenten sermons, a practice which began in the fourteenth century. The custom of preaching a series of sermons on the Epistle and Gospel readings appointed for the Sundays of the Church year also dates from this period.[52]

The many different types of sermons in the late Middle Ages ranged from highly structured scholastic discourses to simple homilies on particular texts of Scripture.[53] By far the most common form of sermon, however, was the thematic sermon, composed for particular feast days and saints' days and known as "sermones de tempore et de sanctis."[54] I have used thematic sermons most frequently as the basis for this study, although other types do appear from time to time.[55]

Late medieval sermons could be quite long, lasting for several hours or more. On certain particularly holy days, sermons might be given in two parts, one in the morning and another in the evening. This was the case with Jean Gerson's famous sermon on the Passion, "Ad deum vadit." The sermons were attended mostly by people of the middle classes, and in

---

(Oxford: Clarendon Press, 1968), 517; Zawart, *History of Franciscan Preaching*, 348–50; Martin, *Métier de prédicateur*, 615.

51. Zawart, *History of Franciscan Preaching*, 245–46.

52. Ibid., 246; Martin, *Métier de prédicateur*, 617. Martin finds evidence of the demand for preaching among civic officials and among the people, whom he describes as "profondement christianisés."

53. Zawart, *History of Franciscan Preaching*, 243–59; Samouillan, *Étude sur la chaire*, 70–71.

54. Zawart, *History of Franciscan Preaching*, 243–59.

55. Bernardino of Busti, for example, often preached symbolic emblematic sermons. These sermons might take each of the letters of Mary's name and use them to stand for one of her personal qualities; or preachers might take objects from the Scriptures which are commonly associated with Mary, such as lilies or pearls, and describe the similarities between the object and the Virgin.

most cases women outnumbered men in the audiences. Preachers usually spoke in churches, but very famous preachers might choose to address the large crowds who came to hear them from open air platforms, as did San Bernardino of Siena. In either situation, there were no pews or chairs for the hearers, who were generally forced to stand or perhaps sit on the ground—unless, of course, they brought their own stools to sit on.[56] Given the length of these sermons, those who listened would have to be accustomed both to standing and to assimilating often very technical spoken language for considerable periods of time. Their listening skills would need to be highly developed.

The content of late medieval sermons could vary as often as the goals of the preachers who delivered them. Some sought to convey the basics of Christian doctrine, while others encouraged the people to confess their sins and lead moral lives. During Lent, sermons often pictured in vivid language the suffering of Christ, and the merciful intercession of Mary on behalf of all Christians.[57]

Preachers were aided in their task by their ability to refer to common iconographic themes associated with Christ, Mary, or the saints which were familiar to most people. Preachers accepted the traditional belief that pictures and statues could function as educational tools for the laity, even though they were less important than preaching or the Eucharist. When preaching about Christ, the most frequent references were to the crucifix as a representation of Jesus' suffering. However, it was in speaking of the Virgin that many preachers kept most closely to the popular motifs which appeared in stained glass windows or other images.[58] Preachers' sermons drew together the various aspects of contemporary religious life and presented them to the people as a unified whole,[59] con-

---

56. Martin, *Métier de prédicateur*, 557–58; Taylor, *Soldiers of Christ*, 28–29.

57. Martin, *Métier de prédicateur*, 304–11, 618–21. In describing Jesus' suffering, some preachers went so far as to list the precise number of wounds he received at 5,475.

58. Ibid., 505, 587–91. The belief that literary or artistic images could serve to educate the laity regarding their faith was usually based on a couple of famous letters of Pope Gregory the Great which may be found in PL 77:990, and 1128–29.

59. People would also have recognized many similarities between sermons and popular drama, because sermons were influential in the development of early public religious plays. See G. R. Owst, *Literature and Pulpit in Medieval England: A Neglected Chapter in the His-*

vinced that they were communicating with their hearers in the most effective way possible, the spoken word.[60] In the context of the primarily oral society of fifteenth-century Europe, they were probably right. The preacher's words certainly would be the most direct means of teaching dogma, while the more skillful might hope to inspire religious devotion and create a sense of community among their hearers.

When it is done effectively, public speaking has the power to unite a group of people through their common experience of the speaker's words. Everyone hears and responds to the same voice and the same ideas simultaneously, joined to each other and to the speaker by the close physical proximity required of sermon audiences and by the omnipresent sound of the human voice.[61] Oral performance, even when relying on a text, also creates bonds between the people and the preacher, because his

---

tory of English Letters and of the English People, 2d ed. (Oxford: Basil Blackwell, 1966), 471–547.

60. Martin, *Métier de prédicateur,* 585. Martin cites an Augustinian preacher of Bayeaux who believed that the preached word, the Eucharist, and Christian art corresponded to the three senses of hearing, taste, and sight. Of the three, this preacher considered hearing to be primary.

61. Walter J. Ong, S.J., *Orality and Literacy: The Technologizing of the Word* (New York: Methuen, 1982), 74. A critique of Ong's belief in the unifying power of public speech has recently been offered by David Chidester, *Word and Light: Seeing, Hearing and Religious Discourse* (Urbana: University of Illinois Press, 1992). Based on an examination of philosophers and theologians from Philo of Alexandria through St. Augustine, St. Bonaventure, and Philip Melanchthon, Chidester argues that in the Western tradition sight, not hearing, is used to represent union. Hearing, he states, has always represented discontinuity, because the ear is essentially passive and must wait to be struck by sound. Unlike the eye it is dependent on *something else* in order to function. Therefore when theologians wish to stress union with the divine as immanent, metaphors of sight are used. He even goes so far as to say that sight indicates presence of the divine, while sound or hearing indicate not only God's transcendence but even absence. If sound exists, however, someone must be present to make it. Chidester also admits that seeing tends to indicate "natural disengagement," while hearing requires "dynamic interaction" (10–11). What Chidester actually proves is that the two modes of perception indicate two different modes of union: sight, one which is continuous, dependent on the individual's perception, and already achieved; hearing, one which must be the result of dynamic action and some kind of mediation, whether the spoken word, the word made flesh, sacraments, burning bushes, etc. In other words, the more one wishes to stress interior, individualized, continuous, and meditative religious experience, the more one tends to rely on metaphors involving light and sight. The more one desires to express the need for interactive, communal religious union with God and with others through mediation of some kind, the more images of the spoken word will prevail. In either case, God is present, but the presence is manifested in a different way.

words place his message automatically in the context of the shared tradition of memories, stories, and experiences common to the lives of all present. By his use of Scripture or familiar phrases and tales, the speaker creates what Ward Parks calls a "dialog of memories" with his hearers, which links the present both with the past and to the future, when these same stories and motifs will be used again.[62]

The late medieval preacher, particularly in the typical Passion sermon, magnified this communal aspect of speech by the frequent use of "we" to unite speaker and hearers,[63] and by often carrying on a dialogue with the audience or presenting various scenes from the Passion in conversation form. It might be an impassioned conversation between the characters of the story, or between the preacher himself and Jesus or Mary, or even with one of the evangelists. In all of these ways, the medieval preacher was able to draw his audience into active participation in the sermon itself and in the drama of the Passion, Annunciation, or other sacred event played out imaginatively in the spoken word and in the mental images those words engendered in the minds of the people. Unfortunately, we do not know precisely what kinds of bodily gestures accompanied the delivery of these sermons, but it is difficult to read them without sensing that the preacher must have been caught up to a certain extent in the stories he presented so vividly. We can assume that medieval preachers were rather lively in their delivery, since the men responsible for hiring preachers in the Middle Ages, as well as those dedicated to the reform of preaching in the sixteenth century, felt it necessary to curb the amount of bodily movement employed in the pulpit. Already in 1434, the city council of Nantes warned preachers in the city against "making terrible outcries, waving their hands about wildly, posturing excessively, and gesticulating outrageously."[64]

---

62. Parks, "Textualization of Orality," 57. Parks is offering a critique of modern literary deconstruction which limits all consideration to the interior of the text. Such a theory cannot deal with the fact that an oral performer, even if relying on a text, is automatically situating the text in the "*con*-text," not only of the present hearers but also of their shared tradition. See also Schaefer, "Hearing from Books," 121.

63. Schaefer, "Hearing from Books," 123. Schaefer believes that the use of "we" in an oral context, or even in a piece of literature designed to be read orally, joins the speaker to his or her hearers and helps to overcome the dichotomy between knower and known.

64. Taylor, *Soldiers of Christ*, 47; Frederick McGinness, *Rhetoric and Counter-Reformation*

The combination of words and gestures used in medieval sermons was still especially effective in the Europe of the fifteenth century, for Europe remained a culture in which the spoken word was the most common means of communication.[65] This feature of European life, however, was changing rapidly as more people, particularly those in the cities, learned to read and write. Increasing literacy gradually led urban people to rely more and more on written words in all areas of life. It was the creation of the printing press which made such a change possible.

The rapid spread of printing and the consequent growth in reliance upon the written word which printing helped to produce is historically unique to Western Europe. The cultural transformation which literacy helped to initiate is one of the most important forces working to change Marian piety and religion generally in the late medieval and early modern periods. The gradual shift in the means of communication inaugurated by the invention of printing around 1450 affected all aspects of social and religious life. Prior to this date, the intense interior reflection and individualism to which literacy and writing can contribute were most often confined to the clergy, to monks and nuns, and to a few well-educated lay people whose constant need to participate in a society structured still by oral discourse meant the their behavior and ways of thinking were shaped by the spoken word as well as by literacy.[66]

Over the course of the sixteenth and early seventeenth centuries, however, the spread of literacy fostered a tendency among some European

---

Rome: Sacred Oratory and the Construction of the Catholic World View, 1563–1621 (Ann Arbor, Mich.: University Microfilms International, 1982), 229–30.

65. Ong, "Orality, Literacy and Medieval Textualization," 9–10. Ong points out that in an oral setting, sometimes the use of the voice itself is as important as what is being said. In reference to oral poetry, he says that it is less like a text than a dance.

66. David R. Olson and Nancy Torrance, eds., *Literacy and Orality* (Cambridge: Cambridge University Press, 1991), 7. In the introduction to the book, Olson and Torrance describe two broad approaches taken by anthropologists, linguists, historians, and others to the issue of literacy and its impact on people and their societies. The "continuity theory" argues that orality and literacy are essentially equivalent linguistic means for carrying out similar functions. Psychologically their differences are not important. The "great divide theory" argues that orality and literacy, while interactive in most cases, really do realign psychological processes and society. These are not, however, the only possible distinctions in method. See below, n. 75.

Christians to adopt a more spiritualized understanding of the faith and to place a greater value on inward prayer and moral convictions and less on external means of communicating with God.[67] While this modification in religious devotion obviously affected Protestantism most completely, it also worked to transform the Catholic tradition as well. As noted above, these changes were most discernable in urban areas, where more people had access both to printed materials and to the sources of education which would allow them to learn to read.[68]

Humanist reformers such as Erasmus and Lefèvre d'Etaples were some of the foremost Catholic promoters of the more inward and ethical approach to Christian prayer and life in all areas of devotion. Both men encouraged European Christians to abandon their reliance on externals such as pilgrimages, relics, and images, and to seek a more contemplative relationship with God through prayer and moral living. Advocates of the superiority of allegorical exegesis of the Bible, they stressed that even the material letter of the text of Scripture must not lead the reader to miss the deeper spiritual meaning beneath.[69] The international popularity of

67. It has become fairly common for historians to point out the ways in which changing religious perceptions in the early modern period resulted in a tendency among some Europeans to exalt the inward and "spiritual" at the expense of the material. See, for example, Carlos M. N. Eire, *War Against the Idols: The Reformation of Worship from Erasmus to Calvin* (New York: Cambridge University Press, 1986); Richard Bauman, *Let Your Words Be Few: Symbolism of Speaking and Silence among Seventeenth-Century Quakers* (New York: Cambridge University Press, 1983); and Sabean, *Power in the Blood.*

68. Thus Sarah Beckwith is able to connect the inward and individualistic piety of Margery Kempe to the "self-authorization" which the process of composing her autobiography granted her. Although unable to read herself, she was immersed in an urban culture in which "the Word" as written was becoming the central expression of religious experience. Margery could also manifest another characteristic which would later come to define religious expression in the early modern world: a concern for fostering moral virtue rather than an interest in the more tangible aspects of the faith. Margery was nevertheless still very much a medieval Christian in her external manifestations of personal religious experience. She is an excellent example of some of the tensions between sacramental and interiorized spirituality that were beginning to be felt by late medieval Christians.

69. In the preface to his *Quincuplex Psalterium*, published in 1509, Lefèvre says that the monks whom he had questioned found little joy or spiritual nourishment in their study of Scripture. Lefèvre believes this is the result of a focus upon the literal rather than the "literal-spiritual" sense intended by the Spirit who inspired the Scriptures. The monks had complained especially about the Psalms, which composed a large percentage of their time both in the liturgy and in private devotions. Lefèvre states, "Et si qui eorum ex sacris litteris

Erasmus in particular meant that his work would be read and absorbed not only by Catholics but by many future Protestant leaders as well, for his works were printed and distributed throughout Europe. But Lefèvre also is considered an influence on Luther himself during his early days as a theologian.[70]

Certainly literacy was not the only social force working to create greater interiority and physical reticence in early modern Europe, and there is no intention here of suggesting that greater literacy alone created the religious changes charted in this study of Marian piety. As we will see, factors such as changing confessional practices, a new stress on civility and manners, the need to engage with the growing Protestant movement, and new pressures from ecclesiastical and secular authorities to conform to prescribed rules of behavior are equally involved in reshaping religious sensibilities. It is nevertheless true that the particular insights into human actions and thought outlined by anthropologists and historians interested in the social implications of literacy are an especially useful tool for aiding our understanding of the changing religious life mirrored in sermons from medieval and early modern European preachers.[71]

Already in 1929 the French historian Lucien Febvre, always sensitive to the power of words to shape mental processes and responses, argued the importance of printing and of vernacular Bibles in helping to form a new type of religious understanding. In his groundbreaking article, "Une question mal posée, les origines de la Réforme," he also sought to turn

---

pastum quaerent, saepius interrogavi quid in illis dulcedinis experirentur, quid saperent. Responderunt plurimi quoties in nescio quem sensum litteralem incidissent, et maxime cum divinorum psalmorum intelligentiam queritarent, se multum tristes et animo deiecto ex illa lectione abscedere solitus." See *The Prefatory Epistles of Jacques Lefèvre d'Étaples and Related Texts*, ed. Eugene F. Rice (New York: Columbia University Press, 1972), 193.

70. See Werner Schwartz, *Principles of Biblical Translation: Some Reformation Controversies and Their Background* (Cambridge: Cambridge University Press, 1955), 167–212; and also Heiko A. Oberman, ed., *Forerunners of the Reformation* (Philadelphia: Fortress Press, 1981), 291. Oberman argues that from 1513–1516 Lefèvre's Psalm commentary was an important help to Luther in the development of his early exegetical principles.

71. Historians are beginning to point out the possible problems with extending conclusions drawn from Western experience to other cultures. The extremely rapid changes brought about by the introduction of printing into Europe in 1450 have no parallel anywhere else in the world. See Graham, *Beyond the Written Word*, 17.

historians of Christianity, and of the Reformation in particular, away from research concerned only with external abuses, institutional affairs, and theological systems, and toward an approach that could explore the broader forces working to change all of European society.[72] In the last few years, historians have at last begun to acquire a greater understanding of the ways in which printing, and the increased exposure to literacy which was its result, slowly but steadily helped to reshape the social forms and mental structures of European culture.[73]

The basic inspiration for examining the effects of cultural transition from primarily oral to literate communication derives from the disciplines of anthropology, history, and literary history and theory.[74] It is certainly

72. Lucien Febvre, "Une question mal posée, les origines de la Réforme," in *Au coeur religieux du seizième siècle* (Paris: SEVPEN, 1957), 33–38, 42–44. Febvre later explored the impact of printing specifically on European culture in Lucien Febvre and Henri-Jean Martin, *L'Apparition du livre* (Paris: Editions Albin-Michel, 1958). Febvre also scolded historians for being bound to old notions of periodization which overlooked historical continuity, and he pointed them toward a study of popular religious practices and devotions, even though he himself did not avoid referring to popular religion in the late Middle Ages as "superstitious."

73. A number of historians have described the impact of literacy and printing on the history of Western Europe during various periods: Lucien Febvre and Henri-Jean Martin, *The Coming of the Book: The Impact of Printing, 1450–1800*, trans. David Gerard (London: Verso Editions, 1984)—this work first appeared in French in 1958 as *L'Apparition du livre;* Henri-Jean Martin, *The History and Power of Writing*, trans. Lydia G. Cochrane (Chicago: University of Chicago Press, 1994); Elizabeth L. Eisenstein, *The Printing Press as an Agent of Change*, 2 vols. (Cambridge: Cambridge University Press, 1979); Clanchy, *From Memory to Written Record;* Stock, *The Implications of Literacy;* Davis, "Printing and the People." Several historians who have more recently used this methodology include John Bossy, *Christianity in the West, 1400–1700* (Oxford: Oxford University Press, 1985); Sabean, *Power in the Blood;* Kristen B. Neuschel, *Word of Honor: Interpreting Noble Culture in Sixteenth-Century France* (Ithaca, N.Y.: Cornell University Press, 1989); David Cressy, *Literacy and the Social Order: Reading and Writing in Tudor and Stuart England* (Cambridge: Cambridge University Press, 1980); Graham, *Beyond the Written Word.*

74. A good summary of the historical development of literacy studies may be found in Eric Havelock, "The Oral Literature Equation: A Formula for the Modern Mind," in Olson and Torrance, eds., *Literacy and Orality*, 11–27. Jack Goody, Walter Ong, and David Warren Sabean have been particularly important for establishing methodologies and principles of understanding that are useful for interpreting sermon literature and changes in religious sensibility. See especially Jack Goody's three books, *The Domestication of the Savage Mind* (Cambridge: Cambridge University Press, 1977); *The Logic of Writing and the Organization of Society* (Cambridge: Cambridge University Press, 1986); *Literacy in Traditional Societies* (Cambridge: Cambridge University Press, 1968); and Walter J. Ong, S.J., *Orality and Literacy*

necessary to take into account recent warnings against assuming that literacy alone must of necessity create particular changes in society or in the minds of those who acquire it. The skills of literacy may have different effects depending on the social and historical forces which shape the culture into which it is introduced. There is, nevertheless, sufficient evidence to suggest that in the context of Western European society, literacy has facilitated the growth of a mindset which favors inner awareness and introspection as well as the individualism which can arise from a heightened sense of the self apart from the group.[75]

For most of the fifteenth and early sixteenth centuries, the impact of printed materials on the majority of people was no doubt indirect and was entwined in a complex relationship with persisting forms of verbal and visual communication. Natalie Davis and Robert Scribner have shown that, even during the height of printed religious propaganda produced by the Protestant Reformation in the sixteenth century, oral traditions of communication persisted and collaborated in the spread of ideas found in books and pamphlets.[76] For quite some time, fly-sheets and tracts employed both the printed word and visual illustrations in an effort to reach as many people as possible.[77] Even so, the gradual transition from a

---

and *The Presence of the Word: Some Prolegomena for Cultural and Religious History* (New Haven: Yale University Press, 1967).

75. Niko Besnier, *Literacy, Emotion, and Authority: Reading and Writing on a Polynesian Atoll* (Cambridge: Cambridge University Press, 1995), 2–7. While not denying the significance of literacy when introduced to various cultures, Besnier distinguishes between two different models for studying effects of literacy. The "autonomous" model, associated most often with Jack Goody and Walter Ong (although Goody disagrees that it represents his position), contends that literacy functions as an independent force that must inevitably result in certain cognitive and social changes. It is essentially the same as the "great divide" theory referred to above in n. 66. The "ideological" model argues that literacy cannot be divorced from the specific social and historical forces shaping the culture in which it develops and is used. Besnier acknowledges that the "autonomous" model is very popular not only among anthropologists but among scholars in a number of disciplines and that it therefore "strikes a particularly enduring chord in Western thinking" (2). The reason for this, perhaps, is that in the context of Western Europe, literacy has in fact worked to develop the type of social and cognitive characteristics identified by Goody and Ong.

76. Natalie Davis, "Printing and the People," 189–226; Scribner, "Oral Culture," 237–56.

77. Robert Scribner analyzes the visual propaganda used to popularize the Reformation among the German people in *For the Sake of Simple Folk: Popular Propaganda for the German Reformation* (Cambridge: Cambridge University Press, 1981).

society organized mentally and socially by the spoken word to one shaped by print was under way, and it brought significant changes to European religious culture. It assisted and probably accelerated the growing privatization and interiorization of religion increasingly favored by Catholic theologians and preachers and institutionalized in the various Protestant churches of the sixteenth century. It also helped to produce a new understanding of the nature of the person.

As a medium, oral communication encourages persons to perceive themselves and others primarily in the context of their objective relationships and shared experiences within the community. Visual, face-to-face contact is necessary to learn the latest news or gossip, and a person's knowledge is acquired as the result of direct personal experience or speech with someone else. Knowledge derives from the concrete, and not from abstract speculation. The work of David Sabean has argued that in such a setting, it is a person's external relationships with others that determine his or her inward emotional state. Feelings of anger, estrangement, and guilt are created within a person because of a specific disagreement or action. When the situation is put right through either private or formal legal settlement, the feelings disappear.[78] Sabean's conclusions concur with the work of John Bossy, who states that throughout most of the Middle Ages "traditional Christianity" understood sin, and therefore guilt, primarily in terms of actions which destroyed the peace and interpersonal relationships of the community. Penance, likewise, was often a specific act designed to make public, and if possible, objective reparation.[79]

The written word, however, requires no person-to-person transmission. Anyone, in the privacy of his or her home, is able to receive information, pursue instruction, or experience the world of literature purely by communing with the words on a page. Private reading and writing work to create people who are more conscious of themselves as autonomous individuals whose ideas, emotions, and sense of self are dependent

---

78. Sabean, *Power in the Blood*, 49–53. For a summary of the characteristics of oral consciousness and social structure, see Ong, "Some Psychodynamics of Orality," chapter 3 in *Orality and Literacy*, 31–77.

79. Bossy, *Christianity in the West*, 45–49.

as much or more upon interior self-reflection as on concrete experience. Not surprisingly, the type of religious thought produced in this environment would prefer to see sin as the result of a person's inward motivations and inclinations. The findings of both Thomas Tentler and John Bossy concerning sin and confession in the late Middle Ages and early modern period reveal just this type of evolving understanding.[80]

By exploring the role of Mary in public sermons with larger cultural changes in mind, we can enhance our understanding of late medieval and post-Tridentine piety and grasp more fully some of the profound social causes for the religious upheavals of the time. Marian devotion is particularly useful for this purpose because it was fully integrated into all aspects of fifteenth and sixteenth-century Catholic religious life, and because the scarcity of Biblical evidence regarding the Virgin caused her cult to be malleable, easily shaped to fit the social and spiritual needs of the Church at any given time.

The remainder of this introduction will demonstrate some of the ways in which Marian piety was woven into the tapestry of late medieval religion, for a complex relationship existed between Marian devotion, popular preaching, and the religious practices and beliefs of the day. The introduction will conclude with a summary of the broad cultural shifts affecting late medieval society and Christianity generally. The following chapters will demonstrate the often sharp contrasts between the portrayal of Mary's role as Mother of God, co-sufferer with Christ at Calvary, and heavenly intercessor in late medieval sermons, and the way she is depicted by late sixteenth and early seventeenth-century Catholic preachers. The concluding chapter will then set this transformation of Marian sermons in the context of larger changes in the culture and society of early modern Europe.

In a study such as this, which attempts to contrast historical periods or climates, there are at least two major dangers. The first is that the historian will exaggerate the changes from one period to the next. The second involves the common historical pitfall of attributing too great a degree of

---

80. Ibid., 48–49; Thomas Tentler, *Sin and Confession on the Eve of the Reformation* (Princeton: Princeton University Press, 1977), 241–49.

homogeneity to European culture and religion in any given era. I have tried to avoid too great an emphasis on change by pointing to the continuing influence of medieval religious themes and practices long after the medieval period has come to a close. I have also tried to show in the second part of the introduction that well before the Protestant Reformation or the Council of Trent, late medieval religious life was beginning to move toward the focus on the inner life which would come to predominate by the late sixteenth century, and that it was perhaps the interaction or even conflict between the concrete and contemplative facets of religious experience, beginning already in the Middle Ages, which caused so much of the religious ferment later on. It is nevertheless the task of the historian to try to envision the order beneath the surface of complex human experiences. To do this, a certain amount of synthesis and generalization is required. Most historians would agree that profound changes took place in the nature of European religious life from the fifteenth through the sixteenth centuries, so that by 1600, the Christian Church and the religious lives of individual Christians would never be the same. I have sought to shed some light on one small corner of that transformation by examining popular Marian sermons. Reading these sermons has been an entertaining, enlightening, and at times a moving enterprise which has created for me a new sense of the dynamic and central place of devotion to Mary in late medieval and early modern life. While I cannot expect to have avoided all of the ills historical work is heir to, I hope that the reader will enjoy and profit from an introduction to the Virgin as she appeared in the public words of these preachers.

Central Themes in Late Medieval Marian Piety

There is nothing more characteristic of late medieval urban piety than its persistent appeals for the guidance, aid, and above all mercy of the Virgin Mary. Medieval Christianity often assigned to Christ the Kingdom of Justice, in light of his future role as judge of the living and the dead, and to Mary the Kingdom of Mercy, expecting her to intercede with her son on behalf of sinners. Marian devotion blossomed as a major part of a religious culture in which boundaries between "popular" and "official" practices and beliefs were often scarcely visible, and in which the development of more systematic theological positions occurred at times in response to a groundswell of lay enthusiasm. The cult of Mary was in essence the result of an active dialogue between, on one hand, the religion of the laity, manifested in miracle stories, popular rituals, commissioned art, and plays, and, on the other, the existing structure of the liturgy and formal ecclesiastical teaching in which medieval piety also found expression.

A principal link between lay piety and formal theology in the late Middle Ages was the popular sermon. As men who were usually trained in the universities and ordained to the priesthood, preachers could and did represent the values and beliefs of the institutional Church. But these preachers were also men who actively participated in the wider religious culture of the day, and they were charged with inspiring the devotion of the laity. Therefore, of necessity, they had to communicate in ways that would be understood and appreciated by their hearers. While it may be assumed that they were not always successful, the fame and widespread popularity of preachers such as San Bernardino of Siena and Jean Gerson suggest both that their reputation spread quickly by word of mouth and that, as speakers, they were skillful in their ability to use the spoken word effectively among all classes of people.

Preaching was one of the most powerful forces shaping and disseminating Marian piety in the cities. Ever since the famous sermons of St. Bernard of Clairvaux in the twelfth century, preachers had been exhorting their congregations to "behold the star and call upon Mary" when they found themselves vexed by sin or temptation.[81] The sermons that St. Bernard delivered for the great Marian festivals became a virtual textbook for Marian homiletics. His themes and even his exact words were repeated again and again in the succeeding centuries by men who may have disagreed with St. Bernard's rejection of the Immaculate Conception, but who could not help being attracted by his eloquent and obviously sincere expression of affection for Mary.[82]

81. "Homiliae Super Missus Est," PL 183:55–88; quoted in Graef, *Mary,* 1:237.

82. St. Bernard's sermons may be found in *S. Bernardi Opera,* ed. J. Leclercq and H. M. Rochais, 8 vols. (Rome: Editiones Cistercienses, 1957–77). Volumes 1–2 were also edited by C. H. Talbot.

It was not until the thirteenth century, however, that preaching became so pervasive in its influence on the cult of Mary. The birth of the mendicant preaching orders, the Dominicans and the Franciscans, inaugurated a new period in the history of the Church and of Marian piety. At the Fourth Lateran Council, convened by Pope Innocent III in November 1215, the Church openly recognized the need for better trained preachers and for preaching on a more regular basis.[83] The Church had an urgent need to do battle with heterodox beliefs, such as those of the Albigensians and Waldensians, which were becoming more popular among the people of southern France. Already, two new religious orders had been formed that would answer in many ways the needs expressed by Innocent III and his council. The Order of Friars Minor received oral confirmation by Innocent himself in 1209. Then in April 1215, Dominic de Guzman's Order of Preachers was given official papal approval.[84] Men from both orders would eventually become important as preachers, confessors, and scholars, and they would leave an indelible mark on Marian devotion in the later Middle Ages.

It was the Franciscans who, from the beginning, made the most lasting contributions to popular Marian piety in the thirteenth century. The Dominicans, on the other hand, were largely involved in developing the official dogmas concerning Mary taught at the universities. In his commentary on the Gospel of Luke, the Dominican Albert the Great advocated belief in Mary's bodily assumption into heaven and taught that all

---

83. Canon X of the IV Lateran Council states, "We decree that bishops provide capable men, powerful in word and work, to exercise fruitfully the office of preaching; who (in place of the bishops, since these cannot do it) diligently visiting the people committed to them, may instruct them by word and example. And when they are in need, let them be supplied with the necessities, lest for want of these they may be compelled to abandon their work at the very beginning"; quoted in William H. Hinnebusch, *The History of the Dominican Order*, 2 vols. (New York: Alba House, 1966), 1:54.

84. James W. Powell, *The Papacy and the Early Franciscans*, Franciscan Studies, no. 36 (St. Bonaventure, N.Y.: Franciscan Institute, 1976). 254. The Franciscans did not receive written confirmation of their order until Honorius III provided it in 1223. Innocent III had hesitated due to the provision adopted at IV Lateran which sought to halt the proliferation of new religious orders. For a general history of the order, see Moorman, *History of the Franciscan Order*. For a sketchy but useful study of Franciscan preaching, which provides information on many lesser known preachers, see Zawart, *History of Franciscan Preaching*. On the founding of the Dominican Order see Hinnebusch, *History of the Dominican Order*, 1:39.

of the graces dispensed by the Church were derived from her merits.[85] Albert's ideas were destined to be significant not only because of his own reputation but also because of his relationship with his student Thomas Aquinas.

St. Thomas, a Dominican like his teacher, was one of the most famous scholastic theologians of the Middle Ages. His *Summa theologiae* was particularly important as a successful synthesis of Christian theology with Aristotelian philosophy. Anything that he had to say concerning Mary would likely have considerable influence, especially within his own order. Thomas is usually credited with helping to slow official acceptance of the doctrine of Mary's Immaculate Conception, for he believed that it detracted from Christ's role as savior of all people. It is important to note, however, that St. Bonaventure, a Franciscan, opposed this doctrine as well.[86] Although the Franciscans would later become the great champions of the Immaculate Conception, they did so in opposition to one of their own most famous theologians.

Meanwhile, thirteenth-century Franciscan efforts encouraged active worship focusing on Mary by introducing in 1263 the Feast of the Visitation,[87] and by giving official support to the popular devotion that has come to be called the Angelus. In 1269, the General Chapter of the Franciscan Order, meeting in Assisi, suggested that Franciscan preachers should teach the people to say the "Ave Maria" each evening when the city bell was rung three times to announce the city's curfew. Later, in 1317, the Dominicans of Frankfurt advocated the same devotion;[88] it received more formal papal support in 1318 when Pope John XXII offered indulgences to those who practiced it.[89] The encouragement given to the Angelus by the Franciscans and the papacy assumes a widespread familiarity with the "Ave" on the part of the people by the later thirteenth century. This assumption was probably well founded, since already in 1210 the Synod of Paris testified to the growing popularity of Mary by recommending that

---

85. Graef, *Devotion*, 50.   86. Ibid., 52.

87. Ibid.   88. Graef, *Mary*, 1:308.

89. Gerard Sloyan, "Marian Prayers," in *Mariology*, 3 vols., ed. Juniper B. Carol (Milwaukee: Bruce Publishing Company, 1961), 3:81.

all of the faithful should learn the "Ave" in addition to the "Credo" and "Pater Noster," thereby symbolically putting the angelic salutation on an equal basis with the prayer of Christ and the Creed.[90]

Popular Marian rituals and festivals promoted by the mendicants were reinforced by the portrayal of Mary found in their own sermons. Hilda Graef, Marina Warner, and Elizabeth Johnson are all convinced that the sermons of the mendicants brought new dimensions to the later medieval cult of the Virgin.[91] These historians find in the Franciscan sermons a more human treatment of Mary that corresponds to the growing emphasis on the humanity of Christ himself. According to Warner, the Franciscans removed Mary from her early medieval pedestal and made of her a humble peasant, immediately recognizable to the people who made up the audience for their sermons.[92] Johnson, too, says that Franciscan preaching provided a more "imaginative" and "human" experience of the Virgin. She became more "mother" than "queen," interceding with her son on behalf of her friends. Johnson, in fact, goes further, to supply a direct link between popular preaching and popular attitudes to Mary in the later Middle Ages. She believes that the popular preaching of the mendicant orders, occurring within the context of the plague, famine, war, and ecclesiastical schism of the time, intensified feelings of sinfulness and guilt already taking root in the popular conscience. Those who were listening to the friars had begun to doubt the possibility of their personal salvation unless Mary should deign to intercede for them with Christ.[93]

There is little doubt that the mendicant orders actively participated in

90. Graef, *Mary*, 1:231.

91. Hilda Graef's two-volume work *Mary: A History of Doctrine and Devotion*, published in 1964, is still the only major work in English covering the entire history of her cult from the standpoint of formal theology. Graef's shorter work, *The Devotion to Our Lady*, is also useful and contains some information not found in the larger study. See pp. 50–52 on the influence of the mendicants. Warner, *Alone of All Her Sex*, 179–84; Elizabeth A. Johnson, "Marian Devotion in the Western Church," in *Christian Spirituality: High Middle Ages and Reformation*, ed. Jill Raitt (New York: Crossroad Publishing Company, 1987), 392–414. Johnson's article is a more recent summary of some of the significant trends in the development of Marian devotion in the medieval period. See also Richard Kiekhefer, "Major Currents in Late Medieval Devotion," in *Christian Spirituality*, 394–414.

92. Warner, *Alone of All Her Sex*, 182.

93. Johnson, "Marian Devotion," 392–93, 400.

the shaping of late medieval Marian piety. Their emphasis on Mary's humanity was crucial for her importance in fifteenth-century religion. Historians are beginning to understand that Mary's bodily human nature was the cornerstone of the entire late medieval edifice of the Virgin's cult. But as Warner and Johnson are aware, Mary was revered by the preachers and by the thousands of people who thronged to her shrines throughout Europe as much more than a humble peasant woman, however holy and favored by God. San Bernardino asserted that Mary had done more for God than God could do for himself.[94] Bernardino of Busti was certain that the Virgin was the mediator between the Trinity and a fallen humanity.[95] Mary's Immaculate Conception was taught not only by its traditional champions, the Franciscans, but also by secular preachers such as Jean Gerson.[96]

Johnson says that, in the later Middle Ages, affection for Mary as Mother merged with a growing sense of need for her protection as Queen of Heaven, so that she was finally exalted as ruler of the universe beside Christ. More and more, people began to think of Mary as Co-Redemptrix—not a completely new idea, but one which was particularly prominent in this period.[97] Warner even goes so far as to assert that belief in Mary's Immaculate Conception removed her from the realm of the human and placed her in such an exalted position that the average person could not identify with her at all.[98] This is a problematical notion, since the Immaculate Conception was a popular belief among the same people who entered so fully into her human anguish at the cross and in the burial of her son. Also, if sinlessness automatically removed Mary from participation in authentic humanity, the same would have to be said of Christ as well. Still, there are certain tensions between exaltation and human lowliness within the Marian devotion of the later medieval period as it was proclaimed by the preachers themselves. As such they are tensions common to the general spirituality of the time, which yearned to experi-

94. San Bernardino of Siena, *Opera omnia*, 2:375.
95. Bernardino of Busti, *Mariale*, Sermon 1: pt. 3, "On the Name of Mary."
96. Gerson, *Oeuvres complètes*, 7:1057–80.
97. Johnson, "Marian Devotion," 405–6.
98. Warner, "The Immaculate Conception," chapter 16 in *Alone of All Her Sex*, 236–54.

ence the most exalted mysteries within the context of tangible human life. Mary was the perfect embodiment of the ability of someone purely human to experience union with the divine; therefore her popularity mingled with almost every aspect of fifteenth-century religious life. There are few religious paintings, plays, sermons, or devotional artifacts dating from this period that do not carry with them the scent, however faint, of roses or lilies.

Most historians, in agreement with Elizabeth Johnson, have concluded that Mary's popularity continued to thrive and even increase during the fourteenth and fifteenth centuries.[99] This accords well with the findings of Bernd Moeller and A. N. Galpern that traditional forms of religious expression not only continued but were especially popular in the years just prior to the Reformation.[100] Galpern speaks of a flowering of late medieval piety in Champagne around 1500.[101] Even Steven Ozment, who believes that late medieval religion was more burden than blessing to believers, agrees that there was a "surge in lay piety" in the late fifteenth and early sixteenth centuries.[102] European religion was entering, nevertheless, a period of profound transformation in the fifteenth century, a change so significant that Lucien Febvre refers to a "crisis" or a "revolution of religious sentiment" experienced not just by one region but by Europe as a whole.[103] While traditional, more concrete forms of piety,

99. Kieckhefer, "Major Currents," 89–93; Graef, *Mary,* 1:265–322. Graef tends to stress what she perceives to be the excesses in the late medieval Marian cult and the efforts by more balanced theologians such as Jean Gerson to curb abuses. All of Warner's *Alone of All Her Sex* confirms Mary's popularity in the late Middle Ages. See also Gail McMurray Gibson, *The Theater of Devotion: East Anglian Drama and Society in the Late Middle Ages* (Chicago: University of Chicago Press, 1989). Especially useful is chapter 6, "Mary's Dower: East Anglian Drama and the Cult of the Virgin," 137–76.

100. Bernd Moeller, "Piety in Germany around 1500," in *The Reformation in Medieval Perspective,* ed. Steven E. Ozment, trans. Joyce Irwin (Chicago: Quadrangle Books, 1971), 50–75; A. N. Galpern, *The Religions of the People in Sixteenth-Century Champagne* (Cambridge: Harvard University Press, 1976). Also important is the traditional negative assessment of the popularity of outward devotions at the close of the Middle Ages in Johann Huizinga, *The Waning of the Middle Ages: A Study of the Forms of Life, Thought and Art in France and the Netherlands in the XIVth and XVth Centuries,* trans. F. Hoffman (London: Arnold, 1924), 166.

101. Galpern, *Religions of the People,* 90. Lucien Febvre also notes the vitality of late medieval religious life in France in "Une question mal posée," 27.

102. Steven E. Ozment, *The Reformation in the Cities: The Appeal of Protestantism to Sixteenth-Century Germany and Switzerland* (New Haven: Yale University Press, 1975), 21.

103. Febvre, "Une question mal posée," 26, 69.

including images and relics, communal processions, and pilgrimages remained popular, some historians point out that personal religious experience and devotional practices were becoming more interiorized and individual. Developments in Mary's cult closely paralleled the more general trends.

There is evidence that more people in the later Middle Ages were attempting to view Mary as an individual with whom they might establish an intimate personal relationship. In the past, in the art and devotion of the Church, Mary was important primarily because of her objective role in the history of salvation; she appeared as a majestic queen, whether holding her son or ruling in heaven. Now, worshipers began to express a subjective interest in Mary as a person with whom they could form intimate, personal bonds. They were interested in her life story as in that of a friend; they looked to her for help and intercession in their individual needs.[104] Those who made wills reveal the personal nature of attachment to Mary. Nicolas Goujon spoke in his will of "my well-beloved mother Mary, dame and mistress"; Adam Maure, a merchant of Bar-sur-Aube called her "the glorious Virgin Mary, my mother."[105]

Books of Hours and Rosaries were two of the most significant popular devotional aids in the later Middle Ages; the use of both points to a movement toward a more interior and individual spirituality. These were even used by worshipers during Mass, indicating the erosion of a sense of communal solidarity during what should have been the supreme sacrament of Christian unity.[106] The Rosary became quite popular in the late fifteenth century, and was widely promoted by the Dominicans. The Dominicans were involved in establishing the first officially recognized confraternity dedicated to the Rosary in 1475, but the honor of creating the first Rosary brotherhood goes to Alanus de Rupe, who founded a

---

104. Johnson, "Marian Devotion," 393–94.

105. Galpern, *Religions of the People*, 50.

106. Francis Rapp, *L'Église et la vie religieuse en occident à la fin du moyen âge* (Paris: Presses Universitaires de France, 1971), 329. John Bossy likewise refers to the change taking place in late medieval attitudes to communion and seems to regret that the older focus on communal unity was being "undermined" by "the use among the devout of the piety of frequent communion: that intimate, interior, even mystical devotion to Christ . . . ," *Christianity in the West*, 72.

Rosary fraternity in Douai in 1470.[107] The Church encouraged the Rosary as a means of allowing worshipers to develop their interior life and avoid too great a reliance on exterior actions.[108]

These two devotions stem from the desire of lay persons to participate in a limited way in monastic forms of worship. Books of Hours, which contained numerous prayers to Mary, were modeled on the round of canonical hours followed in convent communities. The Rosary, known as "Mary's Psalter" or "Our Lady's Psalter," attempted to provide the laity with their own "psalms," since most either could not read or were unlikely to be able to memorize the entire 150 Psalms of the Old Testament or recite them in the course of a week as the monks did.

The practice of sacramental confession, required at least once a year at Easter, was also changing in ways that reinforced the tendency toward interior, individualized feelings of personal shortcoming. Thomas Tentler has examined the confessional manuals and practices in vogue just prior

107. Anne Winston-Allen, *Stories of the Rose: The Making of the Rosary in the Middle Ages* (University Park: Pennsylvania State University Press, 1997), 24–25; Febvre, "Une question mal posée," 28; Warner, *Alone of All Her Sex*, 306. Alanus de Rupe (1428–75), also known as Alain de la Roche, created a Rosary brotherhood in Douai in 1470, but it was not recognized in Rome until 1475, when the Dominican witch-hunter, Jacob Sprenger, founded a similar confraternity devoted to the Rosary at Cologne. Apparently it was the presence of Emperor Frederick III among the founding members of the Cologne group which ultimately assured papal acceptance of both brotherhoods. Jean-Claude Schmitt has studied a Rosary confraternity founded by the Dominicans at Colmar in 1484. He links Dominican support of such confraternities to the desire of the Observants to extend their influence. More to the point in this context, Schmitt confirms the individuality fostered by this devotion. He stresses that there were no communal obligations attached to membership. It sufficed only to recite the Marian psalter once weekly to receive the graces and indulgences conferred on members. This allowed membership to be spread over greater geographical areas and into remote places where travel was difficult. As he states it, "Aucun intermédiaire entre le confrère et la Vierge, à qu'il s'adressait. Il était seul avec sa prière, et de lui seul dépendait aussi qu'il profitat des biens spirituels de la communauté"; "Apostolat mendiant et société: une confrérie Dominicaine a la vielle de la Réforme," *Annales ESC* 26 (1971): 83–104.

108. Winston-Allen, *Stories of the Rose*, 29–30. Winston-Allen stresses that, in addition to the importance of the Rosary as an aid to private and individualized devotion, it is useful to keep in mind that the narrative structure of the devotion itself, which focused on the lives of Christ and the Virgin, was ideally suited to a culture still primarily oral in nature. The narrative can serve as a mnemonic aid enabling the worshiper to remember the necessary parts of the ritual act.

to the Reformation; he concludes that priests were asked to investigate the motives for sin and the repentance of their parishioners according to standards that were much more "exacting" and introspective than formerly.[109] Tentler tries to show that one of the primary motivations for a more detailed confession was social control. The individual was encouraged to discipline his or her own life, beginning with that most difficult-to-control aspect of the human person, thought.[110] Popular vernacular literature of the later Middle Ages was also designed to produce the same result.[111]

A heightened sense of sin, particularly at the personal level, is in part responsible for creating a more fervent devotion to the Passion of Christ. John Bossy attributes an absorption in Christ's suffering to the need for medieval persons to prove to themselves that the Christ whom they knew to be God was also a human being like themselves, experiencing real pain and anguish.[112] As one of the central themes of the Christian faith, the death of Christ might be expected to be of paramount importance in any age of the Church. Yet the intensity of emotion created in the fourteenth and fifteenth centuries by portrayals of Christ's suffering is unique and gives the piety of the late Middle Ages a distinctive character. Paradoxically, the interiorized need to associate with the Passion found its fulfillment in a number of exterior, concrete ways. Images of the suffering Christ proliferated in all forms of artistic, literary, and ritual expression, including the crucifix, the Ecce Homo, Passion plays, and the Stations of the Cross. Popular sermons described in ever more vivid and concrete terms every stage of Christ's Passion, from his arrest in the garden to his

109. Tentler, *Sin and Confession*, 245. Canon XXI of the IV Lateran Council of 1215 decreed that all Christians of both sexes were to confess to their own priest and perform the assigned penance at least once a year prior to receiving the Eucharist at Easter. See Henricus Denzinger and Iohannes Umberg, S.J., eds., *Enchiridion symbolorum definitionum et declarationum de rebus fidei et morum* (Freiburg: Herder and Co., 1937), 204–5.

110. Tentler, *Sin and Confession*, 234–37; Bossy, *Christianity in the West*, 27. Bossy calls the new approach to confession "an incentive for the systematic interior monitoring by the individual of his own life."

111. Coleman, *Medieval Readers and Writers*, 186–87.

112. Bossy, *Christianity in the West*, 6–7. According to Bossy, this need was occasioned by St. Anselm's doctrine of the atonement which required that the person offering satisfaction on behalf of someone else be kin, a member of the family.

burial. The overall trend in later years may have been a more interiorized religious life, but the fifteenth century was pervaded by an almost universal effort to achieve closeness to God and, in particular, to Christ through tangible images of his suffering body.

In the end, it is this need to approach the divine by means of the human and the material which provides the common thread running through all aspects of late medieval religion and most closely links devotion to Mary with that offered to her son. Everywhere one looks in the fifteenth century, there is evidence that people were straining to use all of their senses to apprehend the holy; bodily metaphors abound in the arts and in sermons. Piety is imbued with a sacramental and incarnational quality that does not hesitate to express the experience of God in ways that have seemed at best simplistic and at worst crude to later Catholic and Protestant Reformers and to some modern historians.[113] It is easy to find summaries of some of the more extreme and questionable aspects of medieval devotion and the very real difficulties which they posed for the religious lives of late medieval Christians.[114] And yet in the creative use of religious symbol the late Middle Ages is one of the most fertile periods in Western history. In her important and innovative study *Holy Feast and Holy Fast*, Caroline Walker Bynum has examined attitudes to food and its role in the religious life of late medieval women. She affirms,

In exactly that period of medieval spirituality that scholars have dismissed as "literal" and "degenerate," symbols flowered into a complexity that lifted the full panorama of human experience toward the divine.[115]

Likewise, Gail McMurray Gibson, in her work *The Theater of Devotion*, has identified the "incarnational aesthetic" as the most significant facet of late medieval English art and drama. Gibson is certain that it is for this reason that Mary plays so prominent a part in East Anglian drama in the fifteenth century.[116]

---

113. One of the best descriptions and critiques of this negative view of the fifteenth century is Gibson, *Theater of Devotion*, 2–5.

114. For a fairly recent discussion of the problems associated with late medieval religious life see Eire, *War Against the Idols*, 8–27.

115. Bynum, *Holy Feast and Holy Fast*, 278.

116. Gibson, "Fifteenth-Century Culture and the Incarnational Aesthetic," in *The Theater of Devotion*, 1–18.

Because of this emphasis on the concrete and the sacramental, Mary's bodily relationship to Christ is at the heart of the devotion surrounding her in the period. It was, of course, not a new source of debate or interest. In the early centuries of the Church, there was such a close link between Christology and doctrines concerning Mary that councils called to deal with Christ inevitably issued official statements about Mary as well. The Third Ecumenical Council of Ephesus in 431 provided a significant boost to Mary's increasing popularity by formally declaring her to be the "Theotokos" or "Bearer of God."[117] The Council of Chalcedon, in 451, further enhanced her special bodily nature by proclaiming her to be "ever-virgin." Mary had retained her bodily virginity unimpaired in conception, while giving birth [in partu], and after giving birth [post partum].[118]

Consistent with these developments, almost all of the major Marian festivals were concerned in some way with the purity of Mary's body and its use as the instrument of the Incarnation.[119] Nor was there a shortage of Marian relics in medieval Europe, in spite of the fact that the doctrine of Mary's bodily Assumption into heaven was widely accepted among the people. Locks of her hair, pieces of her dress, her veil, her milk, and even her house were the magnets for some of the most popular shrines in Europe, drawing numerous pilgrims to worship and pray, and to spend their money in the local community.[120] Undoubtedly, much of the ferment of late medieval religious life in general, and of the cult of Mary in

117. Graef, *Mary,* 1:108–11. Referring to the Virgin as "Theotokos" was one means of defending the position that already within the womb, Jesus possessed a divine as well as a human nature.

118. Ibid., 116–18.

119. Gibson, *Theater of Devotion,* 166–68.

120. H. P. J. M. Ahsmann, *Le culte de la Sainte-Vierge et la littérature française profane du Moyen Age* (Paris: Picard, 1930), 21. Ahsmann points out that Marian relics were already popular in France at the time of Gregory of Tours in the sixth century. Famous French shrines with Marian relics included Paris, which claimed to have a lock of her hair; Aix-la-Chapelle, which had a piece of her dress; and Chartres, which had her veil. England claimed one of the internationally popular Marian shrines at Walsingham, where Richelde Faverches had received visions in the twelfth century showing her the very house in which Mary had received the Annunciation and therefore in which she had conceived Christ. Mary commanded Richelde to build an exact replica of the house and even directed her to the proper site. See Colin Stephenson, *Walsingham Way* (London: Darton, Longman and Todd, 1970); and also Gibson, *Theater of Devotion,* 139–43. Even more important, perhaps, was the

particular, may be attributed to the juxtaposition of this intensely sacramental piety beside the newer, more interiorized forms of devotion among the people.[121]

It might seem natural that Mary's body or the body generally should be an important symbol in the context of Christian society. St. Paul led the way in the Christian tradition with his famous comparison of the early Christian community to a body whose members are all necessary and work together toward a common end.[122] But this seeming naturalness can be deceptive. It may be true that certain symbols are used in many cultures and at different times to represent similar social or even religious experiences. However, as Mary Douglas warns in her book *Natural Symbols,* there are, paradoxically, no "natural" symbols, since any image can have meaning only in the context of a specific society and its understanding of itself. All symbols are social.[123]

For a comparative study such as this one, which seeks to compare the

---

Holy House of Loreto, Italy, which was supposed to be not a replica, but the very house in which Jesus was conceived. It had been miraculously transported to Italy in 1295. As late as the seventeenth century, emotional pilgrims were still making the trek to visit it. See Stéphane Boiron, *La Controverse née de la querelle de reliques à l'époque du concile de Trente (1500–1640),* Travaux et recherches de l'Université de droit d'économie et de sciences sociales de Paris, no. 28 (Paris: Presses Universitaires de France, 1989), 111–12.

121. See Eire, *War Against the Idols,* 2, 25. Eire argues that the tensions in late medieval religion are due in part to the fact that "paradoxically, in seeking divinity through more immediate means, late medieval religion only succeeded in making it ever more distant." He believes that late medieval Christians were expecting so much from their view of the immanence of God in the material objects of worship that they were bound to be disappointed. On the other hand, it is clear that not all people in the period were dissatisfied with their religious practices, even in England, which had seen the rise of an intense, if limited, Lollard/Wycliffite movement. See Eamon Duffy, *The Stripping of the Altars: Traditional Religion in England, c. 1400–1580* (New Haven: Yale University Press, 1992). Duffy's book is an extensive refutation of the usual notion that the people of sixteenth-century England were either religiously indifferent or patently anxious to embrace the new Protestant faith.

122. 1 Corinthians 12.

123. Mary Douglas, *Natural Symbols: Explorations in Cosmology* (New York: Pantheon Books, 1982, xix–xx. Peter Brown, for instance, cautions those who are so prepared to see the early Christian patron saints as simple extensions of pagan gods and goddesses, as though both represented the same religious experience. Instead, they belong to two divergent interpretations of reality. While the patron saint may in some ways have been the "heir" of the Roman "genius," the saint was a fellow human being. See Peter Brown, *The Cult of the Saints: Its Rise and Function in Latin Christianity* (Chicago: University of Chicago Press, 1981), 57–60.

presentation of Mary in the fifteenth century with her portrayal in the later sixteenth and seventeenth centuries, Douglas's point is crucial. It means that it will be necessary to determine whether the common fund of bodily symbols and other stylized language used in both periods to describe Mary and her saving role expresses the same or a different meaning. This problem is compounded because of the need to deal with an institutional Church which has always been committed to a book, the Scriptures of the Old and New Testaments, and to a common tradition of interpreting those writings. A fixed body of literature has a way of establishing both form and content, making those institutions which adopt particular writings as authoritative more resistant to cultural change.[124]

Because of their adherence to the specific content of a fixed body of literature, some religions are more likely to create an organized structure which governs both practices and beliefs. Such religions are less likely to modify their teachings and rituals in immediate response to broader social trends. It is also true, however, that the Christian religious texts have always existed not only as written documents to be read intact, either privately or in worship. Parts of them have also been incorporated into the active liturgy of the people and, in that form, can be interpreted and even altered by worshipers and preachers in new ways.[125] The Christian landscape of any period will then be formed by the interaction between the forces for change which are shaping the culture and its ideas at large, the liturgical use of religious books, and official institutional loyalty to a traditional interpretation of those books.

124. Goody, *Logic of Writing*, xvii. Goody states, "In both ways (form and content) religion acquires an increased measure of autonomy in relation to other aspects of the social system. But the emergence of religion as one of the 'great organizations' . . . implies autonomy of the Church as an organization. It is the partial autonomy of these organizations that requires us to qualify . . . as well as to modify those social theories of many different inspirations, that assume religion, even in its ecclesiastical form to reflect the dominant themes of the rest of the socio-cultural system in any tight structural or functional way."

125. Graham, *Beyond the Written Word*, 61, 141–42, 156–57; E. Ann Matter, *The Voice of My Beloved: The Song of Songs in Western Medieval Christianity* (Philadelphia: University of Pennsylvania Press, 1990), 151–52. Matter discusses the way in which liturgical use of the Song of Songs to refer symbolically to Mary eventually led to official Biblical exegesis of the same sort.

The irony of the late fifteenth and sixteenth centuries is that, in this period, it was "the book" itself, understood as both the Bible and other literature, which was altering in deep and permanent ways the religion and society of Western Europe. As literacy increased, and with it an emphasis on inner religious experience, attitudes toward the spiritual value of the concrete body in a religious context began to change. For one thing, the body's necessary role in the passing on of knowledge and information is not as obscured in the arena of the spoken word as in that of writing— first, because one must be bodily present in a group or with someone else for communication to take place; second, because body movements, or a lack of them, are an important part of oral communication, often completing or clarifying the verbal message. As Walter Ong observes, "In oral verbalization, particularly public verbalization, absolute motionlessness is itself a powerful gesture."[126] By its presence alone, the body assists in transmitting the message, and the distinction between the action of the body as a whole and the act of the mouth in speaking is blurred. The word is always incarnate in an active person. The importance of this fact in the history of Judeo-Christian thought is clear. The Genesis account records a God who brings all into existence through his spoken word, which finds form in concrete, material objects. The Gospel of John speaks of the creative Word made flesh in the human form of Jesus. Therefore in spite of a certain tendency within the Christian tradition to speak of the body as a deterrent to the spiritual life or as a source of temptation, for the most part, a Christian society which takes seriously the religious implications of the Incarnation and which is also primarily reliant on speech for communication should logically use the body most often as a positive symbol of spiritual union or nourishment.[127]

126. Ong, *Orality and Literacy*, 68. See also Graham, *Beyond the Written Word*, 61, 141–42. Graham points out that in the Middle Ages people approached even the written word of Scripture as something that speaks because most encountered it orally through the liturgy and preaching. It was an "extension" of the oral word which lives in ritual, in situations in which there is no separation between word and act.

127. Biblical precedents in the Old and New Testament are numerous. For example, Psalm 34:8, "O taste and see that the Lord is good"; Isaiah 55:1–2; 1 Peter 2:2; 1 Corinthians 3:2; and Hebrews 5:13–14 all rely on the bodily symbolism of taste or eating to represent spiritual experience. Psalm 34:8 is a good example of synesthesia, discussed by David

Larissa Taylor provides one of the most striking examples in a sermon of the body's use as a positive symbol of love and nurture. She quotes this story from Michel Menot's Lenten sermons in Tours. The story was intended to illustrate the fulfillment of the commandment to honor father and mother. Menot told of a young woman of the Roman Empire whose mother was arrested for committing a serious crime and imprisoned without food. She obtained permission from the emperor to visit her mother, but was forced to disrobe before entering her mother's cell to prevent the concealment of food that she might want to bring with her. While in the cell, she fed her mother from her own breasts as once her mother had fed her. When the emperor learned of the daughter's great love for her mother, he allowed the mother to go free.[128] If the body of an ordinary woman can become for Menot and his hearers a demonstration of supreme love and devotion through its ability to nourish, how much more will this be true when the body in question is the pure flesh of the Virgin Mary which provided and then nurtured the bodily humanity of Jesus?

The world of the fifteenth century, the world of Jean Gerson, of San Bernardino, of Olivier Maillard and Gabriel Barletta, was a world increasingly familiar with the written word, yet their day-to-day experiences were still largely structured by the rhythms of speech. In this setting, the words of preachers were especially important to people as sources of information, of religious instruction, and even of ecclesiastical and political propaganda. They can tell us much about the place of Mary in the Christianity of late medieval Europe.

In describing the lives of Mary and Jesus, medieval preachers often

---

Chidester in *Word and Light,* 14–24, 144. Synesthesia is especially common in the Christian literary tradition. It combines or crosses the perceptions of the senses. Taste and sight or sound and sight are blended in an attempt to indicate that something out of the ordinary or even transcendent is taking place. Chidester also remarks that such synesthesia represents a more "unified" approach to sense perception. Nevertheless, Chidester argues that "both literate and oral textual traditions have tended to reject smell, taste, and touch as authentic modes of perception, or thought or relation with the sacred." This doesn't always seem to be the case, however, with either the Jewish or Christian Scriptures and it certainly was not the case in medieval sermons.

128. Michel Menot, *Carême de Tours,* 37; quoted in Taylor, *Soldiers of Christ,* 68, 262 n. 109.

employ a style of narration similar to that found in medieval Biblical commentaries. Not content with the few events and explanations provided in the Scriptures, medieval preachers sought to supply all of the necessary details that would enable their hearers to entertain a complete mental picture of the setting, actions, and words of the actors in the historical drama of salvation. By doing so they also came within the tradition already begun by the writers of the apocryphal gospels in the second century. Authors of works like the *Protevangelium of James* had tried to fill in the events of Mary's life omitted by those evangelists who were eventually enshrined in the canon. It is an approach perfectly suited to religious sensibilities accustomed to thinking of God as immanent, the human Jesus enfleshed in the Virgin's womb, dying on the cross, or present in the Eucharist, for it makes the characters a part of the everyday world in much the same way that religious drama did. Such sermon accounts coincide with Erich Auerbach's description of the "foregrounded" style of myth. Mythic narrative seeks to leave no loose ends; all is explained and made to fit into the prescribed pattern of belief. Auerbach likewise contrasted this foregrounded style with the Biblical accounts which portray instead the transcendence and mystery of God by leaving much more to the imagination and in the background, refusing to allow God to be revealed too greatly in tangible, concrete ways.[129] Some scholars might think that it should have been problematic for medieval exegetes to abandon the transcendent, "backgrounded" style employed by the Scriptures in favor of a foregrounded style suitable for myth. Yet what could be more logical for members of a religion which believes that the transcendent Deity has in fact become immanent in the flesh of the historical Jesus, conceived in the body of the Virgin Mary?

Did all of the attention showered by preachers upon Mary and her role in salvation mean that late medieval people saw Mary as a person important even apart from her relationship with Christ? Had she become an independent spiritual power in the life of the individual? Some historians would say "yes." Graef asserts that from the thirteenth through the fif-

129. Erich Auerbach, *Mimesis*, trans. Willard R. Trask (Princeton: Princeton University Press, 1953), pp. 7–11.

teenth centuries, Mariology ceased to be a "section of theology belonging to the incarnation" and became instead "an independent subject in which pious imagination was allowed to run riot."[130] Johnson agrees and says that, after the fourteenth century, popular piety looked to Mary as to an "autonomous being, less and less connected with Christ."[131] John Bossy offers a dissenting opinion, since he ties Mary's importance in the late Middle Ages directly to her kinship relation with Jesus.[132]

In actual practice, it is difficult to see how Mary could have acquired any permanent significance apart from Christ altogether. She was "Notre Dame," but only because Christ was "Notre Seigneur"; "Regina Coeli," because mother or spouse of the "Rex Regum et Dominus Dominorum." Finally, she was "Mater Misericordiae" chiefly because of her ability to stay the punishing hand of God and obtain his mercy by imploring her son for forgiveness for sinners. It is true that in many of the miracle stories associated with Mary, as well as in the plague art generated by the onset of the Black Death in 1348, she appears to act unilaterally, ensuring the salvation of thieves and rogues or the protection of a city from the plague purely because they have offered her worship or praise.[133] The miracle stories and the plague art, however, existed within the context of a popular piety equally familiar with Nativity and Passion plays and with sermons and altarpieces which consistently demonstrated the close rela-

130. Graef, *Devotion*, 65.

131. Johnson, "Marian Devotion," 406. Heiko Oberman agrees and says that, in the devotional works and sermons of Gabriel Biel, "popular Marian piety is stimulated and encouraged to isolate Mary as an individual apart from her son." See Oberman, *Harvest of Medieval Theology*, 301.

132. Bossy, *Christianity in the West*, 8–9.

133. Louise Marshall, "Manipulating the Sacred: Image and Plague in Renaissance Italy," *Renaissance Quarterly* 47 (1994): 485–532. Marshall argues that late medieval devotion tended to see a "specialization of functions" in the patronage of various saints, and that in plague art, Mary often acts as an autonomous protector for those who seek her aid. Both Jesus and God the Father are at times portrayed as Mary's opposition in their desire to punish humankind with the plague. Virginia Reinburg, however, points out that medieval laypersons often did not make clear distinctions among heavenly beings when praying; she asserts that regardless of the saint to whom the prayer is addressed, the person felt God always to be present. See Virginia Reinburg, "Hearing Lay People's Prayer," in *Culture and Identity in Early Modern Europe (1500–1800): Essays in Honor of Natalie Zemon Davis*, ed. Barbara B. Diefendorf and Carla Hesse (Ann Arbor: University of Michigan Press, 1993), 22.

tionship between Mary and Jesus. While it is impossible to know definitely the thoughts of medieval Christians, to suppose that Mary was seen fully autonomous in the minds of the people is perhaps to introduce a mental dichotomy that did not exist at the time, but was created by Protestant and even reforming Catholic attacks on popular practices and religious language later on. It would be closer to the truth to see Mary as approaching equality with Christ, participating alongside him in the ongoing salvation of sinners.

Plays and sermons devoted to the Passion usually give the impression that Mary was a constant companion of Jesus. She was in his thoughts even in those times when her physical presence cannot be documented by the Gospel accounts. In the popular devotion the Stations of the Cross, Jesus encountered his mother as he carried his cross to Calvary, and it is always Mary who is shown receiving the dead body of her son after its removal from the cross. As the Mater Dolorosa of popular art and drama, Mary often appears as a co-sufferer with Christ, her soul's compassion echoing the physical passion which he endured.[134] It should also be remembered that San Bernardino, who is often quoted as someone who made extreme statements about the role of Mary in salvation, was most widely known for popularizing devotion to the Holy Name of Jesus. San Bernardino's love for Mary did not cause him to forget in his preaching the supreme importance of Jesus as the savior. The Virgin Mary was certainly important as an individual to the Christians of the fifteenth century, but the source of her significance was her divine motherhood of Christ who, because of his filial devotion, could deny his mother nothing, even when she chose to intercede for sinners who had shown little remorse for their sin.[135]

134. The best discussion of Mary's compassion and her role as Co-Redemptrix in popular devotion is in Sandro Sticca, *The "Planctus Mariae" in the Dramatic Tradition of the Middle Ages*, trans. Joseph R. Berrigan (Athens: University of Georgia Press, 1988).

135. The notion that Christ could not say no to Mary is especially popular in the miracle stories often used as sermon illustrations. Dominican preacher Gabriel Barletta began his sermon for the first Saturday of Lent with a miracle story concerning a thief who heard Mass every Saturday in honor of the Virgin. He asked her not to allow him to die without contrition and confession. She appeared to him and granted him his request; when he finally died, he was saved. Barletta, *Sermones quadragesimales*, 15v–16r.

At times the complexity and richness of late medieval Marian piety can appear overwhelming, seeming to deny any attempts by the historian to reduce it to logical order. No doubt this explains in part the fact that there are few historical monographs providing a synthesis of the cult of Mary in the Middle Ages. This is the reason that popular sermons are an especially useful source of information. They demonstrate clearly the significance of Marian devotion in the context of late medieval religion and they provide a yardstick for measuring the growth and changes occurring in the Christian Church in the midst of the storms of religious upheaval in the sixteenth century. These sermons are a point of contact between the formal religion of the schools and the religious culture of the laity. They also reflect the tensions between exterior and interior forms of devotion so characteristic of the period. This latter tension appears as early as the sermons of Parisian Chancellor Jean Gerson, in the late fourteenth and early fifteenth centuries. Already he is encouraging his hearers to develop their interior mental creativity, but for the purpose of painting very concrete images. He exhorts his congregation, "Keep before the eyes of your mind, on the canvas of true faith, the picture and sorrowful likeness of Jesus, your savior."[136] Those who heard these words would have thought immediately of the crucifixes, altar paintings, and even dramatic presentations of Jesus' suffering that were well integrated into their common experience. Now, however, the people were being asked to reconstruct them mentally.

Daniel Lesnick identifies the same characteristic in the sermons of Italian Franciscans. He contrasts their popular approach with that of the more formal Dominicans and says that the Franciscans' goal was to reach "the humbler social orders of artisans, craftsmen, and shopkeepers" and to incite them to action. Therefore, their sermons were filled with more concrete examples and with more colorful language. Like Gerson, they sought to help their audience recreate, in the interior of their own minds, solid mental images drawn from their sense of sight. In this way, the Franciscans "fostered a piety based not on abstraction and intellect but

---

136. Gerson, *Oeuvres complètes*, 7:467. "Mets a present devant les yeulx de ta pense, en la carte de vrai foy l'image et la piteuse semblence de ton Sauveur Jhesus."

rather on direct sensible experience that was created by the imaginative process."[137]

Sermons delivered by Franciscans, Dominicans, and secular preachers before large public congregations were an intersection of all of the avenues of later medieval religious life. One of their goals was to kindle religious devotion in the hearts of their individual hearers; to do this they did often try to fuel a sense of guilt that would lead to contrition and confession. At their best, however, medieval preachers could be capable of great sensitivity and warmth. This was never more true than in their references to Mary, Virgin Mother of Christ. They speak of a woman known to all as "Mother," or "Our Lady," "Queen of Heaven," and "Star of the Sea." Love for Mary was sincere, on the part of the preachers and the people. But what did Mary really mean to them and how did the preachers use Marian devotion to attempt to shape the religious lives of those who came to hear them in churches and on open air platforms? To answer these questions, it is necessary to begin with their presentation of Mary's most basic and tangible accomplishment, her bestowal of a fleshly humanity on the Son of God.[138]

137. Daniel R. Lesnick, *Preaching in Medieval Florence: The Social World of Franciscan and Dominican Spirituality* (Athens: University of Georgia Press, 1989), 134–35, 162–63. See also Lochrie, *Margery Kempe*, 28–31. Lochrie finds the same approach in the non-Dionysian mysticism of the late Middle Ages as well as the more popular guides for pilgrims. Both are shaped by the pattern of the Incarnation, which had allowed access to divine truth by means of the human body of Jesus. In the same way, corporeal mental images permit contact with the spiritual in mystical descriptions of union with God and in descriptions of the Holy Land and the places where Jesus suffered.

138. I am indebted to Heiko Oberman's *Harvest of Medieval Theology*, 281, for the idea of constructing this study according to the categories traditionally used for discussions of the life and work of Christ: his Incarnation and earthly life, and his ongoing presence as resurrected ruler of the universe, seated at the right hand of God in heaven. According to Oberman, Biel's formal Mariology was organized in this way. A section of the study has been devoted also to the Passion in order to highlight the special place held by Mary in the Passion sermons of the late Middle Ages and to show more clearly the important changes which occur in presentations of the Passion in the sixteenth century.

One

"From the Very Pure Blood"

Mary's Motherhood and Late Medieval Christianity

This beautiful body (of Christ), created by the work of the blessed Holy Spirit, was so dear, so precious, so noble, so heroic, because it was formed from the very pure blood of blessed Mary.[1]

—Michel Menot

For the immaculate conception of the blessed Virgin became the solid foundation for the salvation of the world, in as much as because of the purity and holy humility of the Virgin herself, the savior of the world was incarnate in her.[2]

—Bernardino of Busti

IN ONE OF HIS SERMONS for the Thursday after Easter, the popular Italian preacher San Bernardino of Siena chose to preach "On the Exceedingly Wonderful Grace and Glory of the Mother of God." As he developed his theme, San Bernardino sought to glorify the shared flesh of Mary and Christ by linking Mary to the whole edifice of the sacramental system.[3]

1. Michel Menot, *Sermons choisis de Michel Menot*, ed. J. Nève (Paris: Bibliothèque du XVe siècle, 1924), 178.

2. Bernardino of Busti, *Mariale* (Milan: Leonardus Pachel, 1493), Sermon 2, "On the Immaculate Conception," pt. 1.

3. San Bernardino was far from being the first to do this. The relationship of Mary to the Eucharist will be discussed fully in Chapter 3. Hilda Graef provides a number of instances in which major theologians sought to tie Mary to the Eucharist because of her shared body with Christ. The earliest person to do so was probably the Syrian deacon

For from the flesh of the blessed Virgin and in the part of her body that was taken from her,[4] the whole glory and weight of the sacraments of the Church of God consists, is perfected, and reaches its end. . . . And so that I might glorify more expressly that most worthy and blessed flesh drawn from the glorious Virgin, I say that the Most High dignified it with such great infinity of nobility, that since it was to be the flesh of true man while Jesus lived, it would be able to lose the form of Man, but never the form of God.[5]

Besides making the Virgin's flesh the original source of sacramental grace, San Bernardino was also suggesting nothing less than the deification of the flesh of Mary through her son, Jesus. Nor was he the only preacher to make such connections in his sermons.

The relationship between Mary's bodily humanity and the central doctrines of the Christian faith was an important consideration for a number of the more prominent preachers of the later Middle Ages; as indicated in the Introduction, bodily metaphors and symbols abounded in the religious culture of the day. The erotic imagery of the Song of Songs resounded throughout the medieval period as an expression of both the union of the soul with Christ and the marriage celebrated between the Virgin Mary and God in the act of Incarnation. For medieval preachers, Mary's ability to participate in human redemption stems from her divine motherhood of Christ and the fact that both mother and son possessed a common flesh and humanity. San Bernardino, who did not hesitate to tie Mary's body to the sacramental system, asserted that Mary's dignity was inescapably tied to her role as Mother of God in the Incarnation because no one else could have fulfilled this duty. The Church's liturgy proves this

---

Ephraem (306–73). Jean Gerson referred to Mary as the "mother of the Eucharist" in his treatise on the "Magnificat." See Hilda Graef, *Mary: A History of Doctrine and Devotion*, 2 vols. (New York: Sheed and Ward, 1964), 1:62, 313.

4. The word "excisa," which San Bernardino used here, literally means "cut off" or "hewn from."

5. San Bernardino of Siena, *Opera omnia*, ed. P. M. Perantoni, 5 vols. (Quaracchi: Collegium S. Bonaventurae, 1950–), 2:380. "De carne enim Virginis benedictae et in parte corporis eius excisa consistit, perficitur et terminatur totium decus et pondus sacramentorum Ecclesiae Dei. . . . Et, ut expressius magnificem illam dignissimam et beatissimam carnem de Virgine gloriosa decisam, dico quod tanta infinitate nobilitatis eam dignificavit altissimus, quod cum esset veri hominis caro, dum vivebat Iesus, formam hominis posset perdere, Dei autem numquam."

when it directs worshipers to sing to Mary, "You have borne in your womb he whom even the heavens cannot contain."[6]

In a slightly more formal way, Dominican Gabriel Barletta's sermon for the fourth Saturday of Lent, "That Mary is the Mother of All Graces," presented Mary's holiness and power as the direct result of her close bodily relationship with Christ. He first quoted St. Thomas, who said that "the Blessed Virgin Mary, because she was Mother of God, has a certain infinite dignity received from the infinite Good which God is." Barletta continued by further explaining Thomas' point with words drawn from the letter to the Colossians which were designed to describe Christ himself. Mary exceeds all others, angels and human beings, in grace, "For in no one else had the fullness of divinity ever dwelt bodily in the same way as in Mary."[7] But it was Jean Gerson, creative as always, who presented this same idea in the most dramatic and poetic way in one of his sermons on the Annunciation.

Today, the first sacrifice or offering for our salvation was made within the sacred temple of the womb of Our Lady. And this offering was accepted by the whole Trinity for our redemption. In this sacred temple, in this worthy and honored chamber of Our Lady, the wedding feast of the divine with our humanity was celebrated. . . . The Holy Spirit celebrated the wedding and Our Lady gave and ministered the materials and the place. She is the hostess . . . the gifts, the dishes of all the virtues are there set forth fully and without measure; and the Holy Spirit is likewise given without measure. And every creature who desires devotedly to make use of these gifts is still seated at this banquet and nourished from this fullness.[8]

---

6. Ibid., 2:387. San Bernardino draws some of this sermon from the works of Peter Olivi.

7. Gabriel Barletta, *Sermones quadragesimales et de sanctis* (Brescia: Jacobus Britannicus, 1497), 71v–72r. "In nullo enim alio habitavit plenitudo divinitatis corporaliter quemadmodum in Maria."

8. Jean Gerson, *Oeuvres complètes,* ed. P. Glorieux, 8 vols. (Paris: Desclée and Cie, 1971), 7:540. "Ad ce jour fu faicte la premiere oblation ou offre pour nostre salut dedens la sacré temple du ventre Nostre Dame. Et fut acceptee ceste oblation par toute la Trinité pour nostre redemption. En ce temple sacré, en ceste sale digne et honnoree de Nostre Dame, furent celebrees les nopces de Divinite avecquez nostre humanité. . . . le Saint Esprit celebre les nopces et Nostre Dame donne et ministre la matiere et le lieu; elle est hostesse. . . . les dons, les metz de toutes vertus y sont pleinement et sans mesure espanduz; datus est spiritus non ad mensuram. Et de ceste plenitude et du relief est assasiee encores et nourrye especialment chascune creature qui devement en veult user."

While he does not refer specifically to the Eucharist, Gerson does use symbols of eating and nourishment to establish Mary's body as a dining chamber where Mary herself provides a banquet at which all of the graces of the Holy Spirit become food for Christian believers.

The Purity of Mary's Body

This emphasis on Mary's concrete physical involvement in human salvation is one of the most common features of late medieval Marian preaching. Her divine motherhood is often mentioned in sermons which otherwise have nothing specifically to do with her. Whenever the body of Christ is spoken of, preachers most often go on to explain that it was formed "ex purissimis sanguinibus beate Marie," "from the very pure blood of blessed Mary." This phrase or a variation of it occurs frequently enough that it must have become a part of the audience's permanent mental stock of phrases and images regarding Mary and her connection with Jesus.[9] This is, interestingly, the one aspect of Marian thought and devotion which Bynum believes to be the most important in the religious lives of late medieval women saints and visionaries.[10] She gives examples of women mystics who felt a special closeness to Christ in his suffering humanity because his flesh was female flesh taken from the body of Mary. Yet this idea will appear in the sermons of male preachers as well. A famous example is the Passion sermon of Jean Gerson.[11] It also found its way into Johannes of Verden's sermon for the second day after Easter. Using the common metaphor for the Incarnation in which Mary weaves the garment of Christ's humanity within her body,[12] Johannes says that Mary "made him a white tunic to put on from her very pure virginal flesh

---

9. San Bernardino of Siena, *Opera omnia*, 4:552; Barletta, *Sermones*, 17r; Menot, *Sermons choisis*, 178; and Bernardino of Busti, *Mariale*, Sermon 1, "On the Nativity of the Virgin Mary," pt. 2.

10. Caroline Walker Bynum, *Holy Feast and Holy Fast: The Religious Significance of Food to Medieval Women* (Berkeley: University of California Press, 1987), 260–69.

11. See below, Chapter 2.

12. For an excellent discussion of this theme in both the plays and iconography of the late Middle Ages, see Gail McMurray Gibson, *The Theater of Devotion: East Anglian Drama and Society in the Late Middle Ages* (Chicago: University of Chicago Press, 1989), 156–66.

. . . But that white garment of his most holy body was, for us, reddened by his blood during his pilgrimage."[13]

A pure white garment splashed with the redness of blood is an effective and memorable visual image for portraying Christ's suffering body; the symbol of weaving or sewing suggests an active, concrete participation by Mary in the formation of Christ's humanity.[14] It is easy to see why such a theme would be significant for the spirituality of medieval women for whom sewing was a common occupation. It was equally important to those theologians and preachers who sought to magnify Mary's part in the miracle of the Incarnation.

To a certain extent, whether or not a theologian presented Mary as active or passive in her maternity depended upon whether or not he drew his biological information from Aristotle or Galen, and this, in turn, could be determined by his loyalty to a particular religious order or theological tradition. In all areas of endeavor, Aristotle had assigned to women a passive role, and to men the sphere of activity and creativity. His logical conclusion was that in the formation of the fetus, the woman's menstrual blood provided only the unformed matter to which the male seed brought form and life. Galen, on the other hand, had envisioned women with sexual organs that were similar to the male but inverted inside their bodies. He therefore believed that women and men contributed in a roughly equal way to forming the child in the womb.

St. Albert the Great and St. Thomas Aquinas set the theological program for the Dominican order in their use of Aristotle in every aspect of their philosophical and theological work. Their Mariology portrayed Mary as the perfect example of the Aristotelian concept of woman. As a passive receptacle for God, she both received a fullness of divine knowledge and became the mother of Christ through the active power of the

13. Johannes of Verden, *Sermones dominicales cum expositionibus evangeliorum, sive Dormi secure de tempore et de sanctis* (Basel: Johann Amerbach, 1484), Sermon 27. "Ita Virgo Maria suo dilecto filio Christo Iesu cuius nativitatem angelus Gabriel praedixit, fecit tunicam albam de purissima virginea carne assumpta. . . . Sed istud vestimentum album sui sanctissimi corporis factum est in peregrinatione pro nobis sanguine rubricatum."

14. Ibid. Johannes goes on to compare Mary's creation of Christ's humanity to the Old Testament patriarch Jacob, who made his son Joseph a coat of many colors which his brothers later reddened with the blood of a wild animal.

Holy Spirit.[15] Indeed, because Thomas believed that original sin could only be passed on by an active power, not by a passive one, he asserted that fathers rather than mothers were responsible for the transmission of original sin to the next generation. As he saw it, there was therefore no need to defend Mary as immune from original sin since, as a passive female, she could not have passed it on to Jesus in any case.[16] For the remainder of the Middle Ages, Dominicans usually adopted both the biology of Aristotle and Thomas's rejection of the Immaculate Conception when discussing Mary. The Franciscans, however, employed Galen because most of them championed belief in the Immaculate Conception and wanted Mary to have as great an involvement in Christ's conception and birth as possible.[17]

The Immaculate Conception was the one aspect of Marian devotion in the late Middle Ages which was therefore capable of stirring up division and discord among her devotees. Virtually all Western Catholic theologians were ready to agree that Mary had in fact led a sinless life, and most would grant that she had received some sort of special sanctification in the womb. Here agreement ended.

Were it not for the fact that interest in Mary's conception had begun two centuries before St. Augustine's time, one would be tempted to say that a focus on the conception of Mary was necessitated by his theology of original sin, since he associated the transmission of sin with the bodily contact of sexual intercourse polluted by lust. Instead, it was the influential apocryphal work, the *Protevangelium* or *Early Gospel of James*, written in the late second century, which first drew popular attention to the relationship between St. Anne and St. Joachim, and to the miraculous circumstances under which Mary's conception occurred. This work, along with the *Gospel of Pseudo-Matthew*, was responsible for presenting most of the stories that would inspire devotion to Mary throughout the medieval

---

15. Prudence Allen, R.S.M., *The Concept of Woman: The Aristotelian Revolution, 750 B.C.–A.D. 1250* (Grand Rapids, Mich.: William B. Eerdmans Publishing Company, 1985), 383, 397.

16. Ibid., 398.

17. Kari Elisabeth Börrensen, *Anthropologie médiévale et théologie mariale* (Oslo: Universitetsforlaget, 1971), 70–90.

period. It supplies, among other information, the names of Mary's parents, the story of Mary's conception and birth, her dedication in the temple at the age of three, and proof of her virginity "in partu." *Pseudo-Matthew*, compiled in the eighth or ninth century and heavily dependent on the *Protevangelium*, adds the story of Mary's vow of virginity made while serving in the temple.[18] Still, even if his theology did not inspire the popular interest in the Virgin's conception, St. Augustine was nevertheless aware of the problems his theology created for belief in a sinless conception of Christ by a sinful woman, for he was willing to consider the possibility that Mary had never sinned.[19]

A feast of Mary's conception was first celebrated in the Eastern Church during the seventh century; most historians agree that the eventual belief in an Immaculate Conception in the West was the result of lay devotion stimulated by the liturgical celebrations of the Church and by popular works concerning Mary's early life. The feast of Mary's conception had already been introduced into the West by the twelfth century, when St. Bernard of Clairvaux spoke out against it. At the time of St. Thomas Aquinas in the thirteenth century, the Feast of the Immaculate Conception was celebrated in parts of England and Normandy, but it was not introduced into most churches until the late fourteenth and fifteenth centuries. By the close of the fourteenth century, even the Dominicans,

18. The most recent edition of these and several other Christian apocryphal works is J. K. Elliot, *The Apocryphal New Testament: A Collection of Apocryphal Christian Literature in an English Translation* (Oxford: Clarendon Press, 1993). Elliot states (pp. 50–51) that throughout the medieval period, the Western Church tended to reject the authority of the *Protevangelium* due to St. Jerome's objections to its contents. St. Jerome was offended by the Gospel's suggestion that the brothers and sisters of Jesus, referred to in the canonical Gospels, were the children of Joseph from a previous marriage. He preferred to believe that they were instead Jesus' cousins and that St. Joseph also had remained a virgin. Strangely enough, *Pseudo-Matthew* was accepted in the West, even though it too asserts that St. Joseph was the father of Jesus' siblings (p. 85).

19. Jaroslav Pelikan, *Mary Through the Centuries: Her Place in the History of Culture* (New Haven: Yale University Press, 1996), 191. Pelikan quotes St. Augustine's *De natura et gratia*, 36:42, where he says that, even though all are born in sin, "we must make an exception of the holy Virgin Mary, concerning whom I wish to raise no question when it touches the subject of sins, out of honor to the Lord. For from him we know what abundance of grace for overcoming sin in every particular [ad vicendum omni ex parte peccatum] was conferred upon her who had the merit to conceive and bear him who undoubtedly had no sin."

who opposed belief in an Immaculate Conception, were celebrating Mary's conception on December 8.[20]

At the Council of Constance, in 1416, Jean Gerson defended publicly the doctrine of the Immaculate Conception.[21] There was no attempt, however, to establish belief in the Immaculate Conception as Catholic dogma until September 17, 1439. At that time, Felix V, who had called the Council of Basel, issued an official declaration to this effect. However, the council was by then meeting illegitimately and so the decree had no binding force.[22] In 1477 Pope Sixtus IV, a former Franciscan, promoted the feast in the papal constitution, *Cum praeexcelsa,* and directed that new propers for it be put into Roman service books for Mass and Office. Bernardino of Busti composed a Mass and Office for the feast in 1480, which Sixtus approved.[23] Finally, the doctrine gained official recognition at the University of Paris when the Theology Faculty decreed on March 3, 1497, that all those who were studying for academic degrees must swear to defend the doctrine of Mary's Immaculate Conception.[24]

The eventual success of the doctrine of the Immaculate Conception is undoubtedly due to the theological creativity of one particular fourteenth-century Franciscan, John Duns Scotus. It was Scotus's success in defending the doctrine against its critics, first at Oxford and then at Paris, which eventually won over a large number of the younger generation of theologians and paved the way for widespread acceptance in the later Middle Ages.[25]

20. Cornelius A. Bouman, "The Immaculate Conception in the Liturgy," in *The Dogma of the Immaculate Conception: History and Significance*, ed. Edward D. O'Connor (South Bend, Ind.: University of Notre Dame Press, 1958), 113–14, 136–39.

21. Roland Gauthier, CSC, "Immaculée Conception de Marie, privilège singulier ou unique? Étude historique sur l'opinion de l'immaculée conception de S. Joseph," *Cahiers de Joséphologie* 2 (1954): 178–79. As the title of Gauthier's article indicates, there was some limited speculation in this period about whether Joseph, too, may have been immaculately conceived.

22. Ignatius Brady, O.F.M., "The Development of the Doctrine of the Immaculate Conception in the Fourteenth Century after Aureoli," *Franciscan Studies* 15 (1955): 202.

23. Bouman, "Immaculate Conception," 151, 153.

24. Brady, "Development of the Doctrine," 201.

25. The following discussion is drawn from Allan B. Wolter, O.F.M., trans., *John Duns Scotus: Four Questions on Mary* (Santa Barbara: Old Mission Santa Barbara, 1988). Wolter provides both the Latin of Scotus's original work, an English translation, and an excellent

In order to defend the Virgin's exemption from original sin, Scotus had to counter a number of theological arguments which can be generally summed up under three categories. First, there could be no doubt that Mary was a daughter of Adam and in Adam all sinned. Did not Mary experience all of the normal and negative effects of a sinful state? She knew hunger, thirst, and pain and suffering. She must have possessed at one point the sin that produced these effects. Second, there was general agreement that the Virgin's conception had occurred in the normal way. This would mean both that concupiscence or lust was present between St. Anne and St. Joachim and also that Mary was conceived of contaminated human seed. Only Jesus had been virginally conceived and therefore could avoid original sin. Finally, and most important of all, St. Thomas Aquinas asserted that to argue for the Immaculate Conception was to demean the saving work of Christ. Christ was the savior of all without exception. If Mary had no original sin, she would be placed outside the need for the salvation provided by her son. Therefore she must have possessed original sin, if only for a brief instant, after which her soul was then purified by God's grace as the future merit of Jesus' death was applied to her.[26]

In reply to the first objection, Scotus countered that the Virgin was certainly a daughter of Adam and therefore her soul, according to nature, possessed no intrinsic merits that would have required God to provide it with the original righteousness lost by Adam. Without grace, her soul would have sinned. There was, nevertheless, an extrinsic cause for preserving her from sin in light of her role as mother of the savior. As far as her suffering and other human experiences were concerned, Scotus argued that her lack of original sin would have caused her to avoid these except that God allowed her to experience such pain and suffering as would be meritorious for her and for others.

---

introduction to the problem. For those not interested in reading the scholastic language of Scotus directly, an excellent summary of Scotus's arguments, as well as those of his opponents, can be found in Allan B. Wolter, O.F.M., and Blane O'Neill, O.F.M., *John Duns Scotus: Mary's Architect* (Quincy, Ill.: Franciscan Press, 1993), 54–84.

26. Wolter, *Four Questions*, 36–39. The reference from St. Thomas is in the *Summa theologiae*, III, q. 27, art. 2, ad 2.

With regard to the objection based on concupiscence and contaminated seed, Scotus chose to reject the traditional argument of St. Augustine concerning the nature of original sin and its transmission, which caused the seed to be contaminated. Instead, Scotus preferred to adopt St. Anselm's view, expressed in the *Cur Deus homo,* that even with the presence of concupiscence, sin resides not in the material seed but in the will. Therefore the seed by which Mary was conceived contained no sin in and of itself. It simply created another daughter of Adam who would have lacked original righteousness and therefore, without grace, would have sinned.[27]

Scotus was then ready to deal with Thomas's belief that the Immaculate Conception detracted from the glory of Christ as savior of all. Scotus replied that Jesus was certainly the savior of all, including the Blessed Virgin. He was indeed the most perfect mediator and savior, but he could only be the most perfect savior if he had saved at least one person in the most perfect manner possible, by preserving them from sin altogether. Therefore, in view of Mary's role as his mother in the drama of salvation, Jesus chose to be her mediator in a perfect way. Consequently, no one is more obligated to him for salvation than his own mother, and no one loves him more.[28]

Scotus's arguments were a brilliant theological tour de force, but of course they did not convince everyone. To the close of the Middle Ages and beyond, there were plenty of preachers and theologians who chose to reject Scotus's position.

Not all medieval preachers felt compelled to discuss such a disputed doctrine in their sermons. Some, perhaps, did not like to encourage too much lay theological speculation, while others may simply have felt that they could sufficiently praise Mary's purity and holiness without reference to it. When it was mentioned, however, most preachers believed that they must support either their rejection or acceptance of it with serious theological argument. One would expect that the Dominican Gabriel Barletta would reject the Immaculate Conception, and he was, in fact, loyal to this tradition of his order. Barletta was prepared to argue that Mary

27. Wolter, *Four Questions,* 43 and 54 n. 8.
28. Ibid., 39–42.

had excelled all the angels and saints and that she had avoided all actual sin.[29] He nevertheless insisted that to support the Immaculate Conception was to remove Mary from the realm of Christ's saving activity. Even if God, in his absolute power, could have preserved Mary from original sin, through his ordained power, Christ had been established as redeemer of all. Mary was no exception. Barletta continued that the Church merely tolerated the feast of Mary's conception because of popular demand, but that, in reality, she had been sanctified in the womb after receiving her soul.[30] This would have meant that the soul would contract original sin from the body and then both soul and body were sanctified together. Defenders of the Immaculate Conception taught instead that both soul and body were purified at the instant of conception, so that Mary's soul had no chance to be polluted by inherited sin. One exception to the Dominican rejection of the Immaculate Conception is the French preacher Guillaume Pepin, who suggested that "the Church commonly holds" Mary to be pure from original sin. The Church thus says of Mary, "You are all fair my love, there is no flaw in you."[31] This verse from the Song of Songs was frequently quoted by advocates of the Immaculate Conception in support of their position.

The Franciscan San Bernardino of Siena should have been inclined to defend the Immaculate Conception along with most members of his order. In actuality, though he saw no objection to it and believed it to be possibly true,[32] he preferred to leave it as an argument to be settled in the schools by formal debate. He did make clear that Mary had been specially sanctified by the Holy Spirit so that her body was completely subject to her reason. Mary had never sinned either venially or mortally.[33]

---

29. Barletta, *Sermones*, 54v. "Peccatum omnem vitavit super omnes sanctos et sanctas immunis ab omni peccato."

30. Ibid., 42v–43r.

31. Guillaume Pepin, *Rosareum aurem B. Mariae Virginis* (Antwerp: Guillelmus Lesteenius and Engelbertus Gymnicus, 1656), 10–11. "Fuit [Mary] itaque pura et hoc mutipliciter. Primò quidem ab originali . . . quod communiter tenet Ecclesia, 'Tota pulchra es amica mea, et macula non est in te.'"

32. San Bernardino of Siena, *Opera omnia*, 2:155. "Fuit enim beata Virgo sine primo 'vae,' hoc est sine tyranno concupiscentiae peccati originalis, quia sine eo concepta est, . . . Aut in ea omnino fuit exstinctum per Spiritus Sancti sanctificationem."

33. Ibid., 4:538, 544, 547.

Chancellor Jean Gerson was an avid defender of all of Mary's powers and privileges, and, as we have seen, had already defended the doctrine of the Immaculate Conception at Constance at the beginning of the fifteenth century.[34] Like San Bernardino, Gerson stressed that Mary's sinlessness meant rational control of her body,[35] but he explicitly defended the Immaculate Conception in a sermon prepared for the feast day and in other sermons as well. Gerson believed not only that Song of Songs 4:7, quoted by Pepin above, proved Mary's purity, but also that the entire book referred to Mary when interpreted allegorically. True, venerable doctors such as St. Augustine and St. Bernard could be quoted in opposition to the Immaculate Conception, but the Holy Spirit did not necessarily reveal everything to them. Doctors in every age have the right to declare the truth that follows from Scripture. The doctrine had not yet been formally accepted only because the Church preferred to move slowly when determining doubtful matters.[36] Besides, he posited in his Christmas sermon, since Mary was exempt from pain in childbirth, the universal curse for sin, why should she not have been exempt from original sin?[37]

Various historians have made much of the idea that the Dominican order promoted the cult of the Virgin's milk because lactation was viewed as part of the curse of original sin. If Mary had breast-fed Jesus, she must have possessed at one time the sin which caused this effect.[38] There is lit-

---

34. Graef, *Mary*, 1:311. Graef explains that, as chancellor, Gerson was bound by an oath required by the university to defend Mary's prerogatives.

35. Gerson, *Oeuvres complètes*, 7:541. ". . . par ce [her title as Mother of God] au jour d'uy Nostre Dame fust confermee royne et dame en soy mesmez c'est a dire que raison fut maitresse de son corps et le corps telement y obeit que nulle rebellion y fut trouvee né que au premier estat de innocence."

36. Ibid., 7:1058–59, 1076–77.

37. Ibid., 7:952. ". . . se la Vierge Marie fut exemptee de ceste maudisson generale je ne voy point pourquoy elle n'ayt esté exemptée de l'autre maudisson que estoit trop plus mauvaise, c'est assavoir du pechié originel."

38. John Bossy, *Christianity in the West, 1400–1700* (Oxford: Oxford University Press, 1985), 8–9; Marina Warner, *Alone of All Her Sex: The Myth and Cult of the Virgin Mary* (New York: Alfred A Knopf, 1976), 204. See also Charles T. Wood, "The Doctor's Dilemma: Sin, Salvation and the Menstrual Cycle in Medieval Thought," *Speculum* 56 (1981): 710–27; and Theresa Coletti, "Purity and Danger: The Paradox of Mary's Body and the En-gendering of the Infancy Narrative in the English Mystery Cycles," in *Feminist Approaches to the Body in Medieval Literature,* ed. Linda Lomperis and Sarah Stanbury (Philadelphia: University of

tle evidence in the sermons of the day, however, that these men necessarily connected Mary's bodily feeding of Jesus with sin in any way. San
Bernardino of Siena, who believed the Immaculate Conception to be at
least possible, and Bernardino of Busti, who accepted it as truth, glorified
Mary's milk as a sublime food from heaven.[39] If it were from heaven,
it could hardly be caused by sin. Jean Gerson, in the same sermon in
which he defended the Immaculate Conception, encouraged women to
imitate Mary and breast-feed their own children.[40] Whatever the reasons
for Dominican support of the lactating Virgin, the widespread popularity
of Mary's milk was much more likely due to the more general late
medieval preference for the sacramental and for symbols of bodily nourishment.

One of the most outspoken advocates of the Immaculate Conception
toward the close of the fifteenth century was Bernardino of Busti. Busti's
popular *Mariale* began with nine sermons designed to defend the Immaculate Conception against every conceivable argument. He chose to use
the nominalist distinction of God's absolute power to support God's ability to preserve Mary from original sin.[41] Busti also argued that it was only
fitting that Christ perfectly fulfill the commandment to honor his mother. He could do this no better than by refusing to allow sin to touch her
in any way. Busti answered the objection that Jesus was born to save all by

---

Pennsylvania Press, 1993), 85–86. Unlike these other historians, Coletti recognizes that
medieval people generally believed fervently both that Mary's body was absolutely pure
and that it had nevertheless experienced some form of childbearing and lactation.
According to Coletti, this meant that people were forced to reconsider their notions of
gender.

    39. San Bernardino of Siena, *Opera omnia*, 2:380–81. ". . . beata Virgo nutrivit Christum
de suo sacratissimo lacte, ubere de caelo pleno, cuius minima stilla praevalet omnibus
fructibus paradisi terrestris ac totius mundi." See also Bernardino of Busti, *Mariale*, Sermon
1, "On the Name of Mary," pt. 2. "De hoc inquit Bernardus in quodam sermone. Omnia
opera misericordie erga filium beata virgo ministravit. Nam ipsum virginea carne vestivit,
eum lacte de celo ministrato potavit et pavit."

    40. Gerson, *Oeuvres complètes*, 7:953.

    41. Bernardino of Busti, *Mariale*, Sermon 1, "On the Immaculate Conception," pt. 3.
". . . beata virgo fuit capacissima gratie preservationis ob originali peccato; cum enim fuerit capax ut esset mater dei et virgo perfecta ante partum, in partu et post partum. Cumque
meruerit elevari super omnes angelicas hierarchias et effici regina celorum; quanto magis
fuit capax huius gratie ut sine peccato originale conciperetur, certe multo plus."

quoting Scotus's position that Jesus was Mary's savior by prevenient grace as he was the savior of everyone else through subsequent grace.[42]

The Immaculate Conception had to wait until 1854 to become official Catholic dogma, but it enjoyed widespread popular support in the fifteenth century among the people and the clergy. There is little evidence from the period to suggest that belief in Mary's Immaculate Conception made her seem remote or unapproachable to those who sought her out through prayer, pilgrimage, or the sacramental viewing of those precious relics associated with her body. The Immaculate Conception provided one more assurance that the virginal body which had conceived and borne the body of Jesus was instrumental in fashioning a new creation in which the material need no longer be a necessary participant in the ancient curse of sin.

It is in this light that one must consider San Bernardino of Siena's famous statements about Mary's power over God. Despite his own cautious reserve, as a Franciscan, with regard to the Immaculate Conception, in his usual enthusiastic way, San Bernardino wanted to make sure that his hearers would not go away unaware of the true power of Mary in cooperating with God in the Incarnation. Surely, no one did. San Bernardino proclaimed,

The Blessed Virgin was able to do more for God than God could do for himself, for there were certain things between God and the Virgin that were contrary, or contradictory, which were able to be reconciled when God came to the Virgin. . . . God was unable to generate anything but God from his own being and yet the Virgin made God a human being.[43]

42. Ibid., pt. 2. ". . . quia respondeo secundum sententiam doctoris subtilis . . . quod Christus fuit redemptor beate virginis per gratiam prevenientem eam preservando quia si illam non preservasset, in originali peccato incidisset. . . . Aliorum autem hominum fuit redemptor per gratiam subsequentem post lapsum." The term "prevenient grace" is generally used in the Middle Ages to refer to grace given prior to any human effort or apart from any human worthiness. Its purpose is to free a person from the inherited bondage of original sin, enabling him or her to live according to the will of God with the aid of the subsequent grace provided by the sacraments. Defenders of the Immaculate Conception after Scotus asserted that God's prevenient grace was given at the moment of Mary's conception, preventing her from contracting original sin at all.

43. San Bernardino of Siena, *Opera omnia*, 2:375. "Plus enim potuit beata Virgo facere de Deo, quam Deus de seipso. Quaedam enim contraria et contradictoria inter Deum et

Later in the same sermon, he made the point again, this time highlighting the holiness of Mary's body.

For the Blessed Virgin alone did more than God, or as much as God did for the whole human race. . . . First because God formed Man from the dust of the earth; but Mary formed him from her most pure blood and her most pure flesh.[44]

Enclosed "Garden of Delights"

San Bernardino's language may sound a bit extreme to modern ears, but then much of the colorful imagery used in connection with medieval Marian devotion would seem out of place in most modern churches. Medieval preachers enjoyed using inventive allegories to illustrate all aspects of Mary's cult. They were at their creative best when interpreting Mary's virginal conception of Jesus at the Incarnation. By far the most striking imagery found in sermons dedicated to Mary and to her conception of Christ is the erotic language drawn from an allegorical interpretation of specific portions of the Old Testament, especially the Song of Songs and the Book of Esther. Use of the Song of Songs as a source of Marian allegory in sermons and Biblical exegesis was first inspired by the book's use to praise Mary in the liturgy. By the twelfth century, the entire book was looked upon as an allegory of the relationship between Mary and Jesus.[45] This is why it seemed so natural for preachers like Gerson to assume that the Song spoke of Mary. He was inheriting a tradition of interpretation that was already over two centuries old. From the Song of Songs and Esther come those passages that refer to Mary's womb as the "hortus conclusus deliciarum," the "enclosed garden of delights," or

---

Virginem erant, quae, dum accessit Deus ad Virginem, concordata sunt. . . . Deus non potuit generare nisi Deum de se; et tamen Virgo Deum fecit hominem."

44. Ibid., 380. "Sola enim benedicta Virgo Maria plus fecit Deo vel tantum, ut sic dicam, quantum fecerit Deus toti generi humano. . . . Primo namque Deus formavit hominem de limo terrae; sed Maria formavit eum de purissimis sanguinibus et purissima carne sua."

45. E. Ann Matter, *The Voice of My Beloved: The Song of Songs in Western Medieval Christianity* (Philadelphia: University of Pennsylvania Press, 1990), 151–77. According to Matter there is a particularly close connection between allegorical use of Scripture in the liturgy and the development of Marian dogma. She demonstrates, for example, that liturgical use of the Song of Songs contributed directly to the development of belief in Mary's Assumption.

describe Mary at times as a virginal temptress, luring God into union with her body through her beauty and virtue.

Allegory was a longstanding part of the medieval tradition of Scriptural exegesis. It had been popular, in fact, since the early Church, with Origen and St. Augustine as two of its most famous advocates. By the medieval period the Church had incorporated the method into a formal fourfold hermeneutic which could be applied to almost every verse of Scripture to arrive at the spiritual meaning hidden beneath the letter of the text.[46] The Marian allegories drawn from the Song of Songs are interesting because of their variation on this procedure. Here we find the use of material imagery, in this case the sexual desire of two lovers, used to express another material truth, Mary's conception of Jesus in her womb. Yes, it is a spiritual idea, the belief in a union of the divine and the human in Jesus, but nothing could be more tangible and physical than the conception and birth of a child.

With the possible exception of some of the more bizarre miracle stories, no other aspect of the late medieval cult of Mary so reveals the vast distance between medieval understanding and sensibilities and modern ones. To see this, we need only imagine the uncomfortable, embarrassed response a preacher today would receive if he or she entered the pulpit and began to speak of Mary as did Gabriel Barletta in one of his Christmas sermons. Barletta described all of the famous women and men of the Bible who had asked God to save the human race to no avail. Finally, a young woman of fourteen entered the throne room of God, knelt, and said to God, "Let my beloved enter his garden and eat the fruit of his fruit trees." The garden, explained Barletta, was her virginal womb; and when the Son heard Mary's words, he replied, "O my Father, I have loved and sought her from my youth and I want to make her my wife. I have fallen in love with her beauty."[47]

46. Medieval exegetes believed that most passages could be explicated according to a literal/historical sense, an allegorical sense which pertained to matters of faith and belief, a tropological sense which could be applied to morality, and an anagogical sense related to teleology.

47. Barletta, *Sermones*, 45r–45v. "'Veniat dilectus meus in ortum suum: ut comedat fructum pomorum suorum.' Ortus fuit uterus virginalis. Audiens autem filius hoc verbum: dixit patri suo, 'O pater, hanc amavi et exquesivi a iuventute mea. Et quesivi eam mihi sponsam assumere; et amator factus sum forme illius.'"

Allegorical use of the Song of Songs often led preachers to speak of Christ as Mary's lover or spouse in the Incarnation. Their intent was not to replace the Holy Spirit as the person of the Trinity responsible for generating Jesus' body in the womb. Rather they simply meant to use this metaphor as one more means of showing the bodily closeness of Mary and her son. It was as intimate as that of a husband and wife.

San Bernardino of Siena presented Mary as someone who actually seduced God.

O unspeakable humility of the Creator! O unthinkable virtue of the Virgin Mother! O incomprehensible height of the mysteries of God! One Hebrew woman invaded the palace of the Eternal King; one young girl, with I do not know what caresses and promises, seduced, deceived, and I might even say wounded God. Wherefore the Lord was conquered by the Blessed Virgin as he says in Cant. 4:9, "You have wounded my heart, my sister, my wife."[48]

Finally, Bernardino of Busti was inspired by the story of Esther to describe Mary's conquest of God and the achievement of union with him. Bernardino used the traditional imagery of the unicorn or rhinoceros,[49] first employed by Pope Gregory the Great in reference to Christ and Mary. It is language suffused with unstated sexual symbolism. Bernardino explained that, even as Esther approached King Ahasuerus with two handmaids, so Mary

went in to the omnipotent God and King accompanied by two handmaids, humility and purity or virginity; and as a rhinoceros, on seeing a holy virgin, puts away his fury and meekly lies in the lap of the virgin, so God, seeing this most holy virgin, touched by love of her, laid aside all indignation and wrath and descended into her womb, laying down the rod of his anger.[50]

48. San Bernardino of Siena, *Opera omnia*, 2:376. "O ineffabilis humilitas Creatoris! O incogitabilis virtus Virginis Matris! O incomprehensibilis altitudo mysteriorum Dei! Una mulier hebraea fecit invasionem in domo Regis aeterni; una puella, nescio quibus blanditiis, nescio quibus cautelis, nescio quibus violentiis, seduxit, decepit, et ut ita dicam, vulneravit et rapuit divinum cor, et Dei sapientiam circumvenit. Propterea conqueritur Dominus de beata Virgine dicens Cant. 4,9: 'Vulnerasti cor meum, soror mea sponsa.'"

49. In the later Middle Ages the words "unicornis" and "rhinoceron" were interchangeable.

50. Bernardino of Busti, *Mariale*, Sermon 1, "On the Annunciation and Incarnation," Introduction. "Intravit ad regem omnipotentem deum sociata duabus ancillis, scilicet humilitate et puritate sive virginitate. Sicut autem rinoceron ad aspectum alicuius sancte

If a modern congregation might feel more than a bit uncomfortable hearing this kind of sermon, it could have produced a sense of incongruity among medieval congregations as well; the theological tradition inherited by the Latin Church from St. Ambrose and St. Augustine invariably tied sexuality and intercourse to the transmission of original sin.[51] Throughout the Middle Ages, sex between married persons was always considered to be at least venially sinful. No one then could have escaped a tendency to feel that sexuality must in some way bring desecration to holy persons, objects, and seasons. The clergy were supposed to be celibate. Marriages were forbidden during Lent; and the married were expected to refrain from intercourse during particular days and seasons of the Church Year.[52]

In the case of Mary, however, the seeming incongruity of erotic imagery tied to the realm of the holy only served to underscore the sense that here something completely new was taking place. Mary's womb, far from being a place where sin was passed from one generation to the next, instead became a temple for the union of divine and human nature. It was, in fact, the locus of nature transformed and assumed into the realm of the divine. As such, the womb of Mary was the scene of a miracle and a transformation as crucial to the divine plan as that which occurred in the tomb of Christ, culminating in the Resurrection on the third day. The French Franciscan Michel Menot drew this parallel explicitly in his Passion sermon. According to Menot, Jesus was buried at the hour of Compline, the same hour in which he had been conceived. Menot continued, "But Jesus, God and Man, made his tomb glorious, by his own will and power he rose living from the enclosed tomb, even as he was born from the enclosed womb of the Virgin."[53] In a similar way, San Bernardino of Siena compared Christ's Incarnation in Mary's womb to his Resurrection from the tomb. In the Song of Songs 7:2, the lover calls the womb of his

---

virginis omnem deponit feritatem et mansuetus ad gremium ipsius virginis accedit sic deus videns hanc sanctissimam virginem, amoris illius tactus omni dimissa indignatione et asperitate descendit in uterum eius, atque virgam furoris sui deponens."

51. Peter Brown, *The Body and Society: Men, Women, and Sexual Renunciation in Early Christianity* (New York: Columbia University Press, 1988), 341–427.

52. Bossy, *Christianity in the West*, 36–37.

53. Menot, *Sermons choisis*, 519. "Sed ipse Iesus, Deus et homo, sepulchrum fecit gloriosum qui voluntate et potestate sua resurrexit vivus clause sepulchro, sicut et natus fuit clauso virginis utero."

beloved an "acervus tritici," a "multitude of wheat." San Bernardino chose to link this to Jesus' words in St. John's Gospel 12:24–25, in which he spoke of his death and Resurrection as a grain of wheat, falling to the earth and bearing much fruit. It was the same, says San Bernardino, at the Incarnation. Christ, the grain of wheat, fell to the earth into Mary's womb.[54]

Mary's body, then, was presented as graced and holy beyond anything possible to another human being except her son. She provided a place for the joining of God with human nature, and she herself supplied the bodily humanity assumed by the eternal Word. Mary's body was holy, first because of its intimate association with divinity for the nine months of her pregnancy. Over and over again, sermons from the period refer to Mary as the "temple of God," the "tabernacle of God," even the "dining chamber of God."[55] Gabriel Barletta describes in one sermon the three persons of the Trinity sending the Angel Gabriel as a messenger to announce to Mary her election for such a high honor. Father, Son, and Holy Spirit all send her greetings and letters. The Spirit instructs Gabriel, "Say to her that I will dwell in her, and she will be my temple."[56] But Mary's bodily holiness was not solely the result of her motherhood. Prior to the Incarnation, indeed from all eternity, she had been destined for her role and given the personal holiness to make her worthy of it. Bernardino of Busti said that God had "formed that most holy tabernacle of the Blessed Virgin in all purity and innocence," and assured his hearers in the same sermon that Mary's body had been predestined for its special role and that, through her body, all human flesh is blessed.[57]

54. San Bernardino of Siena, *Opera omnia*, 2:156–57.

55. Barletta, *Sermones*, 54v. Barletta explains that the Lord dwells in many ways with his creatures but especially in Mary because he was conceived in her womb. Therefore the Church calls her "Totius trinitatiis nobile triclinium."

56. Ibid., 45v.

57. Bernardino of Busti, *Mariale*, Sermon 2, "On the Immaculate Conception," pt. 3. "Profecto sanctissimum illud tabernaculum beate virginis omni puritate et innocentia repletissimum formavit." ". . . namque dei genitricis marie corpus ante secula ad generandum dei filium predestinatum prope finem mundi nasciturum. . . . Nunquid non tibi benedicebatur humanitatis caro; cum inde nasceris gloriosa virgo? Tibi profecto benedicenda erat caro humana in tuis progenitoribus que ex castissimis visceribus illum cras paritura peccatoribus que est super omnia benedictus."

The Reversal of History

If medieval Christians did not find the preachers' juxtaposition of erotic language and references to the holy disturbing, perhaps it was because the sexual metaphors were used to describe a union which everyone knew had bypassed sexuality altogether. What was so crucial to the maternity of Mary was its virginal character. The transformation of human nature which the Incarnation achieved in the womb of Mary was accomplished through suspension of ordinary, natural processes; the flesh which Mary shared with Jesus was virginal flesh, completely free from all taint of sexuality and therefore of sin. It is this fact which makes the virgin birth of Jesus so important to medieval Christianity. In addition, Mary's virginity was one further source of her unquestioned purity and holiness.

Mary's virginal conception of Jesus had reversed the inevitable transmission of sin, making possible a pure, restored humanity. In *The Body and Society*, Peter Brown closes with the growing importance of the cult of Mary and the saints in the mid-fifth century. It was the century which witnessed the deaths of St. Augustine and St. Jerome and the final dissolution of Rome as an empire in the West, and which provided the seedbed for the growth of the medieval outlook. He explains that the attractiveness of Mary in this context lay in her virginal conception of Christ and her ability to give birth while her womb remained miraculously unopened.

Overarching the Christian urban community, the cult of the Virgin offered the luminous inversion of the dark myth of shared, fallen flesh. . . . In the hymns and sermons of the age, the great hope of the accessibility of fallen man to God, of the weak to the powerful, and of each member of the Christian community to each other, as bearers of the common flesh of Adam and Eve, was condensed in the ideal of the shared flesh of Christ and Mary.[58]

In the ancient world, virginity and sexual abstinence had long been associated with prophecy, with ritual purity, and with strength.[59] Under-

---

58. Brown, *Body and Society*, 445–46.

59. Ibid., 67. See also Giulia Sissa, *Le corps virginal* (Paris: J. Vrin, 1987), 76–78. Sissa says that the same is true of Greek prophetesses. She also states that the tendency to link togeth-

stood in this way, however, virginity was less a virtue in and of itself than it was a means to an end. Rome's Vestal Virgins, for instance, were allowed to marry after age thirty.[60] Giulia Sissa argues in *Le corps virginal* that in ancient Greek society, virginity was defined more by a lifestyle of continence than by a physical state. Unlike later Western notions of virginity associated with the hymen, the Greeks saw female virginity largely in terms of sexual abstinence. Therefore a woman's virginity in girlhood and her sexual continence as a widow were much the same. The period of sexual activity and childbirth during marriage was only a temporary interruption. In fact, Sissa points out that neither of the two ancient Greek medical authorities, Aristotle and Galen, were even familiar with the hymen as it was later understood in the West.[61]

Within the mainstream of the early Christian community, through much of the third century, the sexual renunciation advocated for the clergy and for virgins and widows continued somewhat in the ancient tradition. It did not follow from a view of the created order that placed sexuality at the heart of sin. Instead, sexuality remained a symbol of the weakness and fallenness of the world because it made possible the continuation of a fallen society. By renouncing sexual activity, the Christian could participate in the new world order inaugurated by God in Jesus and could remain pure and separated from the worldly concerns of pagan Rome. Also, belief in Mary's virginal conception of Jesus preserved the ancient view that a body closed to sexual union would be more open to divine inspiration and better serve as a link between the spiritual and the material worlds.[62] As Brown has shown, however, by the close of the ancient period, sexuality was seen as sinful in and of itself, a blot on the pristine purity of God's original creation. This view persisted throughout

---

er the openings of the female body is both ancient and widespread, and can be found as far back as Hippocritas, continuing in Aristotle and Galen. Ancients concluded that as a woman should make her body available only to her husband for sexual activity, so she should speak only with and through him. It is this notion that produces the belief in a prophetess, wife of the god, who remains celibate and gives birth to the word of the god through her mouth.

60. Brown, *Body and Society,* 8–9.
61. Sissa, *Corps virginal,* 131–32, 142–43.
62. Brown, *Body and Society,* 183–96.

the Middle Ages. One of the central reasons for St. Bernard of Clairvaux's rejection of the Immaculate Conception of Mary in the twelfth century was that it made God a participant in the sexual union of Anne and Joachim, and therefore a partner in a sinful act.[63]

By the later Middle Ages, most of the ancient and early Christian beliefs regarding virginity had been combined. They surrounded the figure of the Virgin like so many rays of light, so that she became the supreme and shining example of the possibility of human redemption and the conquest of sin through sexual renunciation.

At this point it will be useful to recall that late medieval sermons were heard by members of a religious culture saturated with Christian symbolism. Sermons were delivered for the most part in towns and cities whose people were already familiar with the most popular iconographic motifs portraying Christ, the Virgin Mary, and the saints, motifs which were often repeated and given added power by their inclusion in liturgical dramas and mystery plays. As preacher after preacher referred to Mary's body as intact, an enclosed garden, even uncultivated earth,[64] those who heard would likely recall paintings and stained glass portraits of Mary receiving the angel's message in a locked room, or reading in a high-walled garden. They might have remembered the echoes of this theme in humorous sections of some Annunciation plays in which Joseph, having returned home after a journey, batters on the locked door of Mary's chamber.[65]

In one of his sermons on Mary as birth-giver of Christ, Bernardino of

63. PL 182:335. To the canons of Lyons, who were proposing to establish a feast of the Immaculate Conception, St. Bernard wrote, "Quomodo namque aut sanctitas absque Spiritu sanctificante, aut sancto Spiritu societas cum peccato fuit? Aut certe peccatum quomodo non fuit, ubi libido non defuit? Nisi forte quis dicat de Spiritu sancto eam, et non de viro conceptam fuisse: sed id hactenus inauditum. Lego denique Spiritum sanctum in eam, non cum ea venisse, dicente angelo: Spiritus sanctus superveniet in te (Luc. 1, 35)."

64. Bernardino of Busti, *Mariale,* Sermon 1, "On the Nativity of Mary," Introduction. "Dicitur (Christ) autem flos campi, . . . quod flos horti ut nascitur terra aperitur. Flos autem campi sine terre apertione nascitur; sic et Christus natus est de virgine sine virginitatis eius violatione."

65. Gail McMurray Gibson, "'Porta Haec Clausa Erit': Comedy, Conception and Ezekiel's Closed Door in the *Ludus Coventriae* Play of 'Joseph's Return,'" *Journal of Medieval and Renaissance Studies* 8 (1978): 137–57.

Busti related a story preserved, he said, in the chronicles of the Franciscan order. A certain prior had come to Blessed Egidius to inquire about the manner in which this birth occurred. When he approached, Egidius, holding his staff in his hand, said,

"I know what you are looking for." He then raised his staff, struck the earth and said, "Virgin before giving birth." And behold, suddenly a lily grew up. Then again he said, "Virgin while giving birth," and behold, another lily. He struck the earth a third time saying, "Virgin after giving birth." And suddenly another lily grew up as a sign of virginal chastity.[66]

Johannes of Verden stressed that with God all miracles are possible. If God could create the universe through his word, why could not the Word, conceived in the Virgin, be born without impairing her virginity?[67] In accord with this belief, sermons to celebrate the festival of Mary's Purification on February 2 most often explain that of course Mary had no need to be purified herself since she had retained her virgin state.[68]

The closed nature of Mary's body was an excellent symbol of sinlessness and purity in general, because it suggested no holes or openings to let in sin, uncleanness, or the danger of evil.[69] As in the ancient world, Mary's virginity not only made her particularly receptive to divine inspiration, it also imbued her with spiritual power to overcome sin and evil. Mary's sealed body endowed her with the additional distinction of embodying all of the spiritual advice traditionally given to women in medieval culture who sought to be especially holy. Western patriarchal culture tended to view the female body as dangerous, for its openings were perceived to be subject to outside forces and influences. It was in danger of lacking clearly defined boundaries. Male spiritual writers therefore pictured the ideal female body as closed, intact, not subject to breaches from without. Mary's perpetual virginity thus made her the perfect

66. Bernardino of Busti, *Mariale*, Sermon 1, "On Mary Giving Birth," pt. 3.

67. Johannes of Verden, *Sermones*, Sermon 6.

68. One example may be found in Bernardino of Busti, *Mariale*, Sermon 1, "On the Purification of Mary," pt 3. ". . . nihil enim purificatur nisi immundum, sed ipsa tota erat purissima, tota sanctissima, et tota mundissima. . . . Nam in ea nulla fuit fractio virginitatis."

69. Sissa, *Corps virginal*, 76–78.

model for female spirituality. Guillaume Pepin demonstrated the perfection of Mary's virginal religious life by reminding his hearers that Mary's virginity was inviolate because she had taken a vow to preserve it. She also protected herself from temptation like any good religious, by fasting.[70]

The "porta clausa" or "closed door" of Ezekiel's prophecy was a common metaphor for Mary's body.[71] Perhaps with this in mind, Gabriel Barletta presented an interesting play on words when he spoke of the power Mary attained through her virginity. He proclaimed, "Mary was made more powerful than all others, so powerful that she opened the heaven that Eve had closed; so powerful that she closed the hell Adam had opened."[72] By keeping the gates to her own body completely closed to all encroachments of evil from without or within, Mary acquired the power to open and close the gates of heaven and hell for all those who came after her. She likewise acquired the strength to conquer even Satan through her virginity. Both San Bernardino of Siena and Bernardino of Busti attribute Mary's power to crush the head of the serpent to her virginal birth-giving of Christ.[73]

The special qualities ascribed to Mary's body because of its pure virginal state were not hers alone. They were bestowed upon the body of Christ when Mary conceived him. Occasionally a preacher will attribute the special nature of Jesus' body to its formation by the power of the

70. Karma Lochrie, *Margery Kempe and Translations of the Flesh* (Philadelphia: University of Pennsylvania Press, 1991), 25–26, 41–47; Coletti, "Purity and Danger," 68–71; Pepin, *Roseum aurem,* 10.

71. Ezekiel 44:1–3. "Then he brought me back to the outer gate of the sanctuary, which faces east; and it was shut. And he said to me, 'This gate shall remain shut; it shall not be opened, and no one shall enter by it; for the Lord, the God of Israel, has entered by it; therefore it shall remain shut. Only the prince may sit in it to eat bread before the Lord; he shall enter by way of the vestibule of the gate, and shall go out by the same way.'"

72. Barletta, *Sermones,* 71v. "Maria super omnes fuit potens; tam potens quod celum aperuit; quod Eva clausit. Tam potens quod infernum clausit; quod Adam aperuit. Tam potens; quod demonem suppeditavit."

73. Bernardino of Busti, *Mariale,* Sermon 1, "On Marian similes in Scripture," pt. 2. "Sicut enim mirra conservat carnem a putrefactione, sic eius puritas et virginitas conservat nos ab omni fetore carnalis concupiscentie. Quarto subvenit nobis contra morsus serpentem id est demonum, imperio sue potestatis." San Bernardino of Siena, *Opera omnia,* 4:561. ". . . tu genus humanum, aeternitatis gloria nudatam, per tuum virgineum partum in pristinum statum deduxisti; tu principem mortis evertisti."

Holy Spirit, as did Guillaume Pepin.[74] Most, however, were convinced that Mary's virginal flesh was the central factor. Bernardino of Busti quoted Bernard of Clairvaux to make the point that Mary had "dressed him (Jesus) with virginal flesh and fed him by giving him milk from heaven."[75] San Bernardino of Siena's Passion sermon portrayed the particular harshness suffered by Christ's virginal body on the cross, its "virginal brightness completely discolored." He later exclaims, "O flesh of a most beloved youth, artfully conceived by the Holy Spirit from the most pure womb of the virgin Mother, how torn and mangled!"[76] Michel Menot informed the citizens of Paris in his Passion sermon that while it is not usual for most people to sweat blood, Christ's anguish had that result because "the body of Christ was most excellently comprised, it was formed from the pure blood of the Virgin and therefore very tender."[77]

Olivier Maillard, however, appears to have been most fascinated by the special ties linking the virginal bodies of Mary and Jesus. In his own Passion narrative, he recreates the dialogue between mother and son when Jesus informed Mary that he must go to Jerusalem to fulfill all that was written of him in the Scriptures. Mary responds to the news with a combination of the words of Jesus and those of Ruth: "Thy will and the will of God be done. I ask that where you go, I go and where you die, I will die." Maillard interjects his own comment, "O sinners, what was possible between those two virginal bodies?"[78] Jesus tells Mary that he must depart

74. Pepin, *Roseum aurem,* 374–75. "Fuit nam corpus Christi sanctissimum tenerrimum propter bonitatem complexionis, quae nunquam in aliquo alio tam bona fuit, aut etiam esse potuit. Nam corpus eius veneratissimum formatum est non ex virile semine, non ex carnali commistione, non naturali opere, sed divina spiritus sancti virtute."

75. Bernardino of Busti, *Mariale,* Sermon 1, "On the Name of Mary," pt. 2. "Se hoc inquit Bernardus in quodam sermone. Omnia opera misericordie erga filium beata virgo ministravit. Nam ipsum virginea carne vestivit, eum lacte de celo ministrato potavit et pavit."

76. San Bernardino of Siena, *Opera omnia,* 2:260. ". . . virginali candore totus decoloratus," "O caro amantissimi iuvenis, a Spiritu Sancto de castissimis visceribus Virginis Matris artificiose concepta, quomodo divulsa et dilacerata."

77. Menot, *Sermons choisis,* 493. "Corpus Christi erat excellentissime complexionatum, quia etiam formatum ex puro sanguine virgine et ideo tenerimum."

78. Olivier Maillard, "Passio domini nostri Jesu Christi," in *Sermones quadragesimales* (Paris: Antoine Caillaut, 1498), pt. 1. "O peccatores quid potuit esse inter illa duo corpora virginea?"

for Jerusalem to establish the sacrament of the Eucharist and fulfill the other mysteries. At last, Mary is convinced that he must go. Maillard continues,

Then Jesus embraced the Virgin Mary in his virginal arms, and the Blessed Virgin said to her son, "It will soon be the twenty-fifth of March, the day on which I conceived you. At least for the honor of that day, I have wished that I might dine with you and hear you speak before you go." Christ answered, "You and I will soon be in a harsh cathedral where I will preach, and I will say words that I have never said before, and we will eat together at one most cruel table, where there will be no one but the two of us, it will be the table of the cross."[79]

This is a complex and important passage. In only a few sentences, Maillard has tied together Mary's conception of Christ, the virginal bodies which both possess as a result, and the fact that Mary must then share in the bitter meal of Christ's suffering and final words served on the table of the cross. It is an effective and condensed presentation of almost all of the significant themes relating Mary bodily to Christ's work of redemption. Even though Maillard does not specifically draw the conclusion that the Virgin is the bodily source of the sacraments, it is also easy to see from a sermon such as this the kind of thought that produced San Bernardino's desire to establish Mary as the ultimate provider of the substance of the sacraments, especially the Eucharist. Maillard has here specifically joined the virginal bodies of Mary and Jesus to the ideas both of sacrificial suffering and of nourishment. His sermon is a singular expression of themes that are firmly rooted in the soil of contemporary devotion, for Maillard belonged to an age absorbed by the sacramental and by the special ability of virginal flesh to mediate the spiritual.

This tendency to focus on Mary's virginity continues the religious emphasis established in the first few centuries of the Church, an emphasis which persisted into the early Middle Ages. In that era, it was Mary's

---

79. Ibid. "Tunc brachia virginea Jesu Christi amplexata sunt virginem Mariam et dixit beata virgo filio suo, Erit cras 25, in qua te concepi: saltem ad honorem illius diei quod prandeam simul vobiscum et audiam sermonem vestrum antequam discedatis. Respondit Christus, Ego et vos cras erimus in dura cathedra ubi predicabo et verba quae nunquam dixi dicam et prandebimus in una tabula durissima ubi nullus erit nisi nos duo et erit tabula crucis."

virginal motherhood, rather than her bodily connection to Christ per se, which was lauded as her most significant attribute by many theologians. Her pure, virginal integrity preserved in conceiving and giving birth to Jesus made her at once the supreme symbol of a new creation and its first member. Her body, untouched by sexuality and the physical trauma of childbirth, came to represent the reversal of the age-old continuation of sinful society, and it mirrored the purity and wholeness of the Christian community in the face of the pagan world.[80] Confirmed by an ecumenical council and praised by Church Fathers and theologians, Mary's perpetual virginity never waned as a popular motif in sermons, prayers, and theological works throughout the Middle Ages. St. Anselm's well-known prayers to Mary address her as "Mother with virginity to be wondered at, Virgin with fertility to be cherished," "Virgin venerated throughout the world . . . By your blessed virginity you have made all integrity sacred."[81]

On a more political note, praise of Mary's virgin state and of virginity in general served to support the authority and prestige of the clergy who, more and more, were expected by the Church to remain celibate, whatever their experiences may have been prior to ordination. An emphasis on sexual abstinence was used from the early centuries of the Church to establish a hierarchy within the Church in which preserved virginity ranked first, widowhood second, and marriage third. St. Ambrose used this scale of perfection to urge his clergy to adopt a celibate lifestyle, even if married, and he pointed to the example of Mary as one to be imitated by all Christians. Peter Brown explains that in the late fourth century, it was novel and controversial for the Church to expect Roman men to accept the virtues traditionally reserved for women.[82]

In the late Middle Ages, the clergy were even more concerned to maintain their authority over the religious lives of the laity. During the fifteenth century, reform-minded clerics sought to curb popular religious practice and bring it into line with official ideals of behavior and belief.[83]

---

80. Brown, *Body and Society,* 444–46.
81. Anselm of Canterbury, *The Prayers and Meditations of St. Anselm,* trans. Sister Benedicta Ward, S.L.G., foreword by R. W. Southern (New York: Penguin Books, 1973), 107, 110.
82. Brown, *Body and Society,* 359.
83. This was especially true in Germany. See R. W. Scribner, "Ritual and Popular Reli-

They tried to do this through the sacrament of confession and penance, and by exercising greater control over lay appropriation and use of sacred objects, especially the host.[84] Given the often outspoken anti-clericalism of the period, a focus on the moral superiority of a virgin or celibate life would have been as important a prop to clerical authority as it had been earlier. As one would expect, then, fifteenth-century preachers were not hesitant to use Marian sermons to illustrate divine preference for virginity and sexual restraint.[85] Mary's virginity remained at the heart of her cult and the sermons that supported it.

In the end, however, Mary's most potent appeal in the later Middle Ages, like that of the other saints, lay in her ability to serve as a sacred place to encounter the holy, a place where the purely human might come into contact with the divine. Mary was able to serve in this capacity in a special way because, in the words of the fifteenth-century English carol, "in that Rose contained was, heaven and earth in little space."[86] For nine months, Mary's body had been intimately joined to the body of Jesus, whose body was in turn united to the divine Logos. The holiness of God himself had been in some measure transferred to Mary through so close an association. The sermons from the fifteenth century, examined here, make more and more references to the fleshly unity of Mary with her son and its importance for her ability to aid in the salvation of sinners.

It was also during the fifteenth century that the doctrine of Mary's Immaculate Conception reached the height of its popularity in the Middle Ages. Instrumentally, this may be attributed in part to the many

---

gion in Catholic Germany at the Time of the Reformation," *Journal of Ecclesiastical History* 35 (1984): 47–77; Charles Zika, "Hosts, Processions and Pilgrimages: Controlling the Sacred in Fifteenth-Century Germany," *Past and Present* 118 (1988): 25–64.

84. Thomas Tentler, *Sin and Confession on the Eve of the Reformation* (Princeton: Princeton University Press, 1977), 345. Zika's entire article, "Hosts, Processions and Pilgrimages," deals with this issue.

85. San Bernardino of Siena, *Opera omnia*, 4:464–84. San Bernardino's entire sermon, "De laudibus virginitatis. Et de duodecim mysticis domicellis Virginis Matris Dei," is an attempt to persuade young women to adopt a life of perpetual virginity in imitation of Mary.

86. The authorship of this carol is unknown. The full chorus reads, "There is no Rose of such vertu, as is the Rose that bare Jesu. For in this Rose contained was, heaven and earth in little space, Alleluia."

chances its Franciscan supporters had to promote it in sermons, and also to the accession of a Franciscan pope, Sixtus IV, in 1471. Most scholars agree, however, that there was enormous popular response to this doctrine among the people and that their support was a factor in the successful establishment of an official feast to celebrate it. The idea of Mary's Immaculate Conception must have held a special attraction for the mind and heart of late medieval Christians. Perhaps they were looking for a source of hope and grace in a world increasingly preoccupied with sin and death.

There was much in the fifteenth century to make a person think about death and the afterlife, besides the usual tendency of medieval religion to dwell on this subject. The four horsemen of the Apocalypse made frequent visitations to most of the villages and cities of Europe. Death, of course, had not been a stranger to Europeans prior to the fifteenth century, but the recurring arrival of the plague after 1348 made the possibility of sudden and unpredictable death more pressing. Life must have seemed uncertain at best to those who chose to ponder it. Many popular sermons, especially those preached during Lent, urged moral reform, confession, and penance. As Johnson believes, they may have made the possibility of salvation in the next world appear as unlikely as in this one, without a powerful mediator to speak up for them or to provide a source of hope.[87]

When people did go to confession to be rid of their sins, Tentler argues, they were expected to try to conform to standards not only of behavior but of thought and intention which were more exacting than ever. These clerical standards of confession may even have seemed alien to persons more accustomed to regulating their moral lives according to their interpersonal relationships than according to what went on in their minds. Possibly to help them out, theologians over the course of the later Middle Ages attributed ever more power to sacramental grace and less to individual effort when explaining the importance of confession. More

---

87. Elizabeth A. Johnson, "Marian Devotion in the Western Church," in *Christian Spirituality: High Middle Ages and Reformation,* ed. Jill Raitt (New York: Crossroad Publishing Company, 1987), 393, 400.

theologians of confession tried to offer their penitents some sense of comfort by allowing the grace of the sacrament to make up for human weakness.[88]

Widespread devotion to the sufferings of Christ and Mary in the late Middle Ages testifies to the growing need of Christians to feel that those who are responsible for their salvation were capable of understanding the pain of human life at its worst. Mary, however, offered them something unique. Unlike Jesus, she was purely human. Mary stood as a symbol for the fact that a human being, not divine in any way, could be saved; for as Bernardino of Busti reminded his audience, "Christ was not only man, but also God."[89] The doctrine of the Immaculate Conception made Mary's salvation and holiness totally dependent on the prevenient grace of God and not on any merits she may have acquired of her own volition. This doctrine may have been so popular in the later medieval period because it was perceived to be a source of hope. The possibility of living purely in a world where the reality of sin was making greater inroads into the interior of the personality may have appeared more and more remote. Mary's salvation through prevenient grace offered the hope that for others, sacramental grace offered through confession and penance and the intercession of an immaculate but human Mary with her son would bring salvation for them as well.[90]

88. Tentler, *Sin and Confession,* 281.

89. Bernardino of Busti, *Mariale,* Sermon 1, "On the Immaculate Conception," pt. 2. "Quia vero Christus erat non tantum homo sed etiam deus."

90. Modern Catholic theologians are still finding a similar hope in Mary's Immaculate Conception, but this time it is a hope which sustains the poor. The fullness of God's grace in the poor, humble, but Immaculate Virgin becomes a pledge to the people of God's promise to all who love her son. See Ivone Gebara and Maria Clara Bingemer, *Mary: Mother of God, Mother of the Poor,* trans. Phillip Berryman (Maryknoll, N.Y.: Orbis Books, 1989), 108–13.

Two

The Sword of Compassion

Mary and the Passion in the Middle Ages

Simeon blessed them and said to Mary his mother, "Behold, this child is set for the fall and rising of many in Israel, and for a sign that is spoken against, and a sword will pierce through your own soul also."

—Luke 2:34–35

But standing by the cross of Jesus were his mother, and his mother's sister, Mary, the wife of Clopas, and Mary Magdalene.

—John 19:25

Because the body of Christ was taken from the substance of the virgin, she was therefore closest to him in grief. [1]

—Bernardino of Busti

Mater Dolorosa

APART FROM THOSE SERMONS devoted especially to Mary, there is one kind of sermon in the late Middle Ages in which she is almost certain to appear, and even occupy center stage: the Passion sermon. This might seem a bit strange when one considers that the two New Testament verses quoted above are the only ones in all four Gospels linking Mary to the suffering of Christ. Jean Gerson reprimanded the four evangelists in his Passion sermon for such a lack of information concerning Mary at this crucial time.

1. Bernardino of Busti, *Mariale* (Milan: Leonardus Pachel, 1493), Sermon 1, "On the Passion," pt. 2.

I ask you then, the true recorders and historians of the life and works of Jesus Christ you my lords the evangelists, why have you written nothing of your good lady and mistress, where she was, what became of her?[2]

Gerson then profusely thanked St. John for the meager information provided by his Gospel account. Mary was there at the cross with Jesus, where we would expect her to be. Of course, Gerson, like all other medieval preachers, did not allow the scarcity of details regarding Mary's life to prevent him from supplying his hearers with a full description of Mary's experiences on Good Friday.

The Scriptures may have been relatively silent about the suffering of Mary during the Passion, but as we have seen, the late medieval desire to identify with the humanity of Christ in his pain had produced a parallel need to know that Mary, too, the purely human mother of Christ and advocate of sinners, understood the meaning of mortal anguish. Mary was seen as the perfect imitator of her son in his Passion and, as such, she herself could and should be imitated by Christians who sought, like her, to enter into and experience the suffering of Jesus.[3] Even more, according to Gerson, the Virgin's ability to suffer with her son meant that she, too, was a partner in the suffering that redeemed the world.

Gerson's Passion sermon, "Ad deum vadit," justly became one of his most famous. It could almost be called a one-person play in which Gerson himself took all the parts, for it related the story of the Passion, step by step, accompanied by imaginative details and lively dialogue among the characters. In the second part of the sermon, Gerson set forth the central and most dramatic portion of the Passion narrative, the crucifixion of Jesus. As he had done throughout the story, Gerson sought to recreate what might have been the feelings, responses, and very words of

2. Jean Gerson, *Oeuvres complètes*, ed. P. Glorieux, 8 vols. (Paris: Desclée and Cie, 1971), 7:504.

3. Karma Lochrie, *Margery Kempe and Translations of the Flesh* (Philadelphia: University of Pennsylvania Press, 1991), 177; Gail McMurray Gibson, *The Theater of Devotion: East Anglian Drama and Society in the Late Middle Ages* (Chicago: University of Chicago Press, 1989), 47–51. Gibson demonstrates that throughout most of her religious life, Margery was guided by the spirituality of the *Meditationes vitae Christi*, in which the Virgin plays a significant role. In fact, says Gibson, "the primary devotional model offered by the *Meditationes vitae Christi* is 'imitatio Mariae' instead of 'imitatio Christi.'"

Mary as she witnessed her son's suffering. In Mary's plea to God as presented by Gerson, Mary suffers with Christ as he hangs on the cross. Always the careful theologian, Gerson stopped short of making Mary fully Co-Redemptrix, but he clearly showed her willingness to suffer "like a good mother for her children" if that should be God's will.[4] In words that echo Jesus' own, Mary cries out,

My God, My God, why have you forsaken the flesh which was taken from me with such holiness and purity, conceived and born from the overshadowing and work of the Holy Spirit? I suffer in it. Since it is one flesh with mine, its grief comes back to me. As of old, sin passed by woman to man, thus the grief of man returns to me, a woman; and by it I purchase and buy back the sin of Eve. And I am willing to suffer, since this pleases God. I consent that I be in some small way a partner and cause of redemption for the human race. And considering this, my grief and even greater grief pleases me if God wills to send it.[5]

As with most of the prominent aspects of the Virgin's cult, her active presence at the foot of the cross had enjoyed a long history within the life and worship of the Church. Her first duty was to act as spokesperson for the Christian community. Through her laments at the cross, the Virgin gave public, ritual expression to the people's grief for the innocent suffering of her son on their behalf. A poetic form of Mary's lamentation, enshrined in a "Kontakion," became a part of the official liturgy for Good Friday in the Eastern Church as early as the ninth or tenth century. It was performed as a dramatic dialogue between a soloist and choir.[6]

Beginning in the eleventh century, contact between the Eastern and Western Churches during the crusades brought the cult of the Mater

4. Gerson, *Oeuvres complètes*, 7:510.

5. Ibid. "Mon Dieu, mon Dieu pourquoy as tu deguerpi la precieuse chair qui tres sainctement et tres purement fu de moy prinse, conceue et enfantee par l'abumbration et operation du Saint Esprit? Je souffre en elle. Comme elle est une chair avecques la mienne, sa douleur redescend en moy. Comme jadis le peche passa par la femme a l'homme, ainsi la douleur de l'homme rechiet sur moy, femme, par quoy je compare et achete le forfait d'Eve. Et je le veuil puisqu'ainsi plaist a Dieu estre fait. Bien me consens que je soie aucunement parcionnere et cause de la redempcion de tout l'humain lignage. Et a ceste consideracion me plait bien ma douleur, et plus grande, si Dieu me la veult envoyer."

6. Jaroslav Pelikan, *Mary Through the Centuries: Her Place in the History of Culture* (New Haven: Yale University Press, 1996), 125–26; Marina Warner, *Alone of All Her Sex: The Myth and Cult of the Virgin Mary* (New York: Alfred A. Knopf, 1976), 209.

Dolorosa to the West. Popular devotion to Mary's sorrows began to grow in Italy and France, spreading to Spain, England, and Flanders during the twelfth century.[7] Thirteenth-century Franciscan sermons, often dramatic in their structure and presentation, encouraged further growth of this cult among the people by helping to move the enactment of the Passion and Mary's lament from their liturgical setting to the public arena.[8]

The most fervent dedication to Mary's sorrow came in the fourteenth and fifteenth centuries. Numerous hymns were composed elaborating Mary's griefs, and various religious orders and confraternities began to dedicate themselves to particular contemplation of her seven sorrows. Among these were the Order of Servites, founded in 1304, and the Confrérie de Notre-Dame des Sept-Douleurs, organized in 1490 in Abbenbroek, Flanders, by John of Coudenberg.[9] The pietà became a popular art form during these centuries;[10] and in 1423 Archbishop Thierry de Meurs introduced in Cologne a Feast of Our Lady of Sorrows, with special indulgences for those who participated.[11] One of the most popular religious works of the later Middle Ages was the *Speculum humanae salvationis,* composed at Strasbourg in 1324 by Ludulphus of Saxony, which devoted all of chapter 27 to the lament of Mary. It was common for editions of this work to come with miniature Marian offices for the seven sorrows or "swords" attached.[12] It is clear that even though the Black Death gave an added boost to the cult of Mary's sorrows after 1348, it was not alone responsible for its popularity.[13]

7. Warner, *Alone of All Her Sex,* 210.

8. Sandro Sticca, *The "Planctus Mariae" in the Dramatic Tradition of the Middle Ages,* trans. Joseph R. Berrigan (Athens: University of Georgia Press, 1988), 11–15.

9. Ibid., 60.

10. A. Latrielle, E. Delaruelle, and J.-R. Palanque, *Histoire du Catholicisme en France,* vol. 2, *Sous les rois très Chrétiens* (Paris: Editions Spes, 1963), 131.

11. André Wilmart, *Auteurs spirituels et textes dévots du moyen âge latin: Études 'histoire littéraire* (Paris: Etudes Augustiniennes, 1971), 511; Warner, *Alone of All Her Sex,* 217.

12. Sticca, *Planctus Mariae,* 62; Graef, *Mary,* 1:307.

13. Gordon Leff, *Heresy in the Later Middle Ages,* 2 vols. (New York: Barnes and Noble, 1967), 2:486–87. The ravages of the plague were certainly responsible for a heightened interest in the sorrows of Mary and Jesus. According to Leff, flagellant processions usually began at a local church where members would pray to the Virgin. During the flagellation itself, they sang of the suffering of Christ and of Mary, and sang a hymn to Mary when they

Meanwhile theologians sought to articulate the possible meaning of Mary's suffering in the context of Jesus' own Passion and death. During the twelfth and thirteenth centuries, as Western Christian piety began to develop along more affective lines, the understanding of the Virgin's role at Calvary changed as well. Whereas earlier theologians such as St. Ambrose (339–97),[14] Richard of St. Victor (d. 1173),[15] and Arnauld Bonnaevallis (d. 1160),[16] had seen Mary's participation at Calvary primarily as a stoic willingness to cooperate with the will of God, by the time of Albert the Great (1193–1280), her ability to suffer with Christ was of the greatest significance.[17] It is this belief, that Mary suffered with her son in behalf of sinners, which was portrayed so poignantly in the sermons and art of the late Middle Ages. Preachers, in fact, will often reject specifically the earlier view that Mary's willingness to allow Jesus to be crucified meant that she felt no pain as she watched him die. Instead they will go to great lengths to express the depth of her anguish in body as well as in mind and heart.

Bernardino of Busti provided his audience with a full summary of the arguments against the reality of Mary's suffering and the most effective

---

were finished. Through this self-inflicted penance, they apparently hoped to link their pain to that of Jesus and his mother as a sacrifice that would appease God and cause him to remove the punishment of the plague.

14. St. Ambrose, "De obitu Valentiniani consolatio," PL 16:1371. "Durum quidem funus videtis; sed stabat et sancta Maria iuxta crucem Filii, et spectabat Virgo sui unigeniti passionem. Stantem illam lego, flentem non lego." See also St. Ambrose, "De institutione virginis liber unus," PL 16:318. "Stabat ante crucem mater, et fugientibus viris, stabat intrepida. Videte utrum pudorem mutare potuerit mater Jesu, quae animum non mutavit. Spectabat piis oculis filii vulnera, per quem sciebat omnibus futuram redemptionem. Stabat non degeneri mater spectaculo, quae non metuebat peremptorem."

15. Richard of St. Victor, "De differentia sacrificii Abrahae a sacrificio Beatae Mariae Virginis," PL 196:1047–48. "Jam non miraris, ut arbitror, si sanctarum sanctissima, perpetua Virgo maria in utroque genere hostiae obtulit quod juxta mysterii dignitatem utrobique optimum esse cognovit. Absit ut dicamus vel credamus beatam Virginem mariam propter metum patiendi; vel timorem cadendi mortis desiderio urgeri: de nullo enim sanctorum rectius creditur quam de ipsa quod parata fuerit semper quantum in ipsa fuit, ad omnia tormentorum genera pro christi nomine sustinenda."

16. Arnauld Bonnaevallis, "Tractatus tertius de vii verbis Domini in cruce," PL 189:1693–94.

17. Sticca, *Planctus Mariae.* 22–23, 102–3; Lochrie, *Margery Kempe,* 177–78. Lochrie believes that it was just this open and, to some, excessive grieving that made Mary such a sympathetic character to late medieval Christians.

proofs in favor of it. Some, he says, believe that Mary experienced no true suffering because she was above the limitations that bind other women merely to expressions of sorrow and tears, that she was in all ways so conformed to God's will that she was actually ready to see Jesus die. They try to say that she showed no outward signs of grief and was so full of charity toward the human race that like the mother in II Maccabees 7, she even urged her son to die. This earlier type of portrayal would imply Mary's superiority to others of her sex for the Maccabees passage says that the mother "exhorted each of her sons with a strong patriotic voice, full of wisdom, because she inserted a masculine soul into her feminine thoughts."[18]

Busti counters these arguments with some of his own, the most effective drawn from Ubertino of Casale's *Arbor vitae.* He quotes Ubertino, saying that as Mary was chosen by grace to bear the redeemer, she was elected by the same grace to participate in his Passion. She entered so fully into his pain

that no thought concerning her son occurred to her virginal mind unless transfixed by bitterness and grief . . . she is therefore a mirror and example of all those lamenting the death of Christ, and she is the ark and chest of the bodily sorrows of the good Jesus.[19]

Passion sermons in the later Middle Ages were the product of interaction with many aspects of contemporary piety. They were certainly inspired by popular Passion plays and by accounts of the Via Dolorosa followed in Jerusalem by pilgrims to the Holy Land. The following description of Mary's anguish as she is forced to watch Jesus carry his cross is clearly influenced by accounts from the Holy Land.

Mary, however, followed from the house of Pilate toward Mount Calvary, dissolved in tears, and as she went, she saw the blood of her son sprinkled on the ground. Before they had come to the place of his execution, his mother, sad and

18. Bernardino of Busti, *Mariale,* Sermon 1, "On the Sorrows of Mary," pt 1. "Et singulos eorum hortabatur voce patria fortiter repleta sapientia, quod feminee cogitationi masculinum animam inserens."

19. Ibid. "Tunc menti virginee nulla ratio occurrebat de filio nisi in ratione amaritudinis et transfigentis doloris . . . ideo ipsa est speculum et exemplum. . . . omnium lamentantium mortem Christi, et archa et armarium dolorum corporis boni Yesu."

afflicted, went forward to meet him, wishing to touch him. When her son saw her so beside herself with grief, he fell, exhausted, beneath his cross. She herself, also, the blessed mother, fell to the ground as though dead.[20]

Devotional literature also contributed to the content of sermons. Two of the most important works were the *Meditationes vitae christi*,[21] thought at the time to be by St. Bonaventure, and Ubertino of Casale's *Arbor vitae crucifixae iesu*, quoted above by Bernardino of Busti. Both date from the beginning of the fourteenth century. San Bernardino of Siena borrowed heavily from the *Arbor vitae* in composing his Passion sermon. The *Arbor vitae* is an eloquent work and it has a special emphasis on the sorrow and compassion of the Virgin.[22] Sermons reflected, too, the liturgical experiences of the people. From the thirteenth century, the "Planctus Mariae" was performed in churches on Good Friday or even on Holy Thursday. By the fifteenth century, some churches were using the "Dialogus mariae cum populo," in which the people themselves spoke verses interspersed with Mary's lines.[23]

During the fourteenth and fifteenth centuries, it became the custom for preachers to begin their sermons with the "Ave Maria," asking Mary to obtain for them divine aid that they might speak the word of God effectively and to good result. Their hearers learned, however, that Mary

20. Gabriel Barletta, *Sermones quadragesimales et de sanctis* (Brescia: Jacobus Britannicus, 1497), 123v. "Maria autem de domo Pilati versus montem calvarie vadit tota lachrymabilis et eundo sanguinem filii sparsum in terra videbat. Antequam ad locum devenuissent sue occisionis; mater eius afflicta et mesta obviam illi processit volens ipsum tangere. Quam ut filius aspexit merore confectam in terram cecidit fatigatus sub cruce. Ipsa etiam mater benedicta quasi mortua in terram cecidit." Barletta says that they have now built a chapel on the site where the incident occurred dedicated to "Sancta Maria de Spasmo."

21. Scholars now generally agree that the *Meditationes vitae Christi* was written by the Franciscan Johannes de Caulibus of Gimignano, between 1346 and 1364. The most recent edition is Iohannis De Caulibus, *Meditaciones vite Christi: olim S. Bonaventuro attributae*, ed. M. Stallings-Taney (Brepols: Turnholit Typographi Brepols Editores Pontificii, 1997). For the bibliographic history of attempts to prove de Caulibus' authorship, see Sticca, *Planctus Mariae*, 196 n. 13.

22. Sandro Sticca refers to this work as "one of the most exalted and profound expressions in the Middle Ages of Christocentric and Marian spirituality." See Sticca, *Planctus Mariae*, 109. Ubertinus de Casali, *Arbor vitae crucifixae Jesu*, introduction by Charles T. Davis (Torino: Bottega d'Erasmo, 1961).

23. Ibid., 123, 134–36.

could not be so casually addressed at certain times of the year. Preachers
so entered into the somber and sorrowful mood of Holy Week and Good
Friday that they fully expected Mary, now reigning as Queen of Heaven,
also to participate with them in the reliving of Christ's Passion. Therefore, as a grief-stricken mother, watching her only son slowly die, she
could hardly be expected to be bothered with the usual prayers and peti-
tions ceaselessly offered to her.

At the opening of his Passion sermon, Gabriel Barletta told the people
that since we need the grace of God to accomplish anything of value,
normally we have recourse to Mary. But today, if we should try to address
her with the "Ave," which means "apart from woe,"[24] she will answer us,
"Do not say to me 'Ave,' for what woman is so unhappy as I?" If we say
"gratia plena," she will only respond that "no, but I am full of bitterness
and grief."[25]

This notion may derive from James of Voragine, because Bernardino
of Busti quotes him in support of it in one of his sermons on the suffering of Mary. But Busti goes on to say that he has first-hand evidence that
it is true. On a certain Good Friday, he was preparing to preach to the people on the Passion of Christ and, as is the custom, he wanted to ask the
Virgin for her aid. Instead, Busti had a vision.

There appeared to me, not to my imaginary sight, but in a form visible to my
bodily eyes a certain man dressed in the black robes customary to a prophet with
a long grey beard reaching to his waist who seemed to be Jeremiah. Recognizing
my desire to petition the most holy Virgin, he said to me these words: "O my son
do not bother the piteous Virgin Mary. . . . You will find her bathed in tears." . . .
Having said these things, when he saw that I wished to go to the Blessed Virgin
herself, he took me by the hand and led me into the presence of an image of the
Virgin, dressed in widow's garments and so full of sadness and grief that she
seemed to be disfigured. I prostrated myself before her feet and said, "Why do I
see you O Virgin Mary, all afflicted and full of grief? I have come to keep you
company, and to share with you in your great grief, to be with you as far as Mount

---

24. Barletta is using a common medieval pun on the word "Ave" as a reversal of the
name given the first woman in Genesis, Eva. As Eve brought one woe, in Latin, "vae," so
the angel's greeting to Mary signaled that through her, the world could once more be separated from or apart from woe, "a-vae."

25. Barletta, *Sermones,* 116r.

Calvary." . . . Then with a deep sigh, she groaned, and she seemed to respond to me with these words, "Since I am not able today to find grace for the freeing of my son, how am I able to help you? Where is your discretion? Where is your prudence? Where is your wisdom? You who ought to suffer with and comfort me, you want to find grace? Do not! Do not allow the angelic greeting to be heard today in the ears of this unhappy mother."[26]

Busti does an excellent job of convincing his hearers, or his readers, that he has had an actual vision. Notice he stresses that this was no purely mental vision, but one which he could perceive with his eyes. Jeremiah is dressed in black and has a long grey beard. The Virgin is disfigured by grief. Presumably, the words of the prophet and of Mary were also able to be heard by his ears. Mary speaks sharply to Busti, just as one would expect of a sorrowing mother pestered by one of her other children for attention. This kind of approach, coming at the beginning of the sermon, must have made the common experience of the Passion among his hearers more tangible and immediate, for it suggested that Jesus' death and Mary's grief were not limited to the distant past. They were instead a present reality into which all might enter. Further, all Christians who heard him might hope to have an experience such as Busti's in which they too, were able to see and converse directly with one of the prophets or even with the Virgin herself.[27]

26. Bernardino of Busti, *Mariale*, Sermon 1, "On the Sorrows of Mary," pt. 1. "Apparuit mihi non visione imaginaria sed in forma visibili corporalibus oculis quidam vestitus more prophetico indutus nigris vestibus: barbam habens canam usque ad cingulum qui videbatur Hieremias . . . et intelligens desiderium meum interpellandi sacratissimam virginem: dixit mihi haec verba. 'O fiol mio de non molestare la piatosa vergene maria. . . . Bagnata de lacrime tu la troverai.' . . . Quibus dictis videns quod ego volebam adire ipsam beatam virginem apprehendit me per manum et duxit coram imagine ipsius virginis quae erat vidualibus vestimentis induta ac mesticia plentissima doloribusque quasi deficere videbatur. Ad cuius pedes ego protinus prostratus dixi: Per che vi vedo o Vergene maria. Tuta afflicta e plena di dolore: Sono venuto a farne compagnia. E esser participe del vostro gran merore. Con voi in fino al monte calvario. . . . Tunc illa alta suspiria et gemitus emittens. Tandem visa est mihi in haec verba respondisse. 'Ex quo non possum hodie pro liberatione filii mei gratiam invenire: Quomodo possum tibi succurrere: Ubi est discretio tua? Ubi est prudentia? Ubi est sapientia tua? Qui deberes mihi compati et condolere per me vis gratiam invenire? Noli, noli in auribus huius infelicissime matris hodie salutationem angelicam personare.'"

27. Johannes of Verden made a similar point in a much less dramatic way in his Passion sermon taken from James of Voragine. He compared Mary to a bell which had such a

Clearly, Passion sermons customarily departed from the usual thematic form of the late Middle Ages and included a large amount of narrative. Even San Bernardino of Siena's thematic Passion sermon contained an extended description of the Seven Words from the Cross, during which he presented many of the incidents that appeared in other, less structured sermons. On Good Friday, preachers became storytellers, attempting to depict the suffering of Christ and his mother in a way that would enable the people to appreciate the sacrifice made for them and turn to God in repentance.

Mary's sorrow and compassion were necessarily determined by the sad events of Holy Week. In trying to present her suffering as dramatically as possible, preachers usually said that it began as early as Wednesday, when Mary parted from her son for the last time before he went to Jerusalem, knowing that he would suffer and die. Barletta's description of the Virgin places her squarely within the Biblical tradition of famous persons who have argued with or talked back to God. Mary pleads with Jesus, offering him as many as six reasons why he should not go. Jesus, however, replies with six reasons of his own why he must go.[28] A number of preachers presented this moment in especially tender ways, expressing the common love shared by mother and son and yet the willingness of both to accept God's will. Mary's words often echo those of Jesus in the Garden of Gethsemane. Once she is convinced that Jesus must leave, she is able to say to God the Father along with her son, "Let it be done not as I will, but as you will."[29]

Mary's pain continued throughout the trial, torture, crucifixion, and burial of Jesus and was not ended until the Resurrection of Sunday morning, when most preachers were convinced that Jesus had appeared in person first to his mother. It was only right that she be the first to experience

---

sweet sound that she had been able to call the son of God from heaven. On the day of the Passion, however, the bell lost its sound because it was pierced with the sword of grief. Johannes of Verden, *Sermones dominicales cum expositionibus evangeliorum, sive Dormi secure de tempore et de sanctis* (Basel: Johann Amerbach, 1484), Sermon 25.

28. Barletta, *Sermones*, 119r–119v.

29. Gerson, *Oeuvres complètes*, 7:450. "Soit fait non pas ainsi comme je veuil, mais ainsi comme vous voulez." See also Olivier Maillard, "Passio domini nostri Jesu Christi," in *Sermones quadragesimales* (Paris: Antoine Caillaut, 1498), pt. 1.

this special joy since no one had been so loyal to him or suffered so much with him as she had.[30]

A few early medieval preachers may have depicted Mary as a stern and unemotional servant of the will of God, but by the fourteenth and fifteenth centuries, everyone knew that her suffering was as real as that of Jesus. In sermons, in stories of the Via Dolorosa, and in paintings, the people learned of her unspeakable anguish as she watched her innocent son, already bloody and weakened, carry his cross, fall under its weight, be nailed to its beams, and die. Mary herself had received Jesus' body from the cross,[31] and as she kissed his hands and feet, her own face received the marks of his blood.[32]

Offering the Blessed Host

Mary's pain was set forth in a very human and sympathetic way. She had sorrowed as any mother would under similar circumstances. But Mary was, of course, not "any mother." She was the virgin mother of Christ, and later medieval preachers were never content to portray her as

30. Johannes of Verden, *Sermones*, Sermon 26. Johannes says no one should doubt Christ's appearance to Mary on Sunday even though it is not recorded. He would have kept the commandment to honor his mother. Mary knew this would happen and that is why she did not accompany the other women to the tomb to anoint the body. See also Michel Menot, *Sermons choisis de Michel Menot*, ed. J. Nève (Paris: Bibliothèque du XVe siècle, 1924), 197–98; Gerson, *Oeuvres complètes*, 7:518.

31. It was this incident which inspired the popular art form, the pietà, to which Maillard specifically refers in his Passion sermon. Maillard, "Passio domini nostri," pt. 4. "Et Virgo Maria venit ad digitos et manus osculando. Quando pedes fuerunt dissoluti deposuerunt eum de cruce et posuerunt corpus Iesu in gremio benedicte matris Christi. Et ideo depingitur nostra domina de pietate." San Bernardino also portrays the pietà, comparing Mary's care of Jesus' body at death to her care of him as an infant. San Bernardino of Siena, *Opera omnia*, 2:268. "Nunc vero, ad doloris augmentum, tenet ipsum in suo materno et virginali gremio reclinatum et, officiosa pro funere, cogitur involvere mortuum ex aliena ope sibi praestitis linteis, quem natum infantem involvit vilibis pannis."

32. Descriptions of Mary marked by Jesus' blood were common in sermons. Gerson, *Oeuvres complètes*, 7:516–17. "Vous, Mere douloureuse travaillee et angoisseuse, regardastes despendre le precieux corps de vostre fils et que vous le peustes recevoir entre vos bras. C'est bien a penser que vous l'embrassastes devotement. . . . Vous l'arrosiez de vos larmes a palle chiere, fors en tant que vostre digne face estoit de son precieux sang et de ses playes coloree et noblement tachee." Menot, *Sermons choisis*, 514. "Hunc sanguinem manibus colligens dulcissimum faciem suam liniebat."

a passive victim of circumstances who could only stand by helplessly weeping. She had responded to Gabriel's announcement by declaring, "Behold the handmaid of the Lord"; from that moment she became a willing and active participant in the unfolding of God's plan of redemption. As preachers looked for ways to describe the exact nature of Mary's involvement in the Passion, they placed her at times in the role of priest, offering the sacrificial victim to God, and at others they scarcely distinguished between the physical passion of Christ and what was generally understood to be a reflection of his pain in the compassion of Mary's soul. Most could not refrain from presenting the Virgin's compassion in very bodily and concrete ways.

St. Bernard of Clairvaux had established in the twelfth century a clear precedent for associating Mary with a priestly role in one of his sermons for the festival of the Purification, celebrated by the Church as Candlemas on February 2. As Mary brings her son to be circumcised and dedicated in the temple, St. Bernard compared her to the priest who sacrificially offers the body of Christ in the Mass. He preached, "Offer your son, sacred Virgin, and present the blessed fruit of your womb to God. Offer the blessed host, pleasing to God, for the reconciliation of us all."[33]

This priestly theme was repeated in the popular *Speculum humanae salvationis*. The candles dedicated and offered to God by the faithful on February 2 are symbols of the supreme candle, the light of the world, offered by the Virgin.

> Marye to Godde in that feest offird a candel bright,
> The whilk Seinte Symeon cald thus: "revelacioune of folkes light."
> Jhesu Crist, Marie son, is this candel brynnung. . . .
> This candele to God the Fadere was offrid for hele of man,
> Be Whilk the nyght, of our derknesse was lightened than.[34]

---

33. St. Bernard of Clairvaux, "Sermo III de purificatione B. Mariae," PL 183:370. "Vere, o beata Virgo, vere non habes causam, nec tibi opus est purificatione. Sed nunquid filio tuo opus erat circumcisione? Esto inter mulieres tanquam una earum; nam et filius tuus sic est in numero puerorum. Circumcidi voluit, et non multo magis velit offeri? Offer filium tuum, Virgo Sacrata, et benedictum fructum ventris tui Domino repraesenta. Offer ad nostram omnium reconciliationem hostiam sanctam, Deo placentem."

34. Avril Henry, ed., *The Mirour of Man's Salvation: A Middle English Translation of the "Speculum humanae salvationis,"* 15th cent. ms. (Philadelphia: University of Pennsylvania Press, 1987), 81.

In the service of Candlemas, worshipers took the part of the Virgin Mary offering Christ to God the Father, who then used this sacrificial giving to bestow grace in return. It is no wonder that it seemed so natural for people to return home with their candles and expect them to bless and protect their family and dwelling from danger. The incarnational symbolism was further elaborated when those candles were melted and formed into crosses placed over doors, in stables, or on wagons and ploughs.[35]

Later medieval preachers continued the tradition of attributing to Mary a quasi-priestly office, both in the dedication of Christ in the temple and in his crucifixion. Gabriel Barletta made special use of this idea throughout his sermons. In his sermon on the Purification, he quoted Albert the Great to affirm that the God of the Old Testament was more inclined to justice than mercy and many offerings had been made through the centuries to appease his anger. Mary, on her initiative, made the supreme offering that alone could dispose the Father to mercy and compassion.

But today, walking into the temple, her son enclosed in her arms, was one who said to him, "Receive this offering which your handmaid brings O Holy Father." . . . When God saw this, moved by mercy, he said, "No longer will my spirit remain eternally in indignation against Man."[36]

Elsewhere Barletta declared that even though Mary was much grieved in watching her son die, she nevertheless "wished him to die for the salvation of the human race . . . if no other means had been found, she herself would have killed her own son." Barletta explained that Mary was no less ready than Abraham had been to sacrifice her only son.[37] Michel Menot likewise compared Mary to Abraham in her willingness to offer Jesus at God's command; but he stopped short of Barletta's rather extreme statement. He says he heard it said in a Parisian convent that as a last resort

35. R. W. Scribner, "Ritual and Popular Religion in Catholic Germany at the Time of the Reformation," *Journal of Ecclesiastical History* 35 (1984): 62.

36. Barletta, *Sermones*, 64v. "Sed hodie in templum ingressa cum brachio clauso in quo filius erat dixit illo 'Suscipe oblationem hec quam obtulit ancilla tua O Pater sancte.' . . . Quod videns deus misericordia motus dixit 'Non permanebit spiritus meus in indignatio mea in homine in eternum.'"

37. Ibid., 88v. "Si alius modus non fuisset; ipsamet filium proprium occidisset. Quia non minor erat charitas sua quam Abrahae; qui filium suum erat paratus etc."

Mary would have killed Jesus herself, but such things only serve to scandalize one's hearers.[38] Neither of these two preachers attempts to say that Mary could offer her son in this way because she suffered no real pain. Their statements must be understood in the context of the desire to see Mary as active rather than passive in her priestly office.

Contemporary art depicted Mary as priest in the Presentation and even in Eucharistic settings. Jacques Daret's "Presentation in the Temple" depicts Mary holding her infant son directly above the altar, which is covered in a white cloth similar to the corporal used in the Mass, as though offering him as a sacrifice to God. Surrounding figures carry candles like those used in the Candlemas service. More striking still is the 1437 painting commissioned for Amiens cathedral, "Le sacerdoce de la Vierge." Mary appears dressed as an Old Testament Levitical priest. She holds the hand of her young son, robed as a Christian priest, encouraging him to take part in the Eucharist, a service in which he would become both priest and victim.[39]

Certainly, none of these preachers or artists intended to imply that Mary had ever been ordained a priest or less still that women in general could or should be priests. As Bynum indicates, through this kind of metaphor, preachers as well as mystics could take advantage of the freedom and complexity of medieval religious symbols to express a particular truth. To cast Mary as priest was to place her in a male role with female characteristics. In the place of women, men who are priests must now lay the table and prepare the food for the people to eat. Medieval mystical literature at times used such gender reversal to speak of the clergy as pregnant with Jesus, or as cooks who prepared Christ as food. Since the twelfth century, Christ himself had been described from time to time as a mother who nourishes her young.[40]

38. Menot, *Sermons choisis*, 453.

39. Barbara G. Lane, *The Altar and the Altarpiece: Sacramental Themes in Early Netherlandish Painting* (New York: Harper and Row, 1984), 70–71. Lane's book is especially skillful in uncovering the Marian symbols of the paintings she examines, and the ways in which late medieval art linked Mary intimately with the Eucharist.

40. Caroline Walker Bynum, *Holy Feast and Holy Fast: The Religious Significance of Food to Medieval Women* (Berkeley: University of California Press, 1987), 285, 278, 266; idem, "Jesus as Mother and Abbot as Mother: Some Themes in Twelfth-Century Cistercian Writing," in

The importance of this priestly language and symbolism for the cult of Mary in the fourteenth and fifteenth centuries is the dignity that it bestows on her as co-participant with God in the act of offering Christ for the salvation of the world. As the mother of his human nature, she willingly presented as oblation the body so dear to her and taken from her own flesh. The spouse of God in the Incarnation, Mary the mother, like God the Father, was prepared to suffer the pain resulting from such a sacrifice. The author of the *Speculum humanae salvationis* assured his readers that Mary demonstrated that she loved us even more than she loved Jesus by allowing him to die to save us.[41]

Passion vs. Compassion

Sermons and literature of the late Middle Ages were no less ready to assert with Jean Gerson that Mary shared in the actual atoning sacrifice of Christ itself. To quote the *Speculum humanae salvationis* once again, "And als crist overcome the feende be his seint passoiune, so did eke blissid marie be moderfulle compassioune."[42] The popular fourteenth-century saint Bridget of Sweden (1301–73) said that Christ had spoken to her in a vision, proclaiming, "And therefore I can well say that my mother and I have saved Man as it were with one heart, I by suffering in my heart and flesh, she in the sorrow and love of her heart."[43]

This is the traditional interpretation of Mary's compassion, Christ suffering in body and soul, Mary in heart and soul. It was a comparison that was almost inevitable, since Simeon had predicted that Mary's soul would also be pierced by a sword and everyone knew that Mary herself had not been physically crucified. Arnauld Bonnaevallis referred to two altars, one the body of Christ, the other in the breast of Mary. Only Christ as high priest had the right to give his own body and blood; nevertheless, Mary's pain had assisted in the propitiation of God. Albert the Great, too,

---

Jesus as Mother: Studies in the Spirituality of the High Middle Ages (Berkeley: University of California Press, 1982), 110–69.

41. Henry, *Mirour*, 143.

42. Ibid., 159.

43. Quoted in Hilda Graef, *Mary: A History of Doctrine and Devotion*, 2 vols. (New York: Sheed and Ward, 1964), 1:307.

said that the wounds Christ had in his body, Mary bore in her heart.[44] It was a way of presenting Mary as a participant, while making a clear distinction between Mary and Jesus as to the type of offering and the degree of suffering involved.

As a permanent part of the Church's symbolic tradition, the distinction between Passion of body and compassion of soul remained in the later Middle Ages. But in keeping with the propensity of late medieval imagery to stress the bodily ties between Mary and Jesus and to see Virgin Mother and divine Son as nearly equal, the difference between them in their sacrifice at Calvary became much less discernible. More preachers were prepared to assure their hearers that Mary, too, had experienced acute bodily suffering in a number of ways.

San Bernardino of Siena represents a certain transition from the earlier to the later approach. While maintaining Christ's bodily pain as distinct from Mary's grief, he described the two as so unified by their experience that Mary actually became one with Jesus on the cross. Mary, he declared, came closer to Jesus' cross than anyone else, "because she did not only stand beside the cross, indeed, she truly hung on the cross, for nothing of herself remained in her. All was mingled by love, and while he offered his body, she offered her spirit."[45] In the same sermon, he reminded his hearers of Mary's familiar problem on the day of the Passion: she is unable to attend to prayers from the faithful. Instead we find her "with her beloved son, so horribly despised and crucified, and with all her heart, in all senses and thoughts suffering with him and thereby completely transformed into him."[46]

Another common metaphor for Mary's compassion, first used by St. Bernard of Clairvaux, was to call it a type of martyrdom. Michel Menot

44. Sticca, *Planctus Mariae*, 22–24.

45. San Bernardino of Siena, *Opera omnia*, ed. P. M. Perantoni, 5 vols. (Quaracchi: Collegium S. Bonaventurae, 1950–), 2:246. "Omnino illa plus ad crucem appropinquabat quam quicumque alii, quia non solum iuxta crucem stabat, verum etiam in cruce pendebat; de se enim nihil in se remanserat. Tota commigraverat in dilectum, et dum ille corpus, ista spiritum immolabat."

46. Ibid., 2:188. "Reperiemus eam sic filio suo dilecto, tam horribiliter conculcato et crucifixo, totis visceribus, omnibus sensibus et cunctis cogitationibus compati et sic in eum totaliter transformari."

pictured Mary's heart as transfixed by the sword of compassion, while she railed at Jesus' crucifiers and begged to be crucified with him. "Then gathering his blood in her hands she bathed her sweet face in it." Menot explained that Mary, as St. Bernard had said, experienced the supreme punishment of the martyrs.[47] Gabriel Barletta declared that Mary's martyrdom exceeded that of all other martyrs, "first because hers was a martyrdom of love, theirs of faith. Second, the others were punished in their bodies, but she in her heart. Third because others suffered after Christ, but she with Christ, and in Christ and by the same blows as Christ."[48]

These passages from Barletta, Menot, and San Bernardino fall fully within the mainstream of ideas concerning Mary's compassion, while at the same time emphasizing as much as possible her unity with Christ in suffering. Yet there was also a history of ascribing bodily pain to Mary at least as old as John Damascene (c. 675–749). Bernardino of Busti quoted John as saying that "the griefs which the Virgin avoided in giving birth she sustained in the Passion of Christ."[49] Barletta pictured the ravaged physical appearance of Mary as she wept at the cross: "We see her, mourning, her face dirty, her hair torn." She calls on all to weep with her, "For all the griefs of giving birth and of death were reserved for her today; because she loved her son above all others."[50] Barletta continued by quoting from St. Bernard of Clairvaux, "She herself wanted to suffer with her son for the salvation of the world and as St. Bernard said, 'she desired to add her own blood and with her son to celebrate the evening sacrifice.'"[51]

Jean Gerson and Bernardino of Busti were most explicit in connecting the suffering flesh of Jesus with that of Mary. As we saw at the opening of this chapter, Gerson described Mary as suffering in the flesh of Christ

47. Menot, *Sermons choisis*, 514–15. See above, n. 25.

48. Barletta, *Sermones*, 104r. "Prima quod fuit martyrium amoris: aliorum autem fidei. Secunda quod alii sunt percussi in corpore; ista autem in corde. Tertia quod alii post Christum; ista autem cum Christo et in Christo et eodem ictu quo Christus."

49. Bernardino of Busti, *Mariale*, Sermon 1, "On the Sorrows of Mary," pt. 1. "Dolores quos virgo effugit pariens; hos in passione Christi sustinuit."

50. Barletta, *Sermones*, 116r. "Nam omnes dolores partus et mortis hodie sibi fuere reservati; quod super omnes dilexit filium."

51. Ibid., 104r. "Ipsa pati volebat cum filio pro salute mundi. Unde Ber. 'Optabat ipsa sanguinem suum addere et cum filio sacrificium vespertinum celebrare.'"

because it was one with hers, thereby allowing her to reverse the curse laid on all persons by God because of Eve's sin. Gerson is unique among the preachers of this study for linking the close bodily association of Mary and Christ in the Passion to Mary's claim to be the Second Eve.[52]

Drawing on St. Paul's reference to Christ as the new Adam,[53] Christian theologians as early as the middle of the second century were comparing the mother of Christ to Eve. It was usually some aspect of Mary's role in the Incarnation, however, which was mentioned in this regard. In the Middle Ages, by contrast, Mary's humility, obedience, or the ability of her holiness and merits to attract God to her were most often favorably compared to the pride, disobedience, and sin of Eve.[54] These preachers were simply continuing the ancient tradition of associating Mary's motherhood with her reversal of Eve's curse. Gerson reveals his sensitivity to the growing cult of the sorrows of Mary as well as to the more obvious use of bodily imagery in the later Middle Ages when he joins these two themes.

Like Gerson, Bernardino of Busti believed the perfection of Mary's compassion was the result of her shared flesh with Christ. He stated that "because the body of Christ was taken from the substance of the Virgin, she was therefore closest to him in grief."[55] Busti also quoted several Franciscan scholars to support this point. Alexander of Hales was used to support the notion that while Mary's rational faculties had rejoiced at Jesus' death because in charity she knew that it would bring salvation, the inferior sensual part of her nature caused her to grieve in both body and soul.[56] Busti likewise compared Mary's compassion to martyrdom; but in Nicholas of Lyra he found the most developed argument supporting his belief that her suffering was physical as well as emotional. Mary's martyrdom was more severe than that of all other martyrs

52. Gerson, *Oeuvres complètes*, 7:510.

53. 1 Corinthians 15:21–22.

54. Examples may be found in Barletta, *Sermones*, 16v, 72v; and San Bernardino of Siena, *Opera omnia*, 2:159–60, 373, 4:552.

55. Bernardino of Busti, *Mariale*, Sermon 1, "On the Sorrows of Mary," pt. 2. "Sola una mulier idest mater sua secum fuit passa per perfectam compassionem. . . . Quia vero corpus Christi erat de substanatia virginis, ideo illa ei fuit propinquissima in doloribus."

56. Ibid., Sermon 1, "On the Sorrows of Mary," pt. 1. "Imo in parte superiori rationis in qua ipsum fructum mortis filii summe appetebat et desiderabat, etiam summe gaudebat

because the grief of passion begins with a wound to the flesh, felt by the senses and then overflows into the soul. But the grief of compassion arises and begins in the soul and overflows into the senses and flesh. . . . Therefore since the soul is more powerful and more dominant over the flesh, and the flesh is more delicate and subject to the soul; the overflowing from soul to body is much greater.[57]

Bynum has argued that a spirituality which emphasizes the bodily side of human nature is less likely to insist on a strict dichotomy between body and soul, and more likely to magnify the importance of the bodily human nature which Mary provided for Christ. A number of medieval women mystics, Hildegard of Bingen, Elizabeth of Schönau, and St. Catherine of Siena, often equated "humanity" both with the body and with "woman," because Eve, unlike Adam, was made purely of flesh and was therefore a better symbol for the weakness and fleshliness of humanity. Hildegard went so far as to say that female flesh, the bodily humanity Christ assumed from Mary, had redeemed the world.[58] St. Catherine said of Mary's experience at Calvary,

Oh sweetest love, this was the sword that struck your mother's heart and soul. The Son was physically pierced, and so was his mother, since his flesh was hers. This was only right, since that flesh was her own: he had taken his flesh from her.[59]

In the writings of Hildegard of Bingen and St. Catherine of Siena, and underlying the sermons of Gerson and Busti, there is a common understanding of human nature as essentially bodily and feminine. Mary, therefore, suffered with Christ on the cross because it was her humanity that he bore, hers doubly because of the medieval association of "woman" with human weakness and suffering and because he drew his flesh from

---

quia caritate plena. Sed in parte inferiori et sensuali summe dolebat in corpore et anima ex compassione filii sui ut etiam dicit doctor et theologus irrefragabilis Alexander de Alles."

57. Ibid. "Quia dolor passionis oritur a lesione carnis cum perceptione sensus; et redundat in anima. Dolor vero compassionis oritur et incipit in anima et redundat in sensum et carnem. Quanto igitur anima est potentior et magis dominans super carnem et caro delicatior et magis subiecta anime; tanto fit maior redundantia."

58. Bynum, *Holy Feast and Holy Fast,* 264–65.

59. Catherine of Siena, *The Letters of St. Catherine of Siena,* vol. 1, trans. Suzanne Noffke, O.P., Medieval and Renaissance Texts and Studies, no. 52 (Binghamton, N.Y.: Medieval and Renaissance Texts and Studies, 1988), 38.

her body. Present also is a profound sense of the interconnectedness of body and soul. Experiences affecting the one will necessarily "overflow" into the other, for without a body as well as a soul, human nature remains incomplete. Christ was required to suffer in body and soul to redeem humanity. Mary, then, if she were to be at all a co-participant in his Passion, would have to endure fleshly as well as spiritual pain. Mother and son are presented as persons who share an almost mystical unity in suffering guaranteed by their common flesh. It is a oneness capable of transcending the limitations of space, reminiscent of the mystery of the Eucharist in which the body of Christ may be present on many altars, yet without division. Characteristics usually associated with the spiritual realm, or at least with the transformed and resurrected body of Christ, are here freely attributed to the materiality of normal, if immaculate, human flesh.

The art of the fifteenth century vividly portrays the shared suffering of Mary and Christ in ways that reinforce their unity of body and soul. Most important of these works is the famous "Descent from the Cross," painted by the Fleming Rogier van der Weyden around 1435. As Christ is lowered from the cross, Mary faints into the arms of St. John immediately below the body of her son. The angle of her body and the position of her arms form an exact parallel to those of Jesus.[60]

Because the Passion of Christ was so central to the Christian drama of redemption, every aspect of Jesus' suffering was traditionally understood to convey a special meaning, much of which was subsequently incorporated into the liturgy and popular religious practice. One of the most symbolic events of the Biblical Passion narratives is recorded in John 19:34. A Roman soldier pierces the side of Jesus with his spear and water and

---

60. Lane, *Altar and the Altarpiece*, 89. Lane also presents a similar work by Petrus Christus, "Lamentation," in which the curve of Mary's body as she swoons duplicates that of Jesus, lying on the ground just below her; ibid., Plate 63. See also the entire article by Harvey E. Hamburgh, "The Problem of 'Lo Spasimo' of the Virgin in Cinquecento Paintings of the 'Descent from the Cross,'" *Sixteenth Century Journal* 12, no. 4 (1981): 45–76. Hamburgh demonstrates the continued popularity of this theme in the Italian art of the sixteenth century after many had begun once again to criticize "excessive" portrayals of Mary's grief. He attributes this primarily to the ongoing influence and popularity of San Bernardino of Siena within the Franciscan order.

blood flow from the wound. At their most fundamental, this water and blood are associated with the power of Christ's sacrifice to cleanse the guilt of sin and bring reconciliation with God. At another level, they represent the origin of the two chief sacraments of the Church. Christians are initiated into the Church in the water of Baptism; and they receive the body and blood of Christ in the Eucharist. As a continuing reminder of baptism, the Church developed the custom of encouraging people to make the sign of the cross with fingers dipped in holy water. It was this practice which perhaps caused preachers to link Mary in yet another way to the sacrifice of her son. Here is a portion of Michel Menot's sermon for Palm Sunday. "In processions, a vessel carrying holy water stands next to the cross, thus the Virgin stood beside the cross. The vessel in which the water was placed were her eyes, from which flowed many tears."[61] Bernardino of Busti, describing Mary as a fruitful garden, says that this garden bore much fruit, "For it was well watered by tears of grief for the Passion of her son, by tears of compassion for the affliction of the miserable, by tears of devotion for the desire of heaven, and by tears of lamentation for the desolation of her present miseries."[62]

Few preachers described Mary's vigil under the cross without an emotional portrayal of her tears. San Bernardino exclaimed that Mary's tears fell in such abundance "that you would think her flesh and spirit dissolved in tears."[63] In the sermons and devotional works of the time, Mary's tears show how fully she entered into the suffering of Jesus, like him pouring out the substance of her body in grief. Her tears, like his blood, are a symbol of the death and rebirth made possible by the sacrifice at Calvary, relived by the Church in the rite of baptism.[64]

61. Menot, *Sermons choisis,* 451. "In processione vas aquam benedictam ferens iuxta crucem stat; sic Virgo stabat iuxta crucem. Vas ubi aqua ponitur erant oculi eius, a quibus multe lachryme manabant."

62. Bernardino of Busti, *Mariale,* Sermon 1, "On Marian Similes in Scripture," pt. 1. "Et sic iste hortus fuit fructiferus. Nam primo fuit bene irriguus modo lacrimis doloris pro passione filii. Modo lacrimis compassionis pro miserorum afflictione. Modo lacrimis devotionis pro desiderio celestis patrie. Et modo lacrimis lamentationis pro incolatu presentis miserie."

63. San Bernardino of Siena, *Opera omnia,* 2:267. "Ipsiusque lacrimae in tanta ubertate fluebant, ut carnem cum spiritu totam in lacrimas resolvi putares."

64. Warner, *Alone of All Her Sex,* 222–23.

Depictions of Mary dissolved in tears at the foot of Jesus' cross or receiving his lifeless body after the deposition are representative of the kind of religious devotion with which late medieval Christians were familiar. For instance, the tears or "roarings" which formed such a visible part of Margery Kempe's religious life were not unusual at all, but fairly common among certain types of mystics.[65] Margery may actually have been consciously imitating Mary's own grief, in an attempt to experience what the Virgin experienced and therefore become a more perfect imitator of the Mother of God.[66]

After Jesus' body was laid in the tomb, it would seem that there was little left for Mary to accomplish. Sermons usually state that she returned to the city, leaning on the arm of St. John or accompanied by the other women, to await the triumph of the Resurrection on Sunday morning. Mary's involvement in the drama of Holy Week, however, was not finished. She had yet one task to perform. Those who were devoted to the Virgin in the Middle Ages could not resist making her the supreme symbol of the Church by proclaiming that she alone had retained a firm faith in the Resurrection of Jesus even in the midst of his Passion. Nor had her faith wavered during the bleak hours of Saturday as his body lay in the tomb. While everyone else either fled or lost hope, Mary alone preserved the Christian community in its darkest time. Bernardino of Busti believed this was the only reason Mary had not died of grief along with Jesus. "She was saved by a singular privilege of God, so that the Christian faith might be preserved in her."[67] According to Jean Gerson, Mary was the first to adore Christ after his birth and the first to adore the cross after his death, and from the time of his burial until his Resurrection, Mary received a special grace from God that enabled her "to behold the secrets of God in mystical contemplation."[68] San Bernardino, Gabriel Barletta, and Busti all

---

65. Lochrie, *Margery Kempe*, 177–80, 206–12.

66. Gibson, *Theater of Devotion*, 49–50. Gibson shows that most of Margery's religious experience was determined by her attempt to imitate the Virgin. See above, n. 3.

67. Bernardino of Busti, Mariale, Sermon 1, "On the Sorrows of Mary," pt 1. "Si quis autem querat quare ipsa benedicta virgo in tantis doloribus non est mortua, respondetur quod singulari dei privilegio fuit preservata ut fides Christiana in ea conservaretur."

68. Gerson, *Oeuvres complètes*, 7:017.

point out that Mary Magdalen and the other women remained faithful to Jesus in spite of their weakness as women, because of their great love for him. Only Mary, however, was able to combine a perfect faith with her compassion for his pain.[69]

Mary's continuing grief on Saturday, as well as her steadfast maintenance of the faith are the reasons given by medieval preachers for dedicating each Saturday to her veneration in Mass and office and by fasting.[70] Also in honor of her faith, when all candles are extinguished and the altar is stripped on Good Friday, one candle remains burning. It is a witness that the true faith of the Church was never altogether lost. As Michel Menot explained, "Because only the Virgin remained, one candle only is left; and the images are covered, because there were none who then dared to call themselves apostles."[71] Menot adds that one of the reasons why Mary had to be present at the crucifixion was that someone had to be able to tell the absent apostles the facts of Jesus' death.[72]

Mary's intimate involvement in the drama of salvation from the moment of the Incarnation through the suffering and death of her son gained for her the supreme right of intercession on behalf of sinners and therefore ongoing participation in the active life of the Church. San Bernardino concludes that the Virgin must have stood to the left of Jesus' cross so that she could assume even then her position as advocate and intercede for those sinners who will be placed on Jesus' left at the Last

---

69. San Bernardino of Siena, *Opera omnia*, 2:263. "Devota vero familia Christi, quamquam fragilis sexu, non recedebat. Crucifixo assistebat, excepta Virgine, fide carens et animo timore ac dolore afflicta." Barletta, *Sermones*, 54r–54v. Barletta says that even though Mary Magdalen loved Jesus, she had only compassion for his pain, but not faith in his Resurrection. Bernardino of Busti, *Mariale*, Sermon 1, "On the Sorrows of Mary," Introduction. "O igitur magnum feminarum preconium, ut in solo pectore femineo tota fides recondita fuerit. . . . beata virgo . . . in tollerantia passionis et in constantia fidei et dilectionis et in perspicacia iudicii et actionis quoscumque viros incomparabiliter excessit quod patet ex eo quod discipulis pro timore mortis fugientibus et in fide vacillantibus; ipsa inconcussa stetit et constantissima perseveravit."

70. Barletta, *Sermones*, 17r; Bernardino of Busti, *Mariale*, Sermon 1, "On the Sorrows of Mary," Introduction.

71. Menot, *Sermons choisis*, 502. "Quia sola Virgo remansit, ideo sola candela dimittitur et imagines cooperiuntur, quia tunc non erant ausi se nominare apostolos."

72. Ibid., 183.

Judgment.[73] Gabriel Barletta concluded his Passion sermon with the story of a notorious sinner who nevertheless always saluted the Virgin with the "Ave." On one such occasion, he beheld a vision of Mary, holding the body of her son in her lap as he poured forth the last of his blood. When the man asked her the meaning of the vision, Mary replied that he and other sinners were responsible for Jesus' pain. They are crucifying him all over again and making her a mother of misery rather than a mother of mercy. The man cries out, "O mother, don't say such a thing. Remember that you are the advocate of sinners and pray for me." Mary asks Jesus to be merciful and he answers that since she is his mother, he cannot deny her. Jesus then pardons the sinner.[74] The miracle story illustrates not only Mary's role as intercessor, but also the power that the image of the pietà had in the religious mind of the period.

Michel Menot closed his Passion sermon at Tours by asking his hearers to pray with him to Mary for pardon of sin, "so that our poor souls will be able to enjoy Christ in eternity."[75] Finally, Bernardino of Busti selected for his sermon on the sorrows of Mary a passage from Ubertino's *Arbor vitae* which serves to combine all of the most important aspects of her involvement in the life of Jesus and the right of intercession this procured for her:

Indeed as he himself was the redeemer of all, thus she was the mother of all, the mediator, reconciler, apologist and advocate of all sinners. And therefore since she was to be the advocate of the world, the Holy Spirit poured into her heart such great sorrow that it would suffice to make her mother of all the elect in order to defend the ingratitude of the world, because she delivered her maker, made of her own material, to such a harsh death.[76]

73. San Bernardino of Siena, *Opera omnia*, 2:246. "Sed qua parte stabat Virgo Maria *iuxta crucem*? Utique ad sinistram Christi, secundum Alexandrum de Hales, scilicet ut pro peccatoribus filium exoraret, qui a sinistris Domini sunt."

74. Barletta, *Sermones*, 104v.

75. Menot, *Sermons choisis*, 183. "Je veulx doncques persuader que luy prions qu'elle nous impetre pardon et remission de noz pechez, affin que noz poures ames puyssent une fois Christo frui in eternum."

76. Bernardino of Busti, *Mariale*, Sermon 1, "On the Sorrows of Mary," pt. 1. "Imo sicut ipse fuit omnium redemptor, ita ipsa fuit omnium genitrix, mediatrix, reconciliatrix, excusatrix et advocata omnium peccatorum. Et ideo cum ipsa esset advocata mundi tantum dolorem spiritus sanctus suis infundit visceribus quantum sufficiebat omnium electorum

The Resurrection and Ascension of Jesus, as portrayed in the Gospels and in the Acts of the Apostles, meant that his body, born of Mary, rose to life again and along with his soul returned to heaven. If Mary were to fulfill her purpose as advocate of sinners, she would likewise need to be present in the court of heaven, at least in spirit. Of course, most Christians of the later Middle Ages were sure that Mary's body, like that of her son, now resided in glory. It is to this chapter in Mary's story that we now turn.

---

genetrici ad excusandam ingratitudinem mundi, quia sic dura morte de sui fabrica suum expellebat auctorem."

Three

"Hevenly Conversacion"

Mary as Supreme Intercessor and Mediatrix

For as the Lord did not allow his Holy One, Christ, to see corruption,
likewise he did not allow that Holy One from whom he was born to
see it; but she was assumed, body and soul, into heaven.[1]

—San Bernardino of Siena

By hur hevenly conversacion she maketh erthely men to be the
cytezens of heven.[2]

—John Bromyard

The Assumption of the Virgin

IN THE PRACTICAL, day-to-day experiences of their lives, people of the
Middle Ages encountered the Virgin Mary most often as intercessor.
Through the "Ave" and in other more personal prayers, they sought her
aid in their troubles and asked her to obtain forgiveness of their sins from
her son. They knew that prayers to other saints could be effective, particularly for specific ailments and problems, and it was not uncommon for
them to approach Mary herself through someone close to her: St. Anne,
St. Elizabeth, or St. John. Yet no saint was so certain of receiving a favorable response from God as was Mary, for no saint had enjoyed so intimate
a relationship with him. People had the added assurance that her inter-

1. San Bernardino of Siena, *Opera omnia,* ed. P. M. Perantoni, 5 vols. (Quaracchi: Collegium S. Bonaventurae, 1950–), 2:155–56.

2. Quoted in G. R. Owst, *Preaching in Medieval England* (Cambridge: Cambridge University Press, 1926), 19–20.

cession would be heard, for she was bodily present in heaven.[3] Thus, in 1950, when Pope Pius XII proclaimed Mary's Assumption into heaven an article of faith to be believed by all Catholic Christians, he was doing no more than giving formal assent to a doctrine which had been a virtual certainty to the faithful for centuries.

There is, to be sure, a theological logic to the Assumption of Mary that has caused it to seem reasonable, if not provable, to Catholics in any age, especially given Catholic acceptance of Mary's intact virginity and sinless life. While late medieval preachers spoke of Mary's Assumption and her position as Queen of Heaven and Mediatrix, however, they also associated Mary with the structures and practices of life as they encountered them in the fifteenth century; and they caused their depiction of her role to appear particularly appropriate to their culture and time. As we shall see, an assertion of Mary's Assumption to persons still largely dependent on the spoken word for communication provided a significant boost to her authority as intercessor. People were able to trust her more confidently to act as a mediator between God and themselves.

Common acceptance of the Assumption of the Virgin was made possible by two facts. There is no mention in the canonical Gospels of Mary's death and burial, allowing plenty of room for popular speculation to supply the deficiency of information. And the growth of the cult of the saints in the early Church produced an interest in sites of martyrdom and in relics which, in Mary's case, was initially forced to remain unsatisfied.

Curiosity concerning the events surrounding Mary's last days on earth developed first in the East. Early accounts such as those of the Syriac *Obsequies of the Holy Virgin* and the *Pseudo-Melito* describe Mary as either falling asleep or dying, after which her body is taken to heaven. By 600, these stories had become an accepted part of Christian tradition and the Emperor Maurice proclaimed August 15 as a feast to remember the Vir-

---

3. Mary was not the only saint believed to have been assumed into heaven. Bernardino of Busti gives this as one of the reasons for belief in Mary's Assumption. If other saints' bodies have been assumed, surely the body of the mother of Christ has been taken to heaven. Bernardino of Busti, *Mariale* (Milan: Leonardus Pachel, 1493), Sermon 1, "On the Assumption of Mary," pt. 3. "Cum enim multi sancti iam sint in celo cum corpore glorificato: quare non credamus quod etiam ibi sit beata virgo que est sanctior universis?"

gin's death. This feast made its way by the seventh century to Gaul, where
it was known first as the Feast of the Dormition, a name which reveals
continuing uncertainty concerning Mary's actual death. During the ninth
century, the feast acquired the title of the Assumption and gradually came
to equal Christmas and Easter in importance.[4]

During the Carolingian period in the West, belief in Mary's Assumption could even inspire new ways of interpreting Scripture. In at least one
instance, acceptance of the doctrine resulted in the liturgical rewording of
the text of Scripture itself. Song of Songs 6:9 was traditionally incorporated into the Vespers liturgy for the Assumption. In the Antiphoner of
Compiègne, the word "progreditur" (advances) was actually replaced by
the more powerful and suggestive "ascendit" (ascends), causing the first
part of the verse to read, "Who is this who ascends as the rising dawn?"
This new version of the verse was then used by Paschasius Radbertus in
his popular and influential work, "Cogitis Me," erroneously thought by
later generations to have been written by St. Jerome. Ann Matter believes
that it is essential to place Biblical commentaries on the Song of Songs in
the context of just this type of liturgical practice. Commentators had
already lived their interpretation in the liturgy; and when they wrote,
they did so with "verses from the Song of Songs ringing in their ears."
This is one of the chief reasons that the dialogues of the text seemed so
natural. They were encountered primarily in the context of a liturgical setting, which, by its nature, involves dialogue.[5] Surely, this is one of the rea-

4. Ibid., 81–88. The *Pseudo-Melito* was the most popular of the Greek versions in the
West. It presents Mary as actually dying, not falling asleep. Jesus awakes her by saying,
"Rise up my love and my kinswoman; thou that didst not suffer corruption by union of the
flesh, shall not suffer dissolution of the body . . .": quoted in Marina Warner, *Alone of All
Her Sex: The Myth and Cult of the Virgin Mary* (New York: Alfred A. Knopf, 1976), 85. Pope
Leo IV (847–55) provided the feast with a vigil and an octave; and Pope Nicholas I (858–67)
declared the Assumption to be equal in importance to Christmas and Easter. For additional information on the Assumption, see Eamon R. Carroll, O.Carm., "Mary in the Documents of the Magisterium," in *Mariology*, ed. Juniper B. Carol, vol. 1 (Milwaukee: Bruce
Publishing Company, 1955), 26–27. Carroll states that the word "Assumption" first appeared
in the West during the pontificate of Adrian I (722–95). The festival had earlier been known
as the Dormition. According to Carroll, it was not until the twelfth and thirteenth centuries
that changes in the prayers for the vigil and Mass of the Assumption began to focus more
on Mary's resurrection and less on her death.

5. E. Ann Matter, *The Voice of My Beloved: The Song of Songs in Western Medieval Christianity* (Philadelphia: University of Pennsylvania Press, 1990), 152–58.

sons that preachers as well found it so easy to incorporate Scripture, especially portions of the Song of Songs, into their sermons in the form of involved speaking parts among the characters.

Acceptance of the Assumption grew throughout Europe in the twelfth century as popular devotion to Mary climbed to new heights. Theologians began to defend the doctrine, aided by a work attributed at the time to St. Augustine but actually written in the late eleventh or early twelfth century. This work stated that since the flesh of Jesus was the same as Mary's, where his is, hers must be too. The "potuit, decuit, fecit" argument, later so commonly used to support Marian doctrines, also appears: God was able to assume Mary's body into heaven; it was fitting that he do so; therefore, he did it. Abelard argued acceptance of the Assumption for similar reasons. In a series of sermons delivered at the cathedral of Lausanne, Amadeus of Lausanne (d. 1159) also asserted the truth of Mary's Assumption because "through the mediation of Christ the fullness of the Godhead dwelt in her corporally."[6]

Arguments on behalf of Mary's Assumption clearly follow a pattern we have seen before in medieval devotion. The certainty that so many persons possessed regarding the Virgin's bodily presence in heaven was linked inescapably to the fact that her body had generated the body of Jesus. As Guillaume Pepin expressed it,

There was in her, of course, a manifold dignity . . . and because of this, it was fitting that she be assumed with her body and soul. . . . For the flesh of Jesus is the flesh of Mary. Therefore that most sacred body from which Christ drew his flesh was not delivered over to be food for worms.[7]

---

6. Hilda Graef, *Mary: A History of Doctrine and Devotion,* 2 vols. (New York: Sheed and Ward, 1964), 1:222, 233, 244–47. The work attributed to Augustine, the "Tractatus de assumptione beatae Mariae Virginis," may be found in PL 40:1140–48.

7. Guillaume Pepin, *Rosareum aurem B. Mariae Virginis* (Antwerp: Guillelmus Lesteenius and Engelbertus Gymnicus, 1656), 366. "Fuit nempè in ea multiplex dignitas secundum eundem Augustinum propter quam congruebat, ut assumeretur cum corpore et anima. . . . Caro enim Iesu, caro Mariae est." Caroline Walker Bynum cites Rachel Fulton for evidence that twelfth-century theologians believed Mary's Assumption was guaranteed because of her union with Jesus. Rachel Fulton, "The Virgin Mary and the Song of Songs in the High Middle Ages" (Ph.D. diss., Columbia University, in progress), cited in Caroline Walker Bynum, *The Resurrection of the Body in Western Christianity, 200–1336* (New York: Columbia University Press, 1995), 170 n. 52.

The West generally produced a more forceful interpretation of the Assumption than the East. Eastern apocryphal stories presented Mary as a passive recipient of the power of God. In the West, however, the visions of a German nun, Elizabeth of Schonau (d. 1164), described Mary's ascent into heaven in an active way that helped alter forever the iconography of the event. In her visions, Elizabeth witnessed Mary's body soaring dramatically toward heaven. These visions were recorded by Elizabeth's companions and translated into Latin by her brother. Copies then made their way to both England and France.[8] Artists and preachers of the late Middle Ages were always looking for ways to draw parallels between the lives of Mary and Jesus and would most likely have tried in any event to depict the Assumption as a Marian version of Christ's Ascension.

Mary's Assumption also seemed appropriate to medieval Christians for several reasons besides the explanation it provided for the close of her earthly life. Bodily corruption after death was believed to be the necessary punishment for sin, and was especially fitting for those bodies that had been tainted with sexual lust and intercourse. Mary's body, however, had retained its virginal purity throughout her life, while she herself had never sinned in thought or act. It was, therefore, only right that God preserve her pure body, the body that had carried and given birth to Jesus.[9] As San Bernardino of Siena put it, God would not permit "that Holy One from whom he was born" to see corruption.[10] Nor was Biblical precedent lacking. There was Enoch, who had walked with God and "was not; for God took him."[11] The prophet Elijah was swept into heaven by a whirlwind as Elisha watched.[12] And, based on statements in St. John's Gospel,

8. Warner, *Alone of All Her Sex,* 89.

9. Ibid., 92. Modern Catholic theologians are still making the same argument. See William B. Smith, "The Theology of the Virginity 'in partu' and Its Consequences for the Church's Teaching on Chastity," *Marian Studies* 31 (1980): 99–110. Smith believes that Mary was assumed into heaven because God wanted to preserve her in the perfection in which he had created her. Virginity is a part of the new creation and someone who retains his or her virginity, like Mary, offers to God an "unblemished sacrifice" (109).

10. San Bernardino of Siena, *Opera omnia,* 2:155–56. "Nam sicut non dedit Dominus Sanctum suum, id est Christum, videre corruptionem, sic nec Sanctam suam, de quo natus est Sanctus; sed corpore et anima in caelum assumpta est."

11. Genesis 5:24. Enoch also appears in Hebrews 11:5.

12. 2 Kings 2:11.

it was believed by many in the Middle Ages that St. John, like his foster mother, had been assumed into heaven.[13]

The Virgin was also the supreme representative of the Church. As mother of Christ and co-sufferer with him, she preserved the faith of the Church when the faith of Jesus' other followers failed. Gabriel Barletta told his hearers that "the whole world is obligated to God in Christ for his Passion, and to Mary for sustaining the faith."[14] Since the eventual triumph of the Church meant salvation of body and soul for all its members, surely God had preserved Mary's body from corruption as a foretaste of what all Christians might expect.[15]

Chapter 12 of the Book of Revelation was also used to support belief in Mary's Assumption. St. John there describes a woman "clothed with the sun . . . and upon her head a crown of twelve stars." The woman is clearly intended to represent both the ancient kingdom of Israel, composed of twelve tribes, as well as the Church, the new Israel, which prevails over all its enemies. It has always been easy enough to see also in the woman the triumphant Virgin, received into heaven by Jesus. This text was used constantly in the Middle Ages as proof that Mary had indeed been crowned Queen of Heaven; all of its rich symbolic possibilities were developed to the full by artists and preachers.

As Queen of Heaven after her Assumption, Mary was always portrayed as continuing the same close relationship with Jesus that she had enjoyed on earth, sitting at his right hand and ruling over the kingdom of Mercy as he administered the kingdom of Justice. Richard Kieckhefer observes, however, that particularly during the fifteenth century, artists began to show the Coronation of the Virgin being performed no longer by Christ alone, but by the whole Trinity.[16] Paintings such as these would

13. Warner, *Alone of All Her Sex*, 91. The Gospel reference is John 21:22–23.

14. Gabriel Barletta, *Sermones quadragesimales et de sanctis* (Brescia: Jacobus Britannicus, 1497), 104r. "Et sic totus mundus obligatur deo christo: per passionem: ita marie per fidei sustentationem."

15. For this theme in fifteenth-century English drama, see Gail McMurray Gibson, *The Theater of Devotion: East Anglian Drama and Society in the Late Middle Ages* (Chicago: University of Chicago Press, 1989), 173.

16. Richard Kieckhefer, "Major Currents in Late Medieval Devotion," in *Christian Spirituality: High Middle Ages and Reformation*, ed. Jill Raitt (New York: Crossroad Publishing Company, 1987), 92.

indicate that the Queen of Heaven has received special honors from all three persons of the Trinity and that she is as close to equality with God as any purely human being could ever be. This interpretation is born out by the sermons of the day.

San Bernardino of Siena declared that only God the Father and the Virgin are able to say that they have God for a son;[17] and as many creatures serve the glorious Virgin Mary as serve the Trinity.[18] He described God's welcome to Mary as she entered Heaven:

"Come most beloved wife, mother, and daughter, enter the garden of delights." She was then introduced into the inaccessible secret and to the delight of the divine persons in the midst of the blessed Trinity. The Virgin was crowned above the angels, so that she might be fully raised within the glory of the Trinity, and that she might love, seize, sense and enjoy the glory of the blessed Trinity more than any other pure creature likewise assumed, and after the Son, the whole universe is made a partner to her glory.[19]

Gabriel Barletta managed to turn a sermon based on the parable of the Prodigal Son into a sermon regarding Mary's relationship to the Trinity in heaven. In the story, the forgiving father says to the elder son who never left home, "Son, you are always with me, and all that I have is yours."[20] Barletta explains,

These words are said by Mary to her son. "My son, you are with me." The Father is with Mary in his power. The Son is with Mary in his wisdom; and the Holy Spirit is with Mary through his mercy. Therefore she is called the saint of saints.[21]

---

17. San Bernardino of Siena, *Opera omnia*, 2:376.

18. Ibid., 377. "Tot enim creaturae serviunt gloriosae Mariae Virgini, quot serviunt Trinitate."

19. Ibid., 396. "'Veni dilectissima sponsa, mater et filia, ingredere hortum deliciarum,' ad inaccessibile secretum et ad delectamentum divinarum personarum in medium Trinitatis beatissimae introducta. . . . Virgo super angelos coronatur, ut intra Trinitatis gloriam ipsa sola amplius sit evecta ac plus beatissimae Trinitatis diligat gloriam, capiat, sentiat et fruatur, quam omnis alia pura creature simul sumpta, de cuius gloria post filium participant universi."

20. Luke 15:31.

21. Barletta, *Sermones*, 53v–54r. "Que verba dicuntur a Maria filio suo. Fili: mecum es. Cum Maria est Pater per potentiam. Cum Maria est Filius per sapientiam. Cum Maria est Spiritus sanctus per clementiam. Unde dicitur sancta sanctorum et sancta sanctarum."

Bernardino of Busti described the joy of the whole Trinity at Mary's birth.[22] Barletta told a story designed to show the quasi-divine character of Mary, even while she was still on earth. A certain Dionysius asked the Apostle John to introduce him to Mary after Jesus' Ascension. Although prior to her assumption into glory, he was so struck by Mary's countenance that he fell to the earth as though dead, exclaiming, "If I were not solidly grounded in the faith I would not believe in any other god but she, because such a clear radiance proceeds from her."[23]

Heiko Oberman speculates that the emphasis of Gabriel Biel, and presumably of other preachers, on access to the Son and Father through Mary produced something approaching a new understanding of the Trinity: Mother, Son, and Father.[24] Oberman is aware, however, that neither preachers nor people were likely to attribute divine status to Mary, for it was her purely human nature, as distinct from the divine-human nature of Christ, which made her bodily presence in heaven so compelling for those still on earth. As both human and sinless, the Virgin was the perfect bridge between the sinful humanity of everyone else, and the divine and sinless humanity of Christ.[25] This was true not only for Biel, and for those preachers such as Geiler of Kaisersberg whom he directly influenced,[26] but for others as well. Bernardino of Busti summed this up well in a sermon on the name of Mary. Drawing once more on St. Bernard of Clairvaux, he explained,

She is our mediator of intercession, for she intercedes daily for us. Therefore St. Bernard says in a sermon on the Annunciation: If you are afraid to approach God the Father, flee to the Son, because Mary gave him to you as a brother. But if by

22. Bernardino of Busti, *Mariale*, Sermon 1, "On the Nativity of Mary," pt. 3.

23. Barletta, *Sermones*, 37r. "Nisi solidatus essem in fide non alium deum crederem quam ipsam; quia tantus radius claritatis ab ea procedit."

24. Heiko Oberman, *The Harvest of Medieval Theology: Gabriel Biel and Late Medieval Nominalism*, rev. ed. (Grand Rapids, Mich.: William B. Eerdmans Publishing Company, 1967), 311–12.

25. Ibid., 313–14.

26. E. Jane Dempsey Douglass, *Justification in Late Medieval Preaching: A Study of John Geiler of Keisersberg* (Leiden: E. J. Brill, 1966), 194. According to Douglass, Geiler borrowed directly from one of Biel's sermons on the Assumption to say that Mary is *pura homo*, a daughter of Adam and Eve, yet free of original sin and thus most "worthy" of all human beings.

chance you fear his divine majesty, run to Mary in whom is pure humanity. . . .
Thus the Blessed Virgin has no one above her except the three persons of the
Trinity. But below her she has the three ranks of those who are being saved: virgins, the continent, and the married. And she herself is placed in the middle, joining and uniting those three ranks to the Blessed Trinity.[27]

In spite of the glories attributed to the Virgin in the art and sermons
of the later Middle Ages, her subordination to the Trinity was usually preserved. In paintings, she was consistently placed on a lower level than God
the Father, although in many cases parallel to Jesus. Preachers almost
always declared that the favors she obtained for her followers came ultimately from Jesus, even if, due to filial affection, he was unable to deny
her requests.

Advocate of Sinners

Johannes of Verden's sermon for the Epiphany describes the miracle of
the wedding feast at Cana, in which Jesus turned water into wine to spare
his host from embarrassment.[28] The servants first brought the problem to
Mary's attention and she ordered them to do whatever Jesus instructed
them, "because she knew that Christ would not deny his mother's petition."[29] Gabriel Barletta said that Christ seated Mary next to his kingly
throne and he "concedes to her whatever she desires on behalf of her
devoted followers who salute her." Barletta exclaims, "O how could the
world exist without the supplications of Mary which compel her son."[30]
Mary was believed by medieval Christians to be an extremely powerful

27. Bernardino of Busti, *Mariale*, Sermon 1, "On the Name of Mary," pt. 3. ". . . est mediatrix nostre intercessionis. Ipsa enim pro nobis quottidie intercedit. Ideo Bernardus in sermone de anuntiatione ait, Si ad deum patrem vereris accedere ad filium fuge quia hunc tibi
fratrem Maria dedit. Sed si forte in ipso maiestatem vereris divinam, ad Mariam recurre in
qua est humanitas pura. . . . sic beata virgo non habet supra se nisi tres in trinitate personas.
Sed infra se habet tres status salvandorum, scilicet, virgines, continentes, et coniugatos. Et
ipsa est in medio constituta coniungens et uniens illos tres status beatissime trinitate."

28. John 2:1–10.

29. Johannes of Verden, *Sermones dominicales cum expositionibus evangeliorum, sive Dormi
secure de tempore et de sanctis* (Basel: Johann Amerbach, 1484), Sermon VIII. ". . . quod scivit
quod Christus non negaret petitionem matri."

30. Barletta, *Sermones*, 103v–104r. ". . . ei concedit quicquid vult pro suis devotis eam
salutantibus. O quomodo esset mundus nisi essent marie supplicationes: que filium
cogunt."

and influential, yet solely human, mediatrix and intercessor, able to obtain whatever graces and blessings she asked for her beloved servants.

There are numerous questions that arise from this astonishing portrait of Mary as Queen of Heaven and mediatrix. On what basis did this hierarchical system of mediation work? When preachers and their hearers thought of Mary, how did they picture in their minds her actions on their behalf in the court of heaven? Why did so many sermons and miracle stories freely describe Mary's willingness to intercede for persons whose only offerings were "Aves," the "Little Office of Our Lady," or perhaps fasting, while their lives remained obviously at odds with the moral demands of the faith? In short, where did preachers and tellers of miracle stories derive their model of divine patronage and intercession?

The following paean of praise to Mary is taken from the opening of one of Jean Gerson's sermons on the Annunciation.

Hail Mary, I salute you Mary. This is a very beautiful salutation and a most agreeable blessing, because by this salutation, by such an "Ave" the curse of the human race that came by Eve was destroyed. . . . What, then, should every devoted heart do and think here[?] . . . Well should it strive to remember worthily such a salutation that reverently it might present it today. To whom? To you, most worthy Virgin, honorable and blessed, to you, Queen of the World, through whom have come to us joy, health and salvation, you who are, to speak truly, so courteous that you greet in return all who greet you. . . . If we have recourse to you who are full of grace, full of excellence and superabundance, will you be able to deny us? . . . No indeed.[31]

Gabriel Barletta opened one of his Saturday Lenten sermons with a miracle story about a man who had honored Mary every Saturday by fast-

---

31. Jean Gerson, *Oeuvres complètes,* ed. P. Glorieux, 8 vols. (Paris: Desclée and Cie, 1971), 7:538–39. "Ave Maria, Je te salue Marie. Moult bel salut icy a et moult agreable beneisson quer par iceluy salut par tel Ave fut destruicte la maudisson de l'umain lignage qui vint par Eve. . . . Que doibt doncquez yci faire et penser tout cuer devot, . . . Bien se doibt esjoir de sobre leesse, de especiale consolation. Bien doibt mettre sa peine que dignement puist remembrer tel salut, que reveremment le puist aujourd'hui preseenter. A qui? A vous, Vierge tres digne, tres honnorable et tres benigne, a vous, Royne du monde, par laquelle nous est venue joie, nous est apparu salut et salvation, qui estez telle a vroy dire et si courtoise que qui vous saluera vous le resaluerez. . . . se nous recourons devotement a vous qui estes plaine de grace, plaine par excellence et superabondance, la nous pourrés vous denier? . . . Non voir."

ing. Then one day, he deliberately gave a false alarm to the city and was put in jail by the magistrate. He was scheduled to die the following Saturday but he called out to Mary, "Where is the reward of all my fasting?" Mary opened his cell and he escaped unharmed.[32] Barletta likewise described Mary herself as equally bold and persistent as she intercedes for sinners, reminding Jesus of all she had done for him as a child. "Remember my son, what I did for you. I carried you for nine months, I fed you with my own milk. . . . I offered you in the temple, I followed you to Calvary and stayed with you and did not flee with the rest."[33]

There are two distinct but related beliefs concerning intercession to be found in the preceding sermon excerpts. The first is that praise alone, especially through the "Ave," is sufficient to secure a loving response from Mary, the "Queen of the World." The second is that someone who presents a request, even the Virgin herself, had a right to expect a favorable hearing based on a past record of services rendered.

If we seek a source for the understanding of an exchange of benefits and blessings such as occurs between individual Christians and their saints in later medieval sermons, a likely place to begin is with the German gift-giving economy of the fifth through the tenth centuries. Georges Duby explores this ethos of early Germanic society in *The Early Growth of the European Economy;* he describes there a society bound together in a complex web of exchanges which he labels "necessary generosity."

The exchange of personal wealth and goods was a means of demonstrating loyalty or gratitude for service rendered. It could be used to seal bargains and marriages, to secure the favor of the gods and the dead, and to fulfill obligations to the poor. The bestowal of gifts could also obtain benefits from those more powerful than oneself. Duby calls it "necessary" since the giving of a gift required a gift in return. Failure to reciprocate could produce grave results. All exchanges, however, did not necessarily require the transfer of material objects. When the Germanic tribes con-

---

32. Barletta, *Sermones,* 36r.

33. Ibid., 38r. ". . . fili recordare quod tibi feci. Te portavi 9 mensibus: te lacte pavi: . . . te in templo obtuli: te secuta sum in montem calvarii: te associavi: quia aliis recendentibus non recessi."

quered the Christian West, the gift-giving ethos was absorbed by the entire culture, including the Church; spiritual blessings, too, came to be a part of the system. It began to seem natural that something so non-material as prayers might be offered in return for goods. Lupus, the ninth-century abbot of Ferrières obtained a sizeable quantity of lead from the King of Mercia in exchange for prayers.[34] Perhaps the single most impressive example of religious exchange centered on the great monastery of Cluny and its network of affiliated houses. A major reason for the astonishing success of Cluny was the fact that lay persons donated land and wealth to the monks in exchange for having their names, or those of their loved ones, placed on the lists of persons for whom the monks regularly prayed.[35]

Creating friendships and alliances through gift-giving was also a part of the classical Roman world. As Peter Brown has shown, high-ranking Christian clerics of the late Roman Empire developed networks of patronage between the Eastern and Western Churches through the exchange of relics.[36] Then, too, belief that mutual exchange governs the relationship between human worshipers and their gods was often a characteristic of ancient religions. It was nevertheless the alliance of the Church with a Germanic society dominated by gift-giving at all levels that made this model so pervasive in Christian practice in the West. It helps to explain why the Church would be disposed to interpret the work of the Virgin and the saints in terms of an exchange of favors and rewards for service.

The gift-giving principle alone, however, cannot account for the ability of such seeming intangibles as prayers and ritual praise to be considered on an equal footing with concrete material goods and services, whether by Germanic kings, or by the saints. The answer to this dilemma

34. Georges Duby, *The Early Growth of the European Economy: Warriors and Peasants from the Seventh to the Twelfth Century*, trans. Howard B. Clarke (Ithaca, N.Y.: Cornell University Press, 1978), 48–57.

35. Barbara Rosenwein, *Rhinoceros Bound: Cluny in the Tenth Century* (Philadelphia: University of Pennsylvania Press, 1982), 82.

36. Peter Brown, *The Cult of the Saints: Its Rise and Function in Latin Christianity* (Chicago: University of Chicago Press, 1981), 89.

lies in an understanding of the spoken word itself as act, which was a part of the orally structured society of the early Middle Ages and which persisted throughout the medieval period.

To begin with, the Christian Church had inherited from Judaism a belief in the power of the spoken word to be active and effective in and of itself. The opening chapter of Genesis describes God creating the universe through his spoken word. Jacob was able to "steal" the blessing of his father, Isaac, from his brother Esau by trickery. Once spoken, the blessing could not be recalled.[37] Prophets spoke the word of God, and by their proclamation alone, set in motion the inevitable working out of God's will in the world.[38]

Jewish tradition may have been unique in its tendency nearly always to associate the work of God with the power of speech, but the understanding of speech as act the Jews shared with all primarily oral-aural societies. In a world without radio or television, something must be going on for sound to exist at all. Sound must come from a source that is both present and in action. When that sound is the spoken word, then not only is some-"thing" happening but some-"one" is present who must be dealt with and responded to. In the context of societies primarily reliant on spoken communication, words produce results. They are, in fact, the most certain way of getting things done. The sworn oath, performed in the presence of others is binding. Verbal declarations, accompanied perhaps by a token to represent them, are sufficient to transfer authority or land ownership. Words themselves are therefore interpreted as actions and as such, "they appear of a piece with other actions, including even grossly physical actions."[39]

For people whose world is conditioned by these responses to speech, to offer praises to Mary could be seen as an act which substantively

---

37. A good discussion of this may be found in Richard Lischer, *A Theology of Preaching: The Dynamics of the Gospel,* ed. William D. Thompson (Nashville: Abingdon Press, 1981), 66–81. See also Walter J. Ong, S.J., *The Presence of the Word: Some Prolegomena for Cultural and Religious History* (New Haven: Yale University Press, 1967), 176–91. Jacob's theft of the blessing is recorded in Genesis 27.

38. See Isaiah 55:10–11.

39. Ong, *Presence of the Word,* 111–13.

increased the aura of glory and honor surrounding her in the court of heaven and in Christendom at large. Thus it was an act of service which she would be bound to acknowledge in the future. To then pray to Mary in need was to ask a favor from her in return. She would be obligated to hear it as the request of someone who had served her faithfully in the past.

To be sure, by the fourteenth and fifteenth centuries, a thriving monetary economy had replaced the German gift-giving system. Germanic values involving the exchange of honors and services, however, were alive and well in the culture of Europe's nobility, and nobles as well as the Church continued to understand speech as act. In her innovative study of the sixteenth-century French nobility, *Word of Honor,* Kristen Neuschel is struck by the fact that in noble correspondence, "so much space is devoted to ritual courtesy."[40]

Formal courtesies and concrete favors were linked by the nobles themselves in that one was offered in exchange for the other. . . . this kind of exchange is also an exchange on a simpler, more mechanical level; it is an exchange of words in return for an object (or something else tangible).[41]

If the nobility were still constructing their relationships on this basis in the sixteenth century, it should be no surprise that the fifteenth-century preacher would present the bonds between Christians and saints as held together by similar ties. He was able to draw his inspiration not only from the centuries of ecclesiastical tradition which had passed on these models, but also from their continuing operation in his own world.

A. N. Galpern offers an explanation for the popularity of the Virgin and saints in the later Middle Ages, especially in their intercessory capac-

---

40. Kristen B. Neuschel, *Word of Honor: Interpreting Noble Culture in Sixteenth-Century France* (Ithaca, N.Y.: Cornell University Press, 1989), 72.

41. Ibid., 73. Virginia Reinburg also believes that the current networks of exchange governing sixteenth-century social relations influenced attitudes to prayer as revealed in books of hours. She points out that in one Rouen prayer book, a prayer to Saint Mary Magdalene refers to her as "honorable lady of the manor." Words addressed to religious figures such as the Virgin or St. John at times resemble "a formal and oral declaration of loyalty to a lord." See Virginia Reinburg, "Hearing Lay People's Prayer," in *Culture and Identity in Early Modern Europe (1500–1800): Essays in Honor of Natalie Zemon Davis,* ed. Barbara B. Diefendorf and Carla Hesse (Ann Arbor: University of Michigan Press, 1993), 22–23.

ity, which links heavenly mediation to contemporary political reality. He argues that medieval Christians projected their experience of earthly politics into the heavenly realm, assuming the confused, decentralized structure of late medieval government to be mirrored above.[42] People knew that nobles often competed successfully with the monarch for political loyalty and service at the local level. If it were assumed that the same situation prevailed in the kingdom of heaven, it made sense to turn to the saints for individual and communal protection. Predictably, many saints then waned in popular devotion during the mid-sixteenth century as both Church and state became more centralized and orderly. It was possible for the people to see a less clouded picture of the political hierarchy and they could therefore form a more limited view of the power and authority of the Virgin Mary and other saints in the heavenly hierarchy.[43]

The Bible itself is full of references to God, or to Christ, as king, and to the kingdom of heaven. There is no reason why medieval Christians could not have modeled their understanding of the celestial court and its operations according to what they knew to be true of feudal kingship and society. This would certainly help to explain why so many local communities could have their own special shrines to Mary and feel that she was personally concerned with their problems and traditions. After all, how

42. A. N. Galpern, *The Religions of the People in Sixteenth-Century Champagne* (Cambridge: Harvard University Press, 1976), 70. Galpern's analysis is inspired by Guy Swanson, *Religion and Regime: A Sociological Account of the Reformation* (Ann Arbor: University of Michigan Press, 1967). Swanson's thesis is that the central issue at stake in Catholic-Protestant debates concerned the immanence vs. the transcendence of God. Whether a country remained Catholic or became Protestant and focused on immanence or transcendence was in turn closely related to the political structure of the area. If the government was perceived by people as embodying a single and easily identifiable set of goals and objectives, the country retained the Catholic faith. Where the government was perceived as being the result of the reconciling of a number of different special interests in the political community, the territory became Protestant.

43. Galpern, *Religions of the People*, 74. Virginia Reinburg credits the change to the direct attempts by both Catholic and Protestant clergy to bring order to the "disorderly" world of late medieval prayers. Both groups "wished to eliminate the complex and disorderly language of late medieval patronage—with its complicated hierarchies, overlapping jurisdictions, private laws and outside appeals." For the time being, however, reformers failed because books of hours continued to be published; the reformers only succeeded in creating a new approach to compete with the more traditional one. See Reinburg, "Hearing Lay People's Prayer," 31–34.

many feudal lords governed fiefs in widely disparate places, each with its own set of feudal customs and obligations?

The political approach can be useful in another way. It provides a rationale for understanding the hierarchical system of intercession most late medieval Christians believed to be necessary. As access to honor, power, and benefits was gained on earth through the mediation of those close to the powerful, so it would be in religious matters.[44] It should also be said, however, that the medieval understanding of the communion of the saints also dovetailed nicely with the prevailing communal approach to all aspects of life, religion, economics, and politics.

Yet the political model for medieval religious understanding as Galpern presents it does leave some unanswered questions. It does not account for the enormous devotion to the saints and their relics which began well before the fall of Rome, when the empire was still strong, and continued unabated until the growth of Catholic reform movements in the late fifteenth and early sixteenth centuries. Nor does it explain why people would have perceived the political structure of the late Middle Ages as "confused" when feudal warfare and the complexity of feudal relationships had been political constants for centuries.

John Bossy favors an analysis based rather on family and kinship structure. He believes that people in the fifteenth century viewed the saints not as sources of power but as friends and relatives. He says, "for the individual, the name-saint was not so much a 'patronus,' as a 'patrinus,' or superior godparent, somebody you could talk to."[45] Whatever the relationship between persons and their lesser name-saints may have been, however, the sermons of the fifteenth century paint a picture of the Virgin Mary, yes, as mother of Christians and friend, but most often as a channel for procuring divine power, mercy, and grace. They recount numerous miracle stories that depict sinners, condemned by the Devil or simply by their

44. A major difference between the world of religious patronage and that of secular society is that, among the nobility on earth, no one noble controlled all power and assets. Thus relationships between the nobility were of necessity more complex and less strictly hierarchical than those of the religious realm. See Neuschel, *Word of Honor*, 93–94.

45. John Bossy, *Christianity in the West, 1400–1700* (Oxford: Oxford University Press, 1985), 12.

own actions, standing before the throne of God seemingly without hope. Mary, in her mercy, will then beg God to pardon the person and he or she will be saved. The dominance of this theme should not be surprising, for as we have seen, late medieval Christians often labored under a heightened sense of inner sinfulness which made the existence of a heavenly protectress very appealing.

Bernardino of Busti looked upon Mary as the ultimate fountain of heavenly patronage. Addressing her in one of his sermons, he says, "All of your devoted servants build their foundations on your example and patronage, o humble Virgin, and they make the home of their devotion in you."[46]

Jean Gerson describes the relationship between a person and the saints in words that are taken directly from feudal ceremony and political patronage:

Present yourself in the midst of Jesus, of Mary, and of John, commit yourself into their hands, believe me, you will not perish. Have you sinned by the hands, by the feet, by the mouth . . . or by any other part of your body? Jesus suffered in all parts for your sins. . . . And if you do not dare to go to him without an introduction, his blessed mother, the kind Virgin, and John, his trusty watchman, are present and ready to present you, to make your request for you.[47]

If any are afraid of the court of justice and its laws, Gerson declares, they may ask Mary, the Queen of Mercy, to receive them according to the laws of her court.[48]

Those who were reluctant to approach even Mary directly could take the logical course of appealing to her through her mother, St. Anne. Fifteenth-century English preacher John Mirk directed his congregation,

46. Bernardino of Busti, *Mariale,* Sermon 1, "On Marian Similes in Scripture," pt. 2. "In tuo enim exemplo et patrocinio o virgo humilima omnes devoti tui faciunt suum fundamentum, et nidum sue devotionis in te constituunt."

47. Gerson, *Oeuvres complètes,* 7:508. "Gette toi au milieu de Jhesus, de Marie et de Jehan, commect toi en leurs mains; croy moi, tu ne periras point. As tu peche par les mains, par les pies, par la bouche . . . ou par autre partie du ton corps? Jhesus souffre en toutes pars pour tes peches. . . . Et si tu n'oses sans moyen aller a lui, sa benoite mere, la Vierge debonnaire, et Jehan sa bonne garde, son presens et apprestes pour toi presenter, pour faire ta demande."

48. Ibid., 509.

"Wherefore ᵹe schul now knele adowne, and pray saynt Anne to pray to her holy doghtyr, oure lady ᵽat scho pray to her sonne ᵽat he ȝeve you hele yn body and yn sowle."[49] When Mirk advised the people to kneel, once again the political and the religious overlapped, for the posture for prayer made popular by medieval custom, to kneel with folded hands, was drawn from the feudal ceremony of homage.[50]

Then there were those times, such as approaching death, when a person might feel that he or she needed to seek help anywhere it was offered. Johan Geiler of Kaisersberg told his hearers that, when dying, they should call on God the Father, God the Son, Mary the Mother, the holy angels, their own angel and saint, and all saints.[51]

Michel Menot was probably more cautious than many medieval preachers. He was wary of death-bed conversions. Lest anyone think that they could completely ignore Mary and the saints, live a sinful life, and then expect mercy at the last minute, he told the people to make amends now, while they could, and repent. God, he said, would not allow even Mary to prevent that heedless a soul from going to hell: "For if the Virgin Mary and all the saints would come, since the law stands firm, they could not impede the demons from carrying away that soul." To set an example, Menot then proceeded to say the "Ave."[52] He could be confident of a response, because, according to San Bernardino of Siena,

The glorious Virgin Mary is a most courteous queen, nor, wondrous to say, is it possible to greet her and not be greeted in return. If you say with devotion a thousand "Ave Marias" in a day, a thousand times you will be greeted by the Virgin.[53]

---

49. John Mirk, *Mirk's Festial: A Collection of Homilies,* Publication of the Early English Text Society, ed. Theodore Erbe, no. 96 (London: Oxford University Press, 1905; reprint, Millwood, N.Y.: Kraus Reprint Company, 1973), 216.

50. Late medieval books of hours often pictured persons praying to God or the saints in this posture of homage. See Reinburg, "Hearing Lay People's Prayer," 23.

51. Douglass, *Justification in Late Medieval Preaching,* 191.

52. Michel Menot, *Sermons choisis de Michel Menot,* ed. J. Nève (Paris: Bibliothèque du XVe siècle, 1924), 21. "Nam si Virgo Maria et omnes sancti venirent, lege stante, non impedirent animam quin a demonibus importaretur."

53. San Bernardino of Siena, *Opera omnia,* 2:154. "Est enim curialissima regina gloriosa virgo Maria, nec potest salutari sine resalutatione miranda. Si mille 'Ave Maria' dicis devote in die, millies a Virgine resalutaris."

To this point, we have been concerned primarily with the late medieval understanding of prayers to Mary and the fact that an exchange of honors and favors was involved. Yet every prayer directed to Mary required two actions from her. She not only responded to the person's prayer, but she must also speak to Jesus on their behalf. The way that preachers chose to illustrate the dynamics of Mary's intercession shows how reliant they were on the power of speech, and especially speech accompanied by ritual gesture, to understand her role. At the same time, it will become clear why belief in Mary's bodily Assumption was so important to medieval Christians, apart from either its theological rationale or the hope it provided for the future salvation of their own bodies and souls. The presence of her body enabled her to add to her words the power of ritual gesture.

One might question whether or not people actually believed that Mary "spoke" in audible words to God. As we have seen, however, the spoken word was still the common means of communication in the fifteenth century, and its power to provoke a response made it a most effective way to achieve results. San Bernardino of Siena and Gabriel Biel believed preaching more important even than the Eucharist, since it had the power to convert people to faith.[54] Preachers never failed to present Mary in conversation with Jesus in their sermons. Nothing else could so demonstrate the ongoing interaction between Mother and Son.

Johannes of Verden shows Mary pleading, like Abraham had done, when God wants to destroy the world, which has become as wicked as Sodom and Gomorrah. Mary, along with the priests on earth, turns to God and says, "O Lord, spare the evil for the sake of the good . . . so that by their merits they may encourage sinners to a time of penitence."[55] That Mary is constantly called the "advocate" of sinners shows how closely she was associated with her ability to construct a convincing argument. Gabriel Barletta listed three qualifications for being a good advocate: to be gracious in words, to be bold, to be observant and careful. He then pro-

54. Loman McAodha, O.F.M., "The Nature and Efficacy of Preaching According to St. Bernardine of Siena," *Franciscan Studies* 27 (1967): 231; Oberman, *Harvest*, 23.

55. Johannes of Verden, *Sermones*, Sermon 9. ". . . sacerdotes orant et virgo Maria et Abraam: O domine parce malos propter bonos . . . ut eorum meritis peccatores foveantur ad tempus penitentiae."

ceeded to quote from Seneca, Cicero, and other classical authors on the value of speaking well. "Mary," he said, "had the grace of eloquence, for she spoke wonderfully. Therefore the angel said to her, 'You have found grace with God.'"[56]

As Guillaume Pepin records it, Mary has more than eloquent speech. She also has the ability to understand the subtleties of textual criticism and to manipulate legal terms to the advantage of sinners when she defends them before the divine judge.

Then, however, the devil wanted to prove [to God] through . . . accusations that the accused sinner belonged to him. First, indeed, by the law of the testament God had dictated from his own mouth when he said to Adam: in the hour that you will eat of the fruit of the tree of the knowledge of good and evil you will perish in death. Since, then, this sinner is born of his offspring, by the law of the public testament, he ought to die eternal death. To which the advocate of the human race answered: O malicious serpent, you have falsified that testament when you placed there something worthless of your own. For you have added a gloss which destroys and corrupts the text. Therefore you must be turned from your lying accusation. Second, the devil said that the sinner belonged to him according to the law of prescription: since for many years he had possessed the sinner as a servant. To this, Mary, the advocate of sinners, responded: That prescription, it is said, was often interrupted because reason, or the divine spark of the soul in the man overcame and spoke against the sinner that he had so cruelly dealt with his Lord. Indeed it is also held regarding prescription that a prescription is invalid if it is interrupted. . . . From which it is obvious that your accusation is frivolous.[57]

56. Barletta, *Sermones*, 37r. Barletta attributes this idea to St. Jerome, who said, "Maria . . . habuit gratiam facundie; quia locuta est mirabiliter. Unde angelus ad eam, invenisti gratiam apud deum."

57. Pepin, *Roseum aurem*, 115. "Tunc autem diabolus per quotuor allegationes voluit probare illum esse suum. Primò quidem iure instrumenti, quod ipse de proprio ore dictavit, quando dixit Adae: Quacunque hora comederitis ex fructu ligni scientia bone et male, morte moriemini. Cum ergo iste peccator fit de eius progenie iure instrumenti publici: debet more morte aeterna. Ad quod advocata humani generis respondet O malitiose serpens, illud instrumentum falsificasti quando ibi (nequequam) de tuo proprio apposuisti. Tu enim apposuisti glossam, quae textum destruxit et corrupit. Et ideo tamquam falsarius ab accusatione es repellendus. Secondò, diabolus dixit peccatorem esse suum iure praescriptionis: quia multis annis eum in servum possederat. Ad quod respondit advocata peccatorum Maria, Illa, inquit, praescriptio saepè fuit interrupta, quia ratio seu syderesis in homine peccatore superremurmurabat, et contradicebat, quòd tam crudeli Domino serviebat. Modò ut habetur extra de praescriptionibus, praescriptio si fuerit interrupta, est invalida. . . . Ex quo patet, quòd tua accusatio est frivola."

Mary acts in this passage as both a textual scholar and a lawyer, reproving Satan for attempting to add his own interpretation to the original text and quoting from the law to prove that Satan's argument cannot legally stand. Her argument regarding prescription is drawn ultimately from Roman law and is the same argument used by Tertullian in his famous work, *On Prescription Against Heretics,* to prove to heretics that only the orthodox Church had the right to the Scriptures, for the Church had enjoyed uninterrupted possession of them from the beginning. By law, ownership of property could be determined by whether or not the person in possession had held it without question for a stipulated period of time. If this were the case, then no successful claims could be brought by others who sought to possess it for themselves. Satan thus claims possession of the sinner by right of prescription. Mary argues, however, that Satan has not held uninterrupted possession of the sinner since the sinner's conscience had from time to time reproved him of his sin and he had repented. In this context, Mary possesses not so much the grace of eloquence as sharpness of wit and knowledge of the law. Nevertheless, it is still her ability to defend the sinner through powerful oral testimony that wins forgiveness. Mary *speaks* in a way which produces results. John Bromyard, a fourteenth-century English preacher, summed up Mary's intercessory role in the most direct and expressive way: "By hur hevenly conversacion she maketh erthely men to be the cytezens of heven."[58]

When Christians tried to visualize Mary's acts of intercession for them, knowing that she was present at the court of heaven in body as well as in soul would have made her capacity for speaking more tangible and easy to comprehend. As the Mass for the vigil of the Assumption in the *Liber sacramentorum* proclaimed, Mary has been "borne across" to heaven so that she might "faithfully intercede . . . for our sins."[59] Mary's Assumption served to unite two significant aspects of social and religious life in the late Middle Ages: the fact that in their world bodily presence was necessary for speech to occur, and their incarnational approach to the sacred.

---

58. Quoted in Owst, *Preaching in Medieval England,* 19–20.

59. PL 78:132–33; quoted in Siegfried Wenzel, *Preachers, Poets, and the Early English Lyric* (Princeton: Princeton University Press, 1986), 28 n. 13.

Christians knew that God had "spoken" most fully to the world in Jesus, the enfleshed Word, a principle that was preserved by the Church in the sacraments and in the cult of the relics of the saints as well.

Since the earliest centuries of the Church, relics of the saints' bodies had assured Christians of the saints' presence and power and therefore of Christians' ability to communicate more directly with them. Peter Brown explains that to visit a relic was in fact to visit a person; the "fullness of the invisible person could be present at a mere fragment of his physical remains and even at objects, such as the brandea of St. Peter, that had made contact with these remains."[60] Bodily presence was somehow a more certain guarantee of spiritual presence and of the possibility of personal interaction.

If Mary's body were in heaven, then the fullness of her presence was there in a concrete way not possible for her soul alone, and in a way that maximized the means of communication open to her. Most importantly, the Virgin could add to the strength of verbal intercession the silent eloquence of ritual gestures designed to remind Jesus of his own close bodily ties to her and of her care for his physical needs on earth.

One of the most popular intercessory themes in medieval sermons, and a common motif in visual art was the "Double Intercession" of Mary and Christ.[61] Gabriel Barletta and Guillaume Pepin attribute this idea to St. Bernard of Clairvaux,[62] but it appeared also in the work of twelfth-century theologian Arnauld Bonnaevallis.[63] Barletta, Geiler of Kaisersberg, and San Bernardino of Siena all make use of it in their sermons. San Bernardino promised that if anyone feared to appear in God's presence, they had no need to hesitate.

You have, O Man, a sure access to God. You have there the Mother before the Son and the Son before the Father. The Mother shows the Son her bosom and breasts,

60. Brown, *Cult of the Saints*, 88. The brandea were small cloths that had been allowed to touch the relics of St. Peter.

61. Caroline Walker Bynum, *Holy Feast and Holy Fast: The Religious Significance of Food to Medieval Women* (Berkeley: University of California Press, 1987), 272; plates 28–30.

62. Barletta, *Sermones*, 38r; Pepin, *Rosareum aurem*, 114. St. Bernard was reticent about stating clearly in his sermons that Mary had been assumed into heaven, but his use of the Double Intercession motif indicates, nevertheless, a belief in her bodily presence in heaven.

63. Douglass, *Justification in Late Medieval Preaching*, 190,

the Son shows the Father his wounds and side. Thus no one can be turned away where there are so many symbols of love.[64]

There were also occasions when only Mary was involved in this ritual intercession. One of the popular miracle stories related by Gauthier de Coincy (d. 1236) shows the way in which Mary's bodily gestures could be combined with speech. Mary and Satan are arguing before God concerning the fate of a certain man. For Mary's mercy to prevail, she has only to turn to Jesus and say, "Sweet dear son, behold here the breast with which I nourished you so well."[65]

The combination of words and gestures, of ritual formulas and physical actions, was a common feature of medieval life. But it is easy today to overlook the power of ritual to convince the person who experiences it first hand that something important and perhaps slightly mysterious is taking place. Bodily motion can add to the perception of speech as act by involving, in addition to hearing, the senses of sight and, to a certain degree, vicarious touch. Often in the Middle Ages when people recited the "Ave" outside of the context of the liturgy, each recitation was accompanied by a genuflection.[66] Like speech, gesture can manifest something of the interior thoughts and attitudes of a person, and it is perceived through the movement of time.[67] In effect, the use of ritual gesture serves to unify the entire person, body and mind, in the act of praise or intercession. It would be fascinating to be able to know precisely what physical motions preachers like San Bernardino and Gabriel Barletta used to enhance their description of the Double Intercession. There was certainly ample opportunity here for dramatic performance.

Speaking of Mary's Assumption and her bodily intercession in heaven raises another issue. If Mary had been assumed into heaven, then she, like

64. San Bernardino of Siena, *Opera omnia*, 2:158. "Securum habes, o homo, accessum ad Deum. Ibi habes Matrem ante Filium, Filium ante Patrem. Mater ostendit Filio pectus et ubera, Filius ostendit Patri latus et vulnera. Nulla ergo poterit esse repulsa ubi tot sunt caritatis insignia."

65. Quoted in H. P. J. M. Ahsmann, *Le culte de la Sainte-Vierge et la littérature française du Moyen Age* (Paris: Picard, 1930), 137. "Doulx chier filz, vez cy la mamelle dont je te norry bonnement."

66. Hilda Graef, *The Devotion to Our Lady* (New York: Hawthorn Books, 1963), 54.

67. Ong, *Presence of the Word*, 147.

Jesus, was removed from the sight and touch of those who were left behind. Nor was there a sacrament like the Eucharist to provide access to her presence in a tangible way. Her body in heaven increased her ability to intercede with Christ, but what about those on earth who wanted to speak with her? How could they know that she was on hand to hear?

Of course, sermons were an important means of convincing people that Mary was present and did in fact listen to their prayers. But medieval Christians always longed for something more concrete. As we have seen, there were Marian relics available throughout Europe. The profusion of relics providing access to Mary included clothing, hair, milk, and nail clippings. Relics, however, were extremely valuable and were usually able to be apprehended only through viewing. That people sought to do more than look is obvious from the few accounts that remain describing people's behavior when they were able to achieve physical access. Peter Brown tells of a Carthaginian noblewoman of the early Church, Megetia, who visited the shrine of St. Stephen in Uzalis. The account of her pilgrimage records,

While she prayed at the place of the holy relic shrine, she beat against it, not only with the longings of her heart, but with her whole body so that the little grille in front of the relic opened at the impact; and she, taking the Kingdom of Heaven by storm, pushed her head inside and laid it on the holy relics resting there, drenching them with her tears.[68]

Things had not changed in 1483 when the Dominican Felix Fabri made a pilgrimage to the Holy Land. He describes in a book, published in 1480, the visit of his group of pilgrims to the shrine of Calvary in the Church of the Holy Sepulcher.

Who would not even weep aloud in the place where Christ our God cried with a loud voice as he hung upon the cross. . . . We remained for a long time bowed to the earth in prayer. When we had finished our prayer, we went one after another to the holy rock, which projects above the floor, and each one as best he could, crawled to the socket-hole of the cross, kissed the place with exceeding devotion, and placed his face and mouth over the socket-hole from whence in very truth there breathes forth an exceedingly sweet scent . . . We put our arms and hands into the hole down to the very bottom.[69]

68. Quoted in Brown, *Cult of the Saints,* 88.
69. Quoted in Herbert Thurston, *The Stations of the Cross: An Account of Their History and Devotional Purpose* (London: Burns and Oates, 1914), 149–54.

It is possible that by the fifteenth century, many people were growing more accustomed to apprehending the presence of the holy by sight alone. If so, this would indicate that a gradual shift in the sensorium of European culture was beginning to take place, and that sight was assuming a more prominent role vis-à-vis the other senses.[70] There are two factors which together would account for this shift. Changes were occurring in the way that European Christians were encouraged to take part in the Mass. And literacy, which fosters a reliance on sight for the acquisition of knowledge, was steadily increasing in Western Europe.

Charles Zika has shown that already by the thirteenth century, the Mass was being "restructured" to require visual witness to drama and theophany rather than physical communion. This kind of experience at the Mass would reinforce the sense of sight as a viable means of perceiving God, present on the altar, or Mary and the saints, present in relics. Most Christians were only communing once a year at Easter anyway, as obliged by the Fourth Lateran Council. "Augenkommunion," or communion by the eyes was becoming more and more popular, and was encouraged for those too physically ill to swallow the host.[71] Indeed, the need to see the host and the benefits claimed for such viewing were greatest during the fifteenth century.[72] Everywhere, the host was displayed in monstrances and paraded through the streets in processions.

The growth of literacy toward the close of the fifteenth century and the beginning of the sixteenth would have furthered the emergence of sight as the dominant sense, subordinating sound and touch. Once the ability to read encourages people to think of communication as taking place objectively and at a distance, rather than interactively through speech or immediate physical contact, the notion of "eye-communion"

70. For an in-depth discussion of the relationship of the human sensorium to religious experience, see Ong, *Presence of the Word*. Ong observes (8) that the increased reliance on sight which resulted from a more pervasive use of written documents was especially prominent during the Middle Ages, and then intensified dramatically in the fifteenth century after the invention of printing.

71. Charles Zika, "Hosts, Processions and Pilgrimages: Controlling the Sacred in Fifteenth-Century Germany," *Past and Present* 118 (1988): 31–33.

72. Edouard Dumoutet, *Le desir de voir l'hostie et les origines de la dévotion au saint-sacrement* (Paris: Beauchesne, 1926), 33–34.

appears to be more likely, more direct, and more under the control of the person seeking the communion.[73] John Mirk was even able to declare in a sermon on the Annunciation that "Our lady at hur salutacyon conceyvet by syght,"[74] thereby replacing the older oral-aural belief that Mary had instead conceived through the ear, through hearing and believing the angel's words.

Sight alone, however, could not overtake sound and physical closeness overnight. Even as the clergy were expecting to present the elevated host from a safe distance, worshipers tried to crowd around the altar itself so closely during the consecration that clergy had to insist they move further away.[75] The majority of people continued to want statues or even pictures of Mary and the saints that could be embraced or kissed, in addition to relics that could be viewed. Images, no less than relics, indicated a saint's presence.[76] Statues and icons were, in Peter Brown's words, "holes in the dyke separating the visible world from the divine."[77] In the case of Mary,

73. David Chidester, *Word and Light: Seeing, Hearing and Religious Discourse* (Urbana: University of Illinois Press, 1992), 136–37. According to Chidester, sight, at least when it is used metaphorically, implies immediacy and a sense of continuum between the person seeing and the object of sight, and establishes the sense that nothing outside the self and individual vision is necessary for communication. He criticizes Ong for saying that "sight isolates" while "sound incorporates." Yet Chidester admits (11) that hearing requires more dynamic interaction with the world and others than sight, which encourages solitary contemplation. This seems to suggest that sight, developed by a reliance on literacy would encourage a person toward individualized rather than communal religious experience, exactly the point that Ong is making.

74. Mirk, *Mirk's Festial*, 108. ". . . for our lady at hur salutacyon conceyvet by syght. And þhat was þhe fyrst myracull þhat was wrought yn prevyng of cristys fayth."

75. Dumoutet, *Desir de voir l'hostie,* 33.

76. Edward Muir, "The Virgin on the Street Corner: The Place of the Sacred in Italian Cities," in *Religion and Culture in the Renaissance and Reformation,* Sixteenth Century Essays and Studies, vol. XI, ed. Steven E. Ozment (Kirksville, Mo.: Sixteenth Century Journal Publishers, 1989), 30. According to Muir, the people of Europe saw images as "signs that indicated the presence of the saint, rather than as symbols that brought the saint's spiritual qualities to mind."

77. Peter Brown, "A Dark Age Crisis: Aspects of the Iconoclastic Controversy," in *Society and the Holy in Late Antiquity* (Berkeley: University of California Press, 1982), 260–61. Brown's complete statement reads, "An icon, or a wall painting, might be known to have made St. Gregory of Nyssa weep, it had reminded St. Anastasius, at a crucial moment, of the courage of the martyrs, it might lead the mystical devotee, in a more subtle way, 'by the hand' to contemplate the incarnation of Christ; but it could do more than this. The icon was a hole in the dyke separating the visible world from the divine, and through this

her images and pictures often exhibited visible signs of bodily life, at times weeping or lactating milk or oil.

Through her Assumption, the Virgin Mary was able to enjoy the best of both worlds as intercessor. The "saint of saints," she possessed the effectiveness of communicating with God through her bodily presence in heaven, and with Christians on earth through her relics and images. The added bonus of Mary's close physical ties to Jesus, her son, meant that the favors and graces she could bestow on her faithful servants were of infinite worth. Among them were the gifts of the Holy Spirit, the grace to progress in justification, and access to the body of Jesus himself.

"Everything through Mary"

St. Bernard of Clairvaux delivered one of his most well-known sermons for the festival of Mary's Nativity on September 8. It is sometimes referred to as the "Sermon on the Aqueduct" because here St. Bernard used the metaphor of an aqueduct to clarify Mary's position as mediator. She is herself the conduit through which the waters of grace flow from God to his Church. It is therefore God's will that Christians show proper devotion to her, for he "willed us to have everything through Mary."[78] This last statement became a recurring refrain throughout the remainder of the Middle Ages. Whatever gifts God chooses to offer are finally distributed through the merciful hands of Mary. In a sermon to celebrate the Annunciation to Mary, Jean Gerson said,

Our Lady has received the highest and most perfect name which can be bestowed after the name of her son. She is called Mother of God. . . . Through this honor Our Lady is called our advocate, our mediator, our queen, our bargainer, by whose hands God has ordained to give what he gives to his human creatures, as St. Bernard has said.[79]

---

hole there oozed precious driblets from the great sea of God's mercy: icons were active. . . ."

78. Graef, *Mary*, 1:237–38.

79. Gerson, *Oeuvres complètes*, 7:540. "Au jour d'uy Nostre Dame a receu le plus hault nom et parfait qui puist estre communiqué après le nom de son filz; c'est qu'elle est dicte mere de Dieu. . . . Par ce Nostre Dame est dicte nostre advocate, nostre moyenneresse, nostre royne, nostre empeteresse par les mains de laquelle Dieu a ordonne donner ce qu'il donne a creature humaine selon le dit saint Bernard."

Other theologians were busy developing the same idea during the twelfth century, but using a metaphor destined to become much more popular than St. Bernard's aqueduct. Herman of Tournai (d. After 1147), Amadeus of Lausanne (d. 1159), Godfrey of Admont (d. 1165), and Philip of Harvengt (d. 1183) all chose to elaborate on St. Paul's corporate description of the Church as the body of Christ with Christ as head. If Christ were the head, they reasoned, then Mary is the neck through whom all benefits of the head come to the rest of the body.[80] San Bernardino of Siena and other preachers in the late Middle Ages continued to popularize Mary as the neck of Christ's body. The foremost grace that she channels to the Church is the gift of the Holy Spirit.

Certainly every grace which is bestowed in this age has a triple procession, for it is dispensed in good order from God into Christ, from Christ into the Virgin and from the Virgin into us. . . . The third procession is from the blessed Virgin. For from the time when she conceived God in her womb, she had, I might say, a certain authority or jurisdiction in every temporal procession of the Holy Spirit, that no creature receives any grace of virtue from God except according to the dispensation of the Virgin Mother herself. For since Christ is our head, from whom every stream of divine grace flows into the mystical body, the Blessed Virgin is the neck, through which this stream passes into the members of the body.[81]

It was fairly common for preachers to invoke Mary's aid to procure the power of the Holy Spirit to assist their preaching. John Brevicoxa stated in one of his Easter sermons, "In order to acquire then the grace of the Holy Spirit without which nothing good can be begun . . . we beseech faithfully this glorious Lady, and greet her devotedly."[82]

80. Graef, *Mary*, 1:234, 245–47, 255.

81. San Bernardino of Siena, *Opera omnia*, 2:157. "Omnis nempe gratia, quae huic saeculo communicatae, triplicem habet processum; nam a Deo in Christum, a Christo in Virginem, a Virgine in nos ordinatissime dispensatur. . . . Tertius processus est a Virgine benedicta. A tempore enim quo concepit Deum in utero suo, quamdam, ut sic dicam, iurisdictionem seu auctoritatem habuit in omni temporali processione Spiritus Sancti, ita quod nulla creature aliquam a Deo recepit gratiam virtutis, nisi secundum dispensationem ipsius Virginis Matris. Cum enim Christus sit caput nostrum, a quo omnis influxus divinae gratiae in mysticum corpus fluit, beata Virgo est collum, per quod hic fluxus pertransit ad corporis membra."

82. Jean Courtcuisse, *L'Oeuvre oratoire française de Jean Courtcuisse*, ed. Giuseppe de Stefano (Torino: G. Giappichelli, 1969), 211. "Pour empetrer doncquez la grace du Saint Esperit, senz la quelle nul bien ne peut estre commencé, . . . nous requerons plus feablement ceste glorieuse Dame, et la saluerons devotement."

Mary was also able to grant the virtue of purity,[83] the charity necessary to complete faith and please God,[84] and even protection from the Devil and all kinds of earthly dangers. The Devil may roam the earth seeking someone to devour, but "Mary is always going around seeking someone to save."[85]

Gabriel Barletta provided the most innovative explanation of Mary's willingness to pour out graces on the faithful. She was obeying the canons of the Church. Canon law requires a person who finds something belonging to someone else to return it. The human race lost the grace of God when it fell into sin; but, as the Angel Gabriel said to Mary, she had found grace with God. Therefore, "Mary is compelled to help sinners since she has something that is ours; and she restores grace to the sinner."[86]

Above all others, the one favor sought from Mary by Christians in the later Middle Ages was mercy. Paintings of Mary from the period often depict her as the "Mater Misericordiae," the Mother of Mercy, sinners fleeing beneath her cloak for protection from judgment. As more people were made aware through confession of a greater inward sinfulness, yet were told they should strive still with the aid of grace to perfect themselves, Mary's mercy shone as the one certain light in the darkness; the mother of Christ, the savior and judge, was also the mother of Christians.[87] The most hardened sinners were promised by stories and sermons that if they cried in their distress to Mary, she would hear.[88] Jean Gerson

83. San Bernardino of Siena, *Opera omnia*, 2:371–72.

84. Gerson, *Oeuvres complètes*, 7:1058.

85. Bernardino of Busti, *Mariale*, Sermon 1, "On the Name of Mary," pt. 2. "Quia enim adversarius noster diabolus tamquam leo rugiens circuit querens quem devoret. . . . ideo ipsa semper circuit querens quem salvet."

86. Barletta, *Sermones*, 103v. "Maria cogitur peccatorem adiuvare: cum de nostro habeat: et gratiam peccatori restituat."

87. Elizabeth A. Johnson, "Marian Devotion in the Western Church," in *Christian Spirituality: High Middle Ages and Reformation*, ed. Jill Raitt (New York: Crossroad Publishing Company, 1987), 401. Johnson points out that this idea was already voiced by St. Anselm, who said, "Blessed assurance, safe refuge, the mother of God is our mother. The mother of him in whom alone we have hope, whom alone we fear, is our mother. The mother of him who alone saves and condemns is our mother"; Anselm of Canterbury, "Prayer to St. Mary, to ask for her and Christ's Love," in *Prayers and Meditations of Saint Anselm*, trans. Sister Benedicta Ward (New York: Penguin Books, 1973), 122.

88. One of the most popular Marian legends in the Middle Ages concerned a treasurer

reproved Judas himself for his suicide. Even Judas, the arch-traitor, could have been saved if he had not lost hope. "Truly Judas," said Gerson, "here you acted wrongly to fall into such despair of the infinite mercy of God and his mother."[89] Elsewhere, Gerson referred to Mary as the "mother of mercy," the "temple of mercy," and the "true place of refuge."[90] San Bernardino called Mary "the Queen of Mercy."[91] Quoting St. Bernard he told the people that Mary "opens the bosom of her mercy to all so that the whole universe may receive from its fullness."[92]

Bernardino of Busti set forth a complete summary of all of Mary's intercessory labors for her sinful children. She assists our justification by getting rid of every impediment to good works.

> She aids men at every stage of progress, in life, in death, and after death. There-fore the Church sings, "Mary, Mother of Grace, Mother of Mercy." For she helps in life both the good and the evil; the good by preserving them in grace, where-fore she is called Mary, Mother of Grace; the evil, by leading them back to the mercy of God through penitence. Therefore she is called Mother of Mercy. She aids also in death by protecting from every treachery of the devil. . . . she aids souls after death by taking them up in her hands and leading them into heaven.[93]

St. Bernard of Clairvaux was, characteristically, the one who elo-quently expressed what would become the predominant medieval sense

---

and archdeacon of Cilicia, Theophilus. He sold his soul to the Devil in exchange for world-ly success and wealth. Even though he duly achieves his goal, he cannot enjoy it because of his guilt. He pleads with the Devil to nullify the contract, but to no avail. When he appeals to Mary, however, she appears to him in a dream and gives him back the contract he had signed in his own blood. He awakes to find the contract indeed there beside him. He dies at peace with God shortly thereafter.

89. Gerson, *Oeuvres complètes*, 7:481. "Vraiment, Judas, icy tu fais mal de prendre un tel desespoir de la misericorde infinie de Dieu et de sa mere."

90. Ibid., 1049.

91. San Bernardino of Siena, *Opera omnia*, 2:153.

92. Ibid., 4:543. ". . . omnibus misericordiae sinum aperit, ut de plenitudine illius accipi-ant universi." The same quotation appears in Barletta, *Sermones*, 63r.

93. Bernardino of Busti, *Mariale*, Sermon 1, "On the Name of Mary," pt. 3. "Ipsa quidem adiuvat hominem in omni statu, scilicet in vita, in morte, et post mortem. Unde ecclesia canit, Maria mater gratie mater misericordie. Adiuvat enim in vita tam bonos quam malos. Bonos, scilicet, in gratia conservando, ideo dicitur Maria mater gratie. Malos vero ad mis-ericordiam dei per penitentiam reducendo. Ideo dicitur mater misericordie. Adiuvat etiam in morte ab omnibus invidiis diaboli protegendo. . . . Adiuvat post mortem animas, scilicet, in suis manibus suscipiendo et eas in celum deducendo."

of trust in the Mother of Mercy. In his fourth sermon on the Assumption, St. Bernard exclaimed, "May he be silent about your mercy, Blessed Virgin, if there should exist one who has called on you in his necessities and remembers that you have failed him."[94]

A famous legend about St. Bernard points to one last duty belonging to Mary's role as intercessor and mother of Christians. As any mother, she was charged with providing sufficient nourishment for her children, with food drawn from her own body. The story says that on a certain day, St. Bernard was at prayer, saying the "Ave Maris Stella" before an image of the Virgin in the Church of St. Vorles, Chatillon-sur-Seine. Upon repeating the words, "monstra te esse matrem," "show yourself to be mother," Mary herself appeared and rewarded him with three drops of her milk. Others too, among them the mystic Henry Suso (d. 1365), Alanus de Rupe (d. 1475), and the fourteenth-century Florentine anchorite Blessed Paula, were given the same gift by Mary.[95] Mary's milk was the only Marian relic that appeared frequently in the miracle stories.[96]

In the Old Testament, milk and honey together were the supreme symbols of plenty and abundance, and of the reward of the Promised Land. Newly baptized Christian converts of the early Church were sometimes given milk and honey to eat to show their arrival in a new land, the Promised Land of heaven. In the Middle Ages, however, milk, especially Mary's milk, represented her power to heal and intercede for sinners;[97] it was the grace she poured out on all who sought her blessing.

Women's bodies in general were frequently looked upon as food during the medieval period. An obvious reason for this was the fact that women, as mothers, fed their children from their bodies, often providing the only nourishment available for them. Medieval philosophers added

---

94. Graef, *Mary*, 1:240.

95. Warner, *Alone of All Her Sex*, 197–99.

96. Ahsmann, *Le culte de la Sainte-Vierge*, 142. See also P. V. Bétérous, "A propos d'une des légendes mariales les plus répandues: le 'lait de la Vierge,'" *Bulletin de l'Association Guillaume Budé* 4 (1975): 403–11.

97. Barbara G. Lane, *The Altar and the Altarpiece: Sacramental Themes in Early Netherlandish Painting* (New York: Harper and Row, 1984), 6–7. Lane describes a portrait of Mary from the Turin-Milan Hours in which she "glances toward a kneeling supplicant as she presses milk from her breast."

more weight to this perception by teaching that breast milk was actually the mother's blood, changed by some mysterious process into food for her children. Women who were breast-feeding, therefore, were believed to be sacrificing a portion of their own blood to sustain their offspring.[98]

The importance of Mary's body, and of her blood in particular, could only be enhanced by the medieval understanding of woman's body as food. Hervé Martin finds that one of the more popular themes regarding Mary in the French sermons of the later Middle Ages was that of producer of food (cibum generavit).[99] The "very pure blood" of the Virgin was the material which formed the body and blood of the Son of God and fed him as an infant. San Bernardino of Siena was fond of this motif and used it in several of his sermons to illustrate Mary's ability to provide for Christ. Mary, he said, was perfectly united to Christ in contemplation and action. She was the ideal representative of both Mary and Martha. Just as there has never been a contemplative to surpass her, so there has never been another like her to minister to needs.

Others clothe paupers with a sheep's wool; she truly clothed the highest riches with her very pure blood. Second, others clothe with rags; she with her body. Third, others feed the poor with outward bread, she fed the God made Man with her own milk.[100]

The least drop of Mary's milk, to San Bernardino, "Surpassed all the fruits of the earthly Paradise and of the whole world."[101]

The Virgin could also supply food for her children in the Church through another channel, more indirect than her physical motherhood of

---

98. Bynum, *Holy Feast and Holy Fast*, 270.

99. Hervé Martin, *Le métier de prédicateur en France septentrionale à la fin du moyen âge, 1350–1520* (Paris: Cerf, 1988), 308. Using five Marian sermons, Martin provides a diagram of all the most commonly used metaphors, actions, and associations employed to describe Mary and her role.

100. San Bernardino of Siena, *Opera omnia*, 4:557–58. ". . . alii induunt pauperes de lana ovis; ipsa vero induit summum divitem de purissimis sanguinibus suis.-Secundo, alii induunt de panno; ipsa de corpore suo.-Tertio, alii pascunt pauperem de pane extrinseco; ipsa vero pavit humanatum Deum de lacte proprio . . ."

101. Ibid., 2:381. "Deus nutrivit hominem de fructibus paradisi; sed beata Virgo nutrivit Christum de suo sacratissimo lacte, 'ubere de caelo pleno,' cuius minima stilla praevalet omnibus fructibus paradisi terrestris ac totius mundi."

Christ, but equally profound: the Eucharist. Bynum has noted that the ties between Mary and the Eucharist appeared more frequently in the art and literature of the late Middle Ages as devotion to the host grew stronger.[102] Charles Zika finds that one of the central symbolic uses of the host in this period was as nourishing food.[103] Contemporary religious imagery certainly did not allow anyone to forget that the host, the body of Christ, was derived from the body of Mary.

Eucharistic symbolism in later medieval art wove together a rich tapestry of themes involving Mary's role in the Annunciation and her suckling of the Christ Child. Robert Campin's "Madonna and Child Before a Fire Screen" abounds in religious symbols. The child, for example, is held in Mary's lap close to a chalice standing on the table beside them. Together, the infant Jesus and the chalice form an image of the bread and wine of the Eucharist. The Virgin offers her breast not to the child but to the viewer, showing herself to be intercessor and also the ultimate source of the food in the Mass. Her blood was transformed into both milk for her son and the substance of his flesh.[104] Another of Campin's works, the Mérode altarpiece, places the Annunciation among all the trappings of the Mass. Gabriel even wears the dalmatic of a deacon, assisting at the consecration.[105]

Tabernacles for storing the consecrated host were often designed to represent Mary, again holding within her the body of Jesus as once she had done at the moment of the Incarnation. A Swabian retable of 1440 held a picture of Mary and the Evangelists preparing the host for the priests to receive, an image that beautifully unites the themes of Christ as the Word preached by the apostles and enfleshed by Mary.[106]

Drama could also present numerous opportunities for a symbolic comparison of the Annunciation and the Eucharist. During Annunciation plays, usually performed in December rather than on March 25, the altar was censed to represent the descent of the Holy Spirit on the Virgin to

---

102. Bynum, *Holy Feast and Holy Fast,* 81.
103. Zika, "Hosts, Processions and Pilgrimages," 44.
104. Lane, *Altar and the Altarpiece,* 4, 6–7.
105. Ibid., 41. See also the frontispiece of this book.
106. Bynum, *Holy Feast and Holy Fast,* 81.

effect the Incarnation, just as he descends to perform the miracle of tran-substantiation.[107] In the liturgical drama, "Missa Aurea," performed at Tournai from 1231, a dove was lowered from above over the kneeling Mary as containers for the host were occasionally lowered over the altar at the point of consecration.[108]

The Assumption of Mary could similarly be associated with the host. Gail McMurray Gibson indicates that the plays staged during the Corpus Christi festival in fifteenth-century England were preoccupied with the glorification of Mary's body in her Assumption, celebrated in the drama with "elaborate music and . . . liturgical pageantry."[109] These dramas served as graphic reminders of the source of the body venerated in the Corpus Christi processions.

The network of religious meanings found in these art works and plays, and, as we will see, in sermons as well, is in many ways inherent in the symbolism of the Incarnation and the doctrine of transubstantiation which sprang from it. It was not created by the spirituality of the four-teenth and fifteenth centuries. But in no other period were these ideas so diffused throughout the entire religious culture of Europe. Prior to the

107. Karl Young, *The Drama of the Medieval Church*, vol. 2 (Oxford: Clarendon Press, 1932), 227.

108. Lane, *Altar and the Altarpiece*, 47–50.

109. Gibson, *Theater of Devotion*, 168. Charles Zika, in "Hosts, Processions and Pil-grimages," 44, has stated that he believes those historians who have stressed the importance of Corpus Christi apart from other festivals have been misled by a tendency to see the host as body and therefore an appropriate symbol for the social body of the community. Zika believes that any significant procession could serve to unify the late medieval community, since it was the processional form as such and not Corpus Christi that was important. Instead, he says, people of the later Middle Ages looked upon the host primarily as relic and not as body. Regardless of what the importance of processions other than Corpus Christi may have been, Zika fails to point out that the importance of any relic was its bodily nature. It was either part of a saint's body or an object that had been in close contact with that body; it could therefore guarantee the presence of the saint and his or her power. The fact that it took the host as long as it did to be seen as similar to other relics most likely was due to the fact that transubstantiation was not adopted as the official position of the Church until 1215, and the widespread popularity of the doctrine did not occur until Cor-pus Christi was made an official feast of the Church by Pope Urban IV in 1264. People could now begin to approach the host as a relic, but the most powerful one, since, as the body of Christ, it ensured the presence of Christ himself, God and man, and not of a purely human saint.

fourteenth century, Mary's connection to the Eucharist as the supplier of
the body and blood of Christ was found primarily in the works of theologians.

As early as the fourth century, the Syrian deacon Ephraem (306–73)
claimed that the Eucharistic body is the same as the body received from
Mary. In a sermon on the feast of Mary's Nativity, Peter Damian (d. 1072)
agreed, saying that the "body of Christ, which the blessed Virgin bore,
which she caressed in her lap, which she wrapped in swaddling clothes,
which she nourished with maternal care, is indeed, I say, without any
doubt, none other than that which we perceive now in the sacrament of
the altar, and we drink his blood in the sacrament of our redemption."[110]
Godfrey of Admont (d. 1165) called Mary the "unique matter of all the
sacraments (sacramentorum omnium materia singularis)."[111] Aelred of
Rievaulx, in a sermon on the feast of Mary's Nativity, linked the themes
of the Virgin's milk and her role as provider of food through her motherhood of Christ. According to Aelred, only the angels are able to be
nourished directly by the solid food of the direct presence of the Son of
God. We on earth, who are yet small, need milk. Therefore the bread of
heaven "came into the womb of the Blessed Virgin and there was made
milk, milk of the kind that we are able to suck. . . . That is the milk which
our good mother provided for us."[112] Richard of St. Laurent (d. 1245)

---

110. St. Peter Damian, "Sermo xlv in nativitate beatissimae Virginis Mariae," PL 144:742–
43. "Illum siquidem corpus Christi, quod beatissima Virgo genuit, quod in gremio fovit,
quod in fasciis cinxit, quod materna cura nutrivit: illud, inquam, absque ulla dubietate, non
aliud, nunc de sacro altari percipimus, et ejus sanguinem in sacramentum nostrae redemp-
tionis haurimus."

111. Godfrey of Admont, PL 174:974. Godfrey addresses Mary as "Digne et congrue beata
Maria, mundi domina, coelorum regina, angelorum imperatrix, sacramentorum omnium
materia singularis, tota pulchra, tota formosa describitur, quae ut summi Regis Matrem
decuit, decore et pulchritudine virgineae carnis ipsum Patris Unigenitum induit qui ut est
ineffabilis, ineffabilia operare voluit in matre Virgine, qui in loco peccati peccatum non
adhaererat ullum sive in verbo, aut cogitatione, vel in opere."

112. Aelred of Rievaulx, "Sermo xx in nativitate B. Mariae," PL 195:323–24. "Verbum Dei,
Filius Dei, sapientia Dei, panis est, et solidus cibus est. Et ideo de illo soli illi qui fortes
erant, id est angeli, manducabant. Nos, qui parvi eramus, non potuimus cibum istum
gustare, quia solidus erat; nos qui in terra eramus, non potuimus ad istum panem ascen-
dere, quia in celo erat. Quid ergo factum est? Venit iste panis in uterum B. Virginis, et ibi
factus est lac, et tale lac, quale nos sugere possumus. . . . Istud est lac, quod nobis bona
mater nostra ministravit."

added the final touch in his *De laudibus sanctae Mariae* by asserting that "in the sacrament of her son we also eat and drink her flesh and blood."[113] Richard was basing his statement on the fleshly unity of Mary and Christ which we have already seen used to conclude that Mary suffered on the cross and to argue the necessity of her bodily Assumption. A sermon on the Mass by Robert Ciboule, "Qui manducat me," combined two of these ideas. The body and blood received in the Eucharist, he declared, "are the same substance as the body and blood which were conceived by the work of the Holy Spirit in the virginal womb and hung on the cross." The divinity of Christ "will never abandon the body, the soul, and the blood that he took from the womb of the Virgin."[114] By the fourteenth and fifteenth centuries, Mary was portrayed as the provider of Christ's Eucharistic body and blood in prayers, literary works, and in sermons.

One of the most famous prayers of the medieval Church was the twelfth-century "O Intemerata," customarily addressed to the Virgin and her virginal protector, St. John. Around the beginning of the fourteenth century, an adaptation of this prayer, perhaps the work of Pope John XXII (1318–34), began to appear in collections of prayers and Books of Hours. Addressed to Mary alone it seems to have been intended as a preparation for communion. The prayer salutes the Virgin who formed the flesh and blood of Christ in her womb, uniting them to his divinity. It is the same flesh and blood that are given daily in the Mass, and "whoever does not eat them, will not have eternal life; and therefore we are rightly able to say that through (Mary) after God, the whole world lives."[115]

---

113. Graef, *Mary,* 1:62, 206–7, 248, 266.

114. Robert Ciboule, *Édition critique du sermon "Qui manducat me" de Robert Ciboule (1403–1458),* ed. Nicole Marzac (Cambridge: Modern Humanities Research Association, 1971), 46.

115. André Wilmart, *Auteurs spirituels et textes dévots du moyen âge latin: Études d'histoire littéraire* (Paris: Études Augustiniennes, 1971), 493–94. "O intemerata et in eternum benedicta, singularis atque incomparabilis virgo dei genitrix Maria, gratissimum dei templum, spiritus sancti sacrarium, ianua regni celorum, per quam post Deum totus vivit orbis terrarum: de te enim dei filius verus et omnipotens Deus suam sanctissimam fecit matrem, assumens de te illam sacratissimam carnem per quam mundus qui perditus erat salvatus est, cuius precioso sanguine mundus ipse redemptus est et ipsa peccata remissa sunt: formans eam in preciosissimo utero tuo de purissimo sanguine tuo, uniens eam eterne et incommutabili divinitati sue: a quo bona cuncta procedunt, per quem omnia facta sunt: quem adoro, quoniam sacratissimam carnem suam cum preciosissimo sanguine suo dat

Individual devotion and prayer to the Virgin, like that of St. Bernard, could bring the reward of the body of Christ as well as Mary's milk, since her blood was ultimately the source of both. One miracle story records,

There was a young monk in the monastery of Saint Chrysantus, called Daniel, the master of students there. He used to say this sequence ("Ave, praeclara maris stella") with great devotion every day on his knees in the crypt of the chapel in front of the altar of Blessed Mary. One day, as in singing it he came to the place: "Pray Virgin, that we may become worthy of the bread of heaven," he saw the glorious one come from the altar and offer him bread that was whiter than snow. He was greatly comforted by this vision and continued to be even more devout in her worship.[116]

Even more direct is this passage from the Middle English version of James of Milan's *Stimulus amoris.* The author declares, "& I shal fonde to sowke with him with al ᵭe feith that I have & thus shal I tempore to-gidere ᵭe swete mylke of marie the virgine with ᵭe blood of ihesu and make to myself a drynke ᵭat is ful of hele."[117]

Numerous parallels between Mary and the Eucharist appear also in the *Speculum humanae salvationis.* Mary is called the Ark of the Covenant which contained a golden urn holding manna from heaven. In the chapter on the Mass, Mary's role is compared to the consecration performed by the priest. "Be Marie Jhesu Gods soun was on tyme incarnate, and of(t) be the preest is brede to flesshe transobstanciate." Mary is also the source of the vine, Christ, who gives his blood on the altar.[118]

The preacher Jean Gerson was known for his literary abilities. He com-

---

cotidie fidelibus suis sub specie panis et vini in cibum viaticum et refectionem animarum salutarem et vitalem.-Qui digne manducaverit habet vitam eternam; qui autem indigne, iudicium sibi manducat et bibit: sicut pluries feci, mea culpa . . . Qui autem non manducaverit, non habet vitam eternam; et propterea merito dicimus quia per te post deum totus vivit orbis terrarum."

116. R. B. C. Huygens, "Deux commentaires sur la séquence, 'Ave, praeclara maris stella,'" *Citeaux* 20 (1969): 124; quoted in Wenzel, *Preachers,* 15–16.

117. James of Milan, *The Prickynge of Love,* Salzburg Studies in English Literature: Elizabethan and Renaissance Studies, ed. Harold Kane (Salzburg: 1983), 91:10; quoted in Sarah Beckwith, *Christ's Body: Identity, Culture and Society in Late Medieval Writings* (New York: Routledge, 1993), 58.

118. Avril Henry, ed., *The Mirour of Man's Salvation: A Middle English Translation of the "Speculum humanae salvationis,"* 15th cent. ms. (Philadelphia: University of Pennsylvania Press, 1987), 71–79, 105.

posed a number of poems and religious treatises dedicated to Mary. In his work on the Magnificat, he named Mary the Mother of the Eucharist;[119] and in a poem to the Virgin, he beseeched her, "Give me your bread which makes the heart whole and purifies the soul; this unleavened bread which, drawn from human nature, repairs that nature."[120] This same idea surfaced in one of Geiler of Kaisersberg's sermons when he instructed his listeners to pray to Mary, "Our Mother, who art in heaven, give us this day our own supersubstantial bread."[121]

Gerson's sermons also feature Mary as the provider of Christ's Eucharistic body. Several times in his sermon for the festival of Corpus Christi, Gerson reminds his hearers that the bread of Christ's body was formed in Mary's womb. He says that only with the grace of the Holy Spirit will we be able to do worthy reverence to the body of Christ in our hearts as well as with outward processions. This can happen, "if we run to you glorious Virgin, to beg this grace, you who are the one in whom this bread of life, the bread of the angels was made and formed."[122] Gerson used the metaphor of Mary as the fruit tree whose fruit is Christ's body. In an Easter sermon, he says that "we must also greatly praise the tree, it is the Virgin Mary, who has born this fruit by which we have been refreshed."[123]

Bernardino of Busti concluded that God's desire to give us everything through Mary makes her our almsgiver. Through Mary, God "gives us, so poor and hungry, that heavenly bread who said of himself in John 6, 'I am the living bread, come down from heaven.'" But God also made Mary the keeper of the royal wine cellar to distribute the intoxicating grace of the Holy Spirit to those in heaven and on earth.[124]

---

119. Graef, *Mary*, 1:313.

120. A. L. Masson, *Jean Gerson: sa vie, son temps, ses oeuvres* (Lyons: Emmanuel Vitte, 1894), 209. "Donne-moi ton pain, Qui fait le cuer sain, L'ame toute pure; Ce pain sans levain Qui du genre humain, Refait la nature."

121. Douglass, *Justification in Late Medieval Preaching*, 191.

122. Gerson, *Oeuvres complètes*, 7:699. "Si recorrons a vous, Vierge glorieuse, pour ceste grace empestrer, qui estes celle in laquelle fut fait et forme ce pain de vie le pain des anges."

123. Ibid., 7:660. ". . . l'arbre aussi devons grandeent louer, c'est la Vierge Marie qui a porte tel fruit de quoy nous avons este refectionnes."

124. Bernardino of Busti, *Mariale*, Sermon 1, "On the Name of Mary," pt. 2. "Non solum autem fecit eum [*sic*] deus elemosinariam suam: per quam nobis pauperibus et esurientibus

Of all the preachers in this study, San Bernardino of Siena came closest to saying with Richard of St. Laurent that Mary not only gave the
Eucharistic body but was herself the body received. This is evident in the
portion of his sermon on Mary's glory and grace quoted at the beginning
of Chapter 1. The language that San Bernardino used made the flesh of
Christ, the substance of the Eucharist, literally a part of the Virgin's body,
"excisa" or cut off. It was her flesh, given to her son, which became the
supreme sacrament, the goal and end of all the other sacraments and
sacramentals.[125]

Michel Menot warned the people that they must show due reverence
to God and to the body and blood of Christ in the Eucharist or they will
face the wrath of God. He told of an incident in which someone had
struck the priest carrying the host in a procession, causing him to drop the
host to the ground. No one begged God's forgiveness and no one was
punished. Therefore, shortly after, thousands of people died in ship-
wrecks at sea. Predictably, it was Mary herself who appeared to inform
the people that this tragedy was the direct result of disrespect shown to
the body of her son.[126]

European religious life in the fourteenth and fifteenth centuries was
permeated by a sense of the sacrality of the material and especially of the
human body as a result of the Incarnation. This spirituality is evident in
the cult of relics and the doctrine of transubstantiation adopted by the
Church in 1215. Miraculous images and paintings, as well as portions of

---

dedit panem illum celestem qui de seipso inquit Jo. 6 Ego sum panis vivus qui de celo
descendit. Sed etiam fecit ipsam cellariam suam. Habet enim deus cellam vinariam, scilicet,
spiritus sancti abundantiam in quam introduxit beatam virginem, et fecit eam suam dis-
pensatricem."

125. San Bernardino of Siena, *Opera omnia*, 2:380. "De carne enim Virginis benedictae et
in parte corporis excisa consistit, perficitur et terminatur totum decus et pondus sacramentorum Ecclesiae Dei.-Certum est enim quod omnis institution sacramentorum et
omnia alia sacramenta, tamquam in ultimum finem et ad illud Sacramentum omnium
sacramentorum excellentissimum, quod est Eucharistia, ordinatur."

126. Menot, *Sermons choisis*, 176. Richard Kieckhefer tells of one of Jane Mary of Mail-
lé's dreams which also suggests that Mary was responsible for the blood of her son and its
administration to sinners. The Virgin appeared to her in a dream holding the child, Jesus,
and censed her with a thurible that gave off drops of Christ's blood. See Richard Kieckhefer, *Unquiet Souls: Fourteenth-Century Saints and Their Religious Milieu* (Chicago: University of
Chicago Press, 1984), 167.

the bodies of the saints or objects that had touched their bodies, were the focus of intense devotion as sources of supernatural power and intercession. Chief among all bodily mediators of power and grace was the glorified flesh of Christ himself, present in the Eucharist. The importance of the host and of the saints' bodies as channels of communication with the spiritual world was reinforced by the primarily oral nature of all communication at the time. People were accustomed to meaningful interaction only with other persons who were physically present. No one, perhaps, would have denied the ability of purely spiritual beings such as angels or demons, not to mention God himself, to make their ideas and intentions known and exert their power through less concrete means. Yet their appearance in bodily form was always somehow more reliable. Bernardino of Busti hastened to reassure his hearers that his vision of Jeremiah was not a dream or something ethereal. Jeremiah had been there. He had a long grey beard.[127]

It is this type of piety, so abundantly represented in all manifestations of late medieval Christianity, which best explains the nature of Marian devotion in the period. Mary's body, and above all her bodily unity with Christ as his mother, was the touchstone for the presentation of her role and importance in art, literature, drama, and certainly in the popular sermon. The Immaculate Conception and the Assumption of her body made her the ultimate symbol of human redemption and gave her a bodily presence in heaven that strengthened her ability to speak to Christ for sinners below. It was, however, the oneness of flesh shared by the Virgin and her son which was her greatest source of religious significance and power. It enabled her to suffer with Jesus in his Passion, best assured that her intercessions would be answered favorably, and made her the provider of the most revered object of devotion in the late Middle Ages, the host. No wonder that English Corpus Christi plays might so concern themselves with the role of Mary's body in the history of salvation. Christ was himself the supreme sacrament. But to the eyes of fifteenth-century devotion, it was through Mary that Christ's Incarnation, and the whole sacramental system that flowed from it, became possible.

127. Bernardino of Busti, *Mariale*, Sermon 1, "On the Sorrows of Mary," pt. 1. For a full citation of this passage, see above, n. 27.

Four

Spiritual Mothers

Mary's Motherhood and Post-Tridentine Catholicism

*The Lord desires nothing more than that he have for himself many
spiritual mothers. . . . For if there may be only one mother of Christ
according to the flesh . . . Still Christ has, I might say, enlarged this
title of maternity to others who are obedient, who receive the word of
God with faith.*[1]

—St. Peter Canisius

*When Our Lady humbled herself, and recognized herself to be unwor-
thy of being raised to the high dignity of Mother of God, she was, by
this same act rendered his Mother.*[2]

—St. François de Sales

ST. FRANÇOIS DE SALES was one of the most eloquent and effective rep-
resentatives of the more interiorized Catholic piety which developed in
the sixteenth century, after the Council of Trent. His sermons reflect in a
particularly forceful way the central themes of the Marian devotion of his
day. St. François offers his hearers a Virgin who is humble, quiet, passive,
and submissive, obedient always to the will of God. This obedience was
proclaimed to be her greatest source of blessing, greater even than her
motherhood of Christ. According to St. François, Jesus could have said of

1. Peter Canisius, *Meditationes seu notae in evangelicas lectiones,* 2d ed., ed. Frederick Streicher, S.J., 2 vols. (Munich: 1957), 2, 2:227.

2. François de Sales, *Oeuvres complètes de Saint François de Sales, évêque et prince de Genève,*
16 vols. (Paris: J. J. Blaise, 1821), 10:308.

his mother, "It is true that my mother is blessed, because she has carried me in her womb; but she is even more blessed for the humility with which she has heard the words of my heavenly Father, and kept them." These qualities had made of Mary the "mirror and summary of Christian perfection which we ought to imitate."[3]

As we will see, this portrait of Mary represents precisely the kind of religious devotion sought by the Church in the later sixteenth and seventeenth centuries. By imitating Mary's humble obedience, Catholic Christians could hope to gain, with the Virgin, a share of the blessedness of heaven. In some ways there is nothing new here. Throughout the Middle Ages and into the early modern period, the Virgin had served, along with her son, as a convenient role model for the Christian life. As a woman, Mary was also useful to preachers as a means to illustrate behavior that they felt to be appropriate specifically for women, in the secular or religious sphere. Often, this was accomplished by stressing the differences between the way that Mary lived her life and the ways in which contemporary women chose to conduct themselves. Late medieval preachers, however, had presented Mary in their sermons as active, often even in her participation in the Incarnation, where she sometimes appeared as one who either deliberately sought God's involvement to save the world or who intentionally attracted Christ to her through her beauty and grace. In Passion sermons in particular, Jesus' mother occupied a central position in every incident of the Good Friday narratives. When she interceded for Christians with God, both body and voice were actively engaged in seeking forgiveness and mercy. The Virgin of the late Middle Ages was rather different from the quiet, passive Virgin who will emerge in Catholic preaching after the Council of Trent.

Separated from the World

There is one facet of Mary's life, however, that reflects a different side of her character from that which we have seen in medieval sermons praising her motherhood and suffering under the cross: Mary as quiet, enclosed contemplative. At least since the fourth century, Mary had been

3. Ibid., II:241, 378.

held up as the ideal model for a life of secluded devotion to God, a life such as that led by the consecrated virgins of the early Church. Preachers in both the late Middle Ages and the post-Tridentine era were also convinced, and tried to convince their hearers, that the Virgin had led a life of privacy and prayer prior to her conception of Jesus, scarcely venturing out of her house for any reason. She had avoided public places, preferring to keep to herself in her chamber. This contemplative Virgin will provide an important link between the Marian devotion of both periods. A comparison of the sermons from these two eras demonstrates a remarkable similarity of themes and issues.

San Bernardino of Siena, for instance, was interested in presenting Mary as a model of the virgin life, to be imitated by all virgins, religious or secular. His sermon for the Saturday of Holy Week is an extended exhortation to women to follow in the footsteps of Mary by remaining modest virgins. Mary remained at home, in the quiet of her room, and asked even Gabriel for his identity before admitting him. The Holy Spirit shows us through Mary's life that virgins and women should "not go about and wander to other houses nor go around visiting the sights of the world."[4] San Bernardino advised women to flee all male society, even of brothers and relatives. They should be as wild animals who are frightened by the sight or sound of a man. This is the only way in which women can be ready at all times to listen to God's voice and to desire only God and divine things.[5]

Bernardino of Busti taught exactly the same thing in one of his sermons on the Visitation. Mary remained about three months in Zechariah's house, not traveling around the countryside, to teach us "to flee the conversations of men, which ought to be avoided especially by virgins and other young women."[6] In addition, Michel Menot listed Mary's modesty

---

4. San Bernardino of Siena, *Opera omnia,* ed. P. M. Perantoni, 5 vols. (Quaracchi: Collegium S. Bonaventurae, 1950), 4:474. "In hoc virgines et mulieres, et potissime spirituales, Spiritus Sanctus edocens non circumcursare per alienas domos, non hinc inde ad mundi spectacula circumvagari, sed in secretis thalamis atque monasteriis immorari ad conservandam virginitatem necesse est."

5. Ibid., 4:475–82.

6. Bernardino of Busti, *Mariale* (Milan: Leonardus Pachel, 1493), Sermon 1, "On the Visitation of Mary," pt. 2.

as a reason for the Spirit's presence with her;[7] and Gabriel Barletta insisted that she never even went to the window of her room in order to escape public view.[8]

Finally, Jean Gerson urged the imitation of Mary's virginity and humility. He advised those who would copy her example to shun idleness, strong wine, and occasions for evil. The latter can best be accomplished by remaining at home. The angel, after all, found Mary alone, "not out talking to Berthe or Gaulthier."[9]

Preachers of the late sixteenth century continued the earlier portrayal. St. Lawrence of Brindisi remarks that when Gabriel approached Mary, she was "separated from the world in both mind and spirit; therefore she was found at home, alone."[10] St. Robert Bellarmine also adds that the angel did not find Mary going about to parties and dances where the flames of concupiscence could be fanned. She was "enclosed in her chamber." She always avoided men, and certainly never spoke alone with them in her room. Someone else was always present.[11]

St. François de Sales repeats all of the above arguments: that Mary was always alone, not speaking with men, like someone who had taken religious vows. Unlike the women of early modern Europe, Mary did not leave her home to visit other women for useless conversations. When the Virgin visited Elizabeth, she hastened to her house as soon as possible to shorten her exposure to the eyes of the world.[12] This was asserted in spite of the fact that St. François deliberately used the Visitation as a symbol and example of active service for religious women when he and St. Jeanne

7. Michel Menot, *Sermons choisis de Michel Menot,* ed. J. Nève (Paris: Bibliothèque du XVe siècle, 1924), 425.

8. Gabriel Barletta, *Sermones quadragesimales et de sanctis* (Brescia: Jacobus Britannicus, 1497), 37r.

9. Jean Gerson, *Oeuvres complètes,* ed. P. Glorieux, 8 vols. (Paris: Desclée and Cie, 1971), 7:542–46.

10. Lawrence of Brindisi, *Opera omnia,* 10 vols. (Patavia: Ex officina typographica seminarii, 1928), 1:119. "Separatum a mundo mente et spiritus; hinc domi sola reperitur."

11. Robert Bellarmine, *Roberti cardinalis Bellarmini opera omnia,* 6 vols. (J. Giuliano, 1860), 5:375–78. "Primum igitur singulas virtutes in Virgine breviter ostendamus, non consueverat sancta Virgo cum viris, ac praesertim adolescentibus, et in cubiculo et sine teste sola cum solis confabulari."

12. De Sales, *Oeuvres complètes,* 10:297, 301; 11:242, 264.

de Chantal founded their new religious order for women in the seventeenth century.[13]

So we find that the public portrait of the Virgin as quiet and secluded from the world through much of her life remains a constant during a period in which the account of her participation in the Incarnation and her behavior during the Passion was undergoing a marked change. The Council of Trent is a logical place to begin when seeking to explain the differences which exist between late medieval and early modern Catholic sermons, for the council was quite concerned with the role of preaching in forming the lives of Christians.

The War against Moral Disorder

On June 17, 1546, the Council of Trent completed its decree on reading and preaching the Word of God. The decree was concerned mostly with ensuring that preaching would occur, that it would be done only by those who were well qualified, and that no one would be permitted to disseminate questionable or heretical ideas publicly in Catholic territories.[14] In the Tridentine decrees, there is one brief mention of the content of that preaching which is nevertheless significant, for the fathers at Trent chose to borrow directly from the work of St. Francis of Assisi, whose order was so fully involved in popular preaching on the eve of the Protestant Reformation. The decree instructs all who are responsible for the cure of souls to teach those committed to their charge "what things all must know in order to be saved, and announce to them briefly and clearly in sermons the vices which they are to avoid and the virtues it is right for them to fol-

13. Elizabeth Rapley, *The Dévotes: Women and Church in Seventeenth-Century France* (Montreal: McGill-Queen's University Press, 1990), 35–40, 169–74. Rapley demonstrates that men such as St. François de Sales and St. Vincent de Paul, who wished to encourage religious women to work actively in the world on behalf of the poor used the Visitation as a symbol of Mary's willingness to leave the enclosure of her home and serve her cousin Elizabeth. If the Virgin could do this, then so, presumably, could women in seventeenth-century France. The Church, however, had other ideas. The women organized by François de Sales and Jeanne de Chantal were eventually forced to accept strict enclosure and traditional vows. The only way that St. Vincent was able to preserve his filles de charité was to make certain that they did not claim to be nuns in any sense of the word.

14. *Canons and Decrees of the Council of Trent: Original Text with English Translation*, trans. H. J. Schroeder, O.P. (St. Louis: Herder, 1941), 305–7.

low so that they may be strong to avoid eternal punishment and obtain celestial glory."[15] This admonition was drawn from chapter 9 of the "second Rule" of St. Francis.

Following their founder's advice, Franciscan preachers had long included heavy doses of moral exhortation in their sermons. Prior to the outbreak of Protestant reform in Germany, they were some of the most outspoken and controversial critics in Europe of the moral laxity of the clergy. Their stress, in France, on the need to reform the episcopate foresaw the measures of the Council of Trent itself.[16] What was new after Trent, however, was the methodical discipline with which the Church sought to structure and order its own hierarchy, and the degree to which each member of that hierarchy and of the Church at large was expected to mirror both outwardly and inwardly that discipline and order.

Public preaching continued to be one of the most important weapons in the battle to enforce order among what the Catholic clergy perceived to be an often unruly flock, prone both to superstition and immoral conduct.[17] The war, however, was not concerned only with eliminating these problems. The presence, by the mid-sixteenth century, of a successful Protestant movement in Germany, Switzerland, England, and even France inevitably endowed Catholic interpretations of the traditional "Church Militant" with new meaning.[18] Henceforth, few Catholic preachers would pass up the opportunity to attack Luther, Calvin, and their "heretical" followers, comparing them to famous heretics of the early

15. Ibid., 305. ". . . docendo ea, quae scire omnibus necessarium est ad salutem, annunciandoque eis cum brevitate et facilitate sermonis vitia, quae eos declinare, et virtutes, quas sectari oportet, ut poenam aeternam evadere et coelestem gloriam consequi valeant."

16. John W. O'Malley, S.J., "Saint Charles Borromeo and the 'Praecipuum Episcoporum Munus': His Place in the History of Preaching," in *San Carlo Borromeo: Catholic Reform and Ecclesiastical Politics in the Second Half of the Sixteenth Century*, ed. John M. Headley and John B. Tomaro (Washington: Folger Shakespeare Library, 1988), 141.

17. Frederick McGinness, *Right Thinking and Sacred Oratory in Counter-Reformation Rome* (Princeton: Princeton University Press, 1995), 29–30. McGinness finds a new emphasis on the dignity of the preaching office in the preaching manuals published for Catholic preachers in the late sixteenth century.

18. Ibid., 110–20. According to McGinness, sermons given at the papal court in the sixteenth century present the Church as an army under siege; Carlo Borromeo hoped to create dioceses organized to resemble well-organized armies, trained to follow their superiors.

Church and highlighting the differences between Protestant errors and authoritative Catholic tradition and truth.

Of course, an integral part of Catholic tradition and of popular piety had always been the cult of the saints and, above all, the special devotion accorded to the Virgin Mary. Because Protestant theologians of every sort sought to undermine the theological basis for prayers to the saints, while their supporters often dismantled the cult in more direct and concrete ways, Catholic preachers had to defend the Virgin and saints publicly and forcefully. Yet the particular emphasis chosen by the preachers revealed that their understanding of the faith was being altered by the social and religious pressures of the day. The Virgin Mary who emerges from Catholic sermons of the late sixteenth and early seventeenth centuries is in many ways a more individualized and distant figure than the woman whose images, relics, and bodily participation in all aspects of the life of Jesus had caused her to seem so tangible in the context of fifteenth-century devotion. She will become instead a model for post-Tridentine Christians to imitate: silent, self-controlled, and obedient.

There is no doubt that Catholic preaching, during and after Trent, felt the impact of Italian humanism in both the style and content of the sermons that were delivered. In accordance with the decree of Trent as well as most popular preaching manuals,[19] preachers sought to inspire in the people a zeal for virtue and an abhorrence for vice. Catholic preachers found in the humanist revival of classical rhetoric and in their ethical understanding of Christianity an approach that was well suited to the goals of current popular preaching. To a greater or lesser degree, Catholic preachers at the papal court and throughout Europe constructed their

19. Frederick McGinness, *Rhetoric and Counter-Reformation Rome: Sacred Oratory and the Construction of the Catholic World View, 1563–1621* (Ann Arbor, Mich.: University Microfilms International, 1982), 198–99. Some of the most important preaching manuals were written by Carlo Borromeo, *Instructiones pastorum ad concionandum* (1583); Gabriel Paleotti, *Instruttione per li predicatori destinati alle ville, or terre* (1578); Francesco Borja, *Ecclesiastes sive ratione concionandi instructio* (c. 1572); and Robert Bellarmine, *De ratione formandae concionis* (1593). See also McGinness, *Right Thinking*, 50–52, for other important preaching manuals. McGinness emphasizes the importance of both St. Augustine's *De doctrina christiana* and Erasmus' 1536 *Ecclesiastes, sive de ratione concionandi libri IV* for influencing contemporary preaching manuals.

sermons according to the rules of epideictic oratory, the rhetoric of praise and blame.[20] People were encouraged to model their spiritual lives on the examples of Christ, Mary, and the saints, whose perfect conformity to all Christian virtues was praised as the highest ideal to which any Christian could aspire. Those who imitated the lives of the saints would acquire virtue and gain heaven. Those who chose instead to follow a path of sin and vice, not to mention heresy, could expect to suffer eternally in hell. Although the saints continued to function in an important way as intercessors, their primary role in many sermons came to be that of a model of virtue.[21]

One of the expert propagators of this new view of sainthood was Erasmus, who in his many popular and widely read works suggested that the most important function of the saints was to serve as an inspiration to others. Indeed Erasmus was one of the most important and influential men working to reshape Catholic Christian piety in the sixteenth century; his work was used as well by even more radical Protestants, who embraced Erasmus' preference for the inner life of faith and used it as a reason for abolishing the cult of the saints altogether.[22]

The clergy who were asking people to re-make themselves according to certain holy models of virtue embodied in the saints were in fact pre-

20. McGinness, *Right Thinking*, 32. See also John M. McManamon, S.J., "Renaissance Preaching: Theory and Practice. A Holy Thursday Sermon of Aurelio Brandolini," *Viator* 10 (1979): 355–73. Larissa Taylor's study of French popular sermons prior to the religious wars finds that while the popularity of humanism helped create a simpler, more eloquent style of preaching and caused preachers to rely less on extra-biblical sources, the content of the sermons remained the same. The emphasis both before and after the advent of humanism was the content of orthodox Catholic doctrine. See Larissa Juliet Taylor, "The Influence of Humanism on Post-Reformation Catholic Preachers in France," *Renaissance Quarterly* 50 (1997): 119–35.

21. McGinness, *Rhetoric*, 212–13; and John Bossy, *Christianity in the West, 1400–1700* (Oxford: Oxford University Press, 1985), 96. See also Barbara B. Diefendorf, *Beneath the Cross: Catholics and Huguenots in Sixteenth-Century Paris* (New York: Oxford University Press, 1991), 42. According to Diefendorf, the Catholic catechists and preachers whom she has studied usually portrayed the saints as role models and intercessors, not necessarily connected to their relics or images.

22. See especially Carlos M. N. Eire, "Erasmus as a Critic of Late Medieval Piety," in *War against the Idols: The Reformation of Worship from Erasmus to Calvin* (Cambridge: Cambridge University Press, 1986), 28–53.

suming a high degree of individual self-awareness and interior piety within each of their hearers. What they intended was that every Christian
would do more than conform to a set of common beliefs and moral
expectations. They must also acquire, first, the spiritual sensitivity to
detect and ideally to combat any personal inclinations to sin, and second,
the mental discipline to order their thoughts in ways pleasing to God. The
inspiration for this type of spirituality had already spread through much
of Northern Catholic Europe during the fifteenth century in the movement known as the Devotio Moderna, whose members, the Brethren of
the Common Life, encouraged Christians to model their lives according
to the life of Christ and to devote themselves to the discipline of mental
prayer. Thomas à Kempis's *Imitation of Christ,* the most famous example
of the Brethren's piety, was one of the most popular devotional books of
the fifteenth and early sixteenth centuries.[23]

The perfect embodiment of this Catholic form of interior prayer was
ultimately achieved in the *Spiritual Exercises* of St. Ignatius Loyola, first
published at Rome in 1548.[24] A person who participated in the *Exercises*
should come under the inspiration of God, having his or her heart firmly
fixed on God and resolved, with the aid of grace, to follow God in all
areas of life.[25]

Of course, belief in the freedom of individuals to fashion their lives as
they chose had also been a mark of fifteenth-century Italian humanist
thought. Giovanni Pico della Mirandola's "De hominis dignitate" of 1486
celebrated the God-given ability of the will to overcome seeming human
limitations and to shape the human person according to an infinite array
of possible selves.

23. Lucien Febvre and Henri-Jean Martin, *The Coming of the Book: The Impact of Printing,*
1450–1800 (London: Verso, 1984), 251, 287. After the Bible, the *Imitation of Christ* was "the
most frequently reprinted work" of the day, as popular at the beginning of the sixteenth
century as it had ever been.

24. A. G. Dickens, *The Counter Reformation* (New York: W. W. Norton, 1979), 51, 78. See
also John W. O'Malley, S.J., *The First Jesuits* (Cambridge: Harvard University Press, 1993),
37–50, for a summary of the contents and intent of the *Exercises.* O'Malley points out that
the *Exercises* were devoted to interior prayer and inspiration to such an extent that they
were sharply criticized by some in the Church as advocating a spirituality much like that of
the Castilian "alumbrados," who claimed superior spiritual enlightenment and disdained
traditional Catholic piety.

25. O'Malley, *First Jesuits,* 42.

As priests began to expect their parishioners to embrace the spiritual discipline which the clerical hierarchy was imposing on its own members, the sacrament of penance changed, too, to meet this expectation. We have seen that newer approaches to confession were requiring a stricter, more interior examination of sin. Gradually, a transformation in the very meaning of penance began to take place. The emphasis, as John Bossy describes it, now lay not on the "restitution of exterior relations" with the Church and with one's neighbor, but on "changing the self." Personal discipline prior to confession was considered to be preferable and more effective than performing a penance afterward. Those penances that were assigned were to have a "medicinal" effect to cure the soul, rather than make amends for sin.[26]

The high degree of literacy among members of the Brethren of the Common Life, the Italian humanists, and the reforming Catholic clergy of the sixteenth century would have given them the mental tools necessary to build the acute self-awareness required for thorough self-modeling and change. It could also have contributed to their assumption that others shared that self-awareness, for the literate culture and traditions which shaped both clerical piety and European educational structures had long presumed the desirability of extensive reading and meditation on the Scriptures, the lives of the saints, or the exemplary lives of famous persons as a means of finding the inspiration for living a moral life in the present.

Stephen Greenblatt, however, has suggested that there were addition-

---

26. Bossy, *Christianity in the West*, 126–27. An interesting fact is that the period in which this more privatized and personal view of sin developed is also the one which experienced the triumph of the Ten Commandments and the gradual demotion of the Seven Deadly Sins as a guide to Christian morality (38). The Seven Deadly Sins define sin according to internal states or inclinations such as lust or avarice, whereas the ethical portion of the Ten Commandments, with the exception of the commandment on coveting, deals primarily with exterior acts, such as adultery, murder, or theft. The general desire during the period to return to the authoritative ancient texts was undoubtedly a factor. It is also true that the Ten Commandments put the focus on an individual love of God. The widespread printing of Scripture beginning in 1450 would then have reinforced the value of the Ten Commandments by conferring on them a sense of permanence or unchangeability lacking in more traditional moral formulations. Still, the Seven Deadly Sins seem to dovetail more neatly with the goal of interior discipline and the acquisition of virtue. It was Jesus, after all, who defined murder in terms of hatred and adultery in terms of lust.

al social pressures in the sixteenth century specifically that not only facilitated personal self-fashioning but made it a virtual requirement for those
who were forced to participate in the public realm of government and
politics. In the first chapter of *Renaissance Self-Fashioning*, Greenblatt presents Thomas More as a man deeply troubled by the role he must play in
his public life. As a government official, he was constantly expected to
enter into the glittering, powerful, but morally inane world of the Tudor
court. It was a setting in which a brilliant public display of opulent material wealth masked the harsh and often deadly reality of political maneu-
vering.

The contrast between the values of this public world and More's own
private and deeply held religious beliefs necessitated a mental ability to
distance his public from his private self if he were to keep his sanity.
More, then, constructed a witty, cunning, and urbane self for his forays
into the political arena, a self which he was capable of entering into fully
when the circumstances demanded. It was a self which required enormous personal energy to maintain. As often as possible, therefore, he
retreated to his private world in a building set apart even from his country house at Chelsea, where he could read, meditate, pray, and perhaps
confess his sense of duplicity to God.[27]

Of course the creation of a private, interior world was not the exclu-
sive preserve of the early modern period. Scholars have long claimed that
the Twelfth-Century Renaissance helped foster a new awareness of the
individual;[28] and Brian Stock points out that already by the eleventh century, the growing proliferation of texts was beginning to have a profound

27. Stephen Greenblatt, *Renaissance Self-Fashioning: From More to Shakespeare* (Chicago:
University of Chicago Press, 1979), 45–46.

28. For what is, perhaps, the classic statement of this thesis, see Colin Morris, *The Discovery of the Individual 1050–1200*, Medieval Academy Reprints for Teaching, no. 19 (Toronto:
University of Toronto Press, in association with the Medieval Academy of America, 1995).
In his conclusion, Morris states, "The discovery of the individual was one of the most
important cultural developments in the years between 1050 and 1200. It was not confined
to any one group of thinkers. Its central features may be found in many different circles: a
concern with self-discovery; an interest in the relations between people, and in the role of
the individual within society; an assessment of people by their inner intentions rather than
by their external acts."

impact on society, even on those individuals who were not literate themselves.[29] It is therefore not surprising to discover that even persons who
lack literacy skills but are influenced by the values and thought structures
of a literate society are capable of developing an interior awareness of the
self.[30]

Greenblatt acknowledges that religious leaders had been advising meditative retreats for some time, at least since San Bernardino of Siena. Now,
however, there were additional pressures which made such a retreat less a
spiritual option and more a mental necessity. He argues,

As the public, civic world made increasing claims on men's lives, so, correspondingly, men turned in upon themselves, sought privacy, withdrew for privileged
moments from urban pressures. This dialectic of engagement and detachment is
among those forces that generated the intense individuality that, since Burck-
hardt, has been recognized as one of the legacies of the Renaissance . . . it now
seems clear that both secular and religious impulses contributed to the same psy-
chic structure.[31]

Secular governments, however, were not the only institutions placing
growing demands for obedience and outward conformity on their public
servants. The Catholic Church in the sixteenth century was also putting
more and more pressure on its clergy to conform in every conceivable

29. Brian Stock, *The Implications of Literacy: Written Language and Models of Interpretation
in the Eleventh and Twelfth Centuries* (Princeton: Princeton University Press, 1983), 8–14. See
above, Introduction, n. 41.

30. See above the discussion of Margery Kempe in the Introduction, n. 68. Also important in this context would be St. Catherine of Siena. Although Catherine was not completely illiterate, she came to such literacy as she possessed rather late, and her letters, in
particular, bear the immediacy and the often wandering style of someone more familiar
with the rhythms of oral communication. Catherine nevertheless had not only developed
an intense interior awareness of her own "interior cell" to which she could retreat, but she
recommended that the others to whom she wrote should do the same. Writing to the
abbess of Santa Marta in Siena, Catherine advised, "I don't think it is possible to have virtue
or the fullness of grace without dwelling within the cell of our heart and soul." And in a
letter to Brother Tommaso dalla Fonte, she describes God the Father saying "'Dearest children, if you wish to discover and experience the effects of my will, dwell within the cell of
your soul.'" See Catherine of Siena, *The Letters of St. Catherine of Siena*, vol. 1, trans.
Suzanne Noffke, O.P., Medieval and Renaissance Texts and Studies, no. 52 (Binghamton,
N.Y.: Medieval and Renaissance Texts and Studies, 1988), 38, 44.

31. Greenblatt, *Renaissance Self-Fashioning*, 46.

detail to the guidelines provided by Trent and by the papal curia. Frederick McGinness has examined the sermons delivered before the pope during the height of Catholic reform and finds that their central message was the "revocatio ad disciplinam," a recall to discipline in body and in mind. Only through discipline and obedience to the Church's dictates could advances be made against the Devil and his forces for disorder which were wreaking havoc in the world. It was a battle which began with the inner life of each person and grew to encompass the broader spectrum of ecclesiastical and secular politics.[32]

As public and influential figures, preachers were to be especially careful of the impression they made on their hearers. Preaching manuals were very clear in telling them which topics were suitable for their sermons, how they should be dealt with, and which subjects should be avoided. Carlo Borromeo provided rules governing what preachers should eat, how they should walk, how to hold their head, where it was permissible to look, how to speak, and how to dress. Chapter 26 of his preaching manual was titled "De voce, et corporis motu." It was a catalog detailing both the acceptable and unacceptable physical motions which might accompany the act of preaching.[33] The range of dramatic possibilities open to the preacher was drastically curtailed when compared to the freedom of medieval preachers. The era of the "free preachers," who, prior to the Reformation, spoke as they chose to royalty and commoner alike, was at an end.[34]

Even when they themselves were the pragmatic advocates of conformity and discipline, it is nevertheless easy to see how men such as Borromeo or Robert Bellarmine, a Cardinal of the Church, might have welcomed the chance to retreat, like Thomas More, into an inner piety which could express their religious individuality and serve as a means of escape from their stressful public lives. They were, in fact, in an ambiguous position. The more private devotional life which they sought to develop in

---

32. McGinness, *Rhetoric*, 300–301, 323–25.

33. Ibid., 229–30; McGinness, *Right Thinking*, 42–43.

34. The phrase is taken from Antony Méray, *La vie au temps des libres precheurs ou les devanciers de Luther et de Rabelais*, 2 vols., 2d ed. (Paris: A. Claudin, 1878).

their hearers could become the vehicle for ecclesiastical control of the most intimate aspects of a person's faith, or it could become the final stage for the creation of a personal self, distanced from the corporate and public expectations of either Church or state. In the end, however, the outward discipline of the Church was likely to remain effective in either case. Those who retreat inwardly to deal with their problems are much less likely to rebel overtly against established authority.[35]

In the context of the Church's renewed emphasis on discipline after Trent, the Virgin Mary became the ultimate example of the type of Christian life preachers hoped to inspire in the members of their congregations. Her physical motherhood of Christ was an undisputed fact of Christian history, so she would continue to be praised as the one woman singled out by God to bestow humanity on the eternal Word. But her virtues of humility, absolute obedience, and even her "spiritual" motherhood of Christ began to assume at least an equal importance with her bodily maternity. Finally, Mary's continued virginity during and after the birth of Christ, symbol of all that might seem to differentiate Catholic and Protestant views on human sexuality, assumed a centrality in public sermons which it had not had since the earliest years of the medieval period. In spite of what one might think from reading Catholic sermons, however, some Protestant leaders retained acceptance of Mary's perpetual virginity. Most Protestants were more concerned with what they believed to be the proper nature of worship and of religious reality than with this issue.

Of course the Protestant critique of Catholicism, and of Marian devotion specifically, was not monolithic. It included a broad spectrum of beliefs and liturgical approaches ranging from Luther's somewhat more conservative reform to the iconoclastic fervor of men such as Andreas Karlstadt, Ulrich Zwingli, and Thomas Muntzer. Luther, for instance, continued all his life to believe in Mary's perpetual virginity; and while he

---

35. David Warren Sabean, *Power in the Blood: Popular Culture and Village Discourse in Early Modern Germany* (Cambridge: Cambridge University Press, 1984), chap. 1 and 206–9; and Kristen B. Neuschel, *Word of Honor: Interpreting Noble Culture in Sixteenth-Century France* (Ithaca, N.Y.: Cornell University Press, 1989), 194.

eventually rejected the Immaculate Conception, he also continued to accept that Mary was purified of all sin when she conceived Jesus. Luther was likewise inclined to view the Virgin as an intercessor.[36] Even the more radical reformers, Zwingli and John Calvin, accepted Mary's perpetual virginity but rejected most other aspects of devotion to her, believing them to be the result of human invention rather than a response to divine command.[37]

Still, for the most part, sermons in praise of Mary delivered after the Council of Trent were considerably more subdued in their language than those of the fifteenth century, and Protestant criticism of the "excesses" of late medieval Marian piety was certainly one of the reasons for a more careful treatment of Mary's role. The Jesuits, in particular, founded in 1534, worked to create a Mariology that would answer effectively the most strident criticisms of Marian devotion while preserving those aspects of her cult which were necessary in the context of Catholic theology and tradition.[38] If Catholic preachers wanted to keep their members safely within the fold of the Roman Church and win back converts from various Protestant groups, they would have to answer Protestant charges that Catholic worship accorded more praise to Mary than to her son; they would also need to prove the value and authenticity of devotion to Mary and the saints through arguments supplied by Scripture and the ancient traditions of the Church.

"This Singular Temple of God"

One of the safest means to praise Mary effectively was to single out the one dignity which Protestants as well as Catholics were agreed belonged

36. Hilda Graef, *Mary: A History of Doctrine and Devotion*, 2 vols. (New York: Sheed and Ward, 1964), 2:7–11.

37. Ibid., 2:12–14; Eire, *War Against the Idols*, 73–86, 195–233. For further information regarding various Protestant teachings concerning the Virgin, see Graef, *Mary*, 2:1–16; Kenneth F. Dougherty, "Our Lady and the Protestants," in *Mariology*, ed. Juniper B. Carol (Milwaukee: Bruce Publishing Company, 1961), 3:422–39; Léon Halkin, "La Mariologie d'Erasme," *Archive for Reformation History* 68 (1977): 32–55; Peter Newman Brooks, "A Lily Ungilded: Martin Luther, the Virgin Mary and the Saints," *Journal of Religious History* 13 (1984): 136–49; and J. A. Ross Mackenzie, "Calvin and the Calvinists on Mary," *One in Christ* 16 (1980): 68–78.

38. Graef, *Mary*, 2:27.

to her alone, her motherhood of Christ. As had been the case in the late Middle Ages, Mary will make a brief appearance as Jesus' mother in sermons where she is mentioned nowhere else, as she did in St. Peter Canisius' Epiphany sermons.[39] It is this privilege of divine maternity, said St. Lawrence of Brindisi, which is the root and origin of all her other praises and titles.[40] There could, of course, be only one physical mother of Christ, and Catholic preachers enjoyed pointing out to Protestants that this alone set the Virgin apart from and above all other human beings and angels as well. "There were many patriarchs, many prophets, many kings," said St. Robert Bellarmine, "many apostles, many martyrs, many virgins; but only Mary was mother, virgin, and Mother of God, this was her privilege alone."[41] The Franciscan preacher Francis Panigarola praised the "incomprehensible mystery of divinity and humanity, creator and creature . . . conception and purity, of spotlessness and pregnancy, maternity and integrity, virginity and giving birth," which alone belonged to the "Holy and immaculate Virgin."[42] It became popular to adapt Hebrews 1:5 to speak of Mary's unique honor. Christopher Cheffontaines announced, "For to which of the angels or Archangels has God ever said, you are my mother."[43]

Many of the themes associated with Mary's motherhood which were the favorites of medieval preachers were continued in late sixteenth and early seventeenth-century sermons. Most preachers still referred specifically to Mary's "very pure blood" as the substance from which Christ's

39. Canisius, *Meditationes*, 2,1:111, 122.

40. Lawrence of Brindisi, *Opera omnia*, 1:232. "Haec enim singularis et praecipua est laus Mariae quod vera dignaque Mater extiterit et Genitrix naturalis Unigeniti Filii Dei."

41. Bellarmine, *Opera omnia*, 5:381. "Multi enim patriarchae, multi prophetae, multi reges, multi apostoli, multi martyres, multae virgines fuerint: at mater, et virgo et Mater Dei, sola Maria fuit, ejus hoc solius privilegium est."

42. Francis Panigarola, "Predica di Maria Vergine, e Madre" (Rome: 1589), 211r. "Mistero incomprensibile, di divinità, e humanità, di Creatore, e creatura, . . . ; Concettione, e purità, mondezza, e gravidanza, maternità, e integrità; Virginitade, e parto. Sancta, et immaculata virginitas; anzi, sancta, et immaculata virgo."

43. Christopher Cheffontaines, "Sermo de Virginis Mariae laudibus et honore, qui in qualibet eius festivitate haberi ad populum potest," in *Novae illustrationes Christianae fidei*, pt. 2 (Paris: Sittart, 1586), 39v. "Cui enim angelorum aut Archangelorum dixit aliquando Deus, mater mea es tu, uti huic eum sepius dixisse, matrem suam dulciter illam vocando, certissimum est?"

body was formed. St. Lawrence and St. Robert Bellarmine stressed that Christ's body, formed from Mary's blood, was therefore a real human body and not some sort of phantom.[44] They perhaps had in mind certain extreme radical groups in Italy and Poland who were denying the actual materiality of Christ's flesh, claiming instead that he had possessed an eternally created "celestial flesh."[45] Even Protestant reformers stressed Mary's motherhood of Christ for the same reason.[46] The phrase appears most often, however, where it would be expected, in conventional discussions of the Incarnation. St. François de Sales exclaimed,

> . . . what greater happiness, I ask you, my dear souls, would a woman be able to experience, than to have carried in her womb the one who is equal to the Eternal Father and whom the heavens cannot comprehend, and to whom the Holy Virgin has received the honor to have given her very pure blood to form this sacred humanity of our dear Lord and Savior.[47]

Mary's close bodily connection to Jesus for the nine months of her pregnancy continued to inspire Catholic preachers to speak of her with the traditional Old Testament metaphors common in the Middle Ages. Her womb was called the "City of God," "temple of the Holy Spirit," the "Ark of the Covenant," and the "Holy of Holies."[48] St. Peter Canisius intentionally attributes his praises of Mary's womb and breasts to the tradition of the Church.[49] Christopher Cheffontaines railed at those who

44. Lawrence of Brindisi, *Opera omnia*, 1:64. "Neque enim ipsa Christo phantasticum dedit, non verum, et naturale corpus, ut impii nugabantur Manichaei, sed verum, sed naturale, ex suis purissimis sanguinibus, divina Spiritus Sancti opera, in suo ipsius utero formatum"; Bellarmine, *Opera omnia*, 5:171.

45. Bossy, *Christianity in the West*, 109.

46. Jaroslav Pelikan, *Mary Through the Centuries: Her Place in the History of Culture* (New Haven: Yale University Press, 1996), 156–57.

47. De Sales, *Oeuvres complètes*, 11:492–93. "Car quel plus grand bon-heur, je vous prie, mes cheres ames, pouvoit avoir une femme, que d'avoir porté dans son ventre celuy que est esgal au Pere eternal, et que les cieux ne pouvent comprendre? Et que la Ste Vierge a receu d'honneur, d'avoie donné son plus pur sang pour former cette sacrée humanité de nostre cher Sauveur et maistre"; Bellarmine, *Opera omnia*, 5:170.

48. Bellarmine, *Opera omnia*, 5:170; de Sales, *Oeuvres complètes*, 11:298; Lawrence of Brindisi, *Opera omnia*, 1:196–97, 314.

49. Canisius, *Meditationes*, 2,1:226. "Tantoque constantius veteri ecclesiae catholicae instituto me conformabo, ut castissimum Deiparae uterum et sanctissima eius ubera celebrem."

refused to honor Mary with the "Ave," as though she were unworthy of praise. When the Angel Gabriel declared "The Lord is with thee," he proved her worthy.

What more could be added to her praise? With what greater honor could God treat someone than by dignifying them with his presence? She was worthy for the fullness of divinity to dwell bodily in her womb for nine months.[50]

"Woe to those," he says, "who dishonor this singular temple of God."[51]

None of the sixteenth century preachers in this study can surpass St. Lawrence of Brindisi for the amount of praise he showers on the body of Mary. His sermons are the most like those of the later Middle Ages in this and in all respects. The persistent authority of San Bernardino of Siena in the Franciscan order may have been responsible for this. St. Lawrence was familiar with San Bernardino because he quoted his famous statement that the Virgin Mary "was able to do more for God than God could to for himself."[52] The Franciscans were also the medieval order traditionally responsible for emphasizing the purity and prerogatives of the Virgin Mary. St. Lawrence was simply continuing this custom when he said that the womb of Mary was "not only the true temple of God and treasury of every grace and holiness in the incarnation of Christ, but also a true Paradise of glory."[53]

One of St. Lawrence's most creative developments of the theme of Mary's womb as "house of God" is to see it as also a temple of sacrifice,

---

50. Cheffontaines, "Sermo de Virginis Mariae," 15v. "Et cum dignam dicit, quae sui cordis hospito, hospitem deum recipiat, cum deum secum esse asserit; quid amplius ad eius laudes addi posset? Quo maiori quemquam honore afficere Deus potest, quam sua eum praesentia dignando? Ipsa divinitatis plenitudo corporaliter in huius per novem menses utero habitare dignate est."

51. Ibid., 36r. "Vae qui sic singulare hoc dei templum inhonoratis."

52. Lawrence of Brindisi, *Opera omnia*, 1:199. Harvey Hamburgh mentions the persistent authority of San Bernardino when accounting for the ongoing popularity of portraits of Mary fainting at the cross in Italian art. See Harvey E. Hamburgh, "The Problem of 'Lo Spasimo' of the Virgin in Cinquecento Paintings of the 'Descent from the Cross,'" *Sixteenth Century Journal* 12 (1981), 57.

53. Lawrence of Brindisi, *Opera omnia*, 1: 215. ". . . dicam plenitudinem gratiae Christi in ventre Mariae. . . . dicam de plenitudine scientiae. . . . dicam de plenitudine gloriae, nam . . . ita ut venter Virginis non solum verum Dei templum fuerit et thesaurus omnis gratia et sanctitatis in Christi incarnatione, sed etiam verus paradisus gloriae."

where Christ the true High Priest offered his humanity to God for the salvation of the world. Mary, herself, was a place of prayer and sacrifice.

The house of God is a house of prayer in which Christ the High Priest prayed to the Father. . . . The house of God is a house of sacrifice. . . . in the house of God, sacrifices for sins, for making peace with enemies, and burnt offerings with oblations are offered to God. The High Priest not only carries incense but also the blood of the sacrifice into the Holy of Holies. In the first instant of his conception, Christ knew not only the benefits given to him but also the will of God for the salvation and redemption of the human race through the passion and death of the cross; here and for this reason he offered himself to the Father, to the passion and death of the cross for the salvation of the world.[54]

There is nothing quite like this in the sermons of any of the other sixteenth-century preachers in this study, Franciscan or Jesuit. St. Lawrence's words could have come straight from the late Middle Ages, reminding his congregation that Mary's blood formed the humanity of Christ which was then offered by her son for human salvation. The other preachers are slow to make so tangible a connection between the contributions of mother and son. For the most part, they represent to a greater degree than St. Lawrence the newer trends in Catholic spirituality. Also, perhaps, sensitive to Protestant criticisms, most of them want to distinguish as much as possible between the lesser contribution of Mary to salvation and the supreme act of Jesus.

St. Lawrence is also known for his extravagant treatment of the marriage between the Virgin Mary and God. Although the Council of Trent warned against superstition and the use of images that might lead to false doctrine,[55] there was enough inspiration in the Song of Songs and in

54. Ibid., 149–50. "Domus Dei, domus orationis, in qua Summus Sacerdos Christus oravit ad Patrem. . . . Domus Dei, domus sacrificii . . . In domo Dei offerebantur sacrificia pro peccatis, hostiae pacificae et holocausta cum oblationibus; summus sacerdos in Sancta Sanctorum non tantum incensum, sed etiam sanguinem sacrificii deferebat. Christus in primo instanti suae conceptionis, non tantum cognovit beneficium sibi collatum, sed etiam voluntatem Dei de redemptione et salute generis humani per crucis passionem, et mortem; hinc ex tunc Patri se obtulit ad passionem et mortem crucis pro salute mundi." Gerson suggested this in the fifteenth century, but did not develop the theme of sacrifice quite so fully. See above, Chapter 1, n. 8.

55. The decree concerning the invocation of saints, veneration of their relics, and sacred images was enacted in session twenty-five, 1563. Norman P. Tanner, S.J., ed., *Decrees of the*

Catholic tradition to allow St. Lawrence free rein with his imagination. He was able to declare that when God beheld Mary he was "captured by her beauty and grace and asked for her in marriage through that most honest legate and nuncio, the Archangel Gabriel."[56] He likewise asserted that as the spouse of God, Mary was a "garden of delights and a paradise of pleasure."[57] The Virgin certainly appears as the mother of Christ frequently enough in St. Lawrence's sermons, but the marriage metaphor is much more central to his presentation of Mary than to that of any of the other contemporary preachers.

Aside from St. Lawrence, only St. Robert Bellarmine and St. François de Sales, among the preachers studied here, provide detailed discussion of the marriage of God and the Virgin. Bellarmine says that God sent the Archangel Gabriel to obtain Mary's consent to the marriage since the consent of the bride is required before any marriage can occur.[58] St. François is certain that God bestowed on Mary the divine kiss, causing her to conceive Christ, at the moment when she consented to the words of Gabriel.[59] Both preachers also continue to refer to Mary as the "enclosed garden" familiar to so many medieval preachers.[60]

St. François, however, did not necessarily think first of Mary when he considered the theme of a divine marriage. In an interesting passage in a

---

Ecumenical Councils, vol. 2 (London: Sheed and Ward, and Washington: Georgetown University Press, 1990), 774–76.

56. Lawrence of Brindisi, *Opera omnia*, 1:108. ". . . requisivit eam in matrimonium per honestissimum legatum et internuntium per Gabrielem Archangelum."

57. Ibid., 122. "Sic hodie Deus Virginem Sanctissimam desponsavit, sibique matrimonio copulavit, quoniam eius veluti amore captus fuit, quoniam Virginis pulcritudo summopere ei placuit: Ave gratia plena . . . invenisti gratiam apud Dominum; ut esset hortus deliciarum, paradisus voluptatis Dei." See also Graef, *Mary*, 2:27. The marriage theme is so prominent in St. Lawrence's sermons that Hilda Graef is ready to say that he considered Mary to be more the spouse of God than the mother of Christ. St. Lawrence was even capable of using the very concrete language of dowries and physical union to describe the marriage (1:90). "Sic Deus, volens Mariam sibi sponsam matrimonio copulare, dotavit eam omni plenitudine gratiae et divitiarum coelestium."

58. Bellarmine, *Opera omnia*, 5:369.

59. De Sales, *Oeuvres complètes*, 10:284–85. "Mais quand fust-ce que ce divin baiser fut donné à ceste espouse incomparable? Ce fust aussi-tost qu'elle eut dit à l'ange cette parole tant desirée: Fiat mihi secundum verbum tuum."

60. Ibid., 300; Bellarmine, *Opera omnia*, 5:70.

sermon for the Assumption of Mary, he develops the story of David and Goliath as an allegory for the battle between Christ and the Devil. David inquired about the reward for killing Goliath, and was not content with money only. He wanted to marry the king's daughter, who was also part of the promised reward. So it was with Christ. When he was preparing to come into the world to slay the Devil, he wanted not only a celestial king-ship but the king's daughter as well. Anyone familiar with medieval ser-mon literature would now be waiting for the inevitable reference to Mary and Christ's love for her. Instead, the bride St. François has in mind for Christ is the glory of the Resurrection.[61] All in all, St. Lawrence is the only one of these preachers who preserves in its entirety the medieval approach to the marriage of God and the Virgin Mary in the Incarnation.

The style of St. Lawrence's sermons also differed considerably from that of most of the other preachers. More than the others, his sermons retain the sense that the preacher must aid his hearers, helping them to remember his major points through the frequent repetition of key words and phrases. If he wishes to stress Mary's holiness, over and over he will say, "hail Mary, full of grace." When it is her closeness to God that is important, Gabriel's words, "The Lord is with thee," recur at regular intervals throughout the sermon. It is true that, even in the late sixteenth century, many Franciscan sermons have a more popular style which seems to be directed to large groups of townspeople rather than to cler-gy or religious specifically. Franciscans do not assume their hearers to be well versed in theology and philosophy. Still, the entire mood of St. Lawrence's sermons is reminiscent of a San Bernardino of Siena or a Jean Gerson and is easily distinguished even from the style of his contempo-raries in the Franciscan order, Christopher Cheffontaines and Francis Panigarola.

Since we know that St. Lawrence of Brindisi was one of the most pop-

---

61. De Sales, *Oeuvres complètes*, 11:343–44. "Mais Nostre-Seigneur n'eust esté content de cela, si l'on n'eust encore adjousté, que le roy avoit promis qu'il luy donneroit sa fille en mariage; or la fille du roy, c'est à dire la fille de Dieu, n'eust autre que la gloire. . . . la gloire qu'on luy promettoit, estoit la glorification et resurrection de son corps." Because this was a sermon on the Assumption, St. François adds that Christ also asked for the resurrection of his mother's body.

ular and effective Catholic preachers of his day, capable of conducting successful preaching missions in several languages,[62] it must also be true that there was still a widespread popular desire to hear the kind of sermons that he delivered at the close of the sixteenth century. Reforming Catholic preachers may have been trying to create a new, more restrained and spiritualized Marian piety, but their prospects for success at the level of the local congregation were likely to be tempered by the continued presence of older forms of devotion.

What was largely missing in the post-Tridentine Catholic sermons examined here, including those of St. Lawrence, was the sense, so common in medieval sermons, of present participation by the people or by Christ, Mary, and the saints, in the events of sacred history. We have seen that medieval preachers encouraged the people to enter into the events being portrayed. There was a clear sense that the hearers could participate in sacred history as they listened to impassioned dialogue between the preacher and the Biblical characters. Historical events were carried forward in time to become the contemporary drama of real life with immediate consequences for those present. An obvious example of this is that the people were told on Good Friday that the Virgin, always ready to hear their prayers, was too distraught to respond on that day. Bernardino of Busti had been informed of this by the Virgin herself. There may some disagreement among scholars concerning the overall effectiveness of medieval sermons, particularly those delivered by inexperienced men. There can be no doubt, however, that in the hands of capable preachers, the medieval sermon's use of dramatic dialogue could become a powerful means of delivering an experience of the Biblical stories.

Effective conversations between the preacher and his hearers, between the preacher and the characters of the story, or even among the characters themselves have almost completely disappeared, however, in the later sermons. The speaker addresses his words to his congregation and their only immediate involvement is to answer silently whatever rhetorical questions the preacher might pose. Occasionally, dialogue can occur.

---

62. Anscar Zawart, *The History of Franciscan Preaching and of Franciscan Preachers (1209–1927): A Bio-bibliographical Study* (New York: J. F. Wagner, 1928), 448–49.

When preachers do want to put words into the mouths of the Biblical characters, however, they preface them with a statement such as "When Gabriel said this, he was really saying . . ."; or "Christ said this because he wanted to tell the people. . . ." It is clear to the hearers that the preacher is inventing words and the overall effect is usually more contrived than in medieval sermons. The listener is distanced from the character who is speaking. And even though the people are addressed as "distinguished hearers" or the more familiar "dear Christians" or "dear souls," there is likewise a sense of distance between preacher and people. The drama of sacred history has become truly that, "history," something which took place in the past. One obvious result of this historical emphasis would have been to distance the Virgin and other Biblical persons from the present world of the hearers.

This method of preaching is generally consistent with the post-Tridentine view of the preacher as someone who should maintain an air of authority over his hearers. He was charged with presenting to them the approved version of the faith; any attempt to become too much like one of the people would impair the impression they should have of him as someone possessed of superior knowledge, endowed by God with a special grace to preach his word.

There is also, perhaps, another factor involved here. These sermons were composed and delivered more than a century after the invention of printing. Among persons who communicate mostly through the spoken word, the sense of time can be radically different from the perception of time common to a print culture. The sense of the present, generated by the act of speech, works to incorporate even past events into present experience.[63] Printed materials, on the other hand, foster a tendency in

---

63. Walter J. Ong, S.J., *The Presence of the Word: Some Prolegomena for Cultural and Religious History* (New Haven: Yale University Press, 1967), 23; and idem, *Orality and Literacy*, 98. In *Orality and Literacy*, Ong writes, ". . . persons whose world view has been formed by high literacy need to remind themselves that in functionally oral cultures the past is not felt as an itemized terrain, peppered with verifiable and disputed 'facts' or bits of information. It is the domain of the ancestors, a resonant source for renewing awareness of present existence, which itself is not an itemized terrain either." See also Ruth Finnegan, *Literacy and Orality: Studies in the Technology of Communication* (Oxford: Blackwell, 1988), 20. Even Finnegan, who is extremely cautious about drawing strict lines between "oral" cultures and

the mind to perceive of time, and indeed all ideas, in objective, spatial terms, capable of being itemized and diagramed. Inevitably, the sense of distance from any point in the past is increased, for time is observed as a series of distinguishable "bits" or "pieces" strung out in a long line. It inhabits a "uniform spatial and temporal framework."[64] Preachers of the late sixteenth century would therefore have experienced a sense of separation in time from the Biblical events they described much greater than that experienced by Jean Gerson in the early fifteenth century, or even Olivier Maillard in the early sixteenth, scarcely fifty years after the invention of the printing press. Of course the increased awareness of the passage of time and of distance from historical events in the past is also traditionally seen as one of the central characteristics of Renaissance culture. It accounts for the need perceived by many Renaissance figures such as Petrarch to escape from the present and recover the lost grandeur of the classical past.

Interactive conversation, one of the most effective techniques used by medieval preachers to inspire their congregations, was therefore disappearing. It was, however, a technique that was not so crucial for achieving the goals of post-Tridentine preachers. While all preachers continued to hope that their sermons might encourage devotion, their overriding concern was correct belief.[65] They sought to present to the people a clear understanding of the accepted teachings of the Church and the "errors" of Protestant theologians. At times, this meant defending positions which

those familiar with literacy, accepts the findings of Goody and Watt that describe an instance in which the "history" of the oral Gonja people of Ghana was modified so that it accorded with the current state of the kingdom. Since one of the purposes of past history was to account for present reality, the legendary founder of the kingdom, who had originally been said to have seven sons, each of whom ruled one section of the kingdom, was now credited with only five sons. The reduction in offspring was necessary because two of the seven divisions of the kingdom had been absorbed by the others, leaving five; Jack Goody, ed., *Literacy in Traditional Societies* (Cambridge: Cambridge University Press, 1968), 33.

64. Elizabeth L. Eisenstein, *The Printing Press as an Agent of Change,* 2 vols. (Cambridge: Cambridge University Press, 1979), 301.

65. Diefendorf, *Beneath the Cross,* 147, 149. Diefendorf's analysis of popular sermons given in Paris in the 1550's and 1560's finds that there was an ongoing concern for explaining to the people the correct meaning of Catholic belief and practice. She finds a particular desire to emphasize the importance of the Eucharist and the sacrifice of the Mass.

were under attack by the followers of Luther and Calvin, and certainly nowhere was this more true than in the area of Marian devotion.

The catechism produced by the Council of Trent upheld the traditional teaching that Mary retained her virginity during and after the birth of Christ.[66] In addition, during session twenty-four, the Council of Trent declared virginity and celibacy to be both "better and more blessed than marriage."[67] Belief in the perpetual virginity of Mary, therefore, became one of the distinguishing marks of Catholic as opposed to Protestant beliefs, although, as we have seen, some Protestant reformers continued to endorse this teaching.[68] François Le Picart stated that even though Mary's perpetual virginity was not explicitly stated in Scripture, it must nevertheless be held to be true as certainly as if it had been stated, because "whatever things are elicited from Scripture ought to be believed in the same way as if they were expressly stated."[69]

Francis Panigarola continued to quote Ezekiel 44 to refer to Mary's virginity "ante partum," "in partu," and "post partum" as a "closed door."[70] St. Peter Canisius castigates Luther and Calvin because he believes they have dared to impugn the purity of Mary by doubting her continued virginity: "The constant faith of the Catholic Church must be retained."[71]

66. *The Catechism of the Council of Trent,* trans. J. Donovan (Baltimore: F. Lucas, Jr., 1829), 40–41.

67. *Canons and Decrees,* 453. "Si quis dixerit, statum conjugalem anteponendum esse statui virginitatis vel coelibatus, et non esse melius ac beatius manere in virginitate aut coelibatu, quam, jungi matrimonio: anathema sit."

68. See Pelikan, *Mary Through the Centuries,* 158–59. Most Catholics assumed that Luther as well as Calvin had abandoned belief in Mary's perpetual virginity. Luther, however, continued to refer to Mary as "ever-virgin" and apparently did not abandon the traditional teaching of the Church on this issue.

69. François Le Picart, *Les sermons et instructions chrestiennes, pour tous les jours de caresme, et feriës de Pasques* (Paris: Nicolas Chesneau, 1566), 187r. ". . . car c'est une regle qu'il fault retenir, 'Quae eliciuntur ex scriptura perinde sunt credenda ac si essent expressa.'"

70. Panigarola, "Predica," 118r. "Ezechiele? Eccolo: Porta hac clausa erit, et non aperietur, et vir non transivit per eam, quoniam Dominus Deus Israel ingressus est per illam: quasi, che piu propriamente si potesse dichiarare la virginità di Maria: della quale notano anche gli Auttori, che trè volte si dimanda chiusa la porta, perche Maria fuit virgo ante partum, in partu, et post partum."

71. Canisius, *Meditationes,* 2,1:79. "Mihi vero constans ecclesiae Catholicae fides retinenda est, quam a sanctis et venerandis patribus veluti per manus traditam semperque Defensam accepi."

Canisius then presents a lengthy defense of Mary's virginity, drawing on the works of Origen, St. Ambrose, St. Jerome, and St. Gregory of Nyssa.[72]

As in the Middle Ages, Canisius and the other preachers continue to assert that Mary was the first woman in the Jewish or Christian traditions to have taken a vow of virginity in her youth. St. Lawrence says that she is the first woman in the Bible, with the possible exception of Jeptha's daughter, to be praised for her virginity.[73] Like most such stories, the account of Mary's vow of virginity comes from the apocryphal Gospels of the early Church which so influenced medieval sermons.[74] The story was presented to the people as fact and supported by the interpretation of Scripture as well, but its continued use is somewhat surprising in light of the caution in such matters urged by the Council of Trent.

In a sermon on the marriage at Cana, St. Peter Canisius is careful to defend the married state as honorable, but his extended praise of virginity and celibacy as preferable goes a long way toward negating the ultimate value of marriage. Christ dignified marriage by his presence at the wedding, but he, his mother, the apostle John, and many saints of both sexes spent their whole lives in perpetual celibacy as an example for others to follow.[75]

Robert Bellarmine concludes that Mary's vow was the reason for her confusion when Gabriel announced her coming motherhood. Since Mary was already engaged, why should she have said, "How can this be?" A coming pregnancy would have been perfectly plausible to her if she had

72. Ibid., 79–80.

73. Lawrence of Brindisi, *Opera omnia*, 1:131.

74. The story of Mary's vow of virginity comes from chapter 7 of the apocryphal Gospel of Matthew. According to this Gospel as well as the Proto-evangelium of James, Mary was able to marry Joseph in spite of her promise of virginity because he was an old man, already the father of several children, who promised to protect her virgin state. Mary agreed to marry in obedience to God's will. Also, by the sixteenth century, the Catholic Church had a long tradition of celibate marriages dating back to the early centuries of Christian history. The Virgin was simply believed to have been the first to enter into such a union.

75. Canisius, *Meditationes*, 2,1:137. "Quare sicut Christus cum parente sua et discipulis et primo quid hoc miraculo matrimonium cohonestavit, ita idem Christus cum castissima virgine matre et uterque Ioannes allique complures in utroque sexu vere sancti, vitam in caelibatu perpetuam laudabiliter transegerunt et servandae castitatis exemplum aliis praebuerunt."

not vowed to remain a virgin. When Mary said, "for I know not a man," she was speaking as do members of religious orders who might say "we don't drink wine" or "we don't eat meat." They say this not because they are not eating and drinking at the time but because they have vowed it. Mary's vow of virginity was more pleasing to God than that of anyone else for it was the first of its kind. Those who now vow to remain celibate have the example of Christ and the apostles. Along with Canisius, Bellarmine says that virginity receives a greater reward in heaven than marriage. Virgins will sing more joyful songs to God than others who will only be able to stand by and listen. No wonder Mary responded to Gabriel as she did. She did not want to lose such a reward.[76]

Mary's virgin state occupied an equally significant place in the sermons of St. François de Sales. This could only be expected from someone who preached frequently to groups of women religious.[77] St. François believed that Mary was especially important as an example to women.[78] All Christians do battle under this "captainess," and she is the patron of all who live virtuously. Women, however, have a special attachment to the virgin because of their sex. They also have an advantage over others when they approach her.[79] Mary is the perfect example of the Christian life, especially of the religious life, and of the virtue of obedience. She proved this obedience when she agreed to marry, although vowed to virginity.[80]

76. Bellarmine, *Opera omnia*, 5:389–90; Lawrence of Brindisi, *Opera omnia*, 1:137–38. St. Lawrence uses the same argument about those who abstain from wine to prove that Mary had taken a vow of virginity. See also Le Picart, *Les sermons et instructions chrestiennes*, 188r. Le Picart says that Mary was troubled by Gabriel's announcement because she knew that she had vowed to remain a virgin. Her questioning of Gabriel was as if to say, "Comment se pourra faire que je conçoeive veu que je suis vierge et ay propos ferme et deliberé de demeurer vierge?"

77. Many of St. François de Sales's sermons were preached for the sisters of the Visitation of Holy Mary, the congregation which he and St. Jeanne de Chantal had founded jointly.

78. This was not a new idea. Jean Gerson believed that women had special cause to rejoice in Mary's accomplishments. See Gerson, *Oeuvres complètes*, 5:965.

79. De Sales, *Oeuvres complètes*, 10:294. "O quel honneur pour nous, de pouvoir batailler sous cette vaillante capitainesse? Mais le sexe feminin semble avoir une obligation particuliere à la suivre? Car elle l'a infiniment relevé et honoré. . . . mais pourtant nul ne peut nier que les filles, à cause de la virginité, n'ayent une certaine alliance avec elle plus particuliere que les autres, parce que cette ressemblance de la virginité leur donne une grande capacité, et un avantage tout particulier pour s'approcher de plus pres de cette Vierge."

80. Ibid., 11:378–79; 10:77–78.

As was traditional in Catholic thought, virginity and moral purity go hand in hand. Because of her purity, Mary was able to avoid the curse of Eve and give birth without pain and with no impairment of her virginity.[81] The logic of this was obvious to St. François de Sales, who was convinced Jesus would never have violated his mother's virginal integrity, since he would not have picked her to be his mother if she had not been a virgin to begin with.[82] In line with this, both Canisius and Bellarmine see Christ himself, and not only Mary's purity, as responsible for the preservation of her virginity in giving birth. Christ's ability to be born from a virgin reveals his power over the accustomed operations of nature.[83] Along with the earlier preacher, Michel Menot, Canisius and Bellarmine see Christ's virginal birth as similar to his power to rise from the sealed tomb on Easter.[84]

For Bellarmine, Mary's purity also allowed her to transcend the earthly limitations of her body and acquire an angelic nature. It is worth quoting Bellarmine here, for he provides an instance of the way in which Mary's body, though still highly praised, was beginning to be less important than her soul and spiritual virtues.

---

81. Bellarmine, *Opera omnia*, 5:374; Canisius, *Meditationes*, 2,1:77, 90; de Sales, *Oeuvres complètes*, 11:580; Lawrence of Brindisi, *Opera omnia*, 1:218.

82. De Sales, *Oeuvres complètes*, 11:579. "Quelle apparence, je vous prie, y auroit-il penser que Nostre Seigneur deust violer l'integrité de sa tres sainct Mere, luy qui ne l'a choisie pour estre sa Mere, sinon qu'elle estoit Vierge, et comment luy, qui est la pureté mesme, eust-il pu diminuer sa pureté virginale."

83. Canisius, *Meditationes*, 2,2:71. "Ac sane multa sunt id genus alia, quae Christus supra omnem naturae morem, legem ac ordinem fecit, ut suam adstrueret divinitatem ac nostram fidem probaret mundique sapientiam et supercilium deprimeret. Nam et ingrediens mundum corpus suum ex clauso Virginis matris utero in aliquando ne videri capique posset."

84. Ibid., 2,1:284. "Neque sine ingenti miraculo contigit, corpus hoc perfecte integrum totumque gloriosum, sua vi, per clausum sepulcrum penetrare, quemadmodum et cum nasceretur, e clauso Virginis matris utero in lucem prodiit." Bellarmine, *Opera omnia*, 5:70. "Postremo, non ex quacumque foemina, sed ex virgine natus est. . . . Quibus unquam saeculis auditum est, in quibus generationibus factum, in quibus libris et voluminibus factum est, ut virgo conciperet, virgo pareret et virgo post partum maneret: Exivit domus [sic] de sepulchro clauso." *The Catechism of the Council of Trent*, 40, makes the same point, ". . . he is born of his Mother without any diminution of her maternal virginity: and as he afterwards went forth from the sepulchre whilst it was closed and sealed . . . ; after a like, but more incomprehensible manner, did Jesus Christ come forth from his mother's womb without injury to her maternal virginity."

For although the blessed Mary was Man, in the realm of nature, nevertheless by the purity of her life, she was a terrestrial angel; her body indeed was directed toward the earth, but certainly in life, in morals, in soul, in desire, in contemplation and in the fervor of her mind she dwelt perpetually in heaven.[85]

St. Lawrence agreed that while Mary's flesh and body kept her on earth, "in mind and in spirit she was always in heaven."[86]

St. François believed that Mary's virginity actually surpassed that of the angels because she nevertheless produced a child. Her virginity was fully chosen by her, not hers by nature; and it withstood testing.[87] His thoughts on virginity also reveal the shift in moral and spiritual emphasis away from the body and exterior piety to one centered on the interior acquisition of virtue. For centuries, most preachers had told the people that widowhood must always remain second to virginity in terms of merit because widows had not retained the intact virginity of their youth. Although this continues to be proclaimed, St. François thinks differently. Speaking of all the virgins who will follow in the train of the Virgin Mary, he says widows "ought not to be rejected from this blessed company for no longer having their virginity, since that is able to be repaired by humility."[88] No longer virgins in body, widows may still be virgins in the spiritual purity of their souls. St. François might also have had in mind the devotion of his friend and co-founder of the Visitandines, Jeanne de Chantal, who was herself a widow.[89]

85. Bellarmine, *Opera omnia*, 5:366. ". . . nemo melius et congruentius ad Virginem castissimam et interrimam mitti potuit, quam angelus. Quamquam enim conditione naturae b. Maria homo; tamen vitae puritate angelus terrestris erat, et corpore quidem versabatur in terris, sed certe vita, moribus, animo, desiderio, contemplatione, mentis fervore, perpetuo habitabat in coelo."

86. Lawrence of Brindisi, *Opera omnia*, 1:149.

87. De Sales, *Oeuvres complètes*, 10:303–5.

88. Ibid., 11:465. "Mais ce que dit le sainct prophete que plusieurs vierges seront amenée apres Nostre-Dame, il ne veut pas pour cela en exclure les vefves, lesquelles ne doivent pas estre rejettées de cette bien-heureuse troupe, pour n'avoir plus leur virginité, puis qu'elle se peut reparer par l'humilité."

89. In a letter to the Archbishop of Lyon, Denis-Simon de Marquemont, St. François de Sales defended the spiritual equality of women with men and pointed to the example of the early Apostles, who encouraged both widows and virgins to embrace the religious life and serve the poor. They need not even necessarily observe strict clausura, which was a recent invention not known to the early Church. According to St. François, while the strict

Along with Mary's perpetual virginity, the doctrine of her Immaculate Conception existed as a point of contention between Protestant and Catholic, and remained a source of dispute among Catholic theologians and preachers. It might have helped matters if the Council of Trent had made a decisive statement on the issue, but, burdened with so many other problems, the decrees restrict the Virgin to casual mention in statements about sin in general. Mary is carefully excluded from the decree on original sin,[90] while the decree on justification states that no one can live without venial sin unless, like Mary, they receive a special grace from God.[91] Nowhere, however, do the decrees specifically teach Mary's Immaculate Conception.

Dominicans continued to reject the Immaculate Conception altogether, but it was strongly supported by the new Jesuit order as a means of demonstrating the authority of the Church to determine official doctrine.[92] St. Peter Canisius, St. Robert Bellarmine, and Francisco Suarez all defended the doctrine.[93] This caused some sharp debates between Dominicans and Jesuits. The arguments became so heated that in 1616 Pope Paul V refused to allow the Immaculate Conception to be discussed from the pulpit at all.[94]

In the meantime, no such strictures applied. St. Peter Canisius was free to say that all Catholics were certain that "an immaculate Lord Christ had come forth from an Immaculate Virgin."[95] Bellarmine declared Mary to be "like the red dawn shining over the whole earth, not defiled by the

---

rules of conventional monastic life can be good, they should not be required of all religious, since the life of perfection is, after all, interior and not exterior. See Rapley, *The Dévotes*, 37–40.

90. *Canons and Decrees of the Council of Trent*, 302. "Declarat tamen haec ipsa sancta synodus, non esse suae intentionis comprehendere in hoc decreto, ubi de peccato originali agitur, beatam et immaculatam Virginem Mariam Dei genitricem."

91. Ibid., 323. "Si quis hominem semel justificatum dixerit amplius peccare non posse, neque gratiam amittere, atque ideo eum qui labitur et peccat, nunquam vere fuisse justificatum; aut contra, posse in tota vita peccata omnia, etiam veniala vitare, nisi ex speciali Dei privilegio, quemadmodum de beata Virgine tenet ecclesia; anathema sit."

92. Graef, *Mary*, 2:67.

93. Ibid., 21–25.

94. Marina Warner, *Alone of All Her Sex: The Myth and Cult of the Virgin Mary* (New York: Alfred A. Knopf, 1976), 249.

95. Canisius, *Meditationes*, 2,1:141.

blemish of original sin"; and as the dawn mediates between night and day, she mediates "between the law and grace."[96]

Like the Jesuits, Franciscan Christopher Cheffontaines chose to emphasize the role of the Church in forming doctrine when he preached about Mary's Immaculate Conception. The Church had been guided by the Holy Spirit when it established the festival of her Conception, and it rightly believes that so blessed a fruit as Christ could never have been born from an evil tree.[97] He affirms that "it is sufficient to know that the Roman Church believes her to have been conceived without original sin, and that this is its faith regarding her conception in the aforesaid festival, to preach and confess it before everyone."[98]

François de Sales also believed that Mary was privileged over every other human being because she remained free of all sin, original or actual.[99] Thus she had no need ever to be purified of sin, since her purity exceeded that of the cherubim and seraphim from the moment of conception.[100] Unlike Mary, however, we must work with the grace of God if we want to be saved. Other people cannot expect to receive the privilege she was given, for only she was destined to bear the Savior.[101]

There is little so far in the statements of these preachers to distinguish their presentation of the Immaculate Conception from that of the preachers of the late Middle Ages, but there are differences. The most important change has to do with the extent to which these preachers stress the role of God's grace in this event and to play down Mary's mer-

96. Bellarmine, *Opera omnia*, 5:294. See also Le Picart, *Les sermons et instructions chrestiennes*, 147v–148r. Le Picart defends belief in Mary's Immaculate Conception as something that must be believed on pain of damnation, even if it is not expressly in Scripture. "Ou trouverez-vous en l'Evangile que la glorieuse vierge Marie, mere de Dieu, soit demeurée perpetuellement vierge: qu'elle ayt esté conceuë sans peché originel? Et toutefois c'est article de foy, qu'il le nous fault ainsi croire sur peine de damnation."

97. Cheffontaines, "Sermo de Virginis Mariae," 17r. "Credit ergo Ecclesia benedictum istum fructum, ex nanquam maledicta arbore natum esse, et ideo non solum nativitatis, sed et conceptionis eius festum celebrat."

98. Ibid., 18r–18v. "Sufficit autem nosse ecclesiam Romanam, illam sine peccato originali conceptam fuisse credere, atque hanc suam fidem de eius conceptione, indicto festo, apud omnes confiteri et praedicare."

99. De Sales, *Oeuvres complètes*, 10:426.   100. Ibid., 10:69–70.
101. Ibid., 11:20–21.

its. As they do this, they also begin to focus on the purity of Mary's soul as being of supreme importance while that of her body remains secondary.

Robert Bellarmine proclaims that Gabriel attributed all of Mary's graces to the supreme grace of God and not to Mary herself. When he told Mary not to fear, what he was really saying was,

Do not fear, Mary, . . . you may spy nothing false here, no adulation, no traps, nor should you marvel that I salute you as full of grace and blessed among women; *For you have found favor with God.* He is the one who has made you this way with his grace and blessing, nor do I ascribe it to your merits, which you don't even recognize, but I give and ascribe all to the grace of God.[102]

St. François de Sales explains to his congregation that while Mary did not have to do penance due to her sinless state, she, like everyone else, needed the blood of Christ.[103]

Even St. Lawrence of Brindisi, the most medieval of these early modern preachers, continually reminds the people that Mary would have been nothing in and of herself. She owed all to God. St. Lawrence quotes one of the more frequently used passages in sixteenth-century Marian sermons, referred to as the "Beatus Venter." While Jesus is teaching, a woman cries out, "Blessed is the womb that bore you and the breasts that you sucked." Jesus then replies, "Blessed rather are those who hear the word of God and keep it."[104] This had been a popular passage in the Middle Ages, when preachers usually preferred to dwell on the woman's praise of Mary even if they could not ignore Jesus' words altogether.[105] In

---

102. Bellarmine, *Opera omnia*, 5:381. *"Ne timeas,* inquit, *Maria:* nihil hic fallaciae, nihil adulationis, nihil insidiarum suspiceris, neque mireris, quod te gratia plenam et benedictam in mulieribus salutaverim; *Invenisti enim gratiam apud Deum.* Ille te talem gratia et benignitate sua fecit, qualem dixi. Neque ego id meritis tuis, quae ipsa non agnosces, sed dono gratiae Dei totum adscribo."

103. De Sales, *Oeuvres complètes*, 10:484. "Mais tous generalement sans exception, ouy mesme Nostre-Dame, ont eu besoin du merite du sang de Nostre-Seigneur."

104. Luke 11:28.

105. The importance of Mary's milk in the Middle Ages as both a relic and an iconographic symbol for the grace of God and the body which formed the humanity of Christ would have prevented preachers from dwelling too long on the more negative aspects of this passage.

the later sixteenth century, preachers have no difficulty concluding that Mary's obedience to the word of God was her true glory, preferable even to her physical motherhood of Christ.

St. Lawrence declares that Mary did not achieve such great glory except through grace. Christ's response to the woman's words was intended to mean that his mother "was first blessed because she had heard the word of God and kept it."[106] Lawrence also reveals, perhaps, his familiarity with the new status that Renaissance artists were achieving by comparing Mary herself to a work of art. Praise of Mary cannot detract from her son because "as we praise the work of an artist, we praise the artist himself; so when we praise the work of God, we praise God himself and Christ, the artist and maker of all things."[107] Mary has become a passive recipient of grace and of the creative skill of the divine artist. There is little room in these passages for active holiness on Mary's part.

St. Lawrence and Robert Bellarmine also want to make the point that the souls of both Christ and Mary are superior to their bodies. After praising her womb in a sermon on the Annunciation, St. Lawrence says that Mary and Christ were especially close; it was a closeness "not only of nature and of blood, but also of souls and hearts, of love and charity. Hence we read that Mary was often with Christ."[108] The body, he says, is inferior to the soul for it is formed from the earth and returns to it. "But

106. Lawrence of Brindisi, *Opera omnia*, 1:35. "Hoc nanque indicavit Christus cum mulieri dicenti: 'Beatus venter qui te portavit, et uberae quae suxisti,' respondit: 'Quinimo beati qui audiunt verbum Dei, et custodiunt illud,' hanc, inquit, ob causam Mater mea principio quidem beata est, quia verbum Dei audivit et custodivit." Ibid., 62.

107. Ibid., 303. "Laudando igitur Matrem nihil detraxit de Filii laudibus, quin etiam ausit. Sicut enim cum artificis operam laudamus, ipsum utique laudamus artificem; sic cum Dei laudamus operam, Deum ipsum Christumque laudamus, rerum omnium artificem et conditorem." Gerson, *Oeuvres complètes*, 7:1068. Gerson compared God to Pygmalion in a sermon on the Immaculate Conception. In his sermon, however, the emphasis was less on God as maker than on the beauty and wonder of the woman whom he had created. Gerson said, "Que voulez que plus en die? Tant apparut belle, tant pure, tant nette que le vray Dieu de saincte amour incontinent fut embrasé de son amour et son ymaige comme de Pigmalion faignent les poetes et contenir ne se pot que joyeusement ne chantast cette amoureuse chancon dessus dicte: Ma mie est celle Qui tout est belle."

108. Lawrence of Brindisi, *Opera omnia*, 1:236. ". . . non solum naturae et sanguinis, verum etiam animorum, cordium, amoris, caritatis, hinc saepe Mariam cum Christo legimus."

if God has so greatly adorned the flesh of the Virgin, what ought we to think about her soul?" If God gave Mary's body a noble descent from patriarchs and prophets, beauty, and modesty, and made it the carrier of his only son, "with what graces, with what gifts has he adorned her most holy soul?"[109] Bellarmine praises Mary's womb as the place of the Incarnation, where the glorious body of Christ was formed, "but truly more glorious was that soul, created today in the same workshop by the same Spirit."[110] The art of the seventeenth century will follow this trend, no longer focused on Mary's bodily conception in the womb of St. Anne, but on her perfect existence, prior to creation, in the mind of God. Whereas in the Middle Ages artistic depictions of the Immaculate Conception emphasized Mary's physical relationship to her parents, often showing Mary as an unborn child in St. Anne's womb, as a baby in her arms, or even nursing at her breast, later iconography preferred to illustrate the same doctrine through the motif of the Apocalyptic Woman of the Book of Revelation or some other design which placed Mary clearly in heaven rather than on earth.[111]

It is true that the Church had always believed that the soul is superior to the body, but in medieval sermons this was rarely mentioned in connection with discussions of the Incarnation. Medieval preachers usually referred to the soul of Christ, or of Mary, to point out that neither person's body had to wait for a time in the womb before receiving a soul. Their bodies and souls were present together from the very moment of conception.

Mary's indebtedness to God's grace for all of her virtues and accomplishments was argued most forcefully in the sermons of Christopher Cheffontaines, a surprising fact, given the usual Franciscan defense of Mary's prominent contributions to human salvation. Cheffontaines calls

---

109. Ibid., 200.

110. Bellarmine, *Opera omnia*, 5:172. "Gloriosa dicta sunt de te, civitas Dei. Gloriosum plane corpus illud, quod in utero virginis, tamquam in officina Spiritus sancti, hodie fabricatum est: sed multo profecto gloriosior animus ille, qui in eadem officina ab eodem spiritu sancto hodie conditus est."

111. Mirella Levi d'Ancona, *The Iconography of the Immaculate Conception in the Middle Ages and Early Renaissance* (New York: College Art Association, in conjunction with The Art Bulletin, 1957), 17–18, 39–40; Warner, *Alone of All Her Sex*, 247.

Mary the "temple of God," constructed by the hands of Christ himself to be completely free of all sin of any kind.[112] Her works and merits could therefore not be the cause of the Incarnation; it occurred solely because of the freely given loving-kindness of God.[113] Nor would her bodily actions, the fact that she had conceived Christ in her womb, borne him, and fed him with her own milk, have been a reason for praising Mary if she had not also heard, believed, and kept the word of God. This privilege, along with her Immaculate Conception, she had "not because of her nature, which would be true of Christ alone, but from grace."[114] God chose to regard the humility, weakness, and insignificance of the Virgin's body and create in her someone worthy of praise.[115] This is why Mary herself desired that no homage be given to her body, but to God alone. In a very personal address, Cheffontaines describes Mary in an interior conversation with her own soul. When she said, "My soul doth magnify the Lord," she really meant,

O my soul, it is innate in your nature that through you the body is magnified, and since it would otherwise be incomplete, you are joined to it so that you might rejoice in it, and so that you may not be torn apart from it by force, nor deprived

112. Cheffontaines, "Sermo de Virginis Mariae," 36r–36v. "Nam si caeteras fideles Dei templa, propter inhabitantem in eis spiritum sanctum Apostolus dixit, quid de hac dicemus? Nisi quod singularissimum sit dei templum, quod ipsemet Christus, propriis construxit manibus."

113. Christopher Cheffontaines, "Homilia in die Immaculatae Conceptionis sacratissimae et dignissimae Virginis Mariae Matris Dei," in *Omnes epistolas quadragesimales homiliae* (Louvain: Johannes Bogardus, 1572), 164v. When Mary said that God had regarded her humility, she meant, "Absit ut hominum laudes michi arrogantiam, seu Dei contemptum pariant. Quinpotius vilior fiam in oculis meis. Illa enim beatitudo quam praedicature sunt omnes generationes, non ex operibus meis habet originem. Siquidem ipsa divini verbi incarnatio quae modo in utero meo facta est: ex merito meo non pendet, sed ex mera et gratuita benignitate Dei."

114. Ibid., 165v. "Susceperit incarnationem verbi Dei in utero, portaverit lactaveritque filium Dei. Sed non in hoc venisset laudanda nisi verbum Dei audivisset, credidisset, observassetque quod utique omni facienti voluntatem Dei commune est, tametsi impari forte. Hoc igitur habet super omnes non ex natura (Siquidem soli Christo congruit) sed ex gratia, ut quae in cause, culpam communem cum omnibus traxisset in effectu fuerit praeventa, et a culpa originali intacta, et gratia singulari insignita, cuius plenitudo se illi infudit caeteris vero per partes gratia Dei tribuitur."

115. Ibid., 165r–165v. "Notum est corpus humile, intelligi infirmum et ignobile. Humilitatem igitur ancillae suae respexit dominus, id est, singulari praerogativa eius naturam insignivit."

of it, but having obtained immortality, you may wear it as a garment. . . . Do not, therefore, do not, O soul, thus magnify your companion the body which needs your works and without you is unable to live, which is subject to you and will be separated from you for a time. But magnify the one who does not need your goods. Magnify him from whose glory you will never be separated once you are joined to him. . . . Why is the body magnified, by which the soul is often aggravated? Magnify the Lord through whom you are adorned with many virtues. True, indeed, you are now the companion of the body which is now the dwelling place of the Son of God. But do not attribute to the body that which is done by the work of the Holy Spirit. . . . My soul, therefore, magnifies the Lord (says Mary) and since my soul is with the body, it must magnify the Lord with the body.[116]

It is difficult to imagine a description of Mary's body more distant from those of the later Middle Ages than this one. What is more, Cheffontaines gives it added emphasis by putting the words into the mouth of Mary herself in a sermon on the Immaculate Conception, a doctrine specifically concerned with the sinless purity of her body. Here, however, all glory is given to the soul, and to God the creator. The Virgin's body has become only an aggravating companion, capable of unbelievable dignity through its association with the Incarnation, but of infinitely less importance in the scheme of things than her soul, which is fully capable of life and glory on its own.

Cheffontaines's portrayal of Mary is a fitting prelude to the course that French Marian devotion would take in the early seventeenth century. The French School, of which Cardinal Berulle was a member, was dedicated to celebrating the Incarnation, and Mary's role in it. One of their favorite prayers began, "O Jesu vivens in Maria," a statement which might easily

116. Ibid., 162v–163r. "O anima mea, naturae tuae insitum est ut per te corpus magnificetur, cui cum exiguum esset, iuncta es, ut eo gaudes, ut ab eo non vis divelli nec eo spolieris, sed sancta immortalitate eo supervestiaris. . . . Noli igitur, Noli O anima ita corpus socium magnificare quod tua eget opera nec sine te vivere potest, quod tibi subditum est quod a te separabitur aliquando. Sed magnifica illum qui bonorum tuorum non eget. Magnifica illum, cuius gloria aliquando iuncta nunquam separaberis. . . . Cur magnificatur corpus quo plerumque anima aggravata est? Magnifica dominum per quem tantis virtutibus ornaris. Verumquidem O anima corpori sociaris, quod filii Dei nunc habitaculum est. Sed noli corpori tribuere, quod ope spiritus sancti factum est. . . . Magnificat ergo (inquit Maria) anima mea dominum, quae quia cum corpore est, magnificet dominum cum corpore necessum est."

be interpreted as a reference to the nine months of Mary's pregnancy. Yet, their spirituality was completely directed to the interior life of the Virgin.[117]

Conceiving the Word

In the wake of this new interest in Mary's soul and spiritual virtues, her spiritual motherhood of Christ begins to emerge as an important and central theme. Theologians had been saying for centuries that Mary had conceived Christ in her heart through faith as the immediate prelude to her bodily conception of him. They had also asserted at times that her spiritual conception was superior,[118] but always in the context of sermons, art, and piety that nevertheless glorified her bodily unity with Christ. In the later sixteenth century, amid so many proclamations by Catholic and Protestant preachers alike that the spiritual is vastly more significant than the material, preaching which attributed greater worth to Mary's conception of Christ through faith would likely have fallen on more fertile soil.

In another of his sermons on the "Beatus Venter," St. Lawrence deals with those instances in which Christ turns away praise of Mary as his bodily mother in favor of those who hear and keep God's word. Christ rejected the woman's attempt to glorify his mother's physical participation in his conception because he wanted to show that honor should be given to God the Father before Mary, and that Mary's greatest dignity was not her bodily conception of the Messiah but in being his mother and sister in spirit. Lawrence does defend the woman's courage, however, because she

117. Hilda Graef, *The Devotion to Our Lady* (New York: Hawthorn Books, 1963), 70. Francisco Suarez, the first theologian to present a systematic Mariology, declared that Mary's supreme dignity as Mother of God ought to be understood morally rather than physically. It allowed the Virgin to share in the moral greatness of her son. Suarez wrote, "Haec matris dignitas absolute sumpta moraliter potius quam physice consideranda videtur." Suarez, *De mysteriis vitae Christi*, ed. Vivès (1860), Disp. 1, sec. 2, 7–8: quoted in H.-M. Manteau-Bonamy, *Maternité divine et Incarnation: Étude historique et doctrinale de Saint Thomas à nos jours*, Bibliothèque Thomiste, vol. 27 (Paris: J. Vrin, 1949), 182–83.

118. See Gerson, *Oeuvres complètes*, 7:958. In a Christmas sermon, Gerson responds to the question, was making Mary the Mother of God the greatest grace God could have given her? He says that Mary would rather have been Mother of God spiritually, by grace and charity, than to be Christ's mother corporally, without grace and charity. Still, to have received both gifts was better than to have received one without the other.

was not afraid to praise Christ's mother even though some in the crowd might have objected. This entire passage appears to be directed toward Catholics who may have been convinced by Protestant assertions of the importance of faith and intimidated by Protestant attacks on Marian devotion. Faith is important, but none should fear to honor the Mother of God.[119]

Mary's spiritual motherhood appears most prominently in the sermons of the two Jesuits, Bellarmine and Canisius, as well as the sermons of St. François de Sales. Bellarmine in particular makes it an integral part of his discussions of the Incarnation and of his own role as a preacher of the Word. In a sermon on the threefold birth of Christ, Bellarmine describes the three ways that Christ was born in heaven and on earth. Christ as God was eternally born of the Father in heaven without a mother; as a man, he was born, in time, of the Virgin Mary without the aid of a father; and he is born many times in human hearts as both God and man without either a father or a mother. As a preacher, it is Bellarmine's responsibility to aid in bringing Christ to birth in the human mind. The preacher is like Gabriel, whose job it was to make possible Mary's conception of Christ. In a passage which blends the metaphors of the Church as spotless bride of Christ and as his spiritual mother, Bellarmine explains, "So preachers are sent to the Church, that pure virgin whom the Apostle Paul promised in marriage to one man, in order to show forth Christ, so that she may conceive the Son of God by faith, give birth in charity, and nourish him with good works."[120] This is why, he says, preachers begin their sermons with an "Ave." They want to obtain Mary's prayers to God so they can perform their duty with angelic purity and aid the Church in its conception and birth-giving of Christ.[121]

In accordance with this goal, Bellarmine calls on all Christians to become spiritual mothers of Christ by following a lifestyle like that of Mary prior to her conception of Christ, a life of quiet contemplation

---

119. Lawrence of Brindisi, *Opera omnia*, 1:301–2.

120. Bellarmine, *Opera omnia*, 5:68, 375. ". . . ita concionatores ad ecclesiam mittuntur quam apostolus Paulus despondit uni viro virginem castam exhibere Christo, ut ea quoque Filium Dei fide concipiat, charitate pariat, bonis operibus nutriat."

121. Ibid.

apart from the world. He admonishes those who wish to conceive Christ spiritually,

Let us learn to dwell with ourselves, to love solitude . . . to enter often into the chamber of our hearts and there, away from the tumult of noise of the things of this world, and with the doors and windows of our bodily senses diligently closed, speak with God . . . about things truly great, about eternal life, the salvation of the soul, the magnitude of celestial glory and the horror and eternity of the pains of hell.[122]

Bellarmine knows that this sounds like the advice one would ordinarily give to a monk or nun, someone who sought to follow the higher path to perfection. Not so, he says: ". . . this is the life of Christians, who ought all to be perfect, so that they might be sons of their Father who is in heaven."[123] Bellarmine's implication is that the religious life of the cloister is now to be extended past the convent walls to encompass all Christians.

St. Peter Canisius agreed with Bellarmine that Mary was most to be imitated in her spiritual maternity. He explained that it was only through hearing the word of God with faith, and embracing it with charity, that the Virgin merited her dignity as Mother of God, blessed above all others. Even if Mary's bodily maternity sets her apart from and above the citizens of earth and heaven, what Christ really wants are many spiritual mothers, who, having received the seed of the word of God, keep it, conceive, and give birth to eternal life.[124]

The subordination of Mary's bodily maternity to her obedience was continued by the Genevan bishop St. François de Sales. Once again in reference to the "Beatus Venter," he says it is true that Mary was blessed in carrying Christ in her womb, but she was much more greatly blessed

---

122. Ibid., 376.

123. Ibid. "Neque dixeris mihi, ista est vita perfectorium, non omnes possumus esse perfecti. Haec enim est vita Christianorum, qui omnes perfecti esse debent, ut sint filii Patris sui, qui in coelis est."

124. Canisius, *Meditationes*, 2,1:226–27. "Nihil magis exoptat Dominus, quam ut plurimos habeat sibi matres vere spirituales, hoc est, qui divini verbi caeleste semen mystice concipiant ac retineant, donec in eis pariat vitam aeternam. Et enim licet mater Christi secundum carnem sit unica, quae illum corporaliter conceperit ac generarit eaque ratione homines et angelos omnes excellat, tamen hunc maternitatis, ut sic dicam, titulum, largitur etiam Christus aliis obedientibus, qui verbum Dei cum fide percipiunt et in corde conservant atque sic excolunt, ut 'verbi sumul auditores et factores' iure dicantur."

because of her humility in obeying God's will at all times.[125] This is what places Mary above others who also try to hear and obey God's word. Mary was privileged to have been obedient to God from the moment of her conception.[126]

It has probably become clear that the theme of Mary's spiritual motherhood was a means of introducing Mary as a role model, someone whose piety and receptivity to God's word could be imitated by all Christians. As Bellarmine said in a sermon on the feast of Mary's Nativity, it is not enough simply to avoid vices. Virtues must be actively cultivated. Otherwise one becomes like a farmer who uproots all of the bad plants in his garden but never sows the good seed. It is necessary to learn to "live soberly, justly and piously in this age . . . to love, as is right, both God, one's neighbor, and oneself."[127] St. François de Sales agreed that Mary had already set an example. She "wondrously practiced" love of God and of neighbor in her love for Christ. When he first came into the world through her, she loved and received him as her God. As she provided for his needs, she loved him as her neighbor.[128] Like her son, Mary fulfilled the law as an example for us to imitate. We must add good works to our lofty thoughts.[129] Christopher Cheffontaines also affirmed that the greater glory goes to those who do the most good; no one did more good deeds for God than Mary, as she cared for Jesus over so many years.[130]

As always, Catholic preachers held up Mary as someone who possessed to the full all the possible graces, virtues, and gifts of God.[131] Traditionally, however, no virtues were so characteristic of the Virgin as her

125. De Sales, *Oeuvres complètes*, 11:241. When Christ gave his reply to the woman who cried out, he really meant, "Il est vray que ma Mere est bien-heureuse, parce qu'elle m'a porté en son ventre; mais elle l'est bien davantage, pour l'humilité avec laquelle elle a entendu les paroles de mon Pere celeste, et les a gardes."

126. Ibid., 11:460.

127. Bellarmine, *Opera omnia*, 5:64.

128. De Sales, *Oeuvres complètes*, 11:350.

129. Ibid., 10:68–69.

130. Cheffontaines, "Sermo de Virginis Mariae," 36v–37r.

131. Bellarmine, *Opera omnia*, 5:372. Bellarmine explains that Mary is called full of grace because she was favored by God over every other creature, she carried the fountain of all graces in her womb, and "quod gratiae donis, fide, spe, charitate, prudentia, justitia, temperantia, fortitudine, timore, pietate, humilitate, aliisque magnis virtutibus, muneribusque divinis prae omnibus angelis et hominibus repleta fuerit."

humility and obedience to God, which had overcome the pride
and disobedience of Eve. These were the virtues the Church urgently
wanted to cultivate in the Catholic people of Europe in the sixteenth and
seventeenth centuries. Pride could cause rebellion, as it had in the case of
the followers of Luther and Calvin. Humble obedience, then, continued
in the late sixteenth century to be the crowning glory of Mary's spirituality.

Mention of the Virgin's humility is so frequent in the sermons of the
time that it comes near to eclipsing other Marian themes. St. Peter Canisius declared that without humility it was impossible to please God. This
was true without exception, for the Virgin Mary as well as for John the
Baptist and King David.[132]

Preaching that exalted the lowly humility of Mary reinforced the contemporary inclination to portray her as a passive receiver of God's grace.
Preachers proclaim her "smallness" and sense of "nothingness" when she
heard Gabriel's announcement. Mary said her soul magnified the Lord
"'because he has regarded the humility of his handmaiden.'" In these
words she did not praise her virtue of humility, but "she acknowledged
her abasement, her smallness, her nothingness, her unworthiness." It is
this kind of humility, concluded Robert Bellarmine, "which we ought to
imitate."[133]

For St. François de Sales, it was Mary's humility which had attracted
God to her in the first place; and "she knew well that the humility which
was in her did not come from her," but was given her by God, and was an
effect of his grace.[134] Mary's response to Gabriel in silence, prudence, and
humility convinced Bellarmine that Mary outshone other women in pos-
sessing "manly constancy," even though she was a woman.[135]

---

132. Canisius, *Meditationes*, 2,1:124. When Jesus insisted that John baptize him in the Jordan in order to fulfill all righteousness, he was showing "absolutam videlicet humilitatem,
sine qua nec sacrosancta Virgo mater, nec Ioannes Baptista, . . . nec David eximie iustus
Deo tantopere placuissent."

133. Bellarmine, *Opera omnia*, 5:381. Mary's response to Gabriel was humble and did not
make reference to her holiness but "abiectionem, parvitatem, nihilitatem, nihilum suum
agnoscit."

134. De Sales, *Oeuvres complètes*, 11:236; also 11:253–54; 10:308.

135. Bellarmine, *Opera omnia*, 5:378. "Quis in isto silentio et commotione, tacitque virgi-

Often preachers favorably compare Mary's humility to the pride of Eve, to the pride of other women, or to human pride in general (all common medieval themes). Pride was the worst possible sin. It had caused the fall of Lucifer and his angels, of Adam and Eve, and of Judas. But, according to St. François, Mary "had come into the world to regain by her humility that which our mother Eve lost by her pride and vanity."[136] For Bellarmine, Mary's hesitance in responding to Gabriel was due solely to her humility. She followed, in fact, a perfect via media between the "audacity of Eve" and the "slowness and extreme fear of Zachariah." Because of her complete humility, God dwelt within her, as he will in all persons who follow the example of her humility. It is only pride that keeps God from inhabiting the human heart.[137] Robert Bellarmine and François de Sales are agreed that Mary outshone other women. Most women, St. François says, and not only Eve, are "ambitious for honor and esteem," even more than men. Mary was a daughter of Eve, however, only according to blood and not according to the spirit, hence her complete humility and self-abasement.[138]

To speak of the Virgin's humility and obedience naturally called to mind the same characteristic virtues in the nature of Jesus, her son. This was the way in which post-Tridentine preachers followed the late medieval practice of drawing parallels between the lives of Mary and Jesus. Peter Canisius exclaimed in a sermon on Jesus' Ascension,

> May I learn to burn with the desire and love of the glorified Lord Christ, and learn to cherish and follow the submission and simplicity of his mother Mary, by which she joined herself to the most humble. For there is nothing more worthy

---

nis cogitatione, virgineam teneramque verecundiam, prudentiae zelum singularem, virilem in foemina constantiam, consilium, ac prudentiam admirabilem, veram profundamque humilitatem elucere non videat?"

136. De Sales, *Oeuvres complètes*, 10:72–74; 11:260. "Mais la sacrée Vierge estant venuë au monde pour regaigner par son humilité ce que nostre mere Eve avoit perdu par son orgueil et vanité."

137. Bellarmine, *Opera omnia*, 5:379, 373.

138. De Sales, *Oeuvres complètes*, 10:76. "Considerez, je vous prie, une fille d'Eve, combien elle est ambitieuse d'honneur et d'estime? Et si bien ce mal est general entre les hommes, neantmoins il semble que ce sexe y soit plus enclin. Or Nostre-Dame et glorieuse Maistress, n'estoit nullement fille d'Eve selon l'esprit, ains seulement selon sang."

for the Christian man than this humility, which Christ himself taught with his whole life and Mary never abandoned.[139]

Mary attained the highest grade of human perfection through her humility, said Bellarmine; in this she was like her son, who proved his humility by living as an ordinary man for thirty years.[140]

Most of François de Sales's sermon on Mary's purification was an exhortation to follow the examples of Jesus and Mary in their humble obedience to the will of God. St. François particularly wants to stress that interior humility is the real requirement; merely to appear humble is of no value, "because one should not amuse oneself with practicing a certain appearance of humility, in countenance and words . . . and perform many exterior devotions and humiliations which are something less than humility itself."[141] He makes Mary's own obedience dependent on that of her son, which she had the foresight to perceive. She was actually imitating the obedience of Jesus,[142] and even Mary's humility and reverence for God could not equal Christ's. His reverence for his Father in heaven exceeds not only Mary's but all the angels' as well.[143]

It was not enough, however, to praise Mary's humility. The rise of Protestantism now required that Catholic preachers also emphasize the strength of her faith. Medieval preachers had enjoyed comparing Mary's trust in God to that of Abraham, especially in regard to Abraham's willingness to offer his son at God's request. Mary, like Abraham, was prepared to see her son suffer and die, if such were God's will. This idea can certainly be found occasionally in later sixteenth-century sermons, but

---

139. Canisius, *Meditationes,* 2,1:375. "Discam Christi domini glorificati desiderio et amore flagrare et matris eius Mariae submissionem atque simplicitatem, quae et infimis sese adiungebat, sectari et colere. Hac enim humilitate, quam Christus ipse tota vita docuit et Maria unuquam deseruit, nihil sublimius homineque Christiano dignius esse potest."

140. Bellarmine, *Opera omnia,* 5:379.

141. De Sales, *Oeuvres complètes,* 10:71. ". . . car il ne se faut pas amuser à la pratique d'une certaine apparence d'humilité, de contenance et de paroles . . . et à faire quantité de reverences et, d'humiliations exterieures, que ne sont rien moin que l'humilité."

142. Ibid., 11:464. "Donc la Ste Vierge prevoyant cela (Christ's perfect obedience) se soubmit en toute chose, sans reserve quelconque à tout ce qu'on vouloit d'elle, se donnant et abandonnat totalement à la mercy de la divine volonté."

143. Ibid., 10:442–43.

these Catholic preachers now had reason to want to contrast Mary's faith with Abraham's. Abraham had become, by this time, the symbol of all that Protestants sought to teach and glorify in their understanding of faith. Abraham "believed the Lord; and he reckoned it to him as righteousness," said the writer of Genesis.[144] It was a perfect text to use to defend justification by faith. Catholic preachers, therefore, felt compelled to respond in kind. Abraham had faith, but the Virgin's faith far exceeded his.

When Mary said to Gabriel, "Behold the handmaid of the Lord," she gave abundant evidence of her faith, her obedience, and her charity. It is true, proclaimed Bellarmine, that Abraham had the faith to believe he would father a son in his old age, "but surely how much greater was the faith of Mary than the faith of Abraham. How much more miraculous it is for a Virgin to conceive than for an old man to be a father. Thus how much more did she believe, in hope against hope, that she would become the mother of her Lord."[145]

François de Sales added that not only did Mary's faith encompass her own coming motherhood; she also believed Gabriel's news that her sterile cousin Elizabeth was pregnant.[146] The Franciscan Christopher Cheffontaines came up with two more reasons for asserting Mary's superiority to Abraham. He was found worthy to be the host of several angels, but Mary hosted the creator of the angels in her womb for nine months and in her home for thirty years.[147] Abraham could only see the day of Christ in faith and rejoice in it, but Mary saw its appearing and directly participated in bringing it to pass.[148]

Catholic preachers of the late sixteenth and early seventeenth cen-

---

144. Genesis 15:6.

145. Bellarmine, *Opera omnia*, 5:396. "At certe tanto majorem fides Mariae, quam fides Abrahae, quanto majus et mirabilius est virginem concipere, quam senem generare. Itaque multo ipsa magis contra spem in spem credidit, ut fieret mater Domini sui."

146. De Sales, *Oeuvres complètes*, 11:244–45. "Mais remarquez ces paroles: Vous estes bienheureuse d'avoir creu à tout ce que l'ange vous a dit; d'autant que cela fait voir que vous avez plus de foy qu'Abraham, parce que vous avez creu que la Vierge et la sterile concevroient; bien que ce soit une chose qui surpasse le cours de la nature."

147. Cheffontaines, "Sermo de Virginis Mariae," 37v.

148. Cheffontaines, "Homilia in die immaculatae conceptionis," 162v.

turies faced a formidable challenge when they spoke to the people about the Virgin Mary. They knew from the beginning that they faced congregations who were aware that significant numbers of people in Western Europe had abandoned Marian devotion entirely. The various branches of Protestantism favored a religious understanding that sought to glorify God alone, to deny the efficacy of prayers to the saints, and to exalt a more interiorized and individualized relationship between God and the human person than had existed in the later Middle Ages. Partly in response to these Protestant criticisms, the official Catholic presentation of Mary during and after the Council of Trent was in most cases more subdued. Her position in the scheme of Catholic theology was clarified, and her complete dependence upon God for all of her graces and merits received greater emphasis. Controversial aspects of traditional Marian piety and belief which the Church felt to be essential, such as her perpetual virginity, were retained, and the right of the Church to determine correct doctrine and practice was declared sufficient proof of their validity.

Unlike Protestantism, the Catholic Church remained linked to a tradition which had always proclaimed that the human will must cooperate with the grace of God to achieve salvation. Catholic preachers, therefore, appropriated the same personal, inward piety that so influenced the Protestant movement, as a means of urging Christians, aided by grace, to remake themselves within and without. Always, the primacy of the soul and spiritual life over the body was of major interest. By correcting inward faults and curbing sinful desires, as well as by striving to acquire virtue, Christians could provide themselves with the necessary disposition to perform useful exterior works and avoid sinful behavior. Mary and the other saints were painted in glowing terms as models of virtue. The inner perfection of their hearts had found full expression in their outward works. Imitation of their example would bring a heavenly reward.

While Mary's motherhood of Christ remained the basis for her importance, her virtues of humility, obedience, and love, gifts of God's grace, were said to be the ultimate causes of her glory and preferential treatment by God. Before Mary was able to conceive Christ bodily, she had become his spiritual mother through faith and the willingness to do God's will; this spiritual motherhood was dearer to her son than even her physical conception of him. If it is true that the fascination with the Immaculate Conception in the late Middle Ages represented the people's need to believe that, as Mary had been saved by God's grace, they might also hope for salvation, then the Church's portrayal of Mary had finally coincided perfectly with that hope. While none but the Virgin herself could claim the perfection of an Immaculate Conception, all could receive God's grace in the sacraments and strive to follow in her footsteps as virtuous, spiritual mothers of Jesus.

Five

Wounds of Love

Christ, Mary, and the Passion in the
Late Sixteenth Century

*Mary, however, suffered the most bitter martyrdom, as Simeon had
foretold to her. . . . For love is the measure of grief; the one who loves
more, suffers more, the greatest love is the cause of the greatest grief.*[1]

—St. Lawrence of Brindisi

*But since it is certain that the Son died of love, and that the Mother
died from the death of her Son, it must be true that the Mother died
of love.*[2]

—St. François de Sales

The Sword of Grief

SERMONS ON THE SUFFERING and death of Christ, and on the compassion
of his mother Mary, might well be the last place one would expect to find
abundant evidence of an increasing internalization of piety in the later
sixteenth century. What could better inspire a preacher to dwell on the
bodily torment of Christ than a sermon on the Passion? And how better
to illustrate the Virgin's compassion than by a dramatic presentation of its
physical manifestations? A late medieval preacher would certainly have
reasoned this way, but not so his later colleagues.

1. Lawrence of Brindisi, *Opera omnia*, 10 vols. (Patavia: Ex officina typographica seminarii, 1928), 1:586.
2. François de Sales, *Oeuvres complètes de Saint François de Sales, évêque et prince de Genève*,
16 vols. (Paris: J. J. Blaise, 1821), 11:312.

The catechism of the Council of Trent may have set the stage for a re-working of the Passion as it was presented to the people. In its exposition of the article of the Apostle's Creed which deals with Jesus' death, the catechism chose to stress the importance of his spiritual agony and declared, "It was the peculiar privilege of the Redeemer to have died when he himself decreed to die, and to have died, not so much by external violence, as by internal assent."[3]

St. François de Sales said almost exactly the same thing in a sermon given for the festival of Mary's Assumption. Christ, he said, had suffered more bodily anguish and pain of heart than anyone had ever experienced.

But nevertheless all these griefs, all these afflictions, all these blows, from the crown of thorns, from the whip, from the hammer, from the lance, were unable to cause him to die. Death had not the power to be victorious over such a life. . . . He died of love, this savior of my soul. . . . He was offered, because he himself willed it.[4]

St. François suggests that, unlike other human bodies, the body of Jesus could not be killed by physical violence alone, even by the brutal act of crucifixion. He died not only because he suffered the physical pain of the cross, but because he chose, in love, to allow his body to die when otherwise it would have continued to live. Jesus' death was caused by an inward act of the will.

In keeping with this desire to present the deepest pain of Christ as one of heart and soul, some preachers began to speak of Christ's heart being wounded by the sword of grief which pierced also the heart of his mother, a foretaste perhaps of the soon-to-be-popular cult of the Sacred Hearts of Jesus and Mary. Cardinal Robert Bellarmine emphasized the fact that Christ's own suffering was intensified by that of his mother, for after God the Father he loved no one as much as Mary. The sword of grief pierced

3. *The Catechism of the Council of Trent*, trans. J. Donovan (Baltimore: F. Lucas, Jr., 1829), 45.

4. De Sales, *Oeuvres complètes*, 11:310–11. ". . . mais neantmoins toutes ces douleurs, toutes ces afflictions, tous ces coups de mains, de roseau d'epines, de foüet, de marteaux, de lance, ne pouvoient le faire mourir. La mort n'avoit pas assez de force pour se rendre victorieuse sur une telle vie. . . . Il est mort d'amour, ce Sauveur de mon ame . . . ; Oblatus est, quia ipse voluit."

his heart even before hers, "nor did it come to the heart of the mother un-less through the heart of the Son. This, therefore, is the interior cross, these the nails, this the lance, which wrung that bloody sweat from the Lord's body."[5] St. Lawrence of Brindisi also agreed that Christ's griefs were so many swords, "transfixing his heart."[6] Even the physical thirst Je-sus endured was eclipsed by his spiritual thirst, because, St. François de Sales explains, "he desired with an insatiable thirst that every person be converted and benefit from his Passion."[7]

There was not, of course, a complete lack of attention to Jesus' physi-cal pain. He had suffered terribly, in greater agony than any human had ever endured. Yet, suffer as he did, this was not the cause of his death. Par-ticularly significant is the fact that the severity of Jesus' bodily pain is at-tributed not to its formation from Mary's flesh but to the involvement of the Holy Spirit, who ensured that his body was "more perfect and better organized than the bodies of other men."[8]

Another striking aspect of these later sermons on the Passion is the small amount of attention devoted to Mary's compassion for her son. Of-ten she scarcely appears except in reference to Jesus' words to her from the cross. Only St. François de Sales gives her a place of prominence somewhat comparable to the one that she held in the Passion sermons of

5. Robert Bellarmine, *Roberti cardinalis Bellarmini opera omnia*, 6 vols. (Naples: J. Giu-liano, 1860), 5:179. "Postremo veniebat ad mentem gladius ille his acutus qui viscera aman-tissimae matris penetratus esset; quae cogitatio, quis dubitat, quin frangeret ac dilaceraret pectus Dominicum? Post Deum Patrem neminem ita Dominus diligebat, ut suam optimam et sanctissimam matrem. Itaque cum sciret, quanta vehementia doloris antea a Simeone praedictus ante cor filii quam matris penetravit, neque ad cor matris nisi per cor filii per-transivit. Haec est igitur crux interior, isti sunt clavi, haec ist lancea, quae sudorem illum sanguinem de corpore Domini exprimebat."

6. Lawrence of Brindisi, *Opera omnia*, 5:263.

7. De Sales, *Oeuvres complètes*, 10:460. ". . . cette soif corporelle n'estoit rien en com-paraison de la soif spirituelle de laquelle son ame estoit alterée, car il desiroit avec une soif insatiable, qu'un chascun se convertist et profitast de sa Passion."

8. *Catechism of the Council of Trent*, 48. "His agony was increased by the very constitu-tion and frame of his body. Formed by the power of the Holy Ghost, it was more perfect and better organized than the bodies of other men can be, and was, therefore, endowed with a superior susceptibility of pain." As we have seen, while medieval preachers might attribute the special qualities of Jesus' body to its formation by the Spirit, most were more likely to mention in this connection the fact that it was formed from the virginal and pure blood of Mary.

the late Middle Ages. Preachers will speak with great warmth concerning Mary's suffering, but they do so most often in specifically Marian sermons. For example, there is only one significant mention of the Virgin in the two Passion meditations of St. Peter Canisius.[9] Elsewhere, however, Canisius does speak about Mary's grief in sermons devoted to Christ's circumcision and the Presentation in the temple.[10] François Le Picart says that Mary stood by the cross since she was destined to be the advocate of the sinners for whom her son died, but he offers no detailed discussion of her pain.[11] Even the Franciscan Lawrence of Brindisi pays scant attention to Mary when he preaches on the Passion,[12] although it is true that the volume of his Marian sermons goes a long way toward making up for this.

Whenever they speak of her suffering, most late sixteenth-century preachers describe Mary's compassion as emotional, a blow to the heart rather than the body. Canisius, François de Sales, and Lawrence of Brindisi all continue to quote St. John Damascene that the Virgin suffered at the Passion those griefs she had avoided in childbearing, but they make it clear that only spiritual and emotional pain was involved.[13] Canisius said that Mary "suffered in that part (the soul) which is held to be impassible, therefore . . . because she suffered spiritually and horribly from the sword of compassion for Christ, she was more than a martyr."[14] François de Sales explicitly denied any bodily connection between Mary and Jesus as he hung on the cross:

9. Peter Canisius, *Meditationes seu notae in evangelicas lectiones,* 2d ed., ed. Frederick Streicher, S.J., 2 vols. (Munich: Officina Salesiana, 1957), 2,1:269.

10. Ibid., 2,1:97, 104.

11. François Le Picart, *Les sermons et instructions chrestiennes, pour tous les jours de caresme, et feries de Pasques* (Paris: Nicolas Chesneau, 1566), 148r–148v. "Iesus Christ estant en croix il a constitué la vierge Marie nostre mere: car Saint Jean represente le pecheurs, et la glorieuse vierge Marie est nostre advocate."

12. Lawrence of Brindisi, *Opera omnia,* 5:387, 393, 399. Only in the first of these references is the mention of Mary more than a brief inclusion in a general statement about the actions of Christ on the cross.

13. Canisius, *Meditationes,* 2,1:97; de Sales, *Oeuvres complètes,* 11:261; Lawrence of Brindisi, *Opera omnia,* 1:60.

14. Canisius, *Meditationes,* 2,1:97. "Beata Dei genitrix, quia in ea parte passa est, quae impassibilis habetur, ideo (ut verum fatear) quia spiriitualiter et atrociter passa est, gladio compassionis Christi plus quam martyr fuit."

The body of Our Lady was not joined to, and did not touch that of her son in his Passion, but in her soul, she was inseparably united to the soul, to the heart, and to the body of her son, and if the blows that the blessed body of the Savior received on the cross did not wound the body of Our Lady, they were massive wounds to her soul.[15]

After describing the terrible suffering of Mary at the foot of the cross, Lawrence of Brindisi carefully explains that the Scriptures commonly use the pain of childbirth as a metaphor for extreme grief. No grief, he says, is worse than that of a parent for a child, as the examples of David and Job clearly show.[16]

Not all preachers, it seems, were prepared to reject completely the possibility that the Virgin had suffered in her own body the wounds of Jesus. Robert Bellarmine, usually a champion of the importance of the inward and spiritual, had inherited from his medieval Italian predecessors, San Bernardino of Siena in particular, a tendency to bring up the bodily unity of Mary and Jesus in the context of the Passion. Although elsewhere he speaks of Mary's crucifixion as one of the soul,[17] in a sermon on the Resurrection he speculates that the resurrected Christ would have remembered his mother's sorrow and gone to comfort her with the joy of his presence. After all, was not Mary of one bone and flesh with him and was she not, with him, fixed to the cross?[18] Devotional literature as well could still present a Virgin who suffered bodily. Maria de Agreda de Jesus (d. 1665) declared in her book *The City of God* that Mary had asked for and received a special dispensation of the Trinity allowing her to sense "in exact duplication" every pain that Jesus suffered.[19] Medieval devotional themes

---

15. De Sales, *Oeuvres complètes,* 10:306. ". . . le corps de Nostre-Dame n'estoit pas joint, et ne touchoit pas a celuy de son Fils en la passion; mais quant a son ame, elle estoit inseparablement unie a l'ame, au coeur, et au corps de son Fils, si que les coups que le beny corps du Sauveur receut en la croix, ne firent aucune blesseure au corps de Nostre-Dame; mais ils firent de grands contrecoups en son ame."

16. Lawrence of Brindisi, *Opera omnia,* 1:60–63.

17. Bellarmine, *Opera omnia,* 5:280.

18. Ibid., 197. "At tu, triumphator, posteaquam cum isto pulcherrimo corpore tuo praedam ac spolia divisisti, num moestae matris tuae non recordaberis, quae etiam os tuum et caro tua est? Ea certe tecum affixa fuit cruci?"

19. Maria de Agreda de Jesus, *The City of God.* Abridgement of the *Divine History and Life of the Mother of God,* trans. G. Blatter (Indiana: 1915), 502; quoted in Marina Warner, *Alone of All Her Sex: The Myth and Cult of the Virgin Mary* (New York: Alfred A. Knopf, 1976), 218.

pertaining to Mary's suffering at Calvary were still able to take root and grow in the changed climate of the post-Tridentine Church, but not on a permanent basis. Maria de Agreda's book made such extravagant claims for Mary that Innocent XI forbade Catholics to read it in spite of its popularity.[20] At least outwardly, the Virgin who would appear in future sermons would not pour forth extravagant public displays of grief. She would have to depend on the preachers to articulate her inner pain and love for Jesus. Mary herself would not be permitted to show it.

The sixteenth century, in fact, participated in a revival of the earlier medieval debate regarding Mary's experience at the cross and its public portrayal in art and sermons.[21] Harvey Hamburgh has addressed this issue in the Italian art of the cinquecento. He finds that while the Franciscan Pope Julius II was so devoted to Mary's suffering that he sought to create a new feast to celebrate it, Cardinal Cajetan disagreed.[22] Commissioned by the pope to investigate the subject, Cajetan produced his findings on July 17, 1506, in *De Spasimo gloriossime virginis Mariae matris dei*. He declared Mary's swoon to be unscriptural and a "morbid state" which suggested Mary suffered a "bodily defect." Instead, Mary participated in Jesus' Passion not with her body, but with her mind, the much more noble part.[23]

Hamburgh also indicates that similar attacks on medieval sermon descriptions of Mary's compassion were increasingly frequent in the later sixteenth century. One of them came from the pen of the famous Jesuit St. Peter Canisius. In his treatise on the Virgin, *De Maria Virgine*, Canisius seeks as far as possible to distinguish Mary from the public physical displays of grief common to other women. Instead, Mary completely controlled her passions and "showed nothing which contradicts holy modesty and dignity."[24] While Italian artists during the sixteenth century

---

20. Hilda Graef, *Mary: A History of Doctrine and Devotion*, 2 vols. (New York: Sheed and Ward, 1964), 2:55.

21. The portrayal of Mary as stoic is discussed in Chapter 2.

22. Harvey E. Hamburgh, "The Problem of 'Lo Spasimo' of the Virgin in Cinquecento Paintings of the 'Descent from the Cross,'" *Sixteenth Century Journal* 12, no. 4 (1981): 45.

23. Ibid., 45–46.

24. Peter Canisius, *De Maria Virgine*, vol. I (Ingolstadt: 1577), 4 c. 26; quoted in Hamburgh, "Problem of 'Lo Spasimo,'" 47. The full quotation provided by Hamburgh illustrates just how much Canisius wants to distance Mary from other women and from the way in which "tasteless or foolish preachers" had portrayed her in the past. Canisius says

continued to be influenced by popular piety and the Franciscan tradition of Mary's grief, eventually paintings of Mary at the cross depicted her in a much more "stoic" fashion, emphasizing her priestly role as the one who was willing inwardly to offer her son to achieve the world's salvation.[25]

Mary's love for Christ was the obvious cause of her terrible grief at his death. This love is especially prominent in the sermons of François de Sales and Lawrence of Brindisi. Lawrence concluded that Mary's sorrow was as great as was her love for her son. Since he surpassed all other sons who have ever been, Mary's love and suffering were greater than any other mother's; her suffering brought her true martyrdom at the Passion.[26]

François de Sales explained the actual death of Mary as a result of both her close spiritual union with Jesus and her love for him. Mary died in the death of Jesus because, although they were two persons, they shared "in one heart, in one soul, in one spirit, in one life." Mary's heart was pierced by a "spiritual sword" which wounds "the spirit and not the flesh"; nevertheless, it was the eventual cause of her death.[27] St. François describes Mary's death in highly romantic terms. She could be the heroine of a nineteenth-century novel, pining away with grief for her lost lover. St. François preached these words in a public sermon on the Assumption, delivered at Paris in 1602:

Alas! Her treasure, that is, her Son, was in heaven, her heart was no longer within her . . . In brief, her heart, her soul, her life was in heaven, how could she have remained on earth? Then finally after so many spiritual flights, so many ecstasies, this holy castle of chastity, this fortress of humility, having sustained miraculously thousands of assaults of love was taken captive by one last general assault, the

---

that Mary cannot be compared to "those women who, caught up in their sorrow, cry aloud, beat their breasts with their fists, pluck out their hair, scratch up their cheeks with their nails and proclaim loudly their misery. . . . For she held the human passions in restraint through spiritual greatness, showed nothing which contradicts holy modesty and dignity."

25. Hamburgh, "Problem of 'Lo Spasimo,'" 68–69.

26. Lawrence of Brindisi, *Opera omnia*, 5:255–56; 1:62, 586.

27. De Sales, *Oeuvres complètes*, 11:303–5. ". . . neantmoins puis qu'il s'agit de l'ame, et non pas du corps; de l'esprit et non pas de la chair, il ne faut pas l'entendre d'un glaive materiel et corporel, ains, d'un glaive spirituel et qui puisse atteindre l'ame et l'esprit."

love which vanquished her, led her beautiful soul as his prisoner, leaving only pale, cold death in her sacred body.[28]

Theologians and preachers of the late sixteenth century, like artists from the same period, were generally still inclined to set forth Mary's role at the Passion in priestly language, as though she were making a sacrificial offering. Francisco Suarez (d. 1617) was the first major theologian to develop a systematic Mariology in the sixteenth century. He said of Mary, "The most holy Mother of God has not only the honor of having given the substance of her flesh to the only-begotten God . . . hers was the task, as well, of caring for and nourishing the same victim and even of placing it near the altar at the appointed hour."[29]

Lawrence of Brindisi is most extravagant in his description of Mary's offering of her son. Mary had already offered Christ to God the Father at her Purification, giving back to God what was his to begin with. Mary, like Abraham, and like God the Father himself, was prepared to suffer the loss of her only son to fulfill the will of God and to save humanity from the curse of sin.[30] Mary was a "spiritual priest."

But did Mary not come through for us at the crucial moment of life when she stood next to the cross of Christ, as Abraham, full and more than full of the Spirit, truly sacrificing him in spirit to God, and truly offering him in charity for the salvation of the world? . . . The spirit of Mary was a spiritual priest, as the cross was an altar and Christ the sacrifice; and if the spirit of Christ himself was the principle priest, then the spirit of Mary was one with the spirit of Christ, indeed she was one with him in spirit as one soul in two bodies.[31]

28. Ibid., 312–13. "Helas! Son tresor, c'est à dire son Fils, estoit au ciel, son coeur n'estoit donc plus en elle; . . . Bref son coeur, son ame, sa vie estoit au ciel, comme eut-elle pu demeurer en terre? Doncques enfin apres tant de vols spirituels, apres tant de suspensions et d'extases, ce sainct chasteau de pudicité, ce fort d'humilité ayant soustenu miraculeusement mille et mille assauts d'amour, fut emporté et pris par un dernier et general assaut; l'amour qui en fut le vainqueur, emmena cette belle ame comme sa prisonniere, et laissa dans le corps sacré la pasle et froide mort."

29. Quoted in Warner, *Alone of All Her Sex*, 220.

30. Lawrence of Brindisi, *Opera omnia*, 1:524, 186.

31. Ibid., 183. "An non pro nobis in vitae discrimen Maria venit, cum iuxta crucem Christi stetit, eum, uti vero Abrahae spiritu plena ac superplena, Deo spiritu vere sacrificans, et pro mundi salute vera caritate offerens? . . . Mariae spiritus erat spiritualis sacerdos, sicut crux altare, et Christus sacrificium; licet spiritus ipse Christi esset principalis sacerdos, sed spiritus Mariae una erat cum spiritu Christi, imo unus cum eo spiritus erat, una veluti anima in duobus corporibus."

Like another Abraham, Mary would have crucified Jesus herself if this had been necessary,[32] but Jesus was much more dear to Mary than Isaac was to Abraham. God was aware of the piety of Abraham, but we see here the "infinite charity of Mary."[33] Once again, Mary is compared to Abraham and emerges the winner.

Lawrence of Brindisi wants to make it clear as well that Mary was no stoic, as some would have it, experiencing no real pain during the crucifixion because of her faith in the Resurrection. Mary did not have a heart of stone and truly grieved at Jesus' death.[34] He is careful, however, to refer to Mary's participation as purely spiritual, avoiding any suggestion of bodily unity with Jesus. He explicitly says that while they were joined in spirit, they inhabited two separate bodies.

Robert Bellarmine also compared Mary to Abraham, who had offered Isaac, trusting God to be able to raise him from death. Mary did no less. She offered Christ on the cross and felt no need to return to the tomb with the other women on the third day to anoint his body. Mary had firm faith that he had already risen as he said. In giving up Jesus to be crucified, Mary went even further than the demand of charity to lay down one's life for a friend. She loved Jesus more than her life, yet was willing to sacrifice him for the greater good of all.[35]

The greatest alteration in conventional descriptions of Mary's role in offering Jesus to God for human salvation comes from St. François de Sales's sermon on the Purification. In a startling departure from centuries of tradition, he suggests that it might have been not the Virgin mother but St. Joseph who offered Jesus to God in the temple. Fathers usually do

---

32. Ibid., 64. "Scio perfectissimam in ea extitisse fidem, perfectissimam caritatem, qua ipsamet suis manibus cum Abraham, si opus fuisset, unicum ac dilectissimum Filium suum Deo in sacrificium obtulisset ipsaque crucifixisset."

33. Ibid., 186. "Multo carior erat Mariae Christus, quam Abrahamo Isaac; dedit tamen illum Deo, pro sua in Deum eximia caritate et pietate. Quid non, postulatus, dedisset Deo, si filium carissimum dedit? Ex eo ait Deus se cognovisse pietatem Abrahae: cognoscamus et nos hinc infinitam caritatem Mariae."

34. Ibid., 64.

35. Bellarmine, *Opera omnia*, 5:280. "Si majorem hac dilectionem nemo habet, ut animam suam ponat quis pro amicis suis, quam excellens charitas Mariae fuit, quae filium illum pro amicis posuit, quem multo vehementius, quam animam suam diligebat?"

this, he says, because they "have a greater part than mothers" in their children. He does not explain himself here. Perhaps François de Sales has been reading Aristotle, who believed that mothers contributed only the matter to form the child's body, while fathers brought form and life. Or perhaps he wants to stress the role of fathers in the spiritual upbringing of children. He adds a ritual explanation: that since women would not yet have been purified, they would not have dared approach the altar of God. St. François nevertheless concludes cautiously that it could have been Mary who offered her son.[36]

St. François also denies the Virgin an active role at the cross. Her greatest contribution was in not resisting the will of God in the death of Jesus. Transfixed by sorrow, she still stood obediently at the foot of the cross in "perfect submission" to the divine plan.[37] She did not faint or make an excessive outward show of her grief, as some painters falsely portray. She remained upright and firm, her only grief an inward pain from the interior crucifixion of her soul.[38]

"She Did Not Say a Word"

We have come a long way from the Mary of late medieval sermons whose face was distorted by tears and bathed in the blood of Jesus as it poured from his body, the Mary who fainted at the sight of her son carrying his cross and who swooned once again when his dead body was removed from its beams. That Mary would have cried out in pain, rebuking

36. De Sales, *Oeuvres complètes,* 10:83. "Il est neantmoins plus probable, que ce fut plustost S. Joseph que Nostre-Dame, pour deux raisons. La premiere est, que les hommes venoient offrir leurs enfans, comme y ayant plus de part que les meres; la seconde raison est, que les femmes n'estant pas encore purifiées, elles n'osoient approcher de l'autel au se faisoient les offrandes."

37. Ibid., 77. ". . . et quant à Nostre-Dame, quel acte signalé d'obeyssance ne fit-elle pas à l'heure mesme de la mort do son divin Fils, qui estoit tout son amour; car elle ne resista aucunement; non-obstant qu'elle fust transpercée du glaive de douleur, ains demeura tousjours ferme et constante aux pieds de la croix, avec une parfaite soubmission a la tressaincte volonté du Pere Eternel."

38. Ibid., 452–53. ". . . la troisieme parole de Nostre-Seigneur, fut une parole de consolation qu'il dit à sa sacree Mere qui estoit au pied de la croix toute transpercée du glaive de douleur, quoy que non pasmée ny à coeur failly, comme quelques peintres la represent faussement? Car l'Evangeliste dit clairement le contraire, asseurant qu'elle demeura debout aux pieds de la croix, avec une fermeté nompareille."

Jesus' executioners and lamenting with an eloquence born of grief his un-just death. The Mary of the late sixteenth century is silent.

There is, to be sure, a form of communication between mother and son at the cross. It is a language of the heart, however, in which the souls of Jesus and Mary speak to each other without benefit of the audible word. For this kind of communion, the body is superfluous, as St. Law-rence confirms when he says that, while Mary stood bodily at the cross, she was there "even more in spirit."[39]

Robert Bellarmine echoes a theme heard occasionally in the Middle Ages when he attributes Mary's silence, and Jesus' as well, to grief. He says, "I indeed believe that the tongues of both were as mute because of such great sorrow, and that they were able to speak either not at all or only a little: but nevertheless the natural affection of the son was able to say a great deal to the heart of the Virgin."[40] Jesus' heart then asks his mother why she had come. Her grief only makes his worse. She replies that she cannot leave him unless he leaves her for he is the life of her life and soul of her soul.[41]

For St. François de Sales, Mary's silence at Calvary was a virtue which she had practiced all her life. When there was no room to be had at the inn in Bethlehem for the birth of Jesus, she did not complain or "say a word"; and she did not speak when the Magi came to adore the Christ Child. "But you see that which is most admirable on the mount of Cal-

---

39. Lawrence of Brindisi, *Opera omnia*, 1:68. "Stabat iuxta crucem Iesu mater eius. O sta-tum mirabilem! Imo O divinum miraculum! Stabat corpore, sed magis animo, virtute fide interrima."

40. Bellarmine, *Opera omnia*, 5:183. "Ego quidem arbitror, linguas amborum prae nimio dolore quasi mutas effectas, vel nihil vel omnino partim dicere potuisse; sed tamen ad cor Virginis effectum naturalem filii multum locutum esse." Olivier Maillard also placed a lengthy conversation between Mary and Jesus in Mary's heart, because he agreed with St. Bernard that she was too grief stricken to speak aloud. The overall effect is different from that of Bellarmine or de Sales, however, both because of the many other conversations Maillard attributes to Mary and Jesus, but also because Maillard has already said in the same sermon that on the day of the Passion, Mary is also too sorrowful to answer prayers ad-dressed to her. In other words, her silence is limited to this one occasion, and applies not only to the specific situation of her experience of Calvary, but also to its commemoration each liturgical year. See Olivier Maillard, "Passio domini nostri Jesu Christi," in *Sermones quadragesimales* (Paris: Antoine Caillaut, 1498), Introduction and Pt. 4.

41. Bellarmine, *Opera omnia*, 5:183.

vary, she made no outburst nor said a single word." Instead she sought only to listen to the words of her son.[42] As with St. Robert Bellarmine, St. François is still certain that communication occurred, but inwardly. Unlike Bellarmine, however, St. François's explanation rests not on a sorrow that prevented speech, nor even solely on Mary's virtue of silence. Their communion was silent because their greatest sorrow and pain was an inner torment that could only be shared inwardly.

And how great were the griefs which then pierced the sacred heart of our beloved and divine Savior! No one knows of it except he who suffered them and the holy Virgin Our Lady, who was at the foot of the cross, to whom undoubtedly he communicated them and who pondered them within herself. . . . But in so far as his greatest griefs were interior, they were known only to him who suffered them and to his holy Mother who participated in them.[43]

There are several possible explanations for the Virgin's silence in these sermons. It can be attributed to a greater attempt on the part of Catholic preachers to avoid "excesses" and to say only those things which have support in the Biblical account, or to a desire to focus greater attention on the death of Christ than on Mary's role. Yet there is no hesitancy in providing interior dialogue for Mary and Jesus; and the insistence that precise communication of thoughts and emotions could take place without audible speech reflects as much the changing religious sensibilities of the day as it does Catholic caution in the face of Protestant criticism. This change has already been apparent in the importance given to Mary's soul and

42. De Sales, *Oeuvres complètes*, 11:322–23. "Le sainct evangile fait un particuliere mention du silence de Marie [the sister of Martha]. . . . Is sembloit de mesme, que nostre digne Maistresse n'eust qu'un seul soin; voyez-la dans la ville de Bethleem, ou l'on fit tout ce que l'on pust pour luy trouver un logis, et ne s'en trouvant point, elle n'en dit mot, n'y n'en fait aucune plainte . . . : quelques jours apres les Roys le vindrent adorer, ou l'on peut penser quelles loüanges ils donnerent, et au Fils et à la Mere; neantmoins elle ne dit pas un seul mot . . . Mais ce qui est plus admirable, voyez-la sur le mont de Calvaire, elle ne jette point d'eslans, ny ne dit pas un seul mot."

43. Ibid., 10:456–57. "Et combien grandes furent les douleurs qui transpercerent alors le sacré coeur de nostre tres-aymable et divin Sauveur! Personne ne le sçait que luy qui les souffroit, et la sacrée Vierge Nostre Dame, qui estoit au pied de la croix, à laquelle sans doute il les communiquoit et laquelle les ruminoit en soy-mesme. . . . Mais d'autant que ses plus grandes douleurs estant interieurs, elles n'estoient conniies que de luy que les souffroit, et de sa saincte Mere, laquelle y participoit."

spiritual virtues over her body in discussions of her holiness and birth-giving. Now her soul becomes an instrument of communication as well. Christopher Cheffontaines described a purely interior conversation between the Virgin and her own soul.[44] In the sermons of Bellarmine and de Sales, we see her in spiritual communion and even conversation with Jesus, conducted from soul to soul, apart even from the spoken word. While the notion of a spiritual conversation was not unheard of in the Middle Ages, it had come to seem more and more plausible to the highly literate Churchmen of early modern Europe.

As we have seen, in traditional medieval religious culture, the body had a positive and even dominant role in communicating religious truth and in drawing people together into a common spiritual experience. Sight, touch, taste, and hearing were employed to perceive and appropriate the host, saints' relics, and visual depictions of the sacred in the liturgy, art, and religious drama. While Charles Zika describes late medieval religion as shaped primarily by sight,[45] speech, too, was a significant unifying religious force, in sermons certainly, but also in the sounds of worship and popular plays. Through the sounds of interactive speech, the body enabled persons to join their inmost selves, their ideas, thoughts, and feelings to the interior of another and to acquire knowledge of them. Naturally, Mary would speak as she stood at the cross. Her words, as related by preacher, actor, or at times even the people themselves, enabled those who heard them to share with Mary in a common participation in Jesus' suffering.

Over the course of the sixteenth century, however, people, especially the most literate, began to rely less and less upon speech and more upon printed materials for all sorts of communication. Speech certainly would always remain the primary means of daily human communication, and sermons not only did not disappear but began to be stressed even more as a means of inculcating proper doctrine and virtue in people's hearts and

44. See above, Chapter 4, n. 116 for the complete citation from Cheffontaines's sermon.
45. Charles Zika, "The Devil's Hoodwink: Seeing and Believing in the World of Sixteenth-Century Witchcraft," in *No Gods Except Me: Orthodoxy and Religious Practice in Europe 1200–1600*, ed. Charles Zika (Melbourne: Melbourne University History Monograph Series, 1991), 153.

lives. Even so, the role of the body in the transmission of thoughts and information seems to have become blurred. The increased reliance on sight and visual awareness, and the greater individuality that accompanied the growth of printing and literacy, caused the body to be seen largely as an instrument of individual separation and definition, in fact a barrier to sharing the truly important spiritual and inward truths of the soul.[46] David Chidester argues that, while sight may provide a sense of continuity between the person seeing and the object of sight, it nevertheless encourages individualization because it creates a sense that nothing outside the self and personal vision is necessary for communication.[47] By the sixteenth century, however, the growing European suspicion of the body in virtually all areas of experience, but especially of religious experience, was beginning to include distrust even in the sense of sight.[48] Only a purely spiritualized apprehension of the divine could be considered authentic.

This altered approach to communication and religion, which devalues the bodily senses and exalts the soul and the spiritual, was mirrored precisely in the Marian sermons of the day. Whereas before Mary's bodily unity with Jesus was a factor which ensured her ability to share with him in all aspects of his life, including the Passion, now she is able to share with him in soul, in spite of the fact that the two inhabit separate bodies.

46. Walter J. Ong, S.J., *Orality and Literacy: The Technologizing of the Word* (New York: Methuen, 1982), 80. Ong believes that alphabetic literacy, even without the presence of printing, can produce an approach to knowledge and religion that devalues the body and sense experience. He discusses the impact of writing on Greek philosophy, particularly that of Plato, and argues that it was the growing acquaintance with the written word that made possible the Greek philosophical method. Plato created an epistemological structure in which all true and unchanging knowledge belongs to the soul. Ong is using material drawn from Eric A. Havelock, *Preface to Plato* (Cambridge, Mass.: Harvard University Press, 1963). See also Kristen B. Neuschel, *Word of Honor: Interpreting Noble Culture in Sixteenth-Century France* (Ithaca, N.Y.: Cornell University Press, 1989), 203.

47. David Chidester, *Word and Light: Seeing, Hearing and Religious Discourse* (Urbana: University of Illinois Press, 1992), 136–37.

48. Zika, "Devil's Hoodwink," 153–55. Zika states that both secular and religious intellectuals in the late fifteenth and sixteenth centuries were "engaged in a large-scale reformulation of the relationship between the sensible world of human experience and the eternal realms of the divine." Reliance on sight or on any of the senses was being replaced by inner belief, which could not rely on sight as proof of certainty. Zika credits Protestants but also such Catholic thinkers as Erasmus for insisting on "separation between spirit and flesh, soul and body, man and God."

The entire religious culture of Europe in the sixteenth and seventeenth centuries, in both its Catholic and Protestant forms, was being shaped to a certain degree by what Richard Bauman calls "a progressive interiorization of the word."[49] Bauman's *Let Your Words Be Few* is an analysis of the role of speech and silence in the most extreme variety of inward religion in the period, the Quakers. Quakers distrusted all speech as belonging to the carnal or natural part of human experience. As the Quaker preacher George Fox put it, worldly people "have mouths full of deceit and changeable words."[50] Logically, Quakers developed a form of worship in which those who had been reborn in the Spirit met together for a silent communion, all waiting together patiently for whatever divine inspiration might come.[51] Speech could be a positive means of communicating God's message to others, but only within strict parameters and without undue elaboration.

Bauman states that another implication of silence for the Quakers had to do with the "suppression of self and of self-will" required to maintain the quiet necessary to hear the inward Spirit. It was one more way to "take up the cross."[52] This is certainly one meaning of Mary's silence on Calvary in sixteenth-century Catholic sermons. Her silence is completely passive, the polar opposite of the dramatic speech-act common to the Mary of the Middle Ages. She remains quiet, submissive to the will of God whatever it might be. Once again, it is St. François de Sales who sums up the essence of Mary's role, complete subjection:

Look at the whole course of her life and you will see nothing except continual subjection: she goes to the temple, but it is her parents who take her there, having promised herself there to God. Several years after, she married, she submitted even though she had made a vow of virginity. . . . In sum, you see in all her goings and comings, the holy Virgin in a subjection and admirable compliance which finally came to this, to see her son and her God die on the wood of the cross.[53]

---

49. Richard Bauman, *Let Your Words Be Few: Symbolism of Speaking and Silence among Seventeenth-Century Quakers* (New York: Cambridge University Press, 1983), 29.
50. Ibid., 20–21.   51. Ibid., 121.
52. Ibid., 22.
53. De Sales, *Oeuvres complètes*, 11:394. "Regardez tout le cours de sa vie, et vous ne verrez autre chose qu'une continuelle subjection: elle va au temple, mais ce sont ses parens qui l'y menent, l'ayant ainsi promis à Dieu: quelques annees apres on la marie, elle s'y soub-

Rather than actively offering her son, in St. François's sermon Mary stands by in obedient watchfulness. There is no initiative on her part at the cross or at any of the other turning points in her personal religious life.

Some of the traditional medieval beliefs about Mary's life after the Passion survived into the sixteenth century. Canisius reaffirms that Christ appeared first to his mother after the Resurrection,[54] while Bellarmine promises that the newly resurrected Jesus certainly visited his mother to reassure her of his triumph. In addition, Bellarmine describes Mary visiting, after the Ascension, the places that were more important to Jesus during his earthly life, visiting "if not in body, certainly in spirit and thought."[55] Perhaps even physical pilgrimage can now be replaced by a spiritual journey. Gone, however, is the suggestion that Mary alone preserved the faith of the Church while others deserted Jesus at the cross. The preachers who examined her make no mention of this idea. According to St. François de Sales, Mary did not die with Jesus in the Passion because she had to remain behind to comfort other Christians, to do more good works, and to assure any heretics that Christ actually possessed a human body. As the Church sings, "O Virgin, you have brought to ruin and destroyed all heresies."[56] Mary was the Lady of the Apostles, and without her presence the Church would likely have withered and become a lifeless garden prior to Pentecost.[57] In this way, the Virgin helped sustain the faith of the Church, but not because she alone possessed and preserved it.

Lawrence of Brindisi and Christopher Cheffontaines handed on the tradition, always strong within the Franciscan order, that attributed

---

met nonobstant qu'elle eust fait voue de virginité: . . . en somme vous verrez en toutes ses allés et venuës cette Ste Vierge en une subjection et souplesse admirable, qui arrive en fin jusques-là, que de voir mourir son Fils et son Dieu sur le bois de la croix."

54. Canisius, *Meditationes*, 2,1:284. "His tribus Mariis, ut vulgus illas vocat, Deipara virgo non est annumeranda, cui Christus redivivus iam ante, uti dicemus, seorsim apparuerat et quae in fide utique perfectior cognoscebat."

55. Bellarmine, *Opera omnia*, 5:280.

56. De Sales, *Oeuvres complètes*, 11:300–301. "La Vierge sa Mere demeurant apres luy servoit d'un asseuré tesmoignage pour la verité de sa nature humaine, commencant par là à verifier ce que nous chantons d'elle, cunctas haereses interemisti, O Vierge tu as ruiné et destruit toutes les heresies."

57. Ibid., 15.

Mary's heavenly queenship and authority to her sharing with Christ in the Passion. Mary reigns with Christ because she suffered with him. The impact of Cheffontaines's assertion is lessened, however, by the fact that he likens the suffering and endurance of the Virgin to that of all Christians who are ready to suffer for Christ in the world. Mary reigns with Christ throughout the whole earth because ". . . who among men was ever with him more or suffered more for him than this his mother, whose heart and soul were pierced by the sword of grief because of his passion and death? The one who suffers with Christ, is rightly believed and said to reign with Christ, if Paul is not a liar."[58] Cheffontaines is referring to St. Paul's second letter to Timothy, 2:12, which reads, "if we endure, we shall also reign with him." This would indicate that Mary has received the reward granted to anyone who suffers with Christ. Her added authority comes from the greater degree to which, as his mother, she participated in her son's pain. Cheffontaines's sermons are obviously concerned throughout with defending Catholic teaching against Protestant accusations that it is unscriptural. This is another instance of that defense.

The Passion provided one further element of the reformed Catholic presentation of Mary's importance. There was general agreement among the preachers that Mary is the mother not only of Christ but of all Christians, an understanding of her role which the Church had taught for centuries. As in the past, the preachers believed that Christ had deliberately bestowed this extended motherhood on the Virgin when, from the cross, he gave St. John to her as a son and protector. "In John," declares Christopher Cheffontaines, "Christ commends all his beloved and true disciples to his mother, and he showed in the same place by this example, that all true Christians, all true disciples ought to have her as their Mother."[59]

---

58. Christopher Cheffontaines, "Sermo de Virginis Mariae laudibus et honore, qui in qualibet eius festivitate haberi ad populum potest," in *Novae illustrationes christianae fidei*, pt. 2 (Paris: Sittart, 1586), 31v–32r. "An quisquam, unquam hominum, plus cum eo et pro eo passus est, quam haec eius mater, cuius animam, cuius cor, tot ob eius passionem et mortem, doloris gladii transfoderunt. Quae compassa cum Christo est, recte cum Christo, si Paulus mentitus non est, regnare creditur et dicitur."

59. Ibid., 53r–53v. "In Ioanne autem, omnes suos dilectos et veros discipulos, matri suae Christus commendabat, et e contra quo in loco, matrem suam, omnes veri Christiani, omnes veri eius discipuli, eam deinceps habere deberent, hoc exemplo monstrabat."

Since the Virgin is the spiritual mother of Christians who live by the Spirit, they owe her even greater honor than they do their bodily mothers.[60] St. François de Sales argued that Mary did not resist when Jesus gave her St. John as a son rather than himself because she "knew well that in the person of St. John, she accepted all children of the cross of our Lord as her own, and that she would be from that time on the dear mother of all Christians."[61] All true Christians love the Virgin, and no one can be the brother of Christ who does not acknowledge Mary as mother. St. François adds, no doubt for the benefit of Protestants, that those who are not brothers of Christ cannot inherit with him eternal life.[62]

Post-Tridentine preachers never forgot, even in the midst of a Passion sermon, that one of their duties was to provide the people with virtuous examples to imitate in their everyday lives. They supplied these implicitly whenever they described the spiritual qualities of Jesus and Mary, no matter what the context, but explicit admonitions to imitate the virtues displayed by Christ and his mother at Calvary are also present. The clear message is that Christ's followers must be prepared to suffer and die for him if this is their destiny.

Lawrence of Brindisi catalogued the virtues shown by Christ at his death: poverty, patience, mercy, desire for righteousness, justice, grief, and contempt of the world. Quoting I Peter 2:21, he told his hearers that "Christ suffered for us, leaving you an example so that you might follow in his footsteps."[63]

60. Ibid., 54v. "Quod si matres carnis nostrae eruditrices habemus, et ideo reveremur eas, non multo magis reverebimur spiritum matrem, et vivemus? Ut spiritu ergo vivamus, honoranda haec à nobis est, multo maiori honore, quàm carnis nostrae parentes honorare debemus."

61. De Sales, *Oeuvres complètes*, 10:486–87. "O Dieu: quel eschange du Fils au serviteur, de Dieu à la creature? Neantmoins elle ne le refusa point, sçachant bien qu'en la personne de S. Jean, elle acceptoit tout les enfans de la croix de Nostre-Seigneur pour siens, et qu'elle seroit desormais la chere mere de tous les chrestiens."

62. Ibid., 11:36. "Et ceux qui ne sont pas avortons du christianism aiment cette dame, l'honorent, la loüent en tout. . . . et nul n'aura Jesus-Christ pour frere, qui n'aura eu Marie pour Mere, et qui ne sera point frere de Jesus-Christ, il n'heritera point avec luy." See also Lawrence of Brindisi, *Opera omnia*, 5:369.

63. Lawrence of Brindisi, *Opera omnia*, 5:335. "Christus passus est pro nobis, vobis relinquens exemplum ut sequamini vestigia eius."

In a meditation on the Presentation in the temple, Peter Canisius affirmed that Mary's grief demonstrated that suffering is inevitable for those who belong to God. Her willingness to suffer shows that it is better to die with Christ than have worldly wealth, "for the apostolic doctrine is that which always maintains 'it is fitting that we enter the kingdom of God through many tribulations.'"[64] The other women who remained at the cross with Jesus and then came on Sunday to anoint his body are likewise examples, showing a firm faith in the face of disaster. For this reason, Canisius says he never speaks disparagingly of women. Instead, these women ought to be imitated.[65]

Bellarmine pointed out that God had never loved two people more than Jesus and Mary, but how did he show his love? He gave them the worst crosses of all to bear. When sorrow comes, therefore, it should be born patiently. "If you suffer because of your sins, you bear the cross of the good thief; but if you are innocent, rejoice even more. For you imitate better and more perfectly Christ and Mary."[66]

As Lawrence of Brindisi's quotation of I Peter indicates, admonitions to suffer with Christ are as old as the Church itself. Still, they would have had an especially sharp edge when they were preached against the backdrop of growing religious strife and warfare in the sixteenth century. As they continued to do battle against the enemies of the Catholic faith, preachers sought to prepare the foot soldiers for their part in the conflict.

The Virgin of the post-Tridentine Church remained, as always, the prototype of the Church and the saint of saints, whose example of selfless love should be imitated by all the faithful. But whereas the form of Mary's self-denial in medieval sermons was an active choice to participate as God's partner in the divine plan, lived out in the life of her son from

64. Canisius, *Meditationes*, 2,1:97–98. "Praestat in cruce cum Maria Christo commori, quam sine Christo cum divite epulone in hoc mundo florere et mundi copiis omnibus abundare. Apostolica enim doctrina est, quae semper obtinet: 'Per multas tribulationes oportet nos intrare in regnum Dei.'"

65. Ibid., 287–88.

66. Bellarmine, *Opera omnia*. 5:182. "Nam undecumque veniat tribulatio, modo patienter feratur, et propter Deum, salutaris crux est. Et si quidem pateris propter peccata, crucem portas boni latronis, vero innocens, magis gaude. Nam melius et perfectiusque Christum et Mariam imitaris."

conception to cross, more and more Mary's contribution becomes a quiet choice to allow God to act in her own life and in that of Jesus. The Virgin offers her son at Calvary, but it is a silent, subservient offering allowing no public view of the cross she carries in her heart. Whatever priestly dignity she may possess is highly muted.

The earthy and involved Mary, as presented by Jean Gerson or San Bernardino, had always been humble and obedient, yet she had an authority rising from her vocation which often permitted her to enter prominently into the life of Jesus. Nowhere was this more evident than her vocal laments at the cross and the impassioned conversations that she had with Jesus prior to his crucifixion and at Calvary with any who were present with her.

By the time of Christopher Cheffontaines and St. François de Sales, there are few preachers who, like St. Lawrence, ascribe to Mary the dynamic part she had played in the past; and even he removed it from his sermons on the Passion. The physical mother of Jesus, the Virgin still occupied a place of prominence as the one who had given the substance of her body to form that of the Son of God. But her shared flesh with Christ no longer assured her of her place in his life. In their drive to exhibit the superiority of the spiritual over the material, preachers had now chosen to praise Mary as Jesus' spiritual mother instead, and to assert that the spiritual suffering of Jesus and his mother at Calvary surpassed even the bodily pain of the cross. In her earthly life, Mary has become a woman who possessed primarily the virtue of inner, silent obedience. Her wounds of love, suffered in Jesus' Passion, are, for the most part, tastefully hidden from the world, visible only to God and to the inner spiritual eyes of faith.

Six

Ubi Maria, ibi ecclesia

Marian Prayers and Devotional Societies after Trent

For I dare to say that it is through devotion and veneration for the
Virgin that the Elect are distinguished from the reprobate, the sons of
God from the sons of the devil, and the Church of Christ from the syn-
agogue of Satan.[1]

—St. Lawrence of Brindisi

If anyone comes to you and refuses to say the Ave to the queen moth-
er of the son of God. . . . but nevertheless says he is sent by God to re-
form and restore the true religion, do not believe him.[2]

—Christopher Cheffontaines

The entire ancient Church throughout all the world, in a perfect
agreement of spirit, has always greeted the Mother of God by this an-
gelic salutation, "Hail Mary, full of grace."[3]

—St. François de Sales

"The Infallible Witness of Tradition"

THROUGHOUT THE MIDDLE AGES the Virgin Mary, mother of Christ, was
the most powerful symbol of the Church, mother of Christians. Her As-

1. Lawrence of Brindisi, *Opera omnia*, 10 vols. (Patavia: Ex officina typographica semi-narii, 1928), 1:171.
2. Christopher Cheffontaines, "Sermo de Virginis Mariae laudibus et honore, qui in qualibet eius festivitate haberi ad populum potest," in *Novae illustrationes christianae fidei*, pt. 2 (Paris: Sittart, 1586), 44v–45r.
3. François de Sales, *Oeuvres complètes de Saint François de Sales, évêque et prince de Genève*, 16 vols. (Paris: J. J. Blaise, 1821), 12:66.

sumption into heaven was but a prelude to the future glory of the Church Triumphant; her intercession for sinners mirrored the prayers of the Church on earth on behalf of the faithful. Medieval Christians fully expected Mary to care for her spiritual children and always looked to her for healing and for mercy. There was no reason to suppose that the Catholic Church after the Council of Trent would try seriously to alter so ancient a custom. In the face of Protestant attacks, the decrees of the council and the catechism it produced defended prayers to all the saints as useful, in no way detracting from the supreme glory of God.[4]

Protestant attempts to eliminate Marian devotion did mean that the prayers offered to Mary by loyal Catholics would take on an added layer of meaning. After Trent, they will be so many stones in the boundary wall separating, as Lawrence of Brindisi said, "the Church of Christ from the synagogue of Satan."[5] As the sinless and intact virginity of Mary's body traditionally stood, in the Catholic mind, for the purity of the Roman Church, so the prayers which praised her and sought her aid were manifestations of the seamless and unbroken tradition of Catholic faith and piety.

One important part of the Church's tradition that had a direct bearing on Mary's position as intercessor was the doctrine of her Assumption. In the later Middle Ages, as we have seen, Mary's effectiveness as intercessor was closely tied to her bodily presence in heaven. In the late sixteenth century, Catholic preachers still proclaimed Mary's Assumption as the fitting conclusion to her sinless life as Jesus' mother, even in a period when they often preferred to focus on her soul and spiritual virtues. The Council of Trent's decision to attribute equal authority to both Scripture and the unwritten traditions of the Church enabled the doctrine to continue to be accepted.[6] It was also one more way to assert the Church's right to deter-

4. *Canons and Decrees of the Council of Trent: Original Text with English Translation*, trans. H. J. Schroeder, O.P. (St. Louis: Herder, 1941), 483–84; *The Catechism of the Council of Trent*, trans. J. Donovan (Baltimore: F. Lucas, Jr., 1829), 246–47.

5. Lawrence of Brindisi, *Opera omnia*, 1:171. "Nam audeo dicere quod ex pia devotione et cultu in Virginem vel maxime Electi a reprobis internoscuntur, filii Dei a filiis diaboli, Ecclesia Christi a synagoga satanae."

6. *Canons and Decrees of the Council of Trent*, 297. The decree states that the Church understands the truth of the Gospel to be contained "in libris scriptis et sine scripto traditionibus."

mine doctrine against Protestant allegiance to the principle of "sola scriptura."

Robert Bellarmine and François de Sales continued to promote belief in Mary's bodily Assumption on the grounds that the ancient traditions of the Church are to be trusted. The entire introduction to one of Bellarmine's sermons on the Assumption is an attack on heretics who put their trust in Christ, but not in the Church he founded on the rock of St. Peter.[7] St. François agrees that even if we cannot prove Mary's Assumption through reference to Scripture, the "infallible witness" of tradition and the Church provide sufficient assurances of its truth.[8] Tradition affirms that Mary both died and was raised again.[9] As Mary once received Christ when he came to earth in bodily form, Christ received his mother into heaven at her Assumption.[10] In agreement with the tradition they preach, Bellarmine and St. François ground Mary's right to be assumed into heaven on her bodily motherhood of Christ and on her sinless life. Christ would not have allowed the body that bore him for nine months to suffer decay.[11] Bellarmine emphasizes that the Virgin's Assumption should be the source of joy for everyone, for she is neither God nor angel, but shares the same human nature possessed by all humanity, even the weakest of human creatures, woman.[12]

7. Robert Bellarmine, *Roberti cardinalis Bellarmini opera omnia*, 6 vols. (Naples: J. Giuliano, 1860), 5:276–83.

8. De Sales, *Oeuvres complètes*, 11:303. ". . . mais la verité, est telle qu'elle est morte et trespassé aussi bien que son Fils et Sauveur: car encore que cela ne se puisse prouver par l'Escriture, si est-ce que la tradition et l'Eglise qui sont d'infaillibles tesmoins nous en asseurent."

9. Ibid., 316.

10. Ibid., 330. ". . . scavoir comment cette glorieuse Vierge receut Nostre-Seigneur dans ses chastes entrailles lors qu'il descendit du ciel en terre: et l'autre, comment Nostre-Seigneur la receut lors qu'elle quitta la terre pour aller au ciel."

11. Ibid., 318. ". . . et ne permettez pas que ce corps qui vous a engendré sans corruption, soit maintenant subjet à la mort; mais resuscitez-le, et le saississez sur les aisles de vostre puissance et bonté, pour le transporter du desert de ce monde en la felicité immortelle." See also Bellarmine, *Opera omnia*, 5:281. "Et quis, obsecro, credere posset, arcam sanctitatis, domicilium verbi, templum Spiritus sancti corruisse? Exhorret plane animus meus vel cogitare carnem illam virgineam, quae Deum genuit, peperit, aluit, gestavit, vel in cinerem esse conversam, vel in escam vermibus traditam."

12. Bellarmine, *Opera omnia*, 5:276. "Beata siquidem Virgo, non Deus, non Angelus sed homo tantum erat, ejusdem naturae, ejusdem mortalitatis, cujus nos omnes sumus: quin

Strangely, it was left to St. Lawrence of Brindisi, the preacher who so liked to praise the role of Mary's body in the Incarnation, to say of her Assumption what one would have expected to hear from others in the late sixteenth century: that it was the reward of her fullness of grace, not of her physical motherhood of Christ. Christ's love for his mother was inspired by grace and the spiritual, not the carnal.

Mary was not assumed into heaven and placed by Christ over all the choirs of angels because of affection for her flesh, because she was his fleshly mother. . . . Nor is Christ the giver of glory in so far as he is man, but because he is God: and since on earth he seems never to have cared for Mary out of affection for her flesh. . . . Therefore out of spiritual affection Christ loved his mother, not out of fleshly considerations, but of spiritual, not with respect to nature but to grace, to virtue and to holiness.[13]

Indeed, although while on earth Mary possessed a fleshly body, in mind and in spirit she was always in heaven.[14] Consequently, the glory that belongs to Mary in heaven is the ultimate reward of her merits. She was endowed with more graces than anyone else in the Church Militant; therefore she enjoys the supreme level of glory in the Church Triumphant.[15] Clearly, for all of his continuation of many medieval themes, St. Lawrence, too, has been affected by the emphasis on interior devotion common to his own day.

Whatever reasons these preachers give for the honor of the Virgin's Assumption into heaven, they are clear that her Assumption, unlike Jesus'

---

etiam, quod magis est admirandum, humilioris. Nam foeminarum naturam infirmiorem et humiliorem esse, quam virorem natura sit, quis ignorat? Et tamen hanc ipsam virginem, natura hominem, sexu foeminam, conditione mortalem, ex hominibus natam . . . jam terrae montes, spatia elementorum, collorem regiones transcendisse, et super omnes omnium angelorum choros, ut ecclesia canit, exaltatem, proxime ad divinum Numen accessisse credimus."

13. Lawrence of Brindisi, *Opera omnia,* 1:576–77. "Non fuit a Christo assumpta Maria in coelum et super omnes Angelorum choros collocata ex affectu carnis, eo quod Mater ipsius carnalis fuerit. . . . nec Christus largitor est gloriae quatenus homo est, sed quatenus Deus est, et cum in terris esset ex affectu carnis Matrem nihili curare visus est. . . . Affectu igitur spirituali Christus Matrem diligebat, non intuitu carnis sed spiritus, non respectu naturae sed gratiae, sed virtutis, sed sanctitatis."

14. Ibid., 154. "Maria autem, quae, carne quidem et corpore in terra constituta, mente et spiritu semper erat in coelo."

15. Ibid., 571.

Ascension, was a gift of grace. Mary was unable to rise from death and enter heaven through her power alone. For this reason, the Church has always taught Christians that Mary was assumed, not that she ascended. That honor belonged to Christ alone.[16]

These constant assurances that Mary received all her honors as gifts of grace and that she in no way eclipses the shining brightness of her son continue to reveal the tension felt by Catholic preachers who wanted to express freely the opinions of the Church yet also needed to respond to Protestant criticisms. This dual purpose helped revive and popularize the traditional metaphor of Christ as the sun and the Virgin as the moon. As a creature, and not God, Mary was able to shine only with the glow of a reflected light, the light of Jesus himself. So preached François de Sales. Even so, she could command an honor infinitely greater than all of God's other creatures, though infinitely less than that of her son.[17]

Lawrence of Brindisi could say that the entire Trinity dwells with Mary, that her throne is only one step removed from that of God himself,[18] and that she is more like God in dignity than any creature;[19] but she is to Christ as the moon to the sun, shining by virtue of his light, not her own.[20] Similar statements were made by Bellarmine, and Francis Panigarola depicted Mary as the Dawn, which then gives birth to the "Sun of Righteousness."[21] Of course the lesser light of dawn is soon swallowed up in the full radiance of the day.

Christopher Cheffontaines defends veneration of the Virgin by reaffirming the traditional grades of honor due to God, to the Virgin, and to the other saints: "latria," "hyper-dulia," and "dulia." He refuses even to

16. Bellarmine, *Opera omnia,* 5:234, 276–77; de Sales, *Oeuvres complètes,* 10:292, 11:341–42.

17. De Sales, *Oeuvres complètes,* 11:324.

18. Lawrence of Brindisi, *Opera omnia,* 1:213, 573. "Sedet Christus in throno Dei ad dexteram Patris, Maria autem ad Christi dexteram collocata est, . . . Thronus igitur Mariae in coelo uno gradu distat a throno Dei tanquam Genitrix et vera Mater Dei."

19. Ibid., 144. "Beatissima Virgo gratia plena est, Deo simillima facta in summa altissimaque dignitate, qua maior excogitari non potest, cum facta sit vera Sponsa et Mater Dei."

20. Ibid., 192. ". . . Christum uti solem, qui proprio lumine fulgidissime splendet, et Mariam instar lunae, quae magno quidem lumine decorata est, sed tamen a sole sibi communicato." See also 1:297.

21. Bellarmine, *Opera omnia,* 5:282, 382; Francis Panigarola, "Predica di Maria Vergine, e Madre" (Rome: 1589), 215r.

discuss the validity of this distinction with heretics.[22] In the same way, Lawrence of Brindisi reasons that the truth always seems to lie somewhere between two extremes, just as Christ hung on the cross between two thieves. The Jews believed that God is one; the Gentiles, that there are many gods. Christians know that God is both one and triune. Ancient heretics wanted to call Mary a goddess; new heretics refuse to honor her at all. The true Church of Christ honors her as Mother of God and blessed, yet knowing that she is not God, but a creature of God.[23] These preachers left no doubt about either the praises due to Mary as Mother of God, or her subordinate position to Christ.

"Ave Maria": Weapon of Orthodoxy

Prayers to the Virgin have always constituted the most frequent and pervasive means of honoring her, and among such prayers the "Ave" continued to be the form especially favored by the Church after Trent. The "Ave" remained a powerful weapon in the Catholic Christian's war against sin, for it procured the intercession of the Mother of God on the sinner's behalf. In the late sixteenth century, it became a weapon in the war against heresy as well.

Francis Panigarola declared in a sermon delivered in Rome in 1589 that Mary herself had designated the Roman Church as her own, in as much as her son was the true founder of the greatness of Rome as the Church's capital city.[24] His statement demonstrates perfectly Mary's place in the post-Tridentine Church. Her duty to be the protectress of the Church was being enlarged. The Virgin was to be not only the advocate of Christian sinners before God, but, often portrayed with sword in hand, the defender of the Roman Church against the Protestant heresy, [25] a role which ap-

---

22. Cheffontaines, "Sermo de Virginis Mariae," 40v–41r.

23. Lawrence of Brindisi, *Opera omnia*, 1:322.

24. Panigarola, "Predica," 218v. "Il figlio, Roma, ti ha fatta sua casa, sua Città, sua sede, capo della sua Chiesa, schuola della sua religione, maestra del sue culto, regola della sua disciplina; ove concorre il mondo, ove tutte le patrie fanno una patria sola, ove è fondata la pietra, e base de tutto il Christianesimo: E la madere pare, che ti habbia specialmente fatta sua habitatione suo albergo, sua patria, suo Templo." See also 219r. "Celebratissima Chiesa: Fatta da Romani, e nobili, ma quello, che piu importa, dalla istessa Maria dissegnata."

25. Louis Chatellier, *The Europe of the Devout: The Catholic Reformation and the Formation*

pears to stand in stark contrast to the usual contemporary portrait of Mary as passive and obedient. Apparently, as with the Virgin of the Visitation, post-Tridentine churchmen are prepared to use the Virgin as a model of holy action when the cause is right.

As champion of orthodoxy, Mary was the patron of the numerous sodalities of the Virgin established throughout Catholic Europe by the Jesuits. These religious societies, which included many lay people as well as churchmen, were outposts in the war to regain Europe for Catholicism and to reshape European society by inspiring it with a new sense of religious devotion. The Rosary, composed of fifteen decades of "Aves," was one of the central acts of piety performed by sodality members.[26]

St. Peter Canisius summed up the connection between the Virgin, the "Ave," and the goals of the Jesuit societies in a letter:

It seems to me that we can all the more certainly restore the Catholic religion in Germany if a large number of men yearn in their hearts, in the name of Jesus, to defend the cult of the holy Virgin and to develop the congregation already begun. The heretics may ridicule and mock the children of Christ who sing Hosannas and Ave Marias. The new world which will have restored the honor of the Mother of God with a new zeal in all categories of men will surprise them.[27]

Canisius places the Marian congregations in the vanguard of the Catholic Church's assault against Protestantism in Germany, an assault whose success will be measured by the degree to which devotion to Mary is restored among the people. In this context, the Rosary, understood as both the prayers and the chaplet of beads, was a symbol of loyalty to the Roman Church, the Church whose patron was the Virgin.

The "Ave" had been in use, in one form or another, for hundreds of years, but it was only in the late fifteenth and early sixteenth centuries that, in the form of the Rosary, it became a widely popular devotion. By the 1560's the Rosary had assumed its final form. Pope Pius V was the first

---

of a New Society, trans. Jean Birrell, Editions de la Maison des Sciences de l'Homme (New York: Cambridge University Press, 1989), 6–8.

26. Ibid., 5. Each member was instructed to say the "Salve Regina" when rising, the "Ave Maris Stella" in the evening, and during the day at least five "Paternosters" and fifty "Aves."

27. Ibid., 9. Chatellier quotes Canisius secondarily from Anna Coreth, "Die ersten Sodalitaten der Jesuiten in Osterreich, Geistigkeit und Entwicklung," *Jahrbuch für Mystiche Theologie* (1965): 37–38.

to include in the reformed Roman breviary the complete modern form of the "Ave."[28] His bull of 1569, *Consueverunt,* was the first official Catholic document to describe the Rosary devotion in detail.[29] It was also Pius V who in 1573 established October 7 as the feast of the Rosary. The feast, dedicated to Our Lady of Victories, was intended to commemorate the battle of Lepanto on October 7, 1571. This victory over the Turks by the Holy League, led by Don John of Austria, crushed Turkish power in the Mediterranean. According to Pius, Don John's success was due solely to the intercession of Mary, procured by the many Rosaries which had been said by the Marian congregations of Rome.[30] Once again, the Virgin was victorious over heresy, and the popularity of Marian societies received a tremendous boost.

The first Jesuit Marian society of the century was formed in 1563 by Jean Leunis, professor at the Jesuit College of Rome. It was begun among his students, and their goals were to honor the Virgin by the common practice of devotions and good works.[31] Members pledged to hear Mass and say either the Little Office of the Virgin or the Rosary each day. In 1564, the group was formally placed under the protection of Mary, who was called by the title "Maria Annunciata"; Gregory XIII accorded them special recognition.[32] From Rome, similar congregations spread to Paris and the Collège de Clermont, and then to other cities in France.[33]

These Jesuit groups were the sixteenth-century equivalent of the popular late fifteenth-century Rosary confraternities such as Jacob Sprenger's, founded in 1475 in Cologne, except that their popularity had become even greater and they were concerned with the moral reform of Catholic society as well as with private devotion. While they were not parishes but separate devotional organizations, some Marian societies did hold Masses on their own. At times, these Masses were more popular with the local

---

28. Marina Warner, *Alone of All Her Sex: The Myth and Cult of the Virgin Mary* (New York: Alfred A. Knopf, 1976), 306.

29. Hilda Graef, *The Devotion to Our Lady* (New York: Hawthorn Books, 1963), 69.

30. Hilda Graef, *Mary: A History of Doctrine and Devotion,* 2 vols. (New York: Sheed and Ward, 1964), 2:17.

31. E. Villaret, S.J., "Marie et la Compagnie de Jésus," in *Maria: Etudes sur la sainte Vierge,* ed. Hubert DuManoir de Juaye, vol. 2 (Paris: Beauchesne, 1952), 962.

32. Graef, *Mary,* 2:26.

33. Villaret, "Marie et la Compagnie de Jésus," 963.

people than their own parish services, a situation which could cause considerable jealousy among local priests.

Popular preachers promoted the cult of the Virgin, including the Rosary, for the same reasons as the Jesuit sodalities. In Peter Canisius, the two sources of support for Marian devotion were combined. A famous and successful Catholic preacher in Germany, he also founded or inspired numerous Jesuit societies dedicated to Mary, including the congregation of the Assumption in Fribourg. In addition, he published a work in praise of Mary in 1577, *De Maria Virgine incomparabili*. Canisius was particularly sympathetic to popular religious practices and the devotional needs of the broad spectrum of Catholic laity. He supported those aspects of Marian piety, such as the Rosary, which he felt would best inspire them with loyalty to the Church.[34]

Canisius's sermons certainly encouraged Christians to pray to Mary. Using a standard medieval theme, he illustrated her willingness to speak on behalf of the faithful by showing that she interceded for her friends at Cana, preparing the way for Jesus to transform water into wine. The testimony of the orthodox Church, said Canisius, proved that the Virgin continues to be a successful advocate before her son for those who come to her in prayer. Canisius declared,

And among the saints, indeed I pay tribute to none more fully than to Mary, the Virgin Mother of God, and with the whole orthodox Church, I will honor her as advocate and Mother of Mercy, and with Athanasius the Great, Gregory of Nazianzus and Ephraem and with Basil I will invoke her piously, certain that when she has interceded with her son for me, the water of tribulation and pain will give way to the wine of spiritual grace and consolation.[35]

Lawrence of Brindisi not only declared Marian devotion to be the distinguishing mark of the true Church of Christ,[36] but also reproached

---

34. A. G. Dickens, *The Counter Reformation* (New York: W. W. Norton, 1979), 144–45.

35. Canisius, *Meditationes*, 2,1:140. "Et inter sanctos quidem nulli amplius quam Deiparae virgini Mariae tribuam illamque cum omnibus orthodoxis advocatam ecclesiae et misericordiae matrem honorabo simulque cum Athanasio Magno, Gregorio Nazianzeno et Ephrem, Basilii diacono, pie invocabo, nimirum ut ipsa apud filium intercedente mihi pro aqua tribulationis et angustiae vinum spiritualis consolationis et gratiae concedatur."

36. Lawrence of Brindisi, *Opera omnia*, 1:171.

those Catholics who do not salute Mary, the Ark of God, with proper reverence in the "Ave." There are even many, he says, no doubt in reference to Protestants, who dishonor her with "sacrileges, curses, and with diabolical tongues utter horrible and foul blasphemies."[37]

François de Sales linked the "Ave" to the true Church's unbroken tradition. The entire ancient Church addressed Mary with the angelic words, and the Church continues to do the same in order to please God by honoring his mother. St. François exclaims, "O holy greeting, O fully authentic praise, O rich and modest honors, the great God dictated them, a great angel pronounced them, a great evangelist recorded them, all of antiquity practiced them, and our ancestors have taught them to us."[38]

Among those preachers who proclaimed that the true church is known by its love for Mary, none could surpass Christopher Cheffontaines. This was, in fact, the dominant theme of his Marian sermons. With the other preachers of the day, Cheffontaines rested his certainty of Mary's intercession on the rock of the Church's tradition;[39] he assured the people that honor was first due to God the Father, and only then, to the Virgin.

Our teacher and nurse, the Roman Church, wishes that those whom she has taught and educated and nurtured as adopted children of the race of the sons of God would, early in the morning, salute first God their heavenly Father on bended knee, saying "Our Father, who art in heaven"; and having done that, she wishes that they reverently and humbly salute the queen, the adoptive mother of the sons of God, by saying to her that most beautiful Angelic Ave, the greeting through which she conceived the Son of God.[40]

37. Ibid., 101. "Voluit Deus, ut tanta reverentia haberetur arcae foederis, quia locus habitationis eius erat . . . Sed nos, O Christiani, non solum indigne tangimus hanc sanctissimam Arcam, dum salutationem angelicam irreverenter dicimus, sed multi etiam sacrilegis, maledictis et diabolicis linguis, horrendis blasphemiis foedissime deturpant."

38. De Sales, *Oeuvres complètes,* 12:66. "O loüanges bien authentiques, O riches et discrets honneurs; le grand Dieu les a dictez, un grand ange les a prononcez, un grand Evangeliste les a enregistrez, toute l'antiquité les a prattiquez, nos ayeuls nous les ont enseignez."

39. Christopher Cheffontaines, "Sermo secundus, qui de Virginis Mariae invocatione agit," in *Novae illustrationes christianae fidei,* pt. 2 (Paris: Sittart, 1586), 74v. "Sequamur igitur matris nostrae ecclesiae Romanae consuetudinem atque institutum, et hanc devote precemur, ut quia sancta et Dei mater est et nos peccatores, pro nobis deum orare dignetur."

40. Cheffontaines, "Sermo de Virginis Mariae," 55r–55v. "Sic quos instituendos et educandos, pedagoga et nutrix nostra Ecclesia Romana, generationis filiorum de alumnos suscepit, vult ut summo mane antequam quicquam aliud faciant, patrem suum caelestem

For this reason, the Church has placed the "Ave" directly following the "Pater Noster" in the catechism.[41]

Cheffontaines is unrelenting in his diatribes against those who impugn Mary's dignity. With St. Lawrence of Brindisi, he groups them among the followers of the devil. Held as Satan's captives, they refuse to call the Virgin blessed. Mary had said that all generations would call her blessed, but she spoke only of the true sons of God, not of heretics.[42] Since she was inspired by the Holy Spirit, however, those who refuse to praise her make the Holy Spirit a liar.[43] To be a brother of Christ, one must honor his mother; and there is no surer way to determine if someone is of the true faith and a son of God than by discovering whether they are willing to salute the Mother of God in prayer. He warns those who will not honor the Virgin that she will then refuse to speak to her son on their behalf. The result will be their eternal death.[44]

The Rosary, too, and not just the "Ave" itself, becomes a symbol of the true faith in Cheffontaines's sermons. The orderly counting of prayers on the beads is in keeping with God's desire that all worship be done with due order and consideration. It is hell, Babylon, which is marked by disorder and chaos. The Rosary also enables a person to be certain of rendering to God all the prayers that he or she has promised.[45]

Deum primum, summa cum humilitate flexis in terram poplitibus, salutent, dicendo: Pater noster qui es in caelis etc. Quo facto, vult ut reginam, deinde, matrem filiorum Dei adoptivam, reverenter humiliterque salutent, dicendo illi pulcherrimum illud Angelicum Ave, quo salutata, Dei filium concepit."

41. Ibid., 42v–43r.

42. Ibid., 6v–7v.

43. Ibid., 41r. "Et quorsum, quaeso, haeriticorum nostri temporis conatus tendunt, dum ne eam Christiani laudent, benedicant, et honorent, impedire nituntur: Certè ut falsam reddant spiritus sancti per os eius elatam prophetiam."

44. Cheffontaines, "Sermo secundus," 58v. "Sic istis dixero. Nunc ergo O viri, debitum huic mulieri reddite honorem et orabit pro vobis, quia prophetis est, et plus quam prophetis, quia Dei mater est. Si autem debitos illi non restitueritis honores, eaque intercedente eius filium non placaveritis, scitote quia morte moriemini aeterna, vos et omnes qui vestri sunt."

45. Cheffontaines, "Sermo de Virginis Mariae," 26r. "Omnia enim ordinem et non confusè, fieri à nobis in Dei servitio debent, qui in numero, pondere et mensura omnia ordinatissimè fecit. In inferno, in Babylone nullus ordo, in Ecclesia Dei, omnia secundum ordinem fiunt."

Finally, Cheffontaines prods Catholics to wear their devotion to Mary in public in the form of the Rosary beads. They can serve as a sort of Christian heraldry, showing forth the allegiance of the individual. He explains, "Since Rosaries are among those things made to honor the aforesaid Virgin, when we wear them around the neck or hanging from a belt, they become a certain public testimony by which we confess that we are dedicated servants of the Virgin and Queen Mother of the Son of God, and we glorify her."[46]

Like St. François de Sales, who emphasized the fact that God himself had dictated the words of the "Ave," which were then faithfully recorded in the Gospel, Cheffontaines wants the people to know that his sermon and the "Ave" itself are founded on Scripture, the Word of God. The Angelic Salutation fully contains the message of the Gospel, he says, because it brings the news of Christ's Incarnation for the redemption of humanity.[47]

St. François de Sales and Christopher Cheffontaines are also the two preachers most concerned with defending prayers to Mary and to all the saints on grounds other than ecclesiastical tradition. Both men explain praise of Mary in terms of its reflection on God himself. To honor Mary is to honor the Word made flesh through her. Christ hears the "Aves" along with his mother and is pleased to hear Christians repeating the good news of his conception.[48]

St. François includes a not-so-subtle jibe at Protestant claims to honor God alone, apart from Mary and the saints. "Soli deo gloria" became one of the watchwords of the Protestant Reformation, symbolizing the rejection of the cult of the saints. In his 1602 sermon on the Assumption, delivered at Paris, St. François explained that, as the Queen of Sheba offered gifts to Solomon, so do all the saints, especially Mary, refer their praises to Christ: ". . . all her perfections, all her greetings are attributed, consecrat-

---

46. Ibid., 26v. "Est autem et alius earum usus. Dum enim Rosaria ex illis ad dictae virginis honorem facta, à collo vel cingulo pendentia deferimus, id protestatio quaedam publica est, qua nos Reginae filii Dei matris et virginis, dedititios servos esse fatemur et gloriamur."

47. Ibid., 34r–34v.

48. Ibid., 20r, 34v–35r. See also "Sermo secundus," 57v.

ed and dedicated to the glory of her Son who is their source, their author and their consummation; to God alone be honor and glory."[49] Although his sermon is in French, the phrase "to God alone be honor and glory" appears in Latin, to make sure that no one misses the comparison between his point and the popular Protestant motto. St. François continues by saying, as Lawrence of Brindisi had done, that it is not necessary to deny all honor to Mary in order to honor Jesus, as the heretics claim. Nor should one consider her to be a goddess. Only fools go to such extremes. The true Church follows the middle path of truth.[50]

Although Cheffontaines and St. François agreed on many things, and both argued strenuously that Mary owed all of her honors to God's grace, Cheffontaines preserves, along with Lawrence of Brindisi, more of the medieval understanding that the Virgin sits on a heavenly throne near her son, enjoying a place of honor only slightly less than that of Jesus. The son honors his mother and will not deny her requests. If the prayers of God's faithful servants obtain great results from God, certainly the prayers of his mother are even more valuable.[51]

Cheffontaines describes the nature of Mary's intercession in the traditional political language of the court. She is the queen mother who is to be approached just as one supplicates an earthly ruler, with honorary greetings and praises. Afterward, she is ready to hear the petitioner's requests. True, only Jesus was needed to save the human race; but since it was not good for a man to be alone, it was fitting that both sexes be involved in repairing the corruption that touched both equally. Besides, the grandeur of the divine majesty residing in Christ causes people to fear approaching him. There was a place for someone to act as a mediatrix with the mediator. Quoting extensively from St. Bernard of Clairvaux's sermon on the Assumption, Cheffontaines says,

49. De Sales, *Oeuvres complètes*, 11:322–23. ". . . toutes ses perfections, toutes ses vertus, toutes ses felicitez sont rapportées, consacrées, et dediées à la gloire de son Fils qui en est la source, l'autheur, et le consommateur; Soli deo honor et gloria."

50. Ibid., 323–24. See also 11:325–27. De Sales says that if people want Mary to hear their prayers, they must first obey Christ her son. Marian devotions alone are insufficient.

51. Cheffontaines, "Sermo de Virginis Mariae," 56r. Robert Bellarmine agreed that Mary's name was never called in vain; *Opera omnia*, 5:370.

Eve was a cruel mediator, through whom the ancient serpent poured the deadly poison also into the man himself, but Mary was faithful, and she hands to women and men the antidote of salvation. . . . You have, O man, a sure access to God. You have there the Mother before the Son and the Son before the Father. The Son shows the Father his wounds and side, the Mother shows the son her bosom and breasts. Thus no one can be turned away where there are so many symbols of love.[52]

What could better tie Cheffontaines to the medieval tradition than St. Bernard and the Double Intercession? Cheffontaines, the preacher who is so adamant that Mary's body was of little importance in and of itself, remains convinced that it is useful in the context of intercession. Either that, or he is enamored enough of St. Bernard and his authority that he is unaware of the conflict. In either case, he is the only early modern preacher in this study to use this well-known example from the past.

As in so many other areas, it is St. François de Sales who breaks most completely with medieval tradition when he preaches about Mary's intercessory role, for he places her not on the royal dais with Christ, but below, as spokesperson for all the other knights and nobles at the court of heaven, yet privileged over and above them. In St. François's sermons, the heavenly throne room is likewise changed. Christ is less a medieval monarch, dependent on the loyalty of his principle nobles in order to maintain his power, than the exalted prince of a centralized state. Surrounded by those who seek his favor, he bestows it not so much as a reward for service, but as a demonstration of his might. St. François asks his hearers,

Consider the Church to be like the court of some great prince, who would be surrounded in his palace by numerous lords and knights. Generally, all have been called to court and all share the favor of the prince, but they are nevertheless different, because he has regard for some, he glances more particularly at others. . . .

52. Cheffontaines, "Sermo secundus," 75v–76r, 77v–78r. "Crudelis mediatrix Eva, per quam serpens antiquus pestiferum etiam ipsi viro virus infudit, sed fidelis Maria, quae salutis antidotum et viris et mulieribus propinavit . . . Securum igitur accessum habes o homo apud Deum, ubi habes filium ante patrem, ante filium matrem. Filius ostendit patri latus et vulnera, mater ostendit filio pectus et ubera. Nec ulla potest haberi repulsa, ubi tot occurrunt charitatis insignia."

But among them, one always finds some whom the prince favors much more than the others. . . . Certainly, we can easily say that all Christians are so many knights and lords who are at the court of the sovereign prince Our Lord, a court which is none other than the Church, and our dear Savior, like a king, regards and favors all, although differently; because he dispenses his graces to whomever he pleases and as he pleases. . . . But among all those who have had this grace, the very holy Virgin has been singularly privileged above all others since God has revealed to her more of the highest secrets and deepest mysteries than to any other creature.[53]

St. François also breaks with the common medieval understanding of Mary as an intercessor whose prayers for sinners mingle with those of Jesus before the throne of God, the theme of the Double Intercession. It is Christ alone who is the "advocate of righteousness," pleading for Christians by virtue of his passion and death on their behalf. The Virgin and saints are "advocates of grace," not trying to justify their pleas for forgiveness, but trusting only in Christ.

In brief, they (Mary and the saints) do not join their prayers to the intercession of the Savior, because they are not of the same quality, but to ours. If Jesus Christ prays to heaven, he prays in his own virtue; but the Virgin prays only as we do, by virtue of her Son, but with more credit and favor.[54]

Heretics accuse Catholics of praying to the saints as the ultimate goal of prayer, but they pray instead to join their prayers to those of the saints, to

53. De Sales, *Oeuvres complètes*, 11:496–97. ". . . considerez l'Eglise comme la cour de quelque grand prince, lequel seroit en son palais environné de plusieurs seigneurs et cavaliers; ils sont generalement tous appellez en la cour, et ont tous la grace du prince: mais differemment neantmoins, car il regarde les uns, il jette des oeillades plus particulieres aux autres. . . . Mais entre ceux-là il s'en trouve tousjours quelques-uns que le prince favorise beaucoup plus que les autres. . . . Certes nous pouvons bien dire que tous les chrestiens sont autant de cavaliers et seigneurs, qui sont en la cour de ce souverain Prince, Nostre-Seigneur, cour qui n'est autre que l'Eglise, et nostre cher Sauveur, comme leur Roy, les regarde et favorise tous quoy que differement; car enfin il depart ses graces à qui il luy plaist, et comme il luy plaist. . . . Mais entre tous ceux qui ont eu cette grace, la tres-Ste Vierge a esté singulierement priviligiée au dessus tous les autres, Dieu luy ayant descouvert de plus hauts secrets et profonds mysteres qu'a nulle autre creature."

54. Ibid., 325–26. "Bref, ils ne joignent pas leurs prieres à l'intercession du Sauveur; car elles ne sont pas de mesme qualité, mais aux nostres. Si Jesus-Christ prie au ciel, il prie en sa vertu; mais la Vierge ne prie que comme nous en la vertu de son Fils, mais avec plus de credit et de faveur."

create a "holy confusion," a "sacred blend" which will be better received by God.[55]

The fact that most preachers after Trent prefer to present the Virgin as a humble recipient of grace, highly favored by God, does not mean that they have removed her as an integral part of the process of salvation or of living the Christian life. Most of them believe that she is the one through whom human prayers must eventually pass as they rise toward heaven and through whom the grace of God will flow in its journey earthward.

Both Robert Bellarmine and Lawrence of Brindisi continue the medieval practice of describing Mary as the neck of Christ's body or as an aqueduct for the flow of heavenly grace. It is a metaphor which makes Mary essential to the ongoing process of salvation even as she was the necessary link between heaven and earth in the Incarnation. Bellarmine consistently joins Christ and Mary together in the dispensing of grace. In the human body there are multiple hands, arms, legs, and feet, but only one head and one neck, through which the head controls the body. As we are accustomed to adorn the head and neck more than the rest of the body, so Christ and Mary are adorned with more graces and virtues than the rest of the Church.[56]

St. Lawrence also describes Mary as the "treasurer of all God's treasures," and the neck of the Church, conducting prayers to Christ and graces from God to Christian people.[57] What is more, she is the means of receiving the ultimate grace, the gift of God in the person of the Holy Spirit.[58] St. François agrees with him in this, even though he feels com-

55. Ibid., 10:82. ". . . ains seulement nous les prions de joindre leurs oraisons aux nostres, pour en faire une saincte confusion, afin que par ce sacré melange, elles soient mieux recuës du Pere Eternel."

56. Bellarmine, *Opera omnia*, 5:299. "Nihil est enim in toto corpore, quod magis emineat, et magis ornari soleat, quam caput et collum. Caput ornatur diademate, collum aureo torque. . . . Sic igitur caput nostrum Christus est, onmi gratia et gloria ornatum. Ad ipsum autem proxime Maria, quae collum est, accedit, ut verissime dicatur: Electa, ut sol."

57. Lawrence of Brindisi, *Opera omnia*, 1:588, 578. "Per collum caput inclinatur, per Mariam Dei misericordiam consequimur; per collum descendit influxus capitis in corpus, et ascendunt vapores a corpore in caput; sic per Mariam ascendunt orationes Ecclesiae ad Deum, et descendunt gratiae a Deo in Ecclesiam."

58. Ibid., 194–95.

pelled to say that it would not be necessary to approach God by means of the saints. God himself prefers that we pray through the saints to preserve the union of the Church Militant with the Church Triumphant. For this reason, God shows in the Scriptures that St. Elizabeth received the Holy Spirit through Mary's mediation. Therefore, St. François concludes, whoever wants to have the Holy Spirit, let him join with Mary.[59]

Post-Tridentine preachers nevertheless do modify the medieval view of Mary as Mother of Mercy, "Mater Misericordiae." Medieval preachers were inclined to contrast Mary's disposition with that of Jesus, whose future role as judge of the living and the dead meant a propensity for justice. Mary became the figure who could be counted on to be merciful to sinners and deflect the anger of her son. After the Council of Trent, however, most preachers avoided this contrast, and in none of the sermons examined here does Christ appear as ruler of the Kingdom of Justice while Mary rules the Kingdom of Mercy. Mary is still the Mother of Mercy, but more often than not, her mercy is now simply offered as one of her defining attributes, or it is contrasted to the anger of God the Father.

One of the social assumptions underlying acceptance of Mary as Mother of Mercy is the belief that men, especially fathers, are inclined to punish children for their wrongdoings while mothers are more likely to want to be lenient with their offspring. This association of punishment with fathers and of forgiveness and mercy with mothers received a perhaps unintended boost from Protestant and Catholic reformers in the sixteenth century as they dealt with the fourth of the Ten Commandments. Both branches of the Church interpreted the commandment to "honor thy father and thy mother" to mean that fathers alone were the heads of households, and extended its meaning to include submission to clerical and princely authority as well.[60] If fathers, priests, and princes are re-

---

59. De Sales, *Oeuvres complètes*, 11:267, 37. "Donc qui veut avoir le Sainct-Esprit, qu'il se joigne avec Marie, quia cum in ea non colligit, spargit, car qui ne s'assemble avec elle, il fait plus de perte que de gain."

60. John Bossy, *Christianity in the West, 1400–1700* (Oxford: Oxford University Press, 1985), 116; Joseph Klaits, *Servants of Satan: The Age of the Witch Hunts* (Bloomington: Indiana University Press, 1985), 69. Klaits illustrates the way in which such patriarchal ideas could be carried to extremes in the political work of Jean Bodin, *The Republic*. Bodin's ideal family placed the wife as lowest in status, after husband, children, servants, and even apprentices. See also *Catechism of the Council of Trent*, 271–76.

sponsible for providing order by using their authority to enforce the rules, mothers might indeed seem to be the last hope of mercy.[61]

Of course it was a simple matter for Catholic preachers to apply the same understanding to the heavenly realm, where God the Father and Mary Mother of Christians reigned in eternity. It could only be "natural" that Mother Mary would want the Father to be forgiving of the sins of her spiritual children. Mary thus remained very much the Mother of Mercy for some preachers at the close of the sixteenth century, even for those who had ceased to present Jesus primarily as a righteous judge. The wrath of the Father replaced that of Jesus as the principle antithesis of Mary's mercy. The Franciscan preacher Christopher Cheffontaines understood Mary's intercession in just this way.

When a son offends the father of his family in some way and knows that he is angry with him, and not without cause, he is accustomed to run to his mother, wanting her to intercede by supplicating the angry father for his sake, hoping that through her influence, she will procure the pardon and indulgence of the father for the offense. Thus, adopted sons of God, when their conscience accuses them and they know they have provoked the Father's anger against themselves, have recourse to their mother Mary, so that they might have remission of sins by her intercession.[62]

Robert Bellarmine and Lawrence of Brindisi say essentially the same thing in their sermons. Bellarmine presents an allegorical interpretation of the Old Testament story of King David, Nabal, and Abigail, in which Abigail turned away David's wrath from her husband, Nabal. In the same way, the Virgin also turns away the anger of God. "For who is Nabal if not

---

61. Of course, there are considerable theological problems with this newer approach as well, and they are problems that are as likely to appear in Protestant works as in Catholic. While Jesus now appears in his role as merciful intercessor, there seems to be an implicit assumption that his desire for mercy contrasts in some way with God the Father's desire to punish. This portrayal suggests that the being of God is divided in inclination or will when considering how to respond to human sin. This duality of intent can also appear in presentations of some doctrines of the atonement.

62. Cheffontaines, "Sermo de Virginis Mariae," 23r–23v. "Cum filius familias aliquis patrem suum offendit, eumque sibi iratum non sine cause cognoscit, solet ad matrem recurrere, ipsam precando velit apud patrem iratum pro se intercedere, sperans, in illius gratiam veniam et indulgentiam paternae se impetraturum offensae. Ita adoptivi dei filii ad matrem suam Mariam cum conscientia accusante sciunt iram se dei patris contra se provocasse, recurre habent, ut ipsa intercedente peccatorum remissam obtinere valeant."

a sinful man, and who is David if not God, and who is Abigail if not Mary, the true Mother of Mercy, who turns away from sinners the just anger of God by her prayers and intercession."[63] Lawrence of Brindisi spoke of Mary's ability to save sinners from divine displeasure by using his favorite metaphor for her, the Ark of the Covenant:

For through Mary, many sinners as well as righteous are saved. . . . For she is the cause of salvation for many sinners who are born in her through the pious affection of devotion and who venerate her as much as they are able, just as the Ark of the Covenant protected Abiathar the priest, to whom King Solomon said: "You are a man of death, but I will not kill you, because you have carried the Ark of the Lord God."[64]

Sinners who deserve the wrath of God are protected by their closeness to the Virgin as Abiathar was protected by his past association to the Ark of the Covenant. Those who pray regularly to Mary can trust that she will intercede successfully for them with God, enabling them to be certain of obtaining mercy.

Inward Prayer and Outward Act

From the standpoint of Catholic clergy and preachers, prayers to the Virgin, particularly the Rosary, served one last function in addition to their value as symbols of loyalty to the Roman Church and as a means of procuring the grace and forgiveness of God through her intercession. The Rosary was a way to cultivate among the people a more vital participation in personal and interior prayer, through which they could begin to re-fashion their spiritual lives according to one of the Church's highest approved models, Mary herself.

Anyone who hopes to engage in extended private prayer has to be able to set aside considerable amounts of time to be alone, preferably far from

63. Bellarmine, *Opera omnia*, 5:374–75. The story of David, Abigail, and Nabal is found in 1 Samuel 25:1–35.

64. Lawrence of Brindisi, *Opera omnia*, 1:36. "Nam per Mariam multi enim peccatores tandem iustificati salvantur. . . . Multis quidem peccatoribus, qui pio in eam devotionis affectu feruntur, eamque pro sua virili venerantur, cause salutis est, sicut arca testamenti extitit Abiataro sacerdoti, cui rex Salomon ait: 'Vir mortis es tu, sed non interficiam te, quia portasti arcam Domini Dei.'"

any source of disturbance or interruption. While in the past, this sort of prayer life could be enjoyed most often only by those who were willing to take monastic vows, it will be remembered that Cardinal Bellarmine urged all Christians to prepare themselves to become spiritual mothers of Christ by learning "to love solitude, to flee the assemblies of men" and "to enter the chamber of the heart," in order to speak with God. He insisted that this was not a practice reserved for "the perfect."[65] The success of this program may be due in part to the increasing desire among European Christians in the late Middle Ages to participate more fully in the religious life. It is also the kind of piety which the popular Devotio Moderna sought to encourage throughout much of northern Europe on the eve of the Protestant and Catholic Reformations.

Catholic religious leaders and preachers of the sixteenth century, especially the Jesuits, promoted development of the private devotional lives of the people of Europe more systematically than ever before, largely through their Marian societies devoted to the Virgin and the Rosary. Those who joined such societies hoped "to intensify the interior spiritual life as much as possible, to the point when it would spill over irresistibly into exterior works of charity and zeal."[66] Louis Chatellier's *The Europe of the Devout* probes the religious life and goals of Jesuit Marian congregations in France, southern Italy, Belgium, Switzerland, southern Germany, and the Rhineland. Chatellier finds that the primary objective was to make each member, each "dévot," an "interior man." To do this, the Jesuit superiors prescribed an intense devotional life of interior prayer, daily examination of conscience, and, from 1585, weekly communion. A person was to strive both for inner renewal and complete control of the imagination, whether at worship or in the activities of everyday life.[67]

One aid for controlling the mind during worship was the construction of mental images to accompany virtually every physical act, whether personal acts such as making the sign of the cross, or the movements of the priest as he celebrated Mass. Like Loyola's imaging in the *Spiritual Exer-*

65. See above, Chapter 4, n. 125.
66. Villaret, "Marie et la Compagnie de Jésus," 965.
67. Chatellier, *Europe of the Devout,* 35–42.

cises, the mental pictures were intended to enable the worshiper, who most likely did not understand explicitly the Latin Mass, to enter nevertheless into its drama and experience with Christ the re-enactment of his Passion.[68]

The Rosary devotion itself, so widely practiced among members of Marian societies, was also well suited for nurturing interior prayer, fully in accord with the requirements of Catholic orthodoxy. The Rosary was addressed to Mary, symbol of prayerful devotion and of the militant Church. Also, the repetitive nature of the prayers served to occupy the conscious mind and will, placing the one who recited them in a spiritual trance which allowed the soul greater openness to divine contemplation and illumination. As Eithne Wilkins describes it, "it is the element of mechanical hallucination that allows the mind to free itself from the words and rise into the realm of pure attention."[69] Physical and mental absorption in the Rosary might also be one way of entering into a sense of interior peace and distance from the world, even when its noises and distractions remain close at hand.

St. François de Sales said the Rosary each day to the close of his life in thanksgiving to Mary for conquering his own tendency to despair. It was a devotion that occupied at least an hour of his time.[70] A. G. Dickens attributed St. Peter Canisius's support of the Rosary to his innate sense of those practices which would most appeal to the people on a broad level.[71] It might also be true, however, that men like St. Peter and St. François advocated the Rosary because their own experience had shown them its usefulness as an aid to personal interior prayer.

Jesuit sodality leaders further contended that inward prayer and mental discipline should result in outward control of the body. Just as Carlo Borromeo, who supported the goals of the Jesuits, insisted that churchmen, especially preachers, strictly control the movements of their bodies

68. Ibid.

69. Eithne Wilkins, *The Rose-Garden Game: A Tradition of Beads and Flowers* (New York: Herder and Herder, 1969), 78.

70. Francis Vincent, "Saint François de Sales," in *Maria: Études sur la sainte Vierge*, ed. Hubert DuManoir de Juaye, vol. 2 (Paris: Beauchesne, 1952), 995.

71. Dickens, *Counter Reformation*, 144–45.

so as to appear at all times chaste and devout, the Jesuits required members of their Marian congregations to keep a tight rein on their bodies. To a certain degree, the sixteenth-century Jesuit sodalities preserved something of the late medieval sense of the value of physical actions as symbols with which to communicate spiritual truths. In fact, some historians have argued that the piety of St. Ignatius himself was as much in line with the late Middle Ages as with more modern trends.[72] These sodalities encouraged the proper posture while at prayer to be sure, but they also continued to value public processions and even pilgrimages, which could become an imitation of the Way of the Cross. Pilgrims, trudging the dusty roads to their destination could, by their own hardship, come closer to the God whose Son had suffered similarly on his way to Golgotha.[73]

On the other hand, these Jesuit societies embraced and promoted an understanding of bodily control and the use of language that closely paralleled larger social and religious changes in the period. Exhortations to keep a close guard on all movements of the body, whether by Borromeo and other prominent churchmen or by the writers of manuals for devotional congregations, are the religious expression of a wider inclination within European society to create a more "civilized" form of life, in which manners and deportment are the supreme means of discerning who has been "well brought up." Often, young children learned proper "Christian civility" along with the other more central aspects of the faith when they attended catechism classes.[74] It was a development that grew in popularity throughout the seventeenth and early eighteenth centuries, and as humility was the Marian virtue most desired by Catholic preachers, so handbooks designed to promote Christian civility in Catholic soci-

---

72. Terence O'Reilly, "The Spiritual Exercises and the Crisis of Medieval Piety," in *From Ignatius Loyola to John of the Cross: Spirituality and Literature in Sixteenth-Century Spain* (Brookfield, Vt.: Variorum, 1995), 102–3. O'Reilly argues that while Ignatius was sympathetic to the problems in late medieval religion which so concerned people like Erasmus, who encouraged a more interiorized and evangelical humanist approach, the solution actually offered by Ignatius was couched in the metaphors and practices of the late Middle Ages. O'Reilly concludes that the piety of Ignatius and the exercises is hard to categorize, for there are elements both of the late medieval period and of the more interiorized piety of the humanists.

73. Chatellier, *Europe of the Devout*, 42–43.

74. Bossy, *Christianity in the West*, 120.

ety praised humility as being of supreme worth. Members of Marian congregations were directed to demonstrate their humility in every aspect of their lives, "by a humble and respectful posture of the whole body, by a very correct restraint of every sense," thereby pleasing Jesus, Mary, and the guardian angels who constantly attended them.[75] In this social climate, one can see easily why Canisius would argue against the tradition of Mary's fainting at the cross, for it would have offended current standards of modesty and deportment.

Father Jean Cordier instructed mothers to teach their children that they should "keep their eyes down, their head erect, their face serene and cheerful; that their speech should be mild and respectful; that their gait should not be hurried nor their gestures extravagant."[76] By bringing up their children in this way, women could achieve significant participation in the task of reforming Catholic society.[77]

The regulation of one's speech was an important part of the larger goal of bodily restraint. For a group whose societies were so given to processions and pilgrimages, the teaching of the Jesuit leaders concerning language is curiously reminiscent of the Quakers. Speech was to be used by members only to convey necessary information or spiritual advice. There should be no "vain talk, lacking in spiritual content." Nothing in their conversation should reek of worldly affairs or interests. Members were encouraged to "keep in mind rule six, which tells us to express our thoughts with great simplicity and in a language redolent of the Gospel,

75. *Pratique de Devotion et des vertus chrestiennes suivant les regles de la congrégation de Nostre-Dame* (Paris: 1654), 12; quoted in Chatellier, *Europe of the Devout*, 162.

76. Jean Cordier, *La famille saincte ou il est traité des Devoirs de toutes les personnes qui composent une famille* (Paris: 1643), 363; quoted in Chatellier, *Europe of the Devout*, 162–63.

77. Chatellier, *Europe of the Devout*, 15–17, 141–46. Women were members of these Marian congregations from the beginning and were especially welcomed by Canisius in Freibourg. Toward the close of the sixteenth century, however, the Jesuit authorities decided that since members were required to take a vow of consecration to the Virgin, women, who were under the authority of fathers or husbands, could not join in their own right. Some male authority would have to make the vow for them. Then, by the mid-seventeenth century, official policy did another about-face. The Jesuit Society's push to reform society through the family required the participation of women, especially mothers. This need for reform therefore overrode godly patriarchy to the extent that women were once again permitted to join on their own.

without affecting certain thoughts which are only curious, and without choosing words which might distract or detain the spirit."[78]

Chatellier finds that there were some in French society who believed that even the Jesuit Marian congregations were too involved in public, corporate actions and not concerned enough with the inner life. He believes that the French School of Cardinal Berulle and Jean-Jacques Olier was in part a reaction to the Jesuit model. These men placed an even greater stress on private prayer to the exclusion of most exterior devotions altogether. Two examples of this movement's work, Olier's *Catéchisme chrétien pour la vie intérieure* and his *Vie intérieure de la très Saincte Vièrge,* show by their titles not only what this movement valued above all but also who was to be the supreme model for the ideal Christian life.[79] Another factor in their opposition to the Jesuits, however, might have been simple jealousy at their success in attracting members to their societies.

Finally, the Jesuits expected that the life of interior prayer springing up within each society member would overflow into the larger society, helping to transform it into a disciplined, moral community of the faith. In cities such as Cologne, where Marian congregations were particularly influential, the ideal was to a large extent achieved, at least in the realm of external, observable reform. Not only did the brothers keep watch for any possible manifestation of Protestant sympathy, they also succeeded in pressuring the town council to pass laws against Carnival and popular dances and other pastimes considered to be immoral. Societies in Italy, among them those in Salerno and Barletta, worked equally hard to prevent widows from entering public life too soon after their husband's deaths, to dispel from taverns those who were inclined to drink in excess, and to denounce people who used profane or bawdy language in public.[80]

François de Sales sums up the goals of post-Tridentine Catholic devotional life in a sermon for the Assumption. He used the traditional motifs

78. *Pratique de Devotion et des vertus chrestiennes,* 40–41; quoted in Chatellier, *Europe of the Devout,* 163.

79. Chatellier, *Europe of the Devout,* 155–58.

80. Ibid., 25.

of the story of Mary and Martha to explain the roles proper to the spirit, the "interior man," and the body, the "exterior man."

The spirit is the one who always tends toward union with God, and who engages in the prayers [discours] necessary for achieving that union. The exterior man, which is the body, is the one who sees, speaks, touches, tastes and hears: now it is the body which hurries when, by the instinct of the interior man, it busies itself in the practice of virtue, especially in the virtue of charity, in order to keep the commandment to love one's neighbor, and to occupy oneself in serving him, just as the interior man observes the commandment to love God, and is employed in prayer and other devotional practices. Thus the body and the spirit observe the two principle commandments, on which, as on two columns, are founded all the law and the prophets.[81]

St. François's words illustrate clearly that many Catholics after Trent shared the same goals for the reform of religious life. They sought to develop the interior life, thereby producing also the fruit of ethical living and good works. This ideal was not limited to the Jesuit reformers. St. François describes a soul that achieves union with God through spiritual means and then turns its attention to directing the body toward the appropriate outward responses. He does not suggest here that the body itself may be a means of appropriating the presence of God. Instead, there is a certain dichotomy involved in which the soul alone experiences God and then instructs the body to perform certain acts. The body's proper sphere of action is the exterior world around it. In spite of the fact that St. François used the word "discours" to refer to the prayer of the soul, the fact that he assigns speaking to those acts performed by the body indicates that this "discours" is not outward speech but an internal dialogue, similar perhaps to that by which Jesus and Mary communicated in silence at Calvary.

---

81. De Sales, *Oeuvres complètes*, 11:345–46. "L'homme interieur, qui est l'esprit, est celuy qui tend tousjours à l'union avec Dieu, et qui fait les discours necessaires pour pervenir à cette union. L'homme exterieur, qui est le corps, est celuy qui regarde, qui parle, qui touche, qui gouste et qui escoute: or c'est celuy-là qui s'empresse, lors que par l'instinct de l'homme interieur il s'exerce à la prattique des vertus, specialement à celle de la charité, afin d'observer le commandement de l'amour du prochain en s'occupant à le servir; comme l'homme interieur observe le commandement de l'amour de dieu, en s'employant à l'oraison, et autres exercices de devotion; et par ainsi le corps et l'esprit s'exercent en l'observance des deux principaux commandements, sur lesquels, comme sur deux colomnes, est fondée toute la loy et les prophetes."

One of the effects of encouraging daily devotional acts that are internalized, and of insisting on a correspondingly controlled body, bound by strict ethical standards of deportment and good works, is the enforcement of religious norms that are more like those of monastic life than those observed by most European Catholic lay persons of the Middle Ages. Andrew Barnes has found the standards of religious behavior in lay penitential confraternities in France during the sixteenth century to be the same as those of the Jesuit societies. Their effect was to create a life in which each day was to some extent devoted to prayer and the praise of God. This promoted a "smoothing out of the liturgical year" and was intended to produce the type of piety that in the past only religious could have been expected to experience.[82] Natalie Davis points out that for Catholics generally, religious time is more "bunched" and "irregular" than the Church year of Protestant congregations.[83] Still, in those areas where the guidelines of Catholic reformers set the standards for devotional life in the late sixteenth century, in towns and cities which felt the impact of Marian or penitential societies, the religious lives of many would have mirrored in some respects the day-in, day-out religious routine of the cloister.

There are some suggestions in the sermons of post-Tridentine preachers that older ways of interpreting and encouraging prayers to the Virgin still prevailed. Lawrence of Brindisi tells his congregation that those who "greet, revere, adore and congratulate" Mary through the "Ave" will not fail to be greeted in return. His advice is reminiscent of medieval preachers who attach merit to the number of prayers said as an end in itself and as an offering to the Virgin. He does specify, however, that such prayers are to be accompanied by the "pious affection of internal devotion."[84] Christopher Cheffontaines was even more blatant when he told Parisians that the degree of merit earned before God corresponds directly to the number of prayers repeated.[85] Even so, the larger trend in these sermons

---

82. Andrew E Barnes, "Religious Anxiety and Devotional Change in Sixteenth Century French Penitential Confraternities," *Sixteenth-Century Journal* 19 (1988): 402–5.

83. Natalie Zemon Davis, "The Sacred and the Body Social in Sixteenth-Century Lyon," *Past and Present* 90 (1981): 60–62.

84. Lawrence of Brindisi, *Opera omnia*, 1:170.

85. Cheffontaines, "Sermo de Virginis Mariae," 35v. ". . . quàm magno in numero eius

and in broader religious developments is to prod the Catholic faithful to embrace a lively private and interiorized devotional life.

It still remains to be seen whether this more spiritualized approach affected those aspects of the cult of Mary, and of Christian piety generally, that were obviously linked to the centrality of bodily presence for their effectiveness—that is, to images and relics. To what degree did Catholics continue to rely on external objects to establish contact with the Mother of God?

"The Relics of His Saints in Glory"

As with so many other areas of the Church's life and teaching, the fathers at Trent were likely to feel bound to uphold the ancient customs of the Church with regard to the veneration of images and relics, even though prominent Catholic humanists such as Erasmus had criticized and poked fun at these practices. Failure to do so would have been to accuse the historic Catholic Church and its worship of profound error. It is also true that the Council of Trent's defense of relics and images was constructed in part through the influence of Carlo Borromeo, a Cardinal, who convinced the council of their ultimate value in worship.[86]

The council therefore reaffirmed that since the bodies of the saints and martyrs had been temples of the Holy Spirit in life, would be glorified at the last day, and had been the means whereby God had given benefits to many, they should be honored. In the same way, images and pictures of Christ, Mary, and the saints should be shown due respect and honor, not, however, because they are the dwelling place of power or divinity, but be-

---

recitatio facta fuerit, imo maximè è re nostra esse, et nostra referre, ut in quanto maximo numero possumus eam recitemus: quandoquidem tanti apud deum meriti est."

86. Stéphane Boiron, *La Controverse née de la querelle des reliques à l'époque du concile de Trente (1500–1640)*, Travaux et Recherches de l'Université de droit d'économie et de sciences sociales de Paris, no. 28 (Paris: Presses Universitaires de France, 1989), 67–69. Boiron cites the Acts of the diocese of Milan during Borromeo's tenure as bishop to show his concern both to reform and encourage the veneration of relics. Between 1565 and 1576, regulations were passed which stipulated that relics were to be viewed only in appropriate places where people would take them seriously, and they were not to be used for money-making. Festivals of those saints whose relics were nearby were to be celebrated with particular grandeur and solemnity. The diocese should take care to ensure the authenticity of any relics held, and they should be accompanied by plaques explaining the life of the saint.

cause of those whom they represent. Images can also be of benefit to the people as reminders of the type of life they should seek to fashion for themselves,[87] precisely the role that reforming humanists sought to develop for the saints, with or without images.

Thus while the decrees of Trent continued to affirm that the relics of the saints can serve as conduits for God's power, the ability of images to function in this way is explicitly denied. And nowhere is it suggested that the saints themselves are present through either their relics or images. The council's catechism explains the importance of these physical objects in the same way as its official decrees: Images are useful, but only for inspiring worshipers to love God and imitate the saints' lives and virtues.[88] In defense of relics, however, the catechism declares,

> If the clothes, the kerchiefs, and even the very shadows of the saints, whilst yet on earth, banished disease and restored health and vigor, who will have the hardihood to deny that God can still work the same wonders by the holy ashes, the bones and other relics of his saints who are in glory.[89]

Lucien Febvre confirms the ongoing popularity of images in France long after the invention of printing and the development of a more spiritualized piety that accompanied it.[90] For many, no doubt, in spite of the Council of Trent's injunctions, images, along with relics, remained assurances of the saints' presence. During the first part of the sixteenth century, some relics in France were believed to confer healing power to wine that had been poured over them; as a cure for fever, pilgrims to Sainte-Baume could acquire a piece of the rock on which Mary Magdalen had slept.[91] Even in an increasingly literate and interiorized society, speech is still the primary and most natural form of human communication; therefore bodily presence represented by relics or even images would continue to be an important source of assurance that a saint was truly present and able to hear supplications. In 1528, Parisian Catholics held their first pro-

87. *Canons and Decrees of the Council of Trent*, 483–84.
88. *Catechism of the Council of Trent*, 250.
89. Ibid., 248.
90. Lucien Febvre, "Une Question mal posée, les origines de la Réforme," in *Au coeur religieux du seizième siècle* (Paris: SEVPEN, 1957), 33.
91. Boiron, *Controverse née de la querelle des reliques*, 97–98.

cession to combat growing heresy. The procession was sparked by the desecration of a statue of the Virgin in the rue aux Juifs. The statue was replaced by a silver-plated one, but the original was placed in Saint-Gervais and became known as "Notre-Dame-de-Bonne-Déliverance," or "Notre-Dame-de-Souffrance." It remained especially important for the religious lives of pregnant women; among the miracles attributed to prayers to the Virgin offered at this image was the return to life of a baby believed to be dead in its mother's womb.[92]

Robert Bellarmine provided six reasons for venerating relics in his *Disputationes . . . de controversiis christianae fidei,* published in 1596. The first two reasons are that relics were once used by the souls of the saints to do good works, and that God still uses them to perform miracles.[93] Another Jesuit, Pierre Coton, also defended their use for similar reasons, and added that they can "console . . . us in the absence of the souls which we ought particularly to cherish."[94] Once again, there is the reminder that, however holy the object, it does not mediate the spiritual presence of the saint.

Lawrence of Brindisi assumes that relics, especially those that are hallowed by their association with Christ himself, are the object of devotion. This, he explains, is why the Virgin herself deserves such great honor, for she not only touched Jesus, but conceived, carried, bore, and fed him.[95] By

---

92. Barbara B. Diefendorf, *Beneath the Cross: Catholics and Huguenots in Sixteenth-Century Paris* (New York: Oxford University Press, 1991), 45–46. Diefendorf says that in spite of the attention paid to this particular statue of the Virgin as a symbol of Catholic orthodoxy, it was nevertheless devotion to the host which was the truly powerful statement of anti-heretical belief for sixteenth-century Parisian Catholics.

93. Robert Bellarmine, *Disputationes Roberti Bellarmini e societate Jesu, de controversiis christianae fidei, adversus hujus temporis haereticos* (Ingolstadt: 1596), col. 2203; quoted in Boiron, *Controverse née de la querelle des reliques,* 84 n. 5. "Primum enim corpora Sanctorum fuerunt organa animarum ad omne opus bonum. . . . Secundo, fuerunt, et sunt instrumenta Dei ad miracula."

94. Pierre Coton, *Institution Catholique* (1610); quoted in Boiron, *Controverse née de la querelle des reliques,* 84 n. 5. Coton provides twelve reasons for venerating relics and says that they are useful ". . . pour nous soulager et consoler en l'absence des ames que nous devons particulierement cherir."

95. Lawrence of Brindisi, *Opera omnia,* 1:326. "Sicut autem propter divinam reverentiam summo in honore habentur sacretissimae reliquiae, maxime quae Christi divino contactu consecratae sunt, ut crux, spinea corona, praesepium et sepulcrum Christi; ita etiam Virgo Sanctissima hunc meretur honorem; Christum enim Dominum non solo tetigit, sed concepit, portavit, peperit, lactavit, educavit."

comparing her to the cross and crown of thorns, St. Lawrence suggests that Mary is the relic par excellence. Lawrence makes no mention, however, of specific relics connected to Mary herself. Yet even as the Virgin's milk and other relics associated with her cult were fading in popularity,[96] pilgrims to the Holy House of Loreto were as earnest as any in the Middle Ages. Believed to be the very house in which Mary received the angel's message and conceived Christ, the house at Loreto probably dates to the late fifteenth century. It was first approved as a pilgrimage site by Julius II in 1507.[97] As late as 1627, however, a history of Italy designed for travelers has this to say of those who visited Loreto,

One sees some among them who, carried away by raptures and zeal, attach themselves to the walls of this sacred chamber with such courage and ardor that it is almost impossible to pry them loose. . . . and if, in these holy places the holy Virgin suggests something to these devoted souls, ravished by contemplation, and causes them to experience her help, they catch fire and burn with such ardor and devotion that they would be unable to be satisfied by looking, embracing and kissing this holy place, if they were not forced to leave in order to allow others to enter.[98]

Mary's house was as popular with many at the beginning of the seventeenth century as it had ever been.

There is some evidence that Catholic desire to highlight Mary's contribution as the mother of Christ prompted a few preachers to grant her a place in their discussions of the supreme object of adoration and worship, the body of Christ received in the Eucharist. The Virgin receives scant mention in the Eucharistic or Corpus Christi sermons of either

96. Bossy, *Christianity in the West*, 8–9; Warner, *Alone of All Her Sex*, 203–4. Warner attributes the waning popularity of Mary's milk in particular to the increasingly exalted image of the Virgin as the Immaculate Conception gained acceptance, and also to the growth in modesty on the part of the Counter-Reformation Church. It was now unseemly for Mary to be shown with one breast exposed. The latter is almost certainly the real reason for the decline of this relic. If Mary is now supposed to be so modest that she will not display her grief at the cross in any bodily way, then to expose a breast would surely be unacceptable.

97. Warner, *Alone of All Her Sex*, 295–96.

98. Frans Schott, *Histoire de l'Italie contenant la description de ses singularitez par Mrs. François Schottus, Senateur d'Anvers: et Andre Schottus de la Compagnie de Jésus* (Paris: 1627); quoted in Boiron, *Controverse née de la querelle des reliques*, 111–12.

Lawrence of Brindisi or Peter Canisius.[99] But François de Sales provides an understanding of her bodily union with Christ in the Eucharist which, even though highly logical in light of Catholic teaching on this sacrament, is quite inconsistent with his usual spiritual and even mystical emphases. By receiving the flesh of her son, he says, we are made members of her family.

> Would you like to be a relative of the Holy Virgin? Commune, and in receiving the holy sacrament, you receive the flesh of her flesh and the blood of her blood: because the precious body of the Savior which is in the very holy sacrament of the altar, was made and formed in her chaste womb, from her pure blood, by the operation of the holy spirit.[100]

99. Lawrence of Brindisi, *Opera omnia,* 10:618. The Virgin's only appearance of note is as an illustration of the fact that God can work miracles. If Christ could be enclosed in Mary's womb and be born of her, then Christ's body can be in the Eucharist. Canisius also makes little reference to Mary in discussing the sacrament. He does say that she sang of the Eucharist in the Magnificat when she prophesied that God would "fill the hungry with good things." And he asserts that the whole Christ, body and soul, is present in both the bread and wine, the same Christ who was born of Mary. See Canisius, *Meditationes,* 2,2:66, 83.

100. De Sales, *Oeuvres complètes,* 11:270. ". . . voulez-vous estre parente de la Ste Vierge? Communiez, et en recevant le sainct sacrement, vous recevrez la chair de sa chair, et le sang de son sang: car le precieux corps du Sauveur qui est au tres-sainct sacrement de l'autel, a esté fait et formé dans ses chastes entrailles, de son pure sang, par l'operation du Sainct-Esprit." Close connections between Mary and the Eucharist continued to surface in the Catholic tradition until the twentieth century, and are often associated with those periods in the Church's history when there are social or political threats to its hierarchical authority in general or to the power of the papacy in particular. In 1875, it was necessary for the Church to condemn some Marian devotions which had gotten out of hand, especially that surrounding the Very Pure Blood of Our Lady. Nevertheless, the title Our Lady of the Atonement was permitted in the same period. The iconographic representation of this title depicts Mary wearing "a red mantle, symbolizing the Precious Blood of the Atonement of which she is the Immaculate source and by which men are united to God." In 1910, at an International Eucharistic Congress in Montreal, Msgr. A. Lepicier read a paper entitled "Relations de la Très Sainte Vierge avec le Très Saint Sacrement." See Nicholas Perry and Loreto Echeverría, *Under the Heel of Mary* (New York: Routledge, 1988), 71–76, 333 n. 10. Perry and Echeverría connect the emotional nineteenth-century revival of the Marian cult to the Church's desire to bypass popular attempts to use Jesus to support egalitarian socio-political theories. By encouraging devotion to the Eucharist and to Mary, as well as the relationship between the two, the Church was promoting aspects of its belief and practice specifically dependent upon Catholic tradition and authority. It was one way to counter the "Christocentric, radical anti-clericalism of 1848." Papal decrees concerning Mary's Immaculate Conception and papal infallibility, in 1854 and 1870, were part of the same anti-democratic authoritarian program.

Elsewhere, St. François urges people to identify with the Virgin because in receiving communion, one receives Christ as she did.[101] This passage is very medieval, not only because of the way in which it draws together the Virgin and Jesus through their shared flesh, but also in its focus on the communal nature of the sacrament at a time when many developments in Catholic practice regarding the Eucharist were causing it to become an individualized and private experience.[102]

Christopher Cheffontaines praised Mary's ability to feed the world and preserve it from hunger by bearing Jesus, the Bread of Life. In this she proved her superiority to the Old Testament patriarch Joseph, whose efforts could only produce enough bodily food to save Egypt from famine.[103]

Stephane Boiron's book concerning the "querelle des reliques" in the sixteenth century makes the point that critiques of relics and outward devotional practices by humanists, including Erasmus, or by Protestant Reformers had no effect whatever on people's loyalty to them and could have had the very opposite result of stirring up even greater adherence to their use. People were, after all, long accustomed to hearing Catholic preachers condemn the abuse of relics; they may have tended to view the more serious attacks of the sixteenth century as a continuation of those made by churchmen in the past. Criticisms of relics were at least as old as the time of St. Bernard.[104] Boiron nevertheless traces the beginning of the "slow death" of the popularity of relics to the criticism of excesses in relic devotion and the movement to eradicate inauthentic ones which began during the Council of Trent. According to Boiron, this process of authentication was greatly expanded in the mid-seventeenth century and finally succeeded in "uprooting" the cult of relics from its natural place among the lives of the people and their history.[105]

101. De Sales, *Oeuvres complètes,* 12:136, 139–40.

102. Bossy, *Christianity in the West,* 141–43. Bossy believes that the movement toward an individualized "asocial and mystical" experience of Communion affected Protestants as well as Catholics.

103. Cheffontaines, "Sermo de Virginis Mariae," 38r.

104. Boiron, *Controverse née de la querelle des reliques,* 7, 17, 22, 119–20. Boiron shows that Michel Menot and Olivier Maillard vigorously attacked abuses associated with the cult of relics.

105. Ibid., 119–20.

Marina Warner makes much the same point in reference to the Catholic Reformation's attempt to revitalize reverence for Marian images and icons. The Church sought to repair bridges to the Christian past that had been broken by the explosion of Protestant ideas and criticism. It was a desperate and contrived effort that fell somewhat short of its goal. "Holy things," while still much respected and revered, were starting to lose their ability to mediate spiritual presence.[106]

If holy objects no longer vibrated with quite the aura of supernatural presence they had embodied in the past, the same was not true of visions of the Virgin and the saints. In the aftermath of Protestant and humanist criticism, in a century during which a personalized Catholic piety found its central expression in the private prayers of the faithful, when even devotion to viewing the host was beginning to fade,[107] visions of the Virgin and other saints proved to be the most enduring personal means of encountering the holy which the Middle Ages bequeathed to early modern Europe, apart from the sacraments.

The vision of a saint, however intangible, was one way to establish the saint's presence and to confirm the truth of the Catholic faith in spite of Protestant assertions to the contrary. It was likewise a suitable compromise between the older desire to establish communication with the supernatural through the material, and the interior spirituality of post-Tridentine piety. Although the visions of certain saints such as St. Teresa of Avila were inward, some visions could be apprehended by physical sight. Since sight had already become a prominent means of perceiving the presence of the holy at the close of the Middle Ages, the vision was the most likely of all the traditional external aspects of the cult of the saints to survive. It was best suited to a religious sensibility formed by the visual medium of printed communication, for its emphasis was on seeing rather than either hearing or touching—although hearing was still important since the Virgin has continued to communicate verbally in her

106. Warner, *Alone of All Her Sex*, 298.

107. Edouard Dumoutet, *Le desir de voir l'hostie et les origines de la devotion au saint-sacrement* (Paris: Beauchesne, 1926), 35–36. Dumoutet states that the fifteenth century was the last in which there was a great desire among the people to view the host, although some continued to defend the practice on into the seventeenth century.

modern appearances.[108] Also, as David Chidester argues, from ancient times sight was often believed to provide the most immediate and direct means of establishing spiritual union with the divine without recourse to the materiality of images, relics, or religious rites such as sacraments.[109]

Once they have disappeared, a vision generally leaves no permanent relic behind, apart from the sanctity the vision imports to the general surroundings in which it has occurred.[110] The saint's ongoing presence at the site may be recognized primarily through spiritual sensitivity or through miracles wrought in the persons who have come there on pilgrimage. Place has largely become the substitute for material objects as the gateway to Mary's spiritual presence, although not always. At times visions are credited with leaving behind physical manifestations such weeping or bleeding statues, or they might perhaps create renewed devotion to an image that had been neglected by the people.[111]

108. See Perry and Echeverría, *Under the Heel of Mary,* 76–78. Often, as with the other aspects of the Marian cult in modern times, her words have served to confirm the Church's dogmas or bolster its authority in uncertain times, but only if the Church is able to control the experience. Perry and Echeverría provide an outline and their interpretation of the major features of modern Marian apparitions.

109. David Chidester, *Word and Light: Seeing, Hearing and Religious Discourse* (Urbana: University of Illinois Press, 1992), 1–10. Chidester examines theories of seeing vs. hearing in ancient Greece and demonstrates that for the Greeks, sight represented "continuity, connection, presence, similarity, immediacy and even union between seer and seen." Hearing, however, was associated with a discontinuity between the one making the sound and the hearer, for sound initiated with someone or something outside the person perceiving, whereas sight is initiated by the perceiver. In an environment in which hearing is stressed, union needs to be achieved and therefore requires involved interaction on the part of the hearers and the person speaking.

110. Warner, *Alone of All Her Sex,* 302–9. Warner contrasts visions of the Virgin which have occurred in the Americas, which she labels as "concrete, almost medieval" in spirit, with those of Europe in the period following the Reformation. The latter are more "abstract." Although no relics are associated with visions of the Virgin, at times physical reminders of the vision are produced. In the vision of St. Catherine Labouré in 1830, the Virgin instructed Catherine to commission a medal patterned according to a design revealed to her in the vision itself. The resulting Miraculous Medal has been one of the most popular and successful devotional objects in the modern Catholic world. For full details of this incident and its results, see Perry and Echeverría, *Under the Heel of Mary,* 90–91; or John J. Delaney, ed., *A Woman Clothed with the Sun: Eight Great Appearances of Our Lady in Modern Times* (New York: Doubleday, 1960), 57–77.

111. William A. Christian, *Apparitions in Late Medieval and Renaissance Spain* (Princeton: Princeton University Press, 1981), 8–9.

William Christian's study of visions in Spain during the late Middle Ages and Renaissance finds that even the popularity of visions waned after 1525. He suggests several reasons for this, including the stern presence of the Inquisition, persistently ready to see in popular visions a source of heterodox belief, as well as increasing doubt on the part of the people themselves in the validity of visions, due perhaps to their awareness of the questions raised by the inquisition.[112]

Christian nevertheless finds that private visionaries, as opposed to public, communal ones, remained especially popular, particularly among women. These private visions generally took place while the visionary was in a trance. Indeed the trance became the new means for determining the presence of a vision rather than other external signs. Thus, paradoxically, while the purpose of these visions was usually to provide personal spiritual advice, the vision itself had to occur in the presence of others so that the visionary's trance could be verified by witnesses. Also, the visionary was almost always a woman who had taken formal religious vows. She was not a typical person of the community. Thus, while the significance of visions that would be endorsed by and meaningful to the entire community declined, that of private, individualized visions remained somewhat strong.[113]

Devotion to relics, images, and external practices obviously did not end in the sixteenth and seventeenth centuries. It is well known that many people in the modern world remain intensely loyal to them, particularly in places where people's lives are lived at the intersection of more traditional oral networks of communication and a public discourse shaped by literacy.[114] In such places, the situation remains much as it was during the transitional period of early modern Europe. Also, in any Christian community, the belief that human bodies as well as human souls were created by God and redeemed in the person of Jesus means that worship will

---

112. Ibid., 8–9, 184–86.

113. Ibid., 185–87.

114. For a discussion of the preservation of the bodies of the most famous Catholic saints, in the medieval and in the modern Church, see J. Carroll Cruz, *The Incorruptibles: A Study of the Incorruption of the Bodies of Various Catholic Saints and Beati* (Rockford, Ill.: Tan Books and Publishers, 1977).

usually address itself to the entire person, to the physical as well as to the purely spiritual side of experience. The centrality of the Eucharist and other sacraments in many modern churches is one testimony to this. The Assumption's continued importance as a doctrine rests not simply on the Church's authority to proclaim it but on the fact that, for some Catholics, their own personal hopes of a continued bodily existence in the next world are tied in part to the belief that the Virgin's bodily transfiguration has preceded theirs.

It is still true, however, that Catholic religious practice and understanding underwent a transformation which had begun by the latter part of the fifteenth century and continued throughout the sixteenth and seventeenth centuries. This transformation involved the cultivation of a more individualized and interiorized understanding of Christianity that ultimately left no aspect of piety untouched. The Virgin remained as central to the Catholic Church's piety as she had ever been, but, when she appeared in popular sermons, her personality, like that of many individuals in Western Europe, had been altered. Among Christians living in the late sixteenth or early seventeenth century, Mary was accessible as intercessor chiefly to those who abandoned the crowded streets and public places and sought to commune with her most holy soul in the quiet stillness of their hearts.

Conclusion

"AVE MARIA, GRATIA PLENA, DOMINUS TECUM." "Hail Mary, full of grace, the Lord is with you." Through these words, Catholic Christians have long been accustomed to greet the Virgin Mary, and through them have sought the prayers of Mary on their behalf. This has never changed. But if the supplication remained unaltered, the image of the Virgin Mother held in the minds of Christians as they prayed was certainly transformed over time. No one can enter fully into the mental world of another person, and this is particularly true of persons separated from us by so great a distance into the past. Yet by examining Marian piety in the late medieval and early modern periods through the lens of popular sermons, it is possible to trace subtle alterations in the perception of the Virgin which were due, in large part, to much broader changes within European Christianity and society as a whole. As European religious life began to move away from an externalized piety which valued devotional objects such as relics, images, and material means for encountering God, a new spirituality began to emerge which magnified instead the importance of inner devotion and mental prayer, even as it continued to affirm the necessity of the sacraments and the usefulness of some traditional popular practices. European Christians, Protestant as well as Catholic, embraced an affective devotional life centered on the heart, the inward seat of the will and emotions.[1]

---

1. Ted A. Campbell, *The Religion of the Heart: A Study of European Religious Life in the Seventeenth and Eighteenth Centuries* (Columbia: University of South Carolina Press, 1991). Campbell's entire book is relevant here, for Campbell believes that all religious life in the seventeenth century was affected by a more emotional and internalized spirituality, which used the heart as the supreme symbol of the affective and intentional center of the human religious personality.

A number of factors may have combined to bring about these changes. Among people of the upper and middle classes as well as the clergy, the growth of literacy after 1450 and the mental habits encouraged by extensive acquaintance with reading and writing were important tools for fashioning an interiorized spirituality. Brian Stock finds that as early as the twelfth century, the more literate clergy were beginning to trust texts more than relics and rituals, and in fact were coming to distrust the material in general. These men tended to equate the practices of the largely "oral" society with "the popular," "the inauthentic," and "the disreputable."[2] If such a transformation could already have begun among literate churchmen of the twelfth century, it would likely spread much farther once the creation of printing made it possible to disseminate such views more widely among the people, who were themselves acquiring literacy skills.

This move from orality to literacy in early modern Europe was, however, only one of the important forces for religious change. Alongside it one must place the growing intrusion into the interior world of European Christians brought about by more rigorous confessional practices and the monitoring of the individual conscience that was its necessary corollary. Altered confessional practices would touch the lives of the majority of the people of Europe, literate or not, prompting them to examine their inner inclinations and motivations more meticulously than ever, with a view toward preventing sinful behavior altogether, especially the kind which disrupted the peace and unity of the Christian community. The late medieval Church was thereby helping to create and shape an inner awareness of the self and its characteristics.

In the wake of the Protestant Reformation, the Catholic Church after Trent began to be even more demanding in its expectations for the faithful. As members of a reinvigorated, forceful organization, Catholic Christians were now supposed to exercise the kind of moral discipline and restraint ordinarily prescribed for the clergy. Even as the growing demands of centralized governments created a need for public figures to find

2. Brian Stock, *The Implications of Literacy: Written Language and Models of Interpretation in the Eleventh and Twelfth Centuries* (Princeton: Princeton University Press, 1983), 246–50.

refuge in a private self, the same dynamic could have operated equally within the structure of the Church. As the Church called on its members, clerical and lay, to be more self-aware and committed, many may have welcomed a private, inner space as a place of retreat from the pressure.

Many people in the Church had long considered inward spirituality to be the superior form of religious experience. As a result of the current development of the interior self, the Catholic clergy in the sixteenth and seventeenth centuries was able, through devotional societies, to encourage a movement already taking place. The Church worked to develop the interior life of the people through the many popular Marian congregations and confraternities. These societies often asked for a daily examination of conscience as well as regular recitation of the Rosary, which, as we have seen, is one aid to mental prayer.

Because so little is actually said about Mary, the mother of Christ, in the Scriptures, it has been possible for preachers to describe her and her importance in ways which enlist her as the champion of the Church, whatever its current cause may be. Predictably, therefore, the Virgin became the acknowledged defender of the Catholic Church against the Protestant movement in the sixteenth century.[3] Yet since the Church itself was undergoing the shift in religious sensibilities outlined above, its portrayal of Mary reflected that shift. Nowhere is the alteration of perspective on Mary's role more revealing than in the significance attached to her bodily relationship with Jesus.

In any period of Christian history, the Virgin Mary should be prominent as the one who bestowed a human body on the eternal Word, and who gave birth to him at a specific time and place. During the Middle Ages, that physical contribution became the springboard for the elaboration of a Marian cult which was fully integrated into the sacramental and incarnational emphases of the time. Sermons and devotional literature described her as actively present throughout Jesus' life, speaking up for

---

3. Luther was equally capable of using Mary as an example of the Protestant belief that human nature is weak and sinful, unable to do anything good without the aid of God's grace. See Hilda Graef, *Mary: A History of Doctrine and Devotion*, 2 vols. (New York: Sheed and Ward, 1964), 2:6–12.

her friends and vehemently protesting Jesus' unjust crucifixion. The mystical unity of their shared flesh enabled Mary to experience with her son the suffering of his Passion. Her physical presence with him in heaven after her Assumption contributed to her power to act as mediator for Christians on earth. She could add to her intercession the effectiveness of ritual gestures, reminding Jesus of their intimate relationship as she revealed the breast with which she had nursed him as an infant. Although bodily present in heaven, Mary was still accessible to the faithful through her many images and relics, scattered throughout Europe, and could be counted on to show mercy to any who sought her aid. The Virgin's body was also the ultimate source of the most powerful devotional object of the later medieval period, the host.

By the late sixteenth century, institutional and social pressures worked to modify this concretized participation of Mary in the Church's life. Still the mother of Christ, it was now her spiritual motherhood which many preachers chose to emphasize, some even saying that Jesus loved his mother not because of her physical birth-giving, but because of her spiritual purity and holiness. Mary still grieves at the Passion, but silently, her suffering the result of spiritual communication between mother and son.

When contrasting historical periods, it is necessary to avoid exaggerating the degree of change which took place. The external practices and traditional sensibilities of medieval Europe did not die overnight, and probably lingered among the people much longer than might be expected.[4]

4. All of David Sabean's *Power in the Blood* is significant here, but see especially chapter 6, "The Sins of Unbelief," in *Power in the Blood: Popular Culture and Village Discourse in Early Modern Germany* (Cambridge: Cambridge University Press, 1984), 174–98. Sabean shows that as late as 1796, the Protestant villagers of Beutelsbach were not beyond the use of sympathetic magic, offering the sacrifice of a bull to end an epidemic of hoof and mouth disease. He also illustrates that the people still conceived of truth and knowledge not as systematic abstract entities, separate from life as it is lived, but as ongoing dialogue and discussion about a central issue, "social knowledge" gained from the input of the community which could be the basis for "practical action." Right belief was less important than the practical results of actions in specific situations. Robert Scribner also finds the remnants of late medieval religious piety continuing on among Lutheran pastors and people long after the Reformation. See R. W. Scribner, "Incombustible Luther: The Image of the Reformer in Early Modern Germany," *Past and Present* 110 (1986): 38–68. Scribner points out that Lutheran pastors used images and medals depicting Luther not only as examples to inspire but also as wonder-working objects, as they sought to compete with Catholics who claimed that

Growing literacy and other factors which acted to transform religious understanding also contributed to a renewed respect for the written tradition that enshrined many of the older practices, a tradition which had the support of the Tridentine decrees themselves. In spite of these reservations, there is no mistaking the attempt by Counter-Reformation clergy to establish a more passive and spiritualized Virgin—humble, obedient, prayerful, silent, and devoted to good works while on earth; interceding, still humbly, for the faithful once she reached heaven—as a model for the type of Catholic they hoped to foster after Trent. The Marian relics and images which remained were expected primarily to inspire those who viewed them with the desire to emulate Mary's spiritual virtues. Because these changes were based not solely on the program of one branch of the Church, but on broader alterations in European social and religious life, it is highly likely that private and personal perceptions of the Virgin would gradually grow in new directions to appropriate these changes for the domain of individual spirituality.

Questions concerning the significance of Marian devotion in the history of Western Christianity certainly remain. Based on the rich variety of ways in which late medieval society incorporated the Virgin into its devotional life, one can never assume that the official position of the Church after Trent, whether presented in sermons, catechisms, or other formal doctrinal statements, determined totally the ways in which individual Christians would appropriate Marian piety.

Recently, Caroline Walker Bynum, Gail McMurray Gibson, and Theresa Coletti have demonstrated that a closer scrutiny of Marian themes in specific contexts is essential for obtaining a complete picture of the rich diversity of means by which late medieval women identified with the Virgin. In *Holy Feast and Holy Fast,* Bynum disagrees with Marina Warner's

---

their images could work miracles. Some of the same conclusions can be drawn about the Catholic world from the work of Christiane Klapisch-Zuber, "Holy Dolls: Play and Piety in Florence in the Quattrocento," in *Women, Family and Ritual in Renaissance Italy* (Chicago: University of Chicago Press, 1985), 310–29. Klapisch-Zuber finds that as late as the seventeenth century, confraternities were organized around the cult of the Christ Child, in which actual dolls representing him were washed, clothed, placed in cradles, kissed, and adorned. This was an especially popular devotion in convents of nuns, but the dolls, or "bambini," were also part of the Christmas rituals of monks as well.

view that Mary had a necessarily negative influence on women's lives. Bynum finds that, for women religious, Mary was simply not important as a "representative woman," and did not occupy center stage in women's spirituality. Mary's significance for women was found in her ability to bear the body of Christ. These women, therefore, identified more closely with Christ, who, like themselves, carried with him a weak, fleshly, "female" humanity. Instead of finding in the Virgin an impossible ideal, religious women such as St. Catherine of Siena and Hildegard of Bingen found in Mary's motherhood of Jesus a positive means to emulate the suffering of Jesus in their own lives, joining themselves, as Mary had done, to the mystery of his Passion.[5]

Gibson, too, places the cult of the Virgin firmly in its place as a part of the incarnational piety of East Anglia in the fifteenth century. Her interpretation of the laywoman Margery Kempe's life, in *The Theater of Devotion,* is also a challenge to a negative interpretation of Mary's influence on women, although from a different perspective from Bynum's. Gibson shows that Margery, in her own visionary life, sought deliberately to copy Mary's role as handmaid of the Lord by becoming a handmaid to the Virgin herself and to the Christ Child. Margery's visions clearly were inspired by the spiritual advice given to a thirteenth-century Franciscan nun in the *Meditationes vitae Christi.* In her personal account of her trials and struggles, Margery did not hesitate to move from an understanding of her suffering as like that of Jesus, a theme which would support Bynum's argument, to a vision of her own service to the Christ Child as a mirror of Mary's. In either case, both Jesus and his mother were positive examples, informing Margery's religious life and giving it meaning.[6]

Theresa Coletti's article "Purity and Danger" also concludes that the medieval cult of Mary was much more than a means of ensuring that women would remain in a subordinate position by imitating the Virgin's humility. Particularly in the religious plays of the day, she argues, Mary's paradoxical status as both Virgin and mother resulted in dramatic situa-

5. Caroline Walker Bynum, *Holy Feast and Holy Fast: The Religious Significance of Food to Medieval Women* (Berkeley: University of California Press, 1987), 264–69.

6. Gail McMurray Gibson, *The Theater of Devotion: East Anglian Drama and Society in the Late Middle Ages* (Chicago: University of Chicago Press, 1989), 47–65.

tions which could confront and challenge the gender stereotypes and structures of society.[7]

The work of Bynum, Gibson, and Coletti dovetails nicely with the findings of this study, which have shown that Mary's birth-giving and bodily unity with Jesus were always given a central, forceful, and positive interpretation in late medieval sermons. If a laywoman like Margery Kemp could feel kinship with the Virgin in her own experience of giving birth, as well as in her mental visions, women who had taken religious vows were no less capable of using their sharing of a female nature with Mary to establish a sense of unity with the Savior, who had received his flesh from a woman. Finally, the fact that Mary was a mother, yet virginal and sinless, made it possible to question the traditional notion that motherhood and women in general need be denigrated to a secondary position. Medieval philosophy may have persistently identified men with the superior soul and women with the body, but in the concrete spirituality of the late Middle Ages, some women were able to use this to a positive advantage as they lived out their faith.

All of this concerns the medieval period, however, and the sermon evidence has shown that preachers in the sixteenth century were beginning to view the importance of the Virgin in a different way. More research will have to be done before any firm conclusions may be drawn about the place of Mary in the context of personal Catholic spirituality during the sixteenth and seventeenth centuries. The tendency to exalt Mary's inner spirituality and passive virtue does coincide, however, with a general suspicion of the body, and of women's bodies specifically, in European society as a whole. Elizabeth Rapley suggests that one of the results of French religious education in the period was to inculcate in students "the distrust of the body which was so much a feature of the seventeenth century."[8] As we will see, this suspicion manifested itself in cultural realms as diverse as

7. Theresa Coletti, "Purity and Danger: The Paradox of Mary's Body and the En-gendering of the Infancy Narrative in the English Mystery Cycles," in *Feminist Approaches to the Body in Medieval Literature*, ed. Linda Lomperis and Sarah Stanbury (Philadelphia: University of Pennsylvania Press, 1993), 66–67.

8. Elizabeth Rapley, *The Dévotes: Women and Church in Seventeenth-Century France* (Montreal: McGill-Queens University Press, 1990), 158.

educational treatises, witchcraft trials, art works, and Cartesian epistemology; and it provides one more reason why those who portrayed the
Virgin in their sermons would prefer to dwell on her soul rather than her
body.

Rapley finds that "pudeur," a rather excessive notion of modesty, best
describes the seventeenth-century French ideal of proper women's behavior. This ideal formed part of the education propagated by female
"dévotes," who sought to promote greater inward devotion and control
of the body among all of their pupils, but especially among their female
charges. Catholic women educators often modeled their pedagogical
techniques and goals on those of the Jesuits, thus the high value placed on
"self-discipline" of the emotions and the body. "Restraint" and "control"
were their watchwords. Just as among the Marian devotional societies,
there is the sense that the body, especially the body of a woman, is always
threatening to break free. Only constant vigilance can prevent sinful and
immodest disorder.[9]

Many historians agree that distrust of women was growing in the sixteenth century. In her recent study of fifteenth- and sixteenth-century
French sermons, *Soldiers of Christ*, Larissa Taylor concludes that the sermons of sixteenth-century French preachers express a more negative
view of women and women's nature than earlier ones, rarely praising
women or their contributions to the faith. These men often insisted on
the greater weakness of women than men, and described even Mary Magdalen as an "imbecile" for seeking to touch Christ after the Resurrection.[10]

9. Ibid., 76, 149–50, 157–58.

10. Larissa Juliet Taylor, *Soldiers of Christ: Preaching in Late Medieval and Reformation
France* (Oxford: Oxford University Press, 1992), 171–78. In the sixteenth century, Protestantism perhaps did more than Catholicism to remove feminine influence from religion by
its condemnation of the saints, male and female, and by its elimination of female religious
orders. It is also true that some Catholic women of the sixteenth century were aware of the
importance of maintaining a gender balance when discussing religious matters. See Natalie Zemon Davis, "City Women and Religious Change," in *Society and Culture in Early Modern France: Eight Essays by Natalie Zemon Davis* (Stanford: Stanford University Press, 1975), 88.
Also see Carlos M. N. Eire, *War Against the Idols: The Reformation of Worship from Erasmus to
Calvin* (Cambridge: Cambridge University Press, 1986), 315. Eire points to what he calls the
"masculinization of piety" in the Protestant movement. The Protestant elimination of the
Virgin and other female saints from their prominent place in religious life left worshipers
with only masculine images for devotional inspiration.

Joseph Klaits's analysis of the witch craze in the early modern period, *Servants of Satan*, attributes the sudden explosion of witchcraft trials around 1550 to what he calls a "dramatic rise in fear and hatred of women" during the era of the Reformation, a connection first made by Joan Kelley.[11] This misogyny was fueled by traditional beliefs which held that women were by nature morally weaker than men and that they possessed a stronger inclination to sexual activity. Such beliefs became deadly for women after the late fifteenth century, when a new definition of witchcraft was adopted by the clerical hierarchy primarily responsible for prosecuting witches. Whereas the witch had been seen as a person, male or female, who tampered with natural magic to harm a neighbor, the new definition specified that the witch was someone who had transferred religious loyalty and become a worshiper of Satan. Furthermore, by 1550, witches were characterized as Satan's sexual slaves, who met periodically in witches' Sabbats to engage in perverted sexual practices with each other and with the Devil.[12] This preoccupation with the sexual nature of witchcraft led to the disproportionately higher numbers of women accused of this crime.

Heinrich Kramer and Jacob Sprenger's *Malleus Maleficarum,* a famous witch-hunting manual published during the 1480's, says,

(That a woman) is more carnal than a man is clear from her many carnal abominations. And it should be noted that there was a defect in the formation of the first woman, since she was formed from a bent rib, that is, a rib of the breast, which is bent as it were in a contrary direction to a man. And since through this defect she is an imperfect animal, she always deceives. . . . All witchcraft comes from carnal lust, which is women insatiable.[13]

Without stopping to consider the theological implications of attributing to God a defect in his creative technique, the authors clearly describe the

---

11. Joseph Klaits, *Servants of Satan: The Age of the Witch Hunts* (Bloomington: Indiana University Press, 1985), 52; Joan Kelley, "Early Feminist Theory and the 'Querelle des Femmes,' 1400–1789," in *Women, History and Theory: The Essays of Joan Kelly* (Chicago: University of Chicago Press, 1984), 93–94.

12. Klaits, *Servants of Satan*, 50–56.

13. Heinrich Kramer and James Sprenger, *The Malleus Maleficarum*, ed. and trans. Montague Summers (New York: Dover, 1971), 41–44; quoted in Margaret R. Miles, *Carnal Knowing: Female Nakedness and Religious Meaning in the Christian West* (Boston: Beacon Press, 1989), 121.

female body as inherently perverse and the logical source of witchcraft. It is certainly true that there was nothing new in the use of the Aristotelian notion that women were biologically less perfect than men. Dominicans at least since Albert the Great and Thomas Aquinas had done so. Thomas believed that woman less perfectly reflected the image of God because she was created from man. Traditionally, however, Dominicans had attributed the defects of women in the order of nature to some problem with parentage or to a bad influence on the sexual act; and, even so, such imperfections in individual natures were compensated for by the greater perfection human nature acquired by having two sexes. Here, in the *Malleus Maleficarum,* the authors appear to believe that women were originally created by God to be prone to sin.[14]

Klaits also links increased concern with witchcraft in the sixteenth and seventeenth centuries to the growth of "introspective habits and preoccupation with sin" which, as we have seen, were the outcome of reforms by both Protestant and Catholic leaders. Increased intrusion by confessors and theologians into the private inner self created the psychological necessity of projecting the cause of sin and evil onto an external source. In addition, elite groups within society were becoming more insistent on bodily control and decorum in public places. Thus any "physically spontaneous" act came to appear "dangerous and low." For this reason peasant women, who were viewed as being more unrestrained in the use of their bodies than other women, were the most likely suspects for accusations of witchcraft.[15] It is also true that the often violent struggle between

14. Prudence Allen, R.S.M., *The Concept of Woman: The Aristotelian Revolution, 750 B.C.–A.D. 1250* (Grand Rapids, Mich.: William B. Eerdmans Publishing Company, 1985), 388–92, 406–7. According to Allen, Thomas Aquinas, in his work, *On the Power of God,* specifically rejects the notion that women should be considered naturally evil since women, like men, derive from the first principle, God, who is good. Thomas Aquinas, *Summa theologiae: Latin text and English translation, Introductions, Notes, Appendices and Glossaries,* vol. 13, *Man Made to God's Image,* trans. Edmund Hill, O.P. (New York: McGraw-Hill Book Company, 1988), 37; or ST: Ia, 92, 1. St. Thomas specifically denies that female nature as a whole, which derives from God, is imperfect. The imperfection lies in individual females, and for Thomas "is the result either of the debility of the active power, of some unsuitability of the material, or of some change effected by external influences, like the south wind, for example."

15. Klaits, *Servants of Satan,* 71–77.

rival religious groups following the onset of the Reformation created a climate of suspicion that fostered the tendency to look for the activity of evil in the world.

In *Carnal Knowing*, Margaret Miles describes the way in which female nakedness was used as a convention in Christian art to symbolize the sinfulness and fallen state of human nature generally. This was obviously true of depictions of Eve, but it carried over into portraits of Susanna, Mary Magdalen, and other women. New themes, however, began to occur in sixteenth-century art, according to both Miles and Klaits. For the first time, artists began to associate representations of overt sexuality with the symbols of death. Some of the Protestant artist Hans Baldung Grien's paintings of Adam and Eve actually present the Fall as occasioned by lust. Grien's famous nude paintings of witches, showing them as carnal and lascivious, were, then, the logical extension of his views on women's nature and women's bodies as a whole.[16] Recent scholars have cautioned against assuming that witch-hunting manuals such as the *Malleus Maleficarum* were the direct inspiration for the witches found in the art of Dürer or Hans Baldung Grien. There is nevertheless plenty of room to suspect that their vivid and suggestive portrayal of witches helped generate suspicions against women and may have influenced pow-

---

16. Miles, *Carnal Knowing*, xiv, 117–44; Klaits, *Servants of Satan*, 73–74. See also Thomas Laqueur, "Orgasm, Generation, and the Politics of Reproductive Biology," *Representations* 14 (1986): 1–41. Laqueur's article is an attempt to explain the radical re-evaluation of female nature and sexuality which took place in the eighteenth century as a response to the "equally radical Enlightenment political reconstitution of 'Man.'" In the past, hierarchical views of the nature of human society and of the relationships between various creatures in the Great Chain of Being went hand in hand. Women, therefore, were considered to be a slightly less perfect form of men in the continuum of being. Descriptions of female biology pictured the female sex organs as simply an inverted form of the male. As radical eighteenth-century political philosophy began to teach the equality of all and their consequent right to participate in politics, those who wished to keep women in the private sphere were forced to redefine female biology if they wished to justify this confinement on the basis of natural law. The result was the creation of a "biology of incommensurability" that stressed the great differences between women and men in the area of reproductive biology. Laqueur is probably right in seeing politics during the Enlightenment as the major immediate cause for this new biology, but attempts by men of the sixteenth and seventeenth centuries to link the nature of women's bodies to their participation in witchcraft shows that the ground work for viewing women's bodies as fundamentally different from men's was laid much earlier.

erful churchmen responsible for prosecuting women as witches later in the sixteenth century.[17]

Finally, in what would appear at first glance to be a completely different cultural category, Susan Bordo explains the creation of Descartes's epistemology as the result of the increased interiority and personal self-awareness of the early modern period, coupled with the distrust of the body and senses also current at the time. In *The Flight to Objectivity,* Bordo uses Descartes's *Meditations* to reconstruct the development of his epistemology, beginning with his radical epistemological doubt.[18]

Descartes's doubt about the possibility of acquiring any accurate knowledge was due in part to the overturning of the traditional understanding of the universe caused by the findings of Copernicus and the subsequent work of Galileo. Their publications had called into question the ability of the senses to provide reliable data even about the physical world itself, customarily believed to be the senses' proper sphere of operation. It was this distrust of the senses which caused Descartes to retreat into the realm of pure thought. He sought to rise above the body and its limitations, perceiving the body's passions and needs as a contamination of the mind's rationality. Bordo states that, for the first time in the Western tradition, even though it had always exhibited dualist tendencies, the "body and mind are defined in terms of mutual exclusivity."[19]

The end product of Descartes's system was a "masculine" model of knowledge which eliminated aspects of participatory knowing usually labeled "feminine," involving empathy, association, and knowledge understood as a union between knower and known. Indeed sixteenth- and seventeenth-century scientists themselves affirmed that their goal was to create a "masculine philosophy." Medieval philosophy had included the body in the process of acquiring knowledge, but by the seventeenth century, for Descartes and for other scientists, knowledge became dependent on "detachment, clarity, and transcendence of the body."[20]

17. Margaret A. Sullivan, "The Witches of Dürer and Hans Baldung Grien," *Renaissance Quarterly* 53 (2000): 375, 394–95.

18. Susan R. Bordo, *The Flight to Objectivity: Essays on Cartesianism and Culture* (Albany: State University of New York Press, 1987), 13–31, 45–58.

19. Ibid., 33–37, 76–77, 93.

20. Ibid., 8–9, 104–5. This section of Bordo's book relies heavily on the following three

Bordo then points to the usual association of women with both nature and body in masculine discourse. The belief that it is necessary to control and achieve distance from the body can be translated easily into a desire to control women, who, like the body, will be perceived as unruly, casting an impure shadow over the clarity of rationality and order. Such sentiments only added to the religious suspicion of women in the period and contributed to a climate of opinion which could support and sustain an attack on women as widespread as the witch craze.[21]

In the meantime, accusations of witchcraft were not the only means used to control women's activities in the sixteenth century. New legal restrictions in the professional sphere were used to limit women's access to public participation in business and craft guilds. These limitations eventually touched the lives of women in all social classes.[22]

What place is left for the Virgin Mary to fill in the midst of so much anxiety about women, and was she used as yet another means to try to control them? Klaits and Miles believe that Marian devotion is problematic because she is always presented as the perfect woman, and therefore automatically unlike all other women.[23] We have already seen, however, that neither the Virgin's sinlessness nor her paradoxical status as both virgin and mother prevented her from being a positive influence on the lives of late medieval women. Jesus was both perfect and of a divine-human nature, yet he was "imitated" by countless Christians of both sexes in the Middle Ages.

Miles may be correct in saying that the Virgin was used by women to form an interior self, since she embodied the "range of acceptable appearance, attitudes, and behavior" for women.[24] In the context of the six-

---

works: Brian Easlea, *Witch-Hunting, Magic and the New Philosophy* (Atlantic Highlands, N.J.: Humanities Press, 1980); Evelyn Fox Keller, *Reflections on Gender and Science* (New Haven: Yale University Press, 1985); Karl Stern, *The Flight from Woman* (New York: Noonday, 1965).

21. Bordo, *The Flight to Objectivity*, 108–11.

22. Miles, *Carnal Knowing*, 126–27; Natalie Zemon Davis, "City Women and Religious Change," in *Society and Culture in Early Modern France*, 94; Merry Weisner, "Women's Defense of Their Public Role," in *Women in the Middle Ages and Renaissance*, ed. Mary Beth Rose (Syracuse, N.Y.: Syracuse University Press, 1986), 3.

23. Klaits, *Servants of Satan*, 66, 72; Miles, *Carnal Knowing*, 120.

24. Miles, *Carnal Knowing*, 139.

teenth-century worldview, however, the fallen feminine nature to which the Virgin's perfection is the foil is no longer viewed as perhaps a bit weaker and more prone to sexual sin than men's but within the bounds of normal humanity. The Virgin now has to stand in contrast to the witch, whose very nature is defined in terms of unrestrained carnality and the physically grotesque.[25] The mental construction of the witch and the Virgin as polar opposites is already suggested by the fact that Jacob Sprenger, co-author of the *Malleus Maleficarum,* also founded a Rosary confraternity in Cologne in 1475 and actively promoted devotion to Mary.[26]

In the context of the Catholic Church's need to halt the rising tide of Protestantism in the late sixteenth century, Peter Canisius's statement that an "immaculate Lord Christ came forth from an immaculate Virgin" takes on a greater significance.[27] Mary's sinless body now bears the symbolic weight of the doctrinal, spiritual, and, not least, physical purity required of Catholics in general and of women in particular, as the Catholic Church does battle with the forces of Satan in the form of either heretics or witches.

Witches were usually painted as nudes, their bodies open to physical perversions just as their souls had admitted the spiritual abuse of satanic slavery. When they spoke, it was to utter blasphemies, curse their enemies, or, perhaps worse, lull others into a false sense of security through friendly and flattering words that masked the evil intent within.[28] It would seem that this aspect of the witch would have been especially frightening in a society that was beginning to question the reliability of the senses to convey accurate information about anything. When both hearing and sight were problematic under ordinary circumstances, how much easier it

25. See especially Miles, "'Carnal Abominations': The Female Body as Grotesque," chap. 5 in *Carnal Knowing,* 145–68.

26. Marina Warner, *Alone of All Her Sex: The Myth and Cult of the Virgin Mary* (New York: Alfred A. Knopf, 1976), 306.

27. Peter Canisius, *Meditationes seu notae in evangelicas lectiones,* 2d ed., ed. Frederick Streicher, S.J., 2 vols. (Munich: 1957), 2,1:141.

28. Mary Douglas, *Natural Symbols: Explorations in Cosmology* (New York: Pantheon Books, 1970), 113. Douglas believes that, as perceived by the community, the primary character of the witch is defined by deception, "someone whose external appearance does not automatically betray his interior nature."

would be for someone to deliberately convey false impressions to these senses. If Mary were to represent the opposite of such creatures as witches and remain a symbol of the purity of the Church, she would have to be fully clothed, as far removed from all physical involvement as possible, and speak little. For a woman, unrestricted speech, especially in public, had traditionally been a sign of sexual laxity no less serious than an open display of her body.[29] Not surprisingly, it was during the sixteenth century that artists largely abandoned portraits of the Virgin suckling her child.[30] This historic iconographic motif gave way in the face of society's desire to suppress the public display of bodily functions and the need to distance the Virgin from as many physical associations with other women as possible.

The altered perspective on Mary's participation in the Passion is important here, for in the Middle Ages Passion sermons had been the occasion for the greatest public elaboration of Mary's individual personality. Except for her tears, there is no outward display through words or dramatic actions of her grief. By the late sixteenth century, the Virgin's speech, whether in sermons or other contexts, is largely limited to her role as intercessor and mediatrix between God and the world. She intercedes for her friends at Cana, she performs good works, and she prays. In visions, she communicates a heavenly message to those who remain on earth. But words such as Mary's laments at the cross and her involved conversations with Jesus, words which could serve to reveal her own thoughts and feelings as a particular woman, are largely absent. The Virgin neither faints nor clings to the cross. She is a model of emotional and

29. Miles, *Carnal Knowing*, 165. In the same context, Miles quotes Francesco Barbaro's treatise, "On Wifely Duties," in which he states, "The speech of a noble woman can be no less dangerous than the nakedness of her limbs." Barbaro's treatise can be found, translated by Benjamin G. Kohl, in *The Earthly Republic: Italian Humanists on Government and Society*, ed. Benjamin G. Kohl and Ronald G. Witt with Elizabeth B. Welles (Philadelphia: University of Pennsylvania Press, 1978), 189–228. See also Karma Lochrie, *Margery Kempe and Translations of the Flesh* (Philadelphia: University of Pennsylvania Press, 1991), 25–26. Lochrie points out that St. Bernard in the twelfth century, and the devotional work the *Ancrene Wisse* in the thirteenth, propounded the belief that the ideal female body should be sealed completely, the mouth included.

30. Warner, *Alone of All Her Sex*, 203–4.

physical control. Even the "Aves" offered to her in the Rosary are now described by Christopher Cheffontaines as a way to bring "order" and discipline to the life of prayer.

Catholic leaders promoted the cult of the Holy Family in the seventeenth century, in which the Virgin appears as the ideal mother: humble, quiet, caring, and submissive to Joseph as well as to God.[31] Since the cult of Joseph himself had been on the rise since the fifteenth century, it was easy to portray him as the role model for fathers, authoritative and protective of wife and children.[32] Once again, there is a preference for creating a structure of patriarchal order and obedience.

The religious creativity of late medieval women cautions against the assumption that Catholic women of the post-Tridentine period could not have been equally innovative in incorporating newer models of the Virgin into their spirituality. It is easy to see how Mary might continue to be a useful exemplar, either for secluded religious, men or women, or for the prayer lives of those who had joined one of the Marian devotional societies. Beyond this, however, seventeenth-century French Catholics revealed their spiritual resourcefulness through a creative interpretation of the Visitation, through which Mary surprisingly became the inspiration for religious women who sought to become more actively involved in service to the poor and in the field of education. Against the prevailing trends of the international Church, in which the ecclesiastical hierarchy usually sought to confine religious women in convents according to the historic contemplative model, the Virgin of the Visitation came to represent the triumph of the active life of service over these restrictions. Both men such as François de Sales, Vincent de Paul, and Jean-Jacques Olier and women such as Jeanne de Chantal and Marguerite Bourgeoys appealed to the Visitation as the prototype for a women's "apostolate."[33] Elizabeth Rapley cites this remarkable passage from Jean-Jacques Olier's work, *Vie intérieure de la Très Sainte Vièrge:* "It is from the mystery of the

31. Ibid., 190.

32. John Bossy, *Christianity in the West, 1400–1700* (Oxford: Oxford University Press, 1985), 10.

33. Rapley, *The Dévotes*, 169–74.

Visitation that apostolic men and missionaries ought to draw the graces of their sublime vocation. From the moment that she (Mary) conceived and formed Him in her womb, she, first of all, went out at once to announce Him, and thus did what the Apostles later did by her example."[34] Clearly, not all Catholics allowed the greater emphasis on interior devotion in the seventeenth century to prevent them from developing a model of Mary as someone whose inner spiritual union with God allowed her the freedom to express that union in active works of love, works defined by some in ways that transgressed traditional boundaries separating men's and women's roles. In any case, the Virgin became, for many, the perfect embodiment of François de Sales's description of the proper relation between the "inner" and the "outer" man. Through her inner life of prayer Mary fulfilled the commandment to love God above all else, while through her good works and her proclamation of the arrival of her son, she fulfilled the commandment to love her neighbor as herself.

The most appropriate way to bring this study to a close is to consider one of the most widespread and popular features of Marian piety in the seventeenth century, devotion to her Sacred Heart. The ideals and practices associated with this devotion reveal both the basic transformation in European spirituality which was taking place at that time, as well as the persistence of more medieval forms of religious expression. Based on the widespread enthusiasm for the cult of the Sacred Heart of Mary in the seventeenth century, it is possible to see that European Christians were indeed increasingly attracted by a piety which stressed inner spiritual union with Christ through Mary. They nevertheless continued to be drawn to pronounced concrete and physical manifestations of that union.

The essence of the cult of the Sacred Heart is the mystical unity of love and purpose shared by the Virgin and her son, the same unity which we have seen expressed in numerous sermons of the day. As such, this devotion was closely linked to a twin devotion to the heart of Jesus. That which bound and continues to bind Mary and Jesus together is their common love for human beings, their mutual suffering to bring about hu-

34. Ibid., 172.

man redemption, and their ongoing cooperation to further the will of God in the world.[35]

The human heart was traditionally understood to be the seat of emotion and affection. In the seventeenth and eighteenth centuries, however, Europe experienced an international spiritual movement in which all religion, Catholic and Protestant versions of Christianity and even Judaism, came to be influenced by what Ted Campbell has called "religions of the heart."[36] This approach promoted an inward love of and dedication to God, which was believed to be superior to organized religion, which stressed formal theology or the sacraments. Campbell accounts for this renewed emphasis on inner devotion by pointing to general dissatisfaction with the excessive rationalism of the scientific revolution and the Enlightenment and to the religious division which had shattered the perceived unity of Christendom in the wake of the Protestant Reformation, a division increasingly manifest in the arena of military as well as pulpit warfare. As various Christian groups competed with each other, each basing its claims to authority on external and objective forms such as the Bible, the early Church Fathers, or Christian traditions in worship and creed, many Europeans began to sense a fundamental error in such divi-

35. Nicholas Perry and Loreto Echeverría, *Under the Heel of Mary* (New York: Routledge, 1988), 47. St. Jean Eudes (d. 1680) did the most to develop and popularize the cult of the Sacred Heart. He composed an Office of the Holy Heart of Mary in 1641 and organized several devotional societies dedicated to Mary's heart. According to Eudes, there were three dimensions to Mary's sacred heart: her virginal fleshly heart; her spiritual heart, which was God-like; and a heart that is actually divine and God himself, for it is the love of God dwelling in her.

36. Campbell, *Religion of the Heart*, 144–51. Campbell points to "parallels" between the development of Christian "religions of the heart" and the Hasidic movement within the Jewish faith. Like Western Christians, the Jews of Eastern Europe had experienced religious division and disillusion in the failed messianic movement of Sabbatai Tsevi. They had also suffered warfare and persecution as a result of "the Deluge," in which Poland was successively attacked by Cossacks from the Ukraine, Russians, and finally Swedes, events which parallel the horrors of the Thirty Years War in the West. In the wake of these events, Israel ben Eliezer or Baal Shem Tov (Master of the Good Name) founded the movement which came to be known as Hasidism. He transformed the religion of Judaism by stressing not the study of Scripture but religious practice and the fervent devotion of the individual, demonstrated by emotional prayer and ecstatic trances. Campbell is not arguing for the influence of Christian movements on Judaism, but for the notion that similar conditions produce similar results for religious communities.

sion. They began to seek a means to bypass the arguments and warfare by appealing to an experience of God not determined completely by objective authorities and ecclesiastical hierarchies. In this way, Christians from apparently competing camps might foster a sense of unity in Christ existing beyond the surface division. Indeed, Campbell points out that many Christians involved in these movements, from Quakers, Moravians, and Methodists to Quietists and Jansenists, recognized and applauded the similarity of religious devotion among such seemingly disparate Christian groups in so wide a variety of cultural contexts.[37] Among the Catholic expressions of these "religions of the heart," Campbell sees the Sacred Heart devotion as both the most orthodox and the most influential.[38]

It is true that a piety centered on the Sacred Hearts of Mary and Jesus would appear to be a totally interior devotion which stresses a spiritual union between mother and son. To an extent, this is accurate. There is likewise a spiritual desire on the part of those who are dedicated to the Sacred Heart to unite their own hearts to those of Jesus and his mother in love and service. Those who participated in this movement stressed the development of an intense private prayer life as well as the performance of works of service to the community. The outward practices which this devotion inspired, however, are more reminiscent of the Middle Ages. Often, the physical hearts of those who had outstanding love for Mary were preserved after death, and were believed to possess miraculous powers as a result of their intimate union with her. The hearts of St. François de Sales and St. Jeanne de Chantal, who helped early on to popularize the Sacred Heart devotion, were kept at Chaillot and were later observed to undergo dramatic changes during times when the Church was distressed. Prominent persons desired to have their hearts preserved in shrines dedicated to Mary. The heart of James II of England was placed, at his request, near those of St. François and St. Jeanne at Chaillot.[39] In short, the Sacred Heart devotion is a blending of the current movement toward inner piety with the traditional cult of relics.

37. Ibid., 152.
38. Ibid., 36–40.
39. Perry and Echeverría, *Under the Heel of Mary,* 47–48.

A commonplace of modern history is the notion that the sixteenth century was a period of transition, but this concept remains empty of content without an attempt, however limited, to discover and describe some of the dynamics of the process involved. This is a task on which historians of the period have been laboring for some time, long enough to have demonstrated that religious sensibilities were undergoing a profound change, a change which eventually produced the Protestant Reformation as well as more subdued but equally significant differences in Catholic piety. This study has sought to examine some of the forces for change in the period and their impact on the Catholic faith as exhibited through popular sermons and Marian devotion. A close scrutiny of the symbols and metaphors employed by the Church's preachers to inspire its members with love for Mary shows that by the dawn of the seventeenth century she was a changed individual, no longer quite the same woman who had participated in so dramatic a way in fifteenth-century sermons, artworks, and treatises. She is more distanced from the action, more spiritualized, more passive, and much more silent.

If it had been possible for a pious Catholic layperson of the fifteenth century, devoted to the Virgin, to encounter her once again as she was presented at the opening of the seventeenth century by a preacher such as François de Sales, the experience would no doubt have been similar to that of a person who happens upon a relative whom he or she has not seen in twenty or thirty years: unsettling. The physical appearance is vaguely familiar and the network of family relationships much the same, and yet the personality has been molded both by time and experience. It would be necessary to become acquainted all over again.

Bibliography

Primary Sources

Anselm of Canterbury. *The Prayers and Meditations of Saint Anselm.* Translated and introduced by Sister Benedicta Ward, S.L.G. Foreword by R. W. Southern. New York: Penguin Books, 1973.

Barletta, Gabriel. *Sermones quadragesimales et de sanctis.* Brescia: Jacobus Britannicus, 1497.

Bellarmine, Robert. *Roberti cardinalis Bellarmini opera omnia.* 6 vols. Naples: J. Giuliano, 1860.

Bernardino of Busti. *Mariale.* Milan: Leonardus Pachel, 1493.

Bernardino of Siena. *Opera omnia.* Edited by P. M. Perantoni. 5 vols. Quaracchi: Collegium S. Bonaventurae, 1950–.

Canisius, Peter. *Meditationes seu notae in evangelicas lectiones.* 2d ed. Edited by Frederick Streicher, S.J. 2 vols. Munich: Officina Salesiana, 1957.

Canons and Decrees of the Council of Trent: Original Text with English Translation. Translated by H. J. Schroeder, O.P. St. Louis: Herder, 1941.

The Catechism of the Council of Trent. Translated by J. Donovan. Baltimore: F. Lucas, Jr., 1829.

Catherine of Siena. *The Letters of St. Catherine of Siena.* Vol. 1. Translated by Suzanne Noffke, O.P. Medieval and Renaissance Texts and Studies, no. 52. Binghamton, N.Y.: Medieval and Renaissance Texts and Studies, 1988.

Cheffontaines, Christopher. "Homilia in die immaculatae conceptionis sacratissimae et dignissimae Virginis Mariae Matris Dei." In *Omnes epistolas quadragesimales homiliae,* 161v–165v. Louvain: Johannes Bogardus, 1572.

———. "Sermo de Virginis Mariae laudibus et honore, qui in qualibet eius festivitate haberi ad populum potest." In *Novae illustrationes Christianae fidei,* pt. 2, 1r–56v. Paris: Sittart, 1586.

———. "Sermo secundus, qui de Virginis Mariae invocatione agit." In *Novae illustrationes christianae fidei,* pt. 2, 57r–82r. Paris: Sittart, 1586.

Ciboule, Robert. *Édition critique du sermon "Qui manducat me" de Robert Ciboule (1403–1458).* Edited and introduced by Nicole Marzac. Cambridge: Modern Humanities Research Association, 1971.

Courtecuisse, Jean. *L'Oeuvre oratoire française de Jean Courtecuisse.* Edited by Giuseppe de Stefano. Torino: G. Giapichelli, 1969.

De Caulibus, Iohannis. *Meditaciones vite Christi: olim s. Bonaventuro attributae.* Edited by M. Stallings-Taney. Brepols: Turnholti Typographi Brepols Editores Pontificii, 1997.

Denzinger, Henricus, and Iohannes Umberg, S.J., eds. *Enchiridion symbolorum definitionum et declarationum de rebus fidei et morum.* Editio 21–23. Freiburg: Herder and Co., 1937.

De Sales, François. *Oeuvres complètes de Saint François de Sales, évêque et prince de Genève.* 16 vols. Paris: J. J. Blaise, 1821.

Elliott, J. K., ed. and trans. *The Apocryphal New Testament: A Collection of Apocryphal Christian Literature in an English Translation.* Oxford: Clarendon Press, 1993.

Gerson, Jean. *Oeuvres complètes.* 8 vols. Edited and introduced by P. Glorieux. Paris: Desclée and Cie, 1971.

Henry, Avril, ed. *The Mirour of Man's Salvation: A Middle English Translation of the "Speculum humanae salvationis."* Philadelphia: University of Pennsylvania Press, 1987.

Johannes of Verden. *Sermones dominicales cum expositionibus evangeliorum, sive Dormi secure de tempore et de sanctis.* Basel: Johann Amerbach, 1484.

Lawrence of Brindisi. *Opera omnia.* 10 vols. Patavia: Ex officina typographica seminarii, 1928.

Le Picart, François. *Les sermons et instructions chrestienes, pour tous les jours de caresme, et feries de Pasques.* Paris: Nicolas Chesneau, 1566.

Maillard, Olivier. *Oeuvres françaises d'Olivier Maillard: sermons et poesies.* Edited by A. de la Borderie. Nantes: Société des Bibliophiles Bretons, 1877.

———. "Passio domini nostri Jesu Christi." In *Sermones quadragesimales.* Paris: Antoine Caillaut, 1498.

Menot, Michel. *Sermons choisis de Michel Menot.* Edited by J. Nève. Paris: Bibliothèque du Xve siècle, 29, 1924.

Migne, J. P., ed. *Patrologiae cursus completus: series latina.* 221 vols. Paris: J. P. Migne, 1844–66.

Mirk, John. *Mirk's Festial: A Collection of Homilies.* Edited by Theodore Erbe. Early English Text Society, O.S., 96. London: Oxford University Press, 1905; reprint, Millwood, N.Y.: Kraus Reprint Company, 1973.

Panigarola, Francis. "Predica di Maria Vergine, e Madre." Rome: 1589.

Pepin, Guillaume. *Rosareum aurem B. Mariae Virginis.* Antwerp: Guillelmus Lesteenius and Engelbertus Gymnicus, 1656.

Rice, Eugene F., ed. *The Prefatory Epistles of Jacques Lefèvre d'Étaples and Related Texts.* New York: Columbia University Press, 1972.

Tanner, Norman P., S.J., ed. *Decrees of the Ecumenical Councils.* 2 vols. London: Sheed and Ward, and Washington: Georgetown University Press, 1990.

Thomas Aquinas. *Summa theologiae: Latin Text and English Translation, Introductions, Notes, Appendices and Glossaries.* Vol. 13, *Man Made to God's Image.* Translated by Edmund Hill, O.P. New York: McGraw-Hill, 1988.

Wolter, Allan B., O.F.M., trans. *John Duns Scotus: Four Questions on Mary.* Santa Barbara: Old Mission Santa Barbara, 1988.

Young, Karl. *The Drama of the Medieval Church.* 2 vols. Oxford: Clarendon Press, 1932.

Secondary Sources

Ackerman, Robert W. "The Debate of the Body and the Soul and Parochial Christianity." *Speculum* 37 (1962): 541–65.

Ahsmann, H. P. J. M. *Le culte de la Sainte-Vierge et la Littérature Française Profane du Moyen Âge.* Paris: Picard, 1930.

Allen, Prudence, R.S.M. *The Concept of Woman: The Aristotelian Revolution, 750 B.C.–A.D. 1250.* Grand Rapids, Mich.: William B. Eerdmans Publishing Company, 1985.

Arasse, Daniel. "Fervebat pietate populus: art, dévotion, et société autour de la glorification de Saint Bernardin de Sienne." *Melanges de l'École Française de Rome, Moyen Âge-Temps Modernes* 89 (1977): 189–263.

Barnes, Andrew E. "Religious Anxiety and Devotional Change in Sixteenth-Century French Penitential Confraternities." *Sixteenth Century Journal* 19 (1988): 389–405.

Bauman, Richard. *Let Your Words Be Few: Symbolism of Speaking and Silence among Seventeenth-Century Quakers.* New York: Cambridge University Press, 1983.

Bäuml, Franz H. "Varieties and Consequences of Medieval Literacy and Illiteracy." *Speculum* 55 (1980): 237–65.

Bayley, Peter. *French Pulpit Oratory 1598–1650: A Study in Themes and Styles, with a Descriptive Catalogue of Printed Texts.* Cambridge: Cambridge University Press, 1980.

Beckwith, Sarah. *Christ's Body: Identity, Culture and Society in Late Medieval Writings.* New York: Routledge, 1993.

Belluco, Bartolomeo. *De sacra predicatione in ordine Fratrum Minorum.* Studia Antoniana, no. 8. Rome: Pontificium Athenaeum Antonianum, 1956.

Bernard, Paul. "Un prédicateur populaire aux approches de la réforme, Jean Geiler de Keisersberg (1447–1510)." *Études* 124 (1910): 52–78, 209–26.

Besnier, Niko. *Literacy, Emotion, and Authority: Reading and Writing on a Polynesian Atoll.* Studies in the Social and Cultural Foundations of Language, no. 16. Cambridge: Cambridge University Press, 1995.

Bestul, Thomas H. *Texts of the Passion: Latin Devotional Literature and Medieval Society.* Philadelphia: University of Pennsylvania Press, 1996.

Bétérous, P. V. "A propos d'une de légendes mariales les plus répandus: le 'lait de la Vièrge.'" *Bulletin de l'Association Guillaume Budé* 4 (1975): 403–11.

Blench, J. W. *Preaching in England in the Later Fifteenth and Sixteenth Centuries.* London: Basil Blackwell, 1964.

Boiron, Stéphane. *La controverse née de la querelle des reliques à l'époque du concile de Trente (1500–1640).* Travaux et recherches de l'Université de droit d'économie et de sciences sociales de Paris, no. 28. Paris: Presses Universitaires de France, 1989.

Bordo, Susan R. *The Flight to Objectivity: Essays on Cartesianism and Culture.* Albany: State University of New York Press, 1987.

Börrensen, Kari Elisabeth. *Anthropologie médiévale et théologie mariale.* Oslo: Universitetsforlaget, 1971.

Bossy, John. *Christianity in the West, 1400–1700.* Oxford: Oxford University Press, 1985.

———. "The Social History of Confession in the Age of the Reformation." *Transactions of the Royal Historical Society,* 5th ser., 25 (1975): 21–38.

Bouman, Cornelius A. "The Immaculate Conception in the Liturgy." In *The Dogma of the Immaculate Conception: History and Significance,* edited by Edward D. O'Connor, 113–59. South Bend, Ind.: University of Notre Dame Press, 1958.

Brady, Ignatius, O.F.M. "The Development of the Doctrine of the Immaculate Conception in the Fourteenth Century after Aureoli." *Franciscan Studies* 15 (1955): 175–202.

Brooks, Peter Newman. "A Lily Ungilded: Martin Luther, the Virgin Mary and the Saints." *Journal of Religious History* 13 (1984): 136–49.

Brown, E. Catherine. *Pastor and Laity in the Theology of Jean Gerson.* Cambridge: Cambridge University Press, 1987.

Brown, Peter. *The Body and Society: Men, Women, and Sexual Renunciation in Early Christianity.* New York: Columbia University Press, 1988.

———. *The Cult of the Saints: Its Rise and Function in Latin Christianity.* Chicago: University of Chicago Press, 1981.

———. *Society and the Holy in Late Antiquity.* Berkeley: University of California Press, 1982.

Burke, Peter. "How to Be a Counter-Reformation Saint." In *Religion and Society in Early Modern Europe, 1500–1800,* edited by Kaspar von Greyerz, 45–55. London: George Allen and Unwin, 1984.

———. *Popular Culture in Early Modern Europe.* New York: New York University Press, 1978.

Bynum, Caroline Walker. *Holy Feast and Holy Fast: The Religious Significance of Food to Medieval Women.* Berkeley: University of California Press, 1987.

———. *The Resurrection of the Body in Western Christianity, 200–1336.* Lectures in the History of Religions, New Series, no. 15. New York: Columbia University Press, 1995.

———. "Women Mystics and Eucharistic Devotion in the Thirteenth Century." *Women's Studies* 11 (1989): 179–214.

Cameron, Averil. "The Theotokos in Sixth-Century Constantinople: A City Finds Its Symbol." *Journal of Theological Studies* 29 (1978): 79–108.

Campbell, Ted A. *The Religion of the Heart: A Study of European Religious Life in the Seventeenth and Eighteenth Centuries.* Columbia: University of South Carolina Press, 1991.

Camporesi, Piero. *The Incorruptible Flesh: Bodily Mutation and Mortification in Religion and Folklore.* Translated by Tania Croft-Murray and Helen Elsom. Cambridge: Cambridge University Press, 1983.

Carol, Juniper B., ed. *Mariology.* 3 vols. Milwaukee: Bruce Publishing Company, 1955–1961.

Carroll, Eamon R., O.Carm. "Mary in the Documents of the Magisterium." In *Mariology*, edited by Juniper B. Carol, 1:1–50. Milwaukee: Bruce Publishing Company, 1955.

Carroll, Michael. *The Cult of the Virgin Mary*. Princeton: Princeton University Press, 1986.

Chatellier, Louis. *The Europe of the Devout: The Catholic Reformation and the Formation of a New Society*. Translated by Jean Birrell. Editions de la Maison de Sciences de L'Homme. New York: Cambridge University Press, 1989.

Chidester, David. *Word and Light: Seeing, Hearing and Religious Discourse*. Urbana: University of Illinois Press, 1992.

Christian, William A. *Apparitions in Late Medieval and Renaissance Spain*. Princeton: Princeton University Press, 1981.

Clanchy, M. T. *From Memory to Written Record: England, 1066–1307*. Cambridge: Harvard University Press, 1979.

Coleman, Janet. *Medieval Readers and Writers, 1350–1400*. New York: Columbia University Press, 1981.

Coletti, Theresa. "Purity and Danger: The Paradox of Mary's Body and the Engendering of the Infancy Narrative in the English Mystery Cycles." In *Feminist Approaches to the Body in Medieval Literature*, edited by Linda Lomperis and Sarah Stanbury, 65–95. Philadelphia: University of Pennsylvania Press, 1993.

Combes, André. "La doctrine Mariale du chancelier Jean Gerson." In *Maria: études sur la sainte Vierge*, edited by Hubert DuManoir de Juaye, 2:865–82. Paris: Beauchesne, 1952.

Cressy, David. *Literacy and the Social Order: Reading and Writing in Tudor and Stuart England*. Cambridge: Cambridge University Press, 1980.

Cruz, J. Carroll. *The Incorruptibles: A Study of the Incorruption of the Bodies of Various Catholic Saints and Beati*. Rockford, Ill.: Tan Books and Publishers, 1977.

Cunneen, Sally. *In Search of Mary: The Woman and the Symbol*. New York: Ballantine Books, 1996.

Cunningham, Francis L. B., O.P. "The Relationship between Mary and the Church in Medieval Thought." *Marian Studies* 9 (1958): 52–78.

Daly, Simeon. "Mary in the Western Liturgy." In *Mariology*, edited by Juniper B. Carol, 1:245–80. Milwaukee: Bruce Publishing Company, 1955.

D'Ancona, Mirella Levi. *The Iconography of the Immaculate Conception in the Middle Ages and Early Renaissance*. New York: College Art Association, in conjunction with The Art Bulletin, 1957.

Daniel-Rops, Henri. *The Catholic Reformation*. Translated by John Warrington. London: J. M. Dent and Sons Ltd., 1962.

Dargon, Edwin Charles. *A History of Preaching: From the Apostolic Fathers to the Great Reformers*. London: Hodder and Stoughton, 1905.

Davis, Natalie Zemon. "City Women and Religious Change." In *Society and Culture in Early Modern France: Eight Essays by Natalie Zemon Davis*, 65–95. Stanford: Stanford University Press, 1975.

———. "From 'Popular Religion' to Religious Cultures." In *Reformation Europe: A*

Guide to Research, edited by Steven Ozment, 321–41. St. Louis: Center for Reformation Research, 1982.

———. "Printing and the People." In *Society and Culture in Early Modern France: Eight Essays by Natalie Zemon Davis,* 189–226. Stanford: Stanford University Press, 1975.

———. "The Sacred and the Body Social in Sixteenth-Century Lyon." *Past and Present* 90 (1981): 40–70.

———. *Women on the Margins: Three Seventeenth-Century Lives.* Cambridge, Mass.: Harvard University Press, 1995.

D'Avray, D. L. *The Preaching of the Friars: Sermons Diffused from Paris before 1300.* Oxford: Oxford University Press, 1985.

Delaney, John J., ed. *A Woman Clothed with the Sun: Eight Great Appearances of Our Lady in Modern Times.* Garden City, N.Y.: Hanover House, 1960.

Delaruelle, Etienne. *La piété populaire au Moyen-Âge.* Torino: Bottega d'Erasmo, 1980.

Delumeau, Jean. *Catholicism between Luther and Voltaire: A New View of the Counter-Reformation.* Philadelphia: Westminster Press, 1977.

Dickens, A. G. *The Counter Reformation.* New York: W. W. Norton, 1979.

Diefendorf, Barbara B. *Beneath the Cross: Catholics and Huguenots in Sixteenth-Century Paris.* New York: Oxford University Press, 1991.

Diefendorf, Barbara B., and Carla Hesse, eds. *Culture and Identity in Early Modern Europe (1500–1800): Essays in Honor of Natalie Zemon Davis.* Ann Arbor: University of Michigan Press, 1993.

Doane, A. N., and Carol Braun Pasternack, eds. *Vox intexta: Orality and Textuality in the Middle Ages.* Madison: University of Wisconsin Press, 1991.

Dougherty, Kenneth F. "Our Lady and the Protestants." In *Mariology,* edited by Juniper B. Carol, 3:422–39. Milwaukee: Bruce Publishing Company, 1961.

Douglas, Mary. *Natural Symbols: Explorations in Cosmology.* New York: Pantheon Books, 1982.

Douglass, E. Jane Dempsey. *Justification in Late Medieval Preaching: A Study of John Geiler of Keisersberg.* Leiden: E. J. Brill, 1966.

Duby, Georges. *The Early Growth of the European Economy: Warriors and Peasants from the Seventh to the Twelfth Century.* Translated by Howard B. Clarke. Ithaca, N.Y.: Cornell University Press, 1978.

Duffy, Eamon. *The Stripping of the Altars: Traditional Religion in England, c. 1400–1580.* New Haven: Yale University Press, 1992.

Dumoutet, Edouard. *Le desir de voir l'hostie et les origines de la dévotion au saint-sacrement.* Paris: Beauchesne, 1926.

Dupont, Jacques. "Le sacerdoce de la Vierge: Le Puy d'Amiens en 1437." *Gazette des beaux-arts,* ser. 6., 8 (1932): 265–74.

Duval, André, O.P. "La dévotion Mariale dans l'Ordre des Frères Prêcheurs." In *Maria: Études sur la sainte Vierge,* edited by Hubert DuManoir de Juaye, 2:737–82. Paris: Beauchesne, 1952.

Eire, Carlos M. N. *War against the Idols: The Reformation of Worship from Erasmus to Calvin.* Cambridge: Cambridge University Press, 1986.

Eisenstein, Elizabeth L. *The Printing Press as an Agent of Change.* 2 vols. Cambridge: Cambridge University Press, 1979.

Ellington, Donna Spivey. "Impassioned Mother or Passive Icon: The Virgin's Role in Late Medieval and Early Modern Passion Sermons." *Renaissance Quarterly* 48 (1995): 227–61.

Evennett, H. O. *The Spirit of the Counter-Reformation.* Edited by John Bossy. Cambridge: Cambridge University Press, 1968.

Farge, James. *Orthodoxy and Reform in Early Reformation France.* Leiden: E. J. Brill, 1985.

Febvre, Lucien. "Une question mal posée: les origines de la Réforme." In *Au coeur religieux du seizième siècle,* 3–70. Paris: SEVPEN, 1957.

Febvre, Lucien, and Henri-Jean Martin. *The Coming of the Book: The Impact of Printing, 1450–1800,* translated by David Gerard. London: Verso Editions, 1984.

Finnegan, Ruth. *Literacy and Orality: Studies in the Technology of Communication,* Oxford: Blackwell, 1988.

Flachaire, Charles. *La dévotion à la Vierge dans la littérature catholique au commencement du xviie siècle.* Paris: Apostolat de la Presse, 1957.

Fleischman, Suzanne. "Philology, Linguistics, and the Discourse of the Medieval Text." *Speculum* 65 (1990): 19–37.

Foley, John Miles. "Orality, Textuality and Interpretation." In *Vox intexta: Orality and Textuality in the Middle Ages,* edited by A. N. Doane and Carol Braun Pasternack, 34–45. Madison: University of Wisconsin Press, 1991.

Galpern, A. N. *The Religions of the People in Sixteenth-Century Champagne.* Cambridge: Harvard University Press, 1976.

Garreau, Albert. *Histoire Mariale de la France.* Paris: Editions des Saints Pères, 1946.

Gauthier, Roland, CSC. "Immaculée Conception de Marie, privilège singulier ou unique? Étude historique sur l'opinion de l'immaculée conception de S. Joseph." *Cahiers de Joséphologie* 2 (1954): 177–205.

Gebara, Ivone, and Maria Clara Bingemer. *Mary: Mother of God, Mother of the Poor.* Translated by Phillip Berryman. Maryknoll, N.Y.: Orbis Books, 1989.

Gellrich, Jesse M. *The Idea of the Book in the Middle Ages: Language, Theory, Mythology and Fiction.* Ithaca, N.Y.: Cornell University Press, 1985.

Gibson, Gail McMurray. "'Porta Haec Clause Erit': Comedy, Conception and Ezekiel's Closed Door in the *Ludus Coventriae* Play of 'Joseph's Return.'" *Journal of Medieval and Renaissance Studies* 8 (1978): 137–57.

———. *The Theater of Devotion: East Anglian Drama and Society in the Late Middle Ages.* Chicago: University of Chicago Press, 1989.

Gilmont, Jean-François, ed. *La Réforme et le livre: L'Europe de l'imprimé (1517–v. 1570).* Paris: Les Editions du Cerf, 1990.

Gilson, Etienne. "Michel Menot et la technique du sermon médiévale." *Revue d'histoire Franciscaine* 2 (1925): 301–50.

Goody, Jack. *The Domestication of the Savage Mind.* Cambridge: Cambridge University Press, 1977.

———. *Literacy in Traditional Societies.* Cambridge: Cambridge University Press, 1968.

———. *The Logic of Writing and the Organization of Society.* Cambridge: Cambridge University Press, 1986.

Graef, Hilda. *The Devotion to Our Lady.* New York: Hawthorn Books, 1963.

———. *Mary: A History of Doctrine and Devotion.* 2 vols. New York: Sheed and Ward, 1964.

Graham, William. *Beyond the Written Word: Oral Aspects of Scripture in the History of Religion.* New York: Cambridge University Press, 1987.

Greenblatt, Stephen. *Renaissance Self-Fashioning: From More to Shakespeare.* Chicago: University of Chicago Press, 1979.

Greyerz, Kasper von, ed. *Religion and Society in Early Modern Europe, 1500–1800.* London: George Allen and Unwin, 1984.

Halkin, Léon. "La Mariologie d'Erasme." *Archive for Reformation History* 68 (1977): 32–55.

Hamburger, Jeffrey. "The Visual and the Visionary: The Image in Late Medieval Monastic Devotions." *Viator* 20 (1989): 161–82.

Hamburgh, Harvey E. "The Problem of 'Lo Spasimo' of the Virgin in Cinquecento Paintings of the 'Descent from the Cross.'" *Sixteenth Century Journal* 12 (1981): 45–76.

Harding, Robert. "The Mobilization of Confraternities against the Reformation." *Sixteenth-Century Journal* 11 (1980): 85–107.

Headley, John M., and John B. Tomaro, eds. *San Carlo Borromeo: Catholic Reform and Ecclesiastical Politics in the Second Half of the Sixteenth Century.* Washington: Folger Shakespeare Library, 1988.

Hinnebusch, William A. *The History of the Dominican Order.* 2 vols. New York: Alba House, 1966.

Hoffman, Philip T. *Church and Community in the Diocese of Lyon: 1500–1789.* New Haven: Yale University Press, 1984.

Huizinga, Johann. *The Waning of the Middle Ages: A Study of the Forms of Life, Thought and Art in France and the Netherlands in the XIVth and XVth Centuries.* Translated by F. Hoffman. London: Arnold, 1924.

Iriarte de Aspurz, Fr. Lazaro, O.F.M. Cap. *Franciscan History: The Three Orders of St. Francis of Assisi.* Chicago: Franciscan Herald Press, 1983.

Janelle, Pierre. *The Catholic Reformation.* Milwaukee: Bruce Publishing Company, 1949.

Jedin, Hubert. *A History of the Council of Trent.* 2 vols. Translated by Dom Ernest Graf, O.S.B. New York: Thomas Nelson and Sons Ltd., 1957.

Johnson, Elizabeth A. "Marian Devotion in the Western Church." In *Christian Spirituality: High Middle Ages and Reformation,* edited by Jill Raitt, 392–414. New York: Crossroad Publishing Company, 1987.

Jordan, Mark, and Kent Emery, eds. *Ad litteram: Authoritative Texts and Their Medieval Readers.* South Bend, Ind.: Notre Dame University Press, 1992.

Kelly, Joan. *Women, History and Theory: The Essays of Joan Kelly.* Chicago: University of Chicago Press, 1984.

Kieckhefer, Richard. "Major Currents in Late Medieval Devotion." In *Christian Spirituality: High Middle Ages and Reformation,* edited by Jill Raitt, 75–108. New York: Crossroad Publishing Company, 1987.

———. *Unquiet Souls: Fourteenth-Century Saints and Their Religious Milieu.* Chicago: University of Chicago Press, 1984.

Klaits, Joseph. *Servants of Satan: The Age of the Witch Hunts.* Bloomington: Indiana University Press, 1985.

Klapisch-Zuber, Christiane. *Women, Family and Ritual in Renaissance Italy.* Chicago: University of Chicago Press, 1985.

Koehler, Theodore. "Marie (Vierge): du moyen âge aux temps modernes." *Dictionnaire de spiritualité ascétique et mystique doctrine et histoire* 10 (1977): cols. 440–59.

Krailsheimer, A. J. *Rabelais and the Franciscans.* Oxford: Oxford University Press, 1963.

Ladame, Jean. *Les saints de France et Notre Dame.* Paris: Editions S.O.S., 1983.

Lane, Barbara G. *The Altar and the Altarpiece: Sacramental Themes in Early Netherlandish Painting.* New York: Harper and Row, 1984.

Laqueur, Thomas. "Orgasm, Generation, and the Politics of Reproductive Biology." *Representations* 14 (1986): 1–41.

Latreille, A., E. Delaruelle, and J.-R. Palanque. *Histoire du Catholicisme en France.* Vol. 2, *Sous les rois très Chrétiens.* Paris: Editions Spes, 1963.

Laurentin, René. "Digne vesture au prestre souverain." *Revue du moyen âge latin* 4 (1948): 253–74.

Leclercq, Jean. "Grandeur et misère de la dèvotion Mariale au moyen âge." In *La liturgie et les paradoxes Chrétiens,* 170–204. Paris: Cerf, 1963.

Leclercq, Jean, François Vandenbroucke, and Louis Bouyer. *A History of Christian Spirituality.* Vol. 2, *The Spirituality of the Middle Ages..* Translated by the Benedictines of Holme Eden Abbey, Carlisle. London: Burns and Oates, 1968.

Leff, Gordon. *Heresy in the Later Middle Ages.* 2 vols. New York: Barnes and Noble, 1967.

Lemaître, Nicole. "Confession privée et confession publique dans les paroisses du xvie siècle." *Revue d'Histoire de l'Église de France* 69 (1983): 189–208.

Lesnick, Daniel R. *Preaching in Medieval Florence: The Social World of Franciscan and Dominican Spirituality.* Athens: University of Georgia Press, 1989.

Lischer, Richard. *A Theology of Preaching: The Dynamics of the Gospel.* Edited by William D. Thompson. Nashville: Abingdon Press, 1981.

Lochrie, Karma. *Margery Kempe and Translations of the Flesh.* Philadelphia: University of Pennsylvania Press, 1991.

Mackenzie, J. A. Ross. "Calvin and the Calvinists on Mary." *One in Christ* 16 (1980): 68–78.

McAodha, Loman, O.F.M. "The Nature and Efficacy of Preaching According to St. Bernardine of Siena." *Franciscan Studies* 27 (1967): 221–47.

McGinness, Frederick. "Preaching Ideals and Practice in Counter-Reformation Rome." *Sixteenth Century Journal* 11 (1980): 109–27.

———. *Rhetoric and Counter-Reformation Rome: Sacred Oratory and the Construction of the Catholic World View, 1563–1621.* Ann Arbor, Mich.: University Microfilms International, 1982.

———. *Right Thinking and Sacred Oratory in Counter-Reformation Rome.* Princeton: Princeton University Press, 1995.

McKitterick, Rosamond, ed. *The Uses of Literacy in Early Medieval Europe.* Cambridge: Cambridge University Press, 1990.

McManamon, John M., S.J. "Renaissance Preaching: Theory and Practice. A Holy Thursday Sermon of Aurelio Brandolini." *Viator* 10 (1979): 355–73.

Manoir de Juaye, Hubert du, S.J. *Maria: Études sur la Sainte Vierge.* 8 vols. Paris: Beauchesne, 1949–71; Bruce Publishing Company, 1949.

Manteau-Bonamy, J.-M. *Maternité divine et Incarnation: Étude historique et doctrinale de Saint Thomas à nos jours.* Bibliothèque Thomiste, vol. 27. Paris: J. Vrin, 1949.

Marshall, Louise. "Manipulating the Sacred: Image and Plague in Renaissance Italy." *Renaissance Quarterly* 47 (1994): 485–532.

Martin, Henri-Jean. *The History and Power of Writing.* Translated by Lydia G. Cochrane. Chicago: University of Chicago Press, 1994.

———. *Print, Power, and People in Seventeenth-Century France.* Translated by David Gerard. Metuchen, N.J.: Scarecrow Press, 1993.

Martin, Hervé. *Le Métier de prédicateur en France septentrionale à la fin du moyen âge, 1350–1520.* Paris: Cerf, 1988.

Masson, A. L. *Jean Gerson: sa vie, son temps, ses oeuvres.* Lyons: Emmanuel Vitte, 1894.

Matter, E. Ann. *The Voice of My Beloved: The Song of Songs in Western Medieval Christianity.* Philadelphia: University of Pennsylvania Press, 1990.

Méray, Antony. *La vie au temps des libres precheurs ou les devanciers de Luther et de Rabelais..* 2 vols. 2d ed. Paris: A. Claudin, 1878.

Miles, Margaret R. *Carnal Knowing: Female Nakedness and Religious Meaning in the Christian West.* Boston: Beacon Press, 1989.

———. *Image as Insight: Visual Understanding in Western Christianity and Secular Culture.* Boston: Beacon Press, 1985.

Moeller, Bernd. "Piety in Germany around 1500." In *The Reformation in Medieval Perspective,* edited by Steven E. Ozment, translated by Joyce Irwin, 50–75. Chicago: Quadrangle Books, 1971.

Moorman, J. R. H. *A History of the Franciscan Order from Its Origins to the Year 1517.* Oxford: Clarendon Press, 1968.

Morris, Colin. *The Discovery of the Individual 1050–1200.* Medieval Academy Reprints for Teaching, no. 19. Toronto: University of Toronto Press, in association with the Medieval Academy of America, 1995.

Muir, Edward. "The Virgin on the Street Corner: The Place of the Sacred in Italian Cities." In *Religion and Culture in the Renaissance and Reformation,* 25–40. Vol. XI, Sixteenth Century Essays and Studies. Edited by Steven E. Ozment. Kirksville, Mo.: Sixteenth Century Journal Publishers, 1989.

Neuschel, Kristen B. *Word of Honor: Interpreting Noble Culture in Sixteenth-Century France.* Ithaca, N.Y.: Cornell University Press, 1989.

Oberman, Heiko A., ed. *Forerunners of the Reformation.* Philadelphia: Fortress Press, 1981.

———. *The Harvest of Medieval Theology: Gabriel Biel and Late Medieval Nominalism.* Rev. ed. Grand Rapids, Mich.: William B. Eerdmans Publishing Company, 1967.

O'Connor, Edward D., ed. *The Dogma of the Immaculate Conception: History and Significance.* South Bend, Ind.: University of Notre Dame Press, 1958.

———. "The Fundamental Principle of Mariology in Scholastic Theology." *Marian Studies* 10 (1959): 69–103.

Olin, John C. *The Catholic Reformation: Savonarola to Ignatius Loyola.* New York: Harper and Row, 1969.

Olson, David R. "Literacy as a Metalinguistic Activity." In *Literacy and Orality,* edited by David R. Olson and Nancy Torrance, 251–70. Cambridge: Cambridge University Press, 1991.

O'Malley, John W., S.J. *Catholicism in Early Modern History: A Guide to Research.* Saint Louis: Center for Reformation Research, 1987.

———. "Catholic Reform." In *Reformation Europe: A Guide to Research,* edited by Steven Ozment, 297–319. Saint Louis: Center for Reformation Research, 1982.

———. *The First Jesuits.* Cambridge: Harvard University Press, 1993.

———. *Praise and Blame in Renaissance Rome: Rhetoric, Doctrine and Reform in the Sacred Orators of the Papal Court, c. 1450–1521.* Duke Monographs in Medieval and Renaissance Studies, no. 3. Durham, N.C.: Duke University Press, 1979.

———. "Saint Charles Borromeo and the 'Praecipuum Episcoporum Munus': His Place in the History of Preaching." In *San Carlo Borromeo: Catholic Reform and Ecclesiastical Politics in the Second Half of the Sixteenth Century,* edited by John M. Headley, 139–57. Washington: Folger Shakespeare Library, 1988.

Ong, Walter J., S.J. *Orality and Literacy: The Technologizing of the Word.* New York: Methuen, 1982.

———. "Orality, Literacy and Medieval Textualization." *New Literary History* 16 (1984): 1–12.

———. *The Presence of the Word: Some Prolegomena for Cultural and Religious History.* New Haven: Yale University Press, 1967.

O'Reilly, Terence. *From Ignatius Loyola to John of the Cross: Spirituality and Literature in Sixteenth-Century Spain.* Brookfield, Vt.: Variorum, 1995.

Owst, G. R. *Literature and Pulpit in Medieval England: A Neglected Chapter in the History of English Letters and of the English People.* 2d ed. Oxford: Basil Blackwell, 1966.

————. *Preaching in Medieval England.* Cambridge: Cambridge University Press, 1926.

Ozment, Steven E. *The Reformation in the Cities: The Appeal of Protestantism to Sixteenth-Century Germany and Switzerland.* New Haven: Yale University Press, 1975.

Parks, Ward. "The Textualization of Orality in Literary Criticism." In *Vox intexta: Orality and Textuality in the Middle Ages,* edited by A. N. Doane and Carol Braun Pasternack, 41–61. Madison: University of Wisconsin Press, 1991.

Patterson, Lee. "On the Margin: Postmodernism, Ironic History, and Medieval Studies." *Speculum* 65 (1990): 87–108.

Pelikan, Jaroslav. *Mary Through the Centuries: Her Place in the History of Culture.* New Haven: Yale University Press, 1996.

Perry, Nicholas, and Loreto Echeverría. *Under the Heel of Mary.* New York: Routledge, 1988.

Porter, Roy. "History of the Body." In *New Perspectives on Historical Writing,* edited by Peter Burke, 206–32. University Park: Pennsylvania State University Press, 1991.

Poschmann, Bernhard. *Penance and the Anointing of the Sick.* Translated and revised by Francis Courtney. New York: Herder and Herder, 1964.

Powell, James W. *The Papacy and the Early Franciscans.* Franciscan Studies, no. 36. St. Bonaventure, N.Y.: Franciscan Institute, 1976.

Rapley, Elizabeth. *The Dévotes: Women and Church in Seventeenth-Century France.* Montreal: McGill-Queen's University Press, 1990.

Rapp, Francis. *L'Église et la vie religieuse en occident à la fin du moyen âge.* Paris: Presses Universitaires de France, 1971.

Reinburg, Virginia. "Hearing Lay People's Prayer." In *Culture and Identity in Early Modern Europe (1500–1800): Essays in Honor of Natalie Zemon Davis,* edited by Barbara B. Diefendorf and Carla Hesse, 19–39. Ann Arbor: University of Michigan Press, 1993.

Rose, Mary Beth, ed. *Women in the Middle Ages and Renaissance.* Syracuse, N.Y.: Syracuse University Press, 1986.

Rosenwein, Barbara H. *Rhinoceros Bound: Cluny in the Tenth Century.* Philadelphia: University of Pennsylvania Press, 1982.

Russell, Paul A. *Lay Theology in the Reformation: Popular Pamphleteers in Southwest Germany, 1521–1525.* Cambridge: Cambridge University Press, 1986.

Sabean, David Warren. *Power in the Blood: Popular Culture and Village Discourse in Early Modern Germany.* Cambridge: Cambridge University Press, 1984.

Samouillan, Alexandre. *Étude sur la chaire et la société française au quinzième siècle: Olivier Maillard, sa prédication et son temps.* Paris: E. Privat, 1891.

Schaefer, Ursula. "Hearing from Books: The Rise of Fictionality in Old English Poetry." In *Vox intexta: Orality and Textuality in the Middle Ages,* edited by A. N. Doane and Carol Braun Pasternack, 117–36. Madison: University of Wisconsin Press, 1991.

Schmitt, J.-C. "Apostolat mendiant et société: une confrérie dominicaine à la vielle de la Réforme." *Annales ESC* 26 (1971): 83–104.

Schneider, Robert A. "Mortification on Parade: Penitential Processions in Sixteenth- and Seventeenth-Century France." *Renaissance and Reformation* 10, no. 1 (1986): 123–46.

Schwartz, Werner. *Principles of Biblical Translation: Some Reformation Controversies and Their Background.* Cambridge: Cambridge University Press, 1955.

Scribner, Robert W. "Cosmic Order and Daily Life: Sacred and Secular in Pre-Industrial German Society." In *Religion and Society in Early Modern Europe, 1500–1800,* edited by Kaspar von Greyerz, 17–32. London: George Allen and Unwin, 1984.

———. *For the Sake of Simple Folk: Popular Propaganda for the German Reformation.* Cambridge: Cambridge University Press, 1981.

———. "Incombustible Luther: The Image of the Reformer in Early Modern Germany." *Past and Present* 110 (1986): 38–68.

———. "Oral Culture and the Diffusion of Reformation Ideas." *History of European Ideas* 5 (1984): 237–56.

———. "Ritual and Popular Religion in Catholic Germany at the Time of the Reformation." *Journal of Ecclesiastical History* 35 (1984): 47–77.

Shea, George W. "Outline History of Mariology in the Middle Ages and Modern Times." In *Mariology,* edited by Juniper B. Carol, 1:282–37. Milwaukee: Bruce Publishing Company, 1955.

Sheerin, Daniel J. "'Sonus' and 'Verba': Varieties of Meaning in the Liturgical Proclamation of the Gospel in the Middle Ages." In *Ad litteram: Authoritative Texts and Their Medieval Readers,* edited by Mark Jordan and Kent Emery, 29–66. South Bend, Ind.: Notre Dame University Press, 1992.

Shorr, Dorothy C. "The Role of the Virgin in Giotto's *Last Judgement.*" *Art Bulletin* 38 (1956): 207–14.

Sissa, Giulia. *Le corps virginal.* Paris: J. Vrin, 1987.

Sloyan, Gerard. "Marian Prayers." In *Mariology,* edited by Juniper B. Carol, 3:64–87. Milwaukee: Bruce Publishing Company, 1961.

Smith, William B. "The Theology of the Virginity 'in partu' and Its Consequences for the Church's Teaching on Chastity." *Marian Studies* 31 (1980): 99–110.

Spencer, H. Leith. *English Preaching in the Late Middle Ages.* New York: Clarendon Press Oxford, 1994.

Stallybrass, Peter. "Patriarchal Territories: The Body Enclosed." In *Rewriting the Renaissance: The Discourses of Sexual Difference in Early Modern Europe,* edited by Margaret W. Ferguson, Maureen Quilligan, and Nancy J. Vickers, 123–42. Chicago: University of Chicago Press, 1986.

Stephenson, Colin. *Walsingham Way.* London: Darton, Longman and Todd, 1970.

Sticca, Sandro. *The "Planctus Mariae" in the Dramatic Tradition of the Middle Ages.* Translated by Joseph R. Berrigan. Athens: University of Georgia Press, 1988.

Stock, Brian. *The Implications of Literacy: Written Language and Models of Interpretation in the Eleventh and Twelfth Centuries.* Princeton: Princeton University Press, 1983.

Strauss, Gerald. *Luther's House of Learning: Indoctrination of the Young in the German Reformation.* Baltimore: Johns Hopkins University Press, 1978.

Sullivan, Margaret A. "The Witches of Dürer and Hans Baldung Grien." *Renaissance Quarterly* 53 (2000): 332–95.

Swanson, Guy. *Religion and Regime: A Sociological Account of the Reformation.* Ann Arbor: University of Michigan Press, 1967.

Taylor, Larissa Juliet. "The Influence of Humanism on Post-Reformation Catholic Preachers in France." *Renaissance Quarterly* 50 (1997): 119–35.

———. *Soldiers of Christ: Preaching in Late Medieval and Reformation France.* Oxford: Oxford University Press, 1992.

Tentler, Thomas F. *Sin and Confession on the Eve of the Reformation.* Princeton: Princeton University Press, 1977.

Thurston, Herbert. *The Stations of the Cross: An Account of Their History and Devotional Purpose.* Reprint. London: Burns and Oates, 1914.

Vandenbrouck, F. "Liturgie et piété personnelle, les prodromes de leur tension à la fin du moyen âge." *La Maison-Dieu* (1962): 56–66.

Vauchez, André. *The Laity in the Middle Ages: Religious Beliefs and Devotional Practices.* Edited by Daniel E. Bornstein. Translated by Margery J. Schneider. South Bend, Ind.: University of Notre Dame Press, 1993.

Venard, Marc. "The Influence of Carlo Borromeo on the Church of France." In *San Carlo Borromeo: Catholic Reform and Ecclesiastical Politics in the Second Half of the Sixteenth Century,* edited by John M. Headley and John B. Tomaro, 208–27. Washington: Folger Shakespeare Library, 1988.

Villaret, E., S.J. "Marie et la Compagnie de Jésus." In *Maria: Études sur la sainte Vierge,* edited by Hubert DuManoir de Juaye, 2:935–73. Paris: Beauchesne, 1952.

Vincent, Francis. "Saint François de Sales." In *Maria: Études sur la sainte Vierge,* edited by Hubert DuManoir de Juaye, 2:991–1004. Paris: Beauchesne, 1952.

Ward, Benedicta. *Miracles and the Medieval Mind: Theory, Record and Event, 1000–1215.* Philadelphia: University of Pennsylvania Press, 1987.

Warner, Marina. *Alone of All Her Sex: The Myth and the Cult of the Virgin Mary.* New York: Alfred A. Knopf, 1976.

Weinstein, Donald. "'The Art of Dying Well' and Popular Piety in the Preaching and Thought of Girolamo Savonarola." In *Life and Death in Fifteenth-Century Florence,* edited by Marcel Tetel, Ronald G. Witt, and Rona Goffen, 88–104. Durham, N.C.: Duke University Press, 1989.

Wenzel, Siegfried. *Macaronic Sermons: Bilingualism and Preaching in Late Medieval England.* Ann Arbor: University of Michigan Press, 1994.

———. *Preachers, Poets, and the Early English Lyric.* Princeton: Princeton University Press, 1986.

Wilkins, Eithne. *The Rose-Garden Game: A Tradition of Beads and Flowers.* New York: Herder and Herder, 1969.

Wilmart, André. *Auteurs spirituels et textes dévots du moyen âge latin: Études d'histoire littéraire.* Paris: Études Augustiniennes, 1971.

Winston-Allen, Anne. *Stories of the Rose: The Making of the Rosary in the Middle Ages.* University Park: Pennsylvania State University Press, 1997.

Wirth, Jean. "Against the Acculturation Thesis," translated by John Burke. In *Religion and Society in Early Modern Europe, 1500–1800,* edited by Kaspar von Greyerz, 66–78. London: George Allen and Unwin, 1984.

Wood, Charles T. "The Doctor's Dilemma: Sin, Salvation and the Menstrual Cycle in Medieval Thought." *Speculum* 56 (1981): 710–27.

Zawart, Anscar. *The History of Franciscan Preaching and of Franciscan Preachers (1209–1927): A Bio-bibliographical Study.* New York: J. F. Wagner, 1928.

Zika, Charles. "The Devil's Hoodwink: Seeing and Believing in the World of Sixteenth-Century Witchcraft." In *No Gods Except Me: Orthodoxy and Religious Practice in Europe, 1200–1600,* edited by Charles Zika, 153–98. Melbourne: Melbourne University History Monograph Series, 1991.

———. "Hosts, Processions and Pilgrimages: Controlling the Sacred in Fifteenth-Century Germany." *Past and Present* 118 (1988): 25–64.

Index

Abelard, Peter, 105
Ailred of Rievaulx, St., 2 n.2, 136
Alanus de Rupe, 33–34, 132
Albert the Great, St., 28–29, 51, 81, 89, 91–92, 253
Alexander of Hales, 94
Allen, Prudence, 253 n.14
Amadeus of Lausanne, St., 105, 129
Ambrose, St., 64, 73, 81, 167
Angelus, 29
Anne, St., 52, 102, 118–19, 175
Annunciation, 49, 65, 68, 88, 111, 127–28, 134, 145, 159, 161, 174, 179, 182, 185
Anselm of Canterbury, St., 56, 73
Arbor vitae crucifixae Jesu, 82–83, 100
Aristotle, 51–52, 67, 197, 253
Assumption of the Blessed Virgin Mary, 1–2, 28, 102–8, 120, 122–24, 128, 135, 137, 141, 189, 208–12, 216
Auerbach, Erich, 42
Augustine, St., 52–53, 56, 58, 62, 64, 66, 105
"Ave Maria," 29–30, 83–84, 100, 102, 111–12, 119, 124, 159, 162, 179, 213–19, 233, 244, 259

Barletta, Gabriel, 6, 41, 49, 56–57, 62, 65, 70, 82–84, 89, 93, 98–100, 111–12, 120–21, 123–24, 130, 145
Barnes, Andrew E., 233
Bauman, Richard, 202
Beckwith, Sarah, 9 n. 28, 13 n. 44, 20 n. 68
Bellarmine, Robert, St., 7, 145, 154, 157–58, 161, 167–71, 173–75, 179–80, 181–82, 185, 189–90, 192, 196, 198–99, 200, 203, 206, 210, 212, 223, 225, 227, 236
Bernard of Clairvaux, St., 27, 53, 58, 68, 71, 88, 92–93, 109, 123, 128–29, 131–32, 138, 220–21
Bernardino of Busti, 5–6, 12, 31, 47, 54, 59–60, 63, 65, 69, 70–71, 77, 81–82, 84–85, 93–95, 97–100, 103 n. 3, 109, 118, 131, 139, 141, 144, 163
Bernardino of Siena, St., 5–6, 16, 27, 31, 41, 44, 47–48, 57, 59–61, 63, 65, 70–72, 83, 86,

92, 96 n. 60, 97–99, 102, 106, 108, 119–20, 123–24, 129–30, 131, 133, 140, 144, 153, 159, 162, 192, 207
Besnier, Niko, 23 n. 75
Bible, 20–21, 39–40, 166, 210, 219; and allegory, 20, 61–63, 104, 107
Biel, Gabriel, 46 n. 137, 109, 120
Black Death, 43, 75, 80
Boiron, Stephane, 234 n. 86, 239
Bonaventure, St., 29, 83
Bonnaevallis, Arnauld, 81, 91, 123
Books of Hours, 33–34, 137
Bordo, Susan, 255–56
Borromeo, Charles, St., 154, 228–29, 234
Bossy, John, 24–25, 33 n. 106, 35, 43, 117, 151
Brethren of the Common Life, 150–51, 227
Brevicoxa, John, 129
Bridget of Sweden, St., 91
Bromyard, John, 102, 122
Brown, Peter, 38 n. 123, 66–67, 73, 113, 123, 125, 127
Bynum, Caroline Walker, 3 n. 4, 36, 50, 90, 95, 134, 248–49, 250

Calvin, John, 147, 156, 166, 182
Campbell, Ted, 244 n. 1, 261
Candlemas. *See* Purification
Canisius, Peter, St., 7, 142, 157–58, 166–67, 169, 171, 179–80, 182, 183–84, 191,193, 203, 206, 214, 216, 228, 230, 238
Catherine of Siena, St., 95, 153 n. 30, 249
Chantal, Jeanne de, St., 145–46, 170, 259, 262
Chatellier, Louis, 213–14, 227–28, 230 n. 77, 231
Cheffontaines, Christopher, 6–7, 12, 157–59, 162, 172, 175–77, 181, 185, 200, 203–4, 207–8, 212–13, 216–19, 220, 225, 233, 239, 259
Chidester, David, 17 n. 61, 40 n. 127, 127 n. 73, 201, 241
Christ. *See* Jesus Christ
Christian, William, 242
Ciboule, Robert, 137
Coleman, Janet, 8 n. 26

281

From Sacred Body to Angelic Soul: Understanding Mary in Late Medieval and Early Modern Europe
was designed and composed in Monotype Dante with Cataneo display type by Kachergis Book
Design of Pittsboro, North Carolina, and printed on 60-pound Glatfelter Natural
and bound by Sheridan Books, Ann Arbor, Michigan.